TRAINING IN THE WORKPLACE

Critical Perspectives on Learning at Work

Edited by

Helen Rainbird

First published in Great Britain 2000 by
MACMILLAN PRESS LTD
Houndmills, Basingstoke, Hampshire RG21 6XS and London
Companies and representatives throughout the world

A catalogue record for this book is available from the British Library.

ISBN 0–333–61671–5 hardcover
ISBN 0–333–61672–3 paperback

First published in the United States of America 2000 by
ST. MARTIN'S PRESS, INC.,
Scholarly and Reference Division,
175 Fifth Avenue, New York, N.Y. 10010

ISBN 0–333–61671–5 (cloth)

Library of Congress Cataloging-in-Publication Data

Training in the workplace / edited by Helen Rainbird.
    p. cm.
  Includes bibliographical references and index.
  ISBN 0–333–61671–5
  1. Employees—Training of. I. Rainbird, Helen.

HF5549.5.T7 T682 2000   00–030583
658.3'124—dc21

This book is printed on paper suitable for recycling and made from
fully managed and sustained forest sources.

10   9   8   7   6   5   4   3   2   1
09   08   07   06   05   04   03   02   01   00

Copy-edited and typeset by Povey–Edmondson
Tavistock and Rochdale, England

Printed in Great Britain by
Creative Print & Design (Wales), Ebbw Vale

In memory of Frank and Esmé Rainbird,
Christine Smith, Ernesto Salazar and Rosa Jara

Contents

Acknowledgements

This book has been a long time in the making and I am grateful to all the people who have encouraged its conception and endured its delays. I am particularly grateful to Stephen Rutt who was my initial contact at Macmillan and to Gibson Burrell at Warwick Business School with whom the first discussions took place about the possibility of a book on this subject for the series 'Management, Work and Organisations'.

There are several people who have contributed to this collection in many ways. The idea for an edited collection as opposed to a single-authored text emerged from a discussion with Prue Huddleston, Helen Newell and Paul Marginson one summer's evening. Each author has contributed insights in their own way to the whole. Nevertheless it is the tradition of theoretically informed empirical research of the Industrial Relations Research Unit (IRRU) at the University of Warwick which has played a decisive role in shaping the development of a critical approach to understanding the context of workplace training and learning. I am grateful to colleagues from the Warwick Vocational Education and Training Forum, the Working to Learn network and those who participated in the Economic and Social Research Council (ESRC) seminar series on 'Apprenticeship in education and work' for opening up many different disciplinary perspectives on vocational education and training. In addition, I have enjoyed the support of colleagues at University College Northampton, especially Lesley Holly and Anne Munro who have worked with me on a number of projects at the Centre for Research in Employment, Work and Training. I am grateful to Charlotte Spokes at the Research Centre for preparing the manuscript for publication with her usual professionalism. Thanks are also due to Peter Senker and Jim Sutherland for their insistence that 'learning' should appear in the title as well as 'training'.

As always, Francisco Salazar has been a great source of support to me, especially through the life cycle crises which marked the progress of the book.

HELEN RAINBIRD

Notes on the contributors

Elena Antonacopoulou is currently a Lecturer in Human Resources and Organisational Analysis at Manchester Business School. Her principal research interests include change and learning processes in organisations. She serves on the Executive Board of the Management Education and Development Division of the American Academy of Management, and is co-editor of the *Journal of Management Learning*.

Peter Caldwell is National Co-ordinator, Workplace Learning for the Workers' Educational Association (WEA). He has been involved in the WEA/Unison programmes since their inception in the West Midlands in 1989.

Sonia Carey is an independent consultant. Her research interests lie in the organisation of the training function and the role of trainers in organisations.

Bitten Hansen is a Research Fellow at the Centre for Management under Regulation at Warwick Business School, University of Warwick. She is presently researching management of performance measures and competitive strategies in regulated UK utilities. Her research interests also include cross-country comparative research of public enterprises with particular interest in postal services, industrial relations institutions, workplace level restructuring and training.

Jason Heyes is Lecturer in Industrial Relations at Leeds University Business School. His current research interests include the economic consequences of minimum wage legislation, lifelong learning and trade union involvement in training and development.

Susan Hoddinott has worked as a teacher and researcher in the field of Adult Education in Canada since 1981. She has researched and written about adult literacy policy, public adult education policy and worker basic skills. She has been the principal researcher on national research projects sponsored by the Movement for Canadian Literacy and the Canadian National Literacy

Secretariat, and she has developed position papers for the National Union of Public and General Employees and the Newfoundland Association of Public Employees.

Lesley Holly is a senior lecturer at University College Northampton. She works in the Centre for Research into Employment Work and Training, where her special interest is in low pay and care workers.

Prue Huddleston is Director of the Centre for Education and Industry at the University of Warwick. She has taught in both further and higher education. Her particular areas of academic and professional interest include: the relationship between the curriculum, qualifications and employment; the work-related curriculum; and vocational education and training.

Paul Marginson is Principal Research Fellow at the Industrial Relations Research Unit at the University of Warwick. He has written and researched extensively on employment relations in multinational companies.

Helen Newell is Lecturer in Industrial Relations and a member of the Industrial Relations Research Unit at the University of Warwick. Her research interests include employment relations in greenfield sites.

Helen Rainbird is Professor of Industrial Relations at University College Northampton and an Associate Fellow at the Industrial Relations Research Unit at the University of Warwick. She has written and researched on the relationship between industrial relations and vocational training and the trade union role in workplace learning.

Chris Rees is a Reader in the School of Human Resource Management at Kingston Business School, Kingston University. He has a PhD in Industrial Relations from Warwick Business School. His main areas of research interest are: international employment relations, work organisation, worker perceptions of organisational change and employee participation and involvement.

Peter Senker led research at the Science Policy Research Unit, University of Sussex for over 20 years, on implications of technological change for engineering training. Subsequently, he worked on a study of development of engineers' knowledge in employment.

Jim Sutherland was Director of Education and Training of the public sector union Unison between 1993 and 1998, and of the National Union of Public Employees prior to the creation of Unison.

List of Abbreviations

ABE	Adult Basic Education
AFL–CIO	American Federation of Labor–Congress of Industrial Organizations
ALBSU	Adult Literacy and Basic Skills Unit
BCEL	Business Council for Effective Literacy
CBI	Confederation of British Industry
CBTFL	Canadian Business Task Force on Literacy
CEC	Commission of the European Communities
CEDEFOP	European Centre for the Development of Vocational Training
CEI	Centre for Education and Industry
CIM	computer integrated manufacturing
CLMPC	Canadian Labour Market and Productivity Centre
CVT	continuing vocational training
DES	Department of Education and Science
DfEE	Department for Education and Employment
DTI	Department of Trade and Industry
EDAP	Employee Development and Assistance Programme
EIRO	European Industrial Relations Observatory
ESRC	Economic and Social Research Council
EWC	European Works Council
HR	Human Resources
HRD	human resource development
HRM	Human Resource Management
ICT	Information and Communication Technology
ID	individual development
IIP	Investors in People
ILAs	Individual Learning Accounts
ILO	International Labour Office
IRRU	Industrial Relations Research Unit
JIT	just-in-time
LEA	local education authorities
MBO	Management by Objectives

MD	management development
MNCs	multinational companies
NAGCELL	National Advisory Group on Continuing Education and Lifelong Learning
NALS	National Adult Learning Survey
NIESR	National Institute for Economic and Social Research
NUPE	National Union of Public Employees
NVQs	National Vocational Qualifications
OD	organisational development
OECD	Organisation for Economic Co-operation and Development
PDPs	Personal Development Plans
PEL	paid educational leave
PRP	performance related pay
QCA	Qualifications and Curriculum Authority
QWL	quality of working life
R2L	Return to Learn
SMEs	small and medium-sized enterprises
SNVQs	Scottish National Vocational Qualifications
TECs	Training and Enterprise Councils
TGWU	Transport and general Workers' Union
TQM	Total Quality Management
TUC	Trades Union Congress
UfI	University for Industry
ULF	Union Learning Fund
UNESCO	United Nations Educational, Scientific and Cultural Organisation
USDAW	Union of Shop, Distributive and Allied Workers
VEAs	voluntary education advisers
VET	vocational education training
WEA	Workers' Educational Association

CHAPTER 1

Training in the workplace and workplace learning: introduction

Helen Rainbird

Introduction

The workplace is enormously significant as a site of learning, both for accessing formal learning opportunities and for many informal learning opportunities which result from the nature of work and from social interaction with work groups. But it is also highly problematic: its primary purpose is not learning, but the production of goods and services, involving the creation of profit in the private sector, or delivery within budget in the case of the public sector. Although it is often assumed that employers and employees have a mutual interest in investing in training and in developing workforce skills, the unitarist assumptions of Human Capital Theory and Human Resource Management (HRM) are not borne out by empirical research, as many of the chapters in this book demonstrate. The relatively low levels of investment by British employers in workforce development compared to their economic competitors are well known. The nature of financial markets, competitive strategy, organisational structures and labour market deregulation have all been identified as contributing to an environment in which there are disincentives to employers to invest in workforce development. Within organisations, the weak role of training and development within corporate structures, the absence of a 'champion' at board level, the tendency for training and development to be seen as an operational rather than strategic issue and conflicts between corporate Human Resource (HR) strategy and operational management contribute to the difficulties of oper-ationalising workforce learning strategies. At the level of the workplace, this is compounded by issues relating to the management, socialisation and control of the workforce. Individuals are located within occupational hierarchies which provide differential access to formal learning opportunities and in jobs which provide differential access to informal learning opportunities and career pro-gression. As a result, some workers enter employment with expectations of access to learning and career progression and will find opportunities to learn informally in the work environment. Others will enter jobs with few opportuni-ties for learning and progression, and low aspirations for themselves which are reinforced by the low expectations of their managers. Their jobs may be nar-rowly constructed, and the pace of work, staffing levels and physical isolation may restrict opportunities for informal learning. Power relations between man-agers and workers and between different groups of workers have a significant impact on learning opportunities, both formal and informal. Moreover, the training and development of staff has symbolic dimensions: it may be regarded as a reward, giving status where there was previously little; it may serve as recognition for effort and a signal of value to the organisation; and it may indi-cate suitability for promotion. Equally, it may be perceived as a threat, an indi-cator of poor performance or the forerunner of work intensification. Therefore when students and researchers analyse training and development in the work-place and the many forms of informal learning which occur in the work envi-ronment, they are confronted by many challenges.

Five challenges

The first of these challenges lies in the need to 'deconstruct the consensus' on the relationship between training, skills and the competitiveness of national economies that Jackson and Jordan have identified (1999). They argue that in many countries a new consensus is guiding public policy in relation to skill formation and labour market programmes which emphasises the need for increased productivity and greater employee flexibility as the key to competi-tive survival. This is leading to the reshaping of training systems in ways which are 'more responsive' to employers' needs, to the decline of older forms of apprenticeship in which the trade unions played a part, and the buying, selling and marketing of training programmes as a commodity. They point out that the connections between skill development and competitiveness on the one hand, and productivity and prosperity on the other, are unclear. In partic-ular, they argue that the perception that training needs to be made responsive to the needs of industry through marketisation and privatisation of training provision raises fundamental questions: how is skill being used in this discourse and by whom? Who decides, and in whose interests (Jackson and Jordan, 1999:232)? To this, the question 'What is the real issue of concern behind the discussion and why is it an issue now?'¹ could be added. The context is that of globalisation of production, the increasing intensity of competition, the social dislocations caused by these processes on regions and local communities, and the nature of the insertion of national economies in the international division of labour. A number of the chapters in this book, in particular those by Carey, Marginson, Newell and Rees, explicitly address the ways in which this wider context impinges on companies' Human Resource and training strategies.

So what is meant by 'making the training system more responsive to the needs of industry' and how is it manifested in policy discourse and interventions? A number of different elements need to be identified. First, we are dealing with a range of different policy arenas which include formal education, vocational training, labour market programmes for the unemployed, the lifelong learning of employees and those outside the labour market as well as a whole gamut of measures to make the labour market more 'flexible'. Second, the concept of 'responsiveness to the needs of industry' assumes that employers have a common understanding of their needs with respect to education and training and are able to articulate them clearly to policy-makers. As Keep and Huddleston's work has shown, in practice they either do not know what their needs are, or they have a range of differing needs which varies according to sector, levels of technology or types of production process (1998). Moreover, it is not self-evident that the needs of employers do equate to 'the needs of industry', or that the unfettered operation of the market is the best way to meet these needs. In turn, this question poses more fundamental issues about access to learning, which concern the relationship between the economy and society, and broader questions about citizenship, democratic participation and the purposes of education. Third, there is a strong strand emphasising the need for individuals to take responsibility for their own training and development in concepts such as 'employability' and 'lifelong learning', yet this is often juxtaposed with silence on legal entitlements to education and training leave and the responsibilities of employers to facilitate them. These themes are explored in several chapters, in particular those by Caldwell, Heyes, Rainbird and Sutherland, and Huddleston. Fourth, although an emphasis on individual responsibility may be appropriate for successful learners, it is inappropriate for those whose experiences of formal education have been unsuccessful. They have least access to formal training in the workplace and are least likely to engage in education outside work on their own initiative (McGivney, 1997). Therefore, any consideration of issues of equity and equality must also include the case for collective frameworks and entitlements. Fifth, there are a number of underlying assumptions about the trend towards job insecurity (the end of 'jobs for life'), its desirability and the extent to which it creates incentives to invest in training and development. Again, it is not self-evident that job insecurity creates incentives to employers or to individuals to invest in training for employability. On the contrary, Arulampalam and Booth's analysis of the British Household Panel Survey data suggests that workers in more flexible forms of employment are significantly less likely to be involved in work-related training to improve or increase their skills (1998).

In attempting to develop an understanding of these issues, it is important to recognise that the regulation of the employment relationship and the training system have consequences for the ways in which labour is deployed in the workplace. This reflects a more general relationship between the construction of skill and the balance of power between labour and capital, at the macro- and micro-levels. Streeck's work on the role of social institutions and economic performance involves a critique of neo-liberal labour market and training policies. It points to the ways in which these broader regulatory structures are related to the composition of workforce skills. He argues that strong institutions, as opposed to deregulated markets, can contribute to economic performance; that trade unions' involvement in these structures allows them to promote training in 'high and broad skills' which improve members' bargaining power in the wider labour market; and that this constraint on employers forces them to invest at a higher level in skills than they would on a voluntary basis which, paradoxically, serves their long-term needs for an adaptable workforce best. In contrast, in a deregulated training system, employers' uncertainty of recouping investment in training in a free market for labour encourages the poaching of labour (the 'free rider' problem) and chronic underinvestment in workforce skills. Where investment in training takes place, it tends to be job- and company-specific (Streeck, 1989). Maurice, Sellier and Silvestre's classic comparative study of workforce skills in France and Germany (1986) shows that the quantity and nature of formal qualifications in the labour market has qualitative implications for the way in which work is organised, the hierarchy of occupations and levels of supervision. At this level too, the definition and exercise of skill is characterised by conflict. Thompson, in an introduction to debates on the labour process, argues that 'skill is largely based on knowledge, the unity of conception and execution, and the exercise of control by the workforce' (1983:92). His concern is with the nature and transformation of craft labour: skilled male manual labour formed through the tradition of craft apprenticeship. Contemporary definitions of skill also incorporate notions of the exercise of responsibility, expertise derived from formal education and learning derived from on-the-job experience. As Gallie points out:

> The very complexity of the task of defining skill, however, makes it implausible that skill classifications in industry reflect in an unproblematic way some objective hierarchy. Rather, they are likely to be the product of a continuous negotiation between employers and employee, in which both relative power resources and prevalent cultural beliefs will influence the grading structure. (1988:8)

Not only are there individual, collective and class political aspects to skill, but it also plays a part in the power relations between women and men (Cockburn, 1983:116). Ironically, those analysing the exercise of skill in the labour process tradition rarely give training consideration. Equally, those who analyse training policy and institutions rarely make explicit their assumptions about the nature of skill (Rainbird, 1997:189) or focus on the workplace.

The second challenge is to examine critically what is happening within organisations and to probe beneath the rhetoric of management gurus and Human Resource managers. What happens with respect to training and development in the workplace is partly unexplored territory. Much of the literature is prescriptive in nature rather than based on the analysis of the empirical evidence. Given managers' often cited claim that 'our people are our most important resource', the ways in which training strategy is formulated and delivered, the support it receives from corporate management, and the resources allocated to it are significant indicators of the extent to which these claims are reflected in practice (Rainbird, 1994). Although the concept of the learning organisation has been promoted as a blueprint for organisational strategies (Senge, 1990), the underlying assumptions relating to the relationship between learning and business competition are problematic. Evidence of the existence of such organisations and the adoption of product market strategies which would warrant such development is weak (Keep and Rainbird, 2000).

As with any element of management strategy, there are always problems of implementation of training strategies due to the tensions between different management functions and the ability of individuals to resist centrally formulated objectives. The extent to which they are undermined by corporate structures and strategy themselves is the subject of Chapter 2. Carey points to the range of activities covered by the term 'training', including the satisfactory completion of a single task, interpersonal skills, organisational socialisation, and the analysis and application of complex data. She argues that unless they are seen as core activities and training personnel as core workers, it is unlikely that the training culture sought by many organisations is likely to be achieved. If training strategy is to be a central feature of Human Resource Management it must be incorporated into strategic decision-making at corporate level. According to large companies' business strategies, they may have greater or lesser capacity for identifying long-term business objectives, centralised planning procedures and for the central planning of their Human Resources. In some cases, corporate objectives and structures will militate against the existence of a corporate training function and company-wide training strategies.

In order to assess the effectiveness of Human Resource strategies it is useful to investigate particular management tools and techniques which have been designed to promote the effective use of labour. Quality assurance systems such as the Investors in People (IIP) award are designed to ensure that training procedures and strategies are appropriate to business needs. They promote the use of tools such as appraisal, which are designed to contribute to the identification of employees' training and development needs. Nevertheless, caution is needed in assessing their significance because they have the difficult task of reconciling the identification of organisational and individual needs, usually to the benefit of the former. In a discussion of managers' self-development in Chapter 3, Antonacopoulou points to the asymmetrical power relationship between the individual and the organisation. Managers have a key role in managing organisational change and their development has often been seen as central to organisational development. Systems of management development are increasingly emphasising managers' own role in identifying their own training and development needs. From evidence from the retail banking sector, she analyses three main approaches which each generate their own tensions. She characterises them as the 'do-it-yourself' approach, and approaches which either integrate or separate personal development from assessment. She shows how these conflicting objectives result in managers internalising corporate goals in identifying their development needs: despite the emphasis on self-development, managers do what the organisation expects them to do.

These contradictions are intensified where the same tool has multiple objectives: measuring and rewarding performance on the one hand, and identifying development needs on the other. As Hansen shows in Chapter 4, the timescale and underlying logic of performance management are short term in nature. There are tensions in its operationalisation, which result in conflicting managerial priorities. Performance management can be seen as part of a more general process of individualisation of the employment relationship. As a management tool, it also suffers from the assumption that managing is a rational process of planning and goal-setting which leads unproblematically to enhanced performance, rather than the realities of organisational politics, conflicts over resources and questions such as release from work for training and development. These realities, alongside the absence of a long-term business strategy (a characteristic of many British companies, as Carey points out in Chapter 2), systematically undermine the objective of identifying development needs, which are, by definition, long-term in their nature and in terms of the results they can deliver.

The third challenge is the critical examination of some of the assumptions underlying this discourse about the nature of work modernisation, its effect on employers' demand for skills and new forms of management. Multinational companies are often seen as trend setters in this respect. In Chapter 5, Marginson explores the factors behind their location decisions and the extent to which this results in innovation in labour practices, the undermining of labour conditions, or adaptation to local conditions. He argues that the rationale for multinational expansion may be significant in determining the labour practices adopted: companies may seek resources and labour; they may be driven by a strategic advantage (technology or management techniques) or new markets for goods and services. Moreover, company structure and organisation may affect capacity for innovation. Using Perlmutter's typology (1965), he argues that ethnocentric companies are likely to be innovators in the countries they operate in; polycentric companies are likely to adapt to local conditions; whilst geocentric companies are most likely to experience two-way flows of innovation. Through an analysis of multinational companies' reasons for location in the UK, he points to factors which are linked to the availability of skills and qualifications, proximity to European markets, the scope for implementing innovatory practices, and ease of exit due to weak employment regulation, as well as factors relating to the insertion of the national economy in the international division of labour.

When companies enter new markets they may do this through acquiring an existing site or building a new site from scratch. In Chapter 6, Newell examines the unique opportunities presented to managers by greenfield sites to plan their operations and Human Resource strategies on an integrated basis. Here, they can introduce new technology and new patterns of work organisation without the complications which arise in brownfield sites. More importantly, they have scope for adopting new management practices across the range of procedures concerning the selection, training and socialisation of new employees. She explores the role of training in the commissioning phase of new plants and the tensions encountered in transferring to normal operation. Some of the problems, for example, the absence of a training champion, failures to establish internal progression routes and the difficulties of developing skills if machinery is not working, are remarkably similar to those experienced in brownfield sites where new forms of work organisation are being introduced. She points to the significance of the trade union in acting as an advocate of employee training to employees' perception of its ability to provide an employee voice more generally. Although trade unions tend to be absent or more docile than normal in greenfield sites, the question of employee voice on training and development is one that is returned to in a number of chapters.

Debates on the changing nature of work have influenced the assumptions underlying policy. Of particular significance is the extent to which assembly line production based on Taylorist principles of work organisation, the fragmentation of tasks and the deskilling of labour is being replaced by changes in work organisation based on computer-controlled production technologies, which increase requirements for skills and worker autonomy. This also requires a trade union response (Ackers, Smith and Smith, 1996). The evidence of transformation is limited. Whilst there is no doubt that significant developments have been taking place in work organisation, as Hyman points out this is based on a manufacturing model which accounts for a declining proportion of employment. The outcome is not universal success: some companies may go out of business, resulting in redundancies. Different sections of the workforce will be affected in different ways: increased levels of skill in the core workforce may be accompanied by the casualisation of those on the periphery (1988). Parts of manufacturing and the services sector continue to rely on routinised work. Moreover, the extent to which flexible forms of employment have been adopted has been much debated (see Pollert, 1991, for example). As the Industrial Relations Research Unit (IRRU) points out: 'Competitive success based on quality and up-skilling is only one of a number of strategies available to organisations. Others include seeking protected or monopoly markets; growth through take-over and joint venture; shifting operations overseas; cost-cutting and new forms of "Fordism" '(1997:7).

Work modernisation is examined in more detail by Rees in Chapter 7. He examines, in turn, scientific management which resulted in the breaking down of jobs into simplified tasks, the Quality of Working Life movement which attempted to address the alienation of assembly line work, and more recent developments in high performance work systems which create a demand for multi-skilled labour, reduced supervision and enhanced employee involvement. It is the links between economic efficiency, forms of employee participation and job satisfaction which underpin many assumptions underlying European and British policy debates. He points to case study evidence which shows that employees are most supportive of programmes for enhancing quality where they have been trained in quality ideas or teamwork principles, rather than training *per se*. He points to the significance of social partnership to work modernisation, given the limited ability of individual employees to influence their organisation's use of skills. He concludes that the work modernisation agenda as promoted by the European Commission's Green Paper *Partnership for a New Organisation of Work* (1997), in suggesting a convergence between competitiveness and quality of working life, seriously underestimates the institutional structures and workers 'rights needed to promote change of this nature. How do changes in work organisation translate into employers' investment in training on the one hand, and their demand for skills in terms of employee recruitment on the other? Provision in the form of apprentice training in Great Britain dropped from 218 000 to 53 600 between 1970 and 1990 (Keep, 1994:310), but these figures represent initial training for skilled jobs and partly reflect the declining proportion of manufacturing employment in the economy. In 1998, only 12 per cent of the employers questioned in the Workplace Employee Relations Survey reported that their employees received five days' training a year and 27 per cent that most supervisors received training in employee relations skills (Cully *et al.*, 1998:10). These figures refer to organisations with over 25 employees, representing the larger employers which are more likely to have a specialist training function and strategies for training and development.

Nevertheless, trends in the nature of labour supply and skill usage require a nuanced interpretation. The Skills Survey, conducted in Britain in 1997, examines the skills people use in work and provides an indication of the extent to which employees' training and qualifications match their responsibilities and tasks at work (Ashton *et al.*, 1999). It compares the level and distribution of skills with those reported in the Social Change and Economic Life Initiative (SCELI) survey, which was conducted in 1986. Using three measures of skill –

(the required qualification, the learning time and the training time needed for the job) – it found that there had been an increase in skills over this period. There has been a decrease in work requiring a short period (three months) of training; an increase in the proportion of workers whose jobs required more than two years' training; and a fall in the number of jobs which it took less than a month to learn to do well. Over the same period, there has been increasing use of computing, communication, social and problem-solving skills. The numbers of jobs for which a degree is now considered 'essential' or 'fairly necessary' has also increased. But when qualifications required for the job are compared with actual qualifications, the overall supply of qualifications 'appears to outstrip the demand by a comfortable margin' (Ashton *et al.*, 1999:63). The imbalance is evident for all groups of workers, but is greatest in jobs held by women part-time workers. The authors argue that this is consistent with the conclusions of commentators such as Keep and Mayhew (1996) who have argued that skill deficiencies are attributable to low levels of employer demand. Similarly, a survey carried out under the ESRC's Future of Work Programme of employees' learning experiences in manual and routine work in the public sector found that employees in these jobs on the lowest salary scales are less well qualified than the representative sample in the Skills Survey. What is striking, though, is that employees of all ages have more qualifications than those required for the job, but the divergences are greatest in younger age groups (Rainbird *et al.*, 1999). These findings, in turn, provide challenges for interpreting the relationship between changes in labour supply, evident in increased staying-on rates in post-compulsory education, changes in labour demand and patterns of class reproduction (Brown, 1995).

The fourth challenge is to recognise explicitly that the workplace is a site of conflict between labour and management, and that the procedures, resources and outcomes of formal and informal learning opportunities must be analysed in this context. Both Human Capital Theory and Human Resource Management operate with unitarist assumptions, a theme explored by Heyes in Chapter 8. The former assumes that management and labour have a joint interest in investing in labour as an asset, and the latter that they have joint interests in developing labour as a resource. Training is often seen as an arena in which management and employees' interests have some overlap. Indeed, in many countries the institutions for regulating initial training and labour market programmes involve corporatist arrangements, whereby the state devolves responsibilities for the development and implementation of policy to the interest groups of labour and capital. This does not mean that their interests are the same. As Heyes points out, there is evidence that unions have a positive role in encouraging training by providing a channel for employee 'voice', but employees are more likely to receive training and positive benefits from it where unions have an active role in decision-making. Training is situated in the broader context of reward, effort and control over production, and to ignore this is to depoliticise it. Management may fear the cost implications of providing employees with training which gives them more bargaining power on the external labour market and a greater role in training decisions within the organisation. In the context of work re-organisation and multi-skilling, conflicts over the distribution of financial rewards may give rise to conflicts between different groups of workers, organised by different trade unions, and can undermine the existing bases of cooperation. He points to the need to develop a better understanding of the objectives of workplace actors in relation to training and how new skills are utilised.

Nevertheless, it is important to emphasise that the conflict between labour and capital is intrinsic to the employment relationship; conflict is already present in the workplace and this is a factor that trade unionists, trainers and adult educators need to take on board.[2] In addition, there may be conflict in relation to the formal content of training and conflict in relation to the deployment of skills acquired, but this is not restricted to formal training programmes and their outcomes. Developments in work organisation such as job enlargement, which may create informal learning opportunities, may be perceived in positive or negative ways by employees according to whether they are initiated by management, by the employee, by the employee with the manager, or by the union and management (Rainbird *et al.*, 1999). Therefore, the questions 'Who initiates?' and 'Who benefits?' should be added to those raised earlier.

Trade unions owe it to their members to retain a critical appreciation of where their interests lie. This is particularly the case with workers who may have literacy problems on lower salary grades or whose experiences of education mean that they are unlikely to engage in lifelong learning on their own initiative. As Hoddinott argues in Chapter 9, a clear distinction is needed between access to training and development in the workplace and a pathology of blaming low-paid workers for low levels of productivity. All workers need access to training and development to do their jobs efficiently and safely, and low-paid workers often have least access to this. The moral panic over the crisis in workers' basic skills in North America in particular has had the effect of increasing the vulnerability of sections of the workforce whose labour market position was already weak. It has created a climate which allowed workplace literacy programmes, in some cases of dubious educational content, to replace the public provision of literacy programmes in the community. More importantly, the dangers lie in the potential for scapegoating workers on the basis of a deficiency, rather than establishing an entitlement and collective systems of support.

As argued above, work modernisation is often dependent on more participative management styles, 'employee empowerment' and, in particular, forms of social partnership on training and development. Trade unions need to formulate strategies towards the work modernisation agenda which encompass workplace learning. In the broader context, this concerns the way in which they relate to the changing nature of their membership bases and, in particular, the growing proportion of women, service sector and professional workers in the labour market. It also concerns how they appeal to new and potential members through the provision of individual services and traditional collectivist approaches. In the workplace, their strategies towards training and development will draw on a range of mechanisms for dealing with employers: collective bargaining, joint problem-solving approaches, consultation and information. These issues are explored in the chapter by Sutherland and Rainbird. They argue that some mechanisms have greater potential than others for setting the workplace learning agenda, as opposed to responding defensively to the management agenda. Equally, some have greater capacity for inclusiveness and promoting new union roles and forms of activity.

The fifth and final challenge to researchers and students is to recognise the complexity of learning in the workplace. This is evident in the title of the book, which stresses both formal instruction (training) and informal learning processes. Indeed, the report of the Workplace Learning Taskforce which reported to the National Advisory Group on Continuing Education and Lifelong Learning (NAGCELL) defined its remit as 'learning in, for and through the workplace' (Sutherland, 1998), encompassing both formal and informal learning, that which is directly work-related and more developmental, as well as forms which are accessed by entitlement through the employment relationship.

The workplace is a significant site of socialisation, including gender socialisation, after the family and school (Purcell, 1988). It is here that workers learn about appropriate work roles, about power relations in the workplace, discipline and control. The social and contextual nature of learning has been emphasised by writers in the anthropological tradition, such as Lave and Wenger (1991). They conceptualise apprenticeship as a form of participation in communities of practice, whereby new workers gradually acquire skills which are increasingly central to practice through learning from work groups, skilled practitioners and masters. The workplace is a valuable site of learning for young people. As Huddleston argues in Chapter 11, work experience programmes aim to tap into these sources of learning although they have multiple, conflicting and sometimes unrealistic objectives. These conflicting objectives make the success of the placement on the one hand, and the quality of the student's learning experience on the other hand, difficult to assess. Teachers, students and employers will have conflicting objectives for engaging in work placement. Though the rationale for its incorporation into the school curriculum has changed over time, its principal aim is to promote employability and a smooth transition from school to work. Huddleston points out that the formal allocation of time to work experience in the school curriculum in this way fails to recognise that many young people are already be engaged in work outside school hours and that this also provides them with 'naturally occurring learning opportunities'. The challenges for teachers are how to make them meaningful for young people. Work placements for the unemployed on training programmes also exploit the workplace as a site of learning but, in both these examples, the employer may have multiple objectives for involvement with them. Both can serve as an extended recruitment process and contribute to good relations with the local community and educational establishments.

The capacity of placements to facilitate learning will be dependent on the quality of the working environment and the abilities of teachers, trainers and mentors to enhance and complement these sources of learning. Nevertheless, it is also important to emphasise that school children on work placements and trainees on labour market programmes will receive other powerful messages from the employer, concerning wages and conditions of employment and the potential for career progression, which may be positive or negative. As Huddleston points out, to know that you do not want to work with a particular employer or in a specific occupation is an equally valid learning experience. In particular, trainees on labour market programmes will quickly perceive whether they are being exploited on a temporary basis as a substitute for trained workers, or are seen as potential new recruits to the organisation.

An emphasis on learning as opposed to formal training programmes allows the ways in which people actually learn at work to be explored. Formal training programmes can serve many purposes, some of them symbolic, to participants and non-participants, as outlined earlier. There are many ways in which people learn from each other in work (Eraut *et al.*, 1998). Equally, the relationship between formal learning in educational establishments and the use of different types of knowledge in the workplace is a complex one. In engineering workplaces, the possession of a university degree may be as useful in terms of the experience of working to deadlines or doing project-based work as in providing a body of scientific knowledge. In Chapter 12, Senker explores the ways in which engineers learn to do their jobs, highlighting the role of trial and error, problem-solving activities and the use of mentors. Many of these learning opportunities are generated by the nature of the work environment itself. Jobs are constructed in different ways; some are richer and others poorer in the opportunities that they afford for learning. He questions the assumption that learning only takes place in formal settings and that inputs and outputs can be measured unproblematically in terms of cost, time and qualifications. He argues that a focus on formal education and training and the measurement of achievement of qualifications has a role in the setting of national targets, but should not be the only basis for policy development. Much learning at work is informal and cannot be quantified in this way. One consequence of a focus on informal learning is to point to the significance of job design and the social relations of the workplace in creating learning opportunities. It also points to the usefulness of job shadowing, secondments and 'acting up' as sources of learning. The latter are relatively low in cost, but require managers to be creative in dealing with any disruption that they may cause to normal work routines.

Whereas Senker's chapter focuses on the highly qualified, it is non-traditional learners in the workplace who are the focus of Chapter 13. Taking a perspective from adult education, Caldwell examines how changes in work are challenging the relationship between vocational education and training (VET) and general education, particularly as regards some of the lowest-paid workers. Although the lifelong learning agenda is primarily driven by the competitiveness agenda, there is also an emphasis on widening participation which poses some fundamental challenges to employers, trade unions and adult educators if the workplace is to become a site for facilitating learning for all employees. In some occupations, particularly those involving contact with the public and caring skills, there are new demands for written and verbal communication skills and, in some cases, the establishment of new career paths driven by skill shortages amongst the more highly qualified. It is this context in which liberal education is being seen both as a bridge into more formal study and as a means of providing workers with more self-confidence in dealing with the challenges of their jobs and the wider labour market. Given adult educators' experience of dealing with non-traditional learners, they have a particular contribution to make to teaching and learning in the workplace.

Given the complexities of analysing workplace learning outlined above, the difficulties of measuring of attainment, especially in relation to informal learning, will be appreciated. Clearly, there are mechanisms for evaluating formal training interventions and this is the subject of the final chapter by Holly and Rainbird. Although there are a number of factors driving the use of evaluation, it operates most effectively with simple processes. For example, statistical process control can identify faults and so it may be relatively easy to attribute reductions in faults to training undertaken. The nature of the training intervention or programme will determine the most appropriate forms of evaluation and the extent to which they are able to contribute to further improvement. Interventions which are aimed at cultural change or improving customer service may be much harder to isolate from other developments in the work environment and to assess. Naturally, any attempt to identify mechanisms for measuring and raising attainment in the workplace must first grapple with the problem of identifying the complexity of learning in work settings.

Conclusion

In an analysis of the need to redirect the research agenda on skill formation, Ashton argues that 'many of those directly involved in the process of learning at work, both managers and individuals, still tend to see learning as relatively unproblematic, a natural occurrence which requires little support'(1998:68). He points to the importance of understanding learning as a process embedded in organisational structures. This book, with its focus on the workplace, attempts to locate both formal training and development and informal learning in the context of complex organisational processes and the conflict embedded in the employment relationship.

In this introduction, five challenges have been identified to the analysis of formal and informal learning in the workplace. The first of these refers primarily to the policy arena and to the need to deconstruct the consensus on the primacy of the employers' agenda on training and competitiveness. Since it deals primarily with the assumptions underlying the decisions made by policy-makers, it impacts on the workplace through the ways in which it affects the financial resources, legal entitlements, rights and responsibilities available to employers, employees, their representatives and to teachers and trainers. Insofar as the book is concerned with the workplace, policy developments and debates and the political spaces they create form the backdrop to the issues explored in the chapters.

The remaining four challenges define the structure of the book. The next three chapters (2, 3 and 4) concern organisational processes and an examination of the empirical evidence rather than abstract rhetoric, ideal systems and prescription. In this section, the tensions within organisations, in their structures and conflicting corporate objectives are examined. They may either facilitate or undermine strategies towards training and development. More fundamentally, the underlying tensions in management tools such as appraisal and performance management are analysed which, on closer inspection, have difficulty in reconciling organisational and individual development objectives. The following three chapters (5, 6 and 7) concern the development of a critical understanding of the nature of work modernisation and its relationship to training and development strategies. The relationship between organisational context and innovation in Human Resource and training strategies is explored in the chapters on multinational companies (MNCs), greenfield sites and work modernisation.

Chapters 8, 9 and 10 concern what counts as effective learning in the workplace. This varies according to perspective: employers, employees and their organisations all have legitimate interests in workplace learning. Their perceptions of who benefits from particular types of interventions will vary. Decisions on training take place against the broader backcloth of workplace industrial relations and questions of effort, control and reward, but training is also a strand running through its fabric. The relationship between management and labour is significant both as context and for the mechanisms adopted for dealing with workplace learning. A focus on learning, as opposed to training at work, is the subject of Chapters 11, 12 and 13. This implies looking at the informal opportunities for learning afforded by job design and the social relations of the workplace, as well as learning accessed through the employment relationship. Any assessment of what constitutes effective learning must recognise that workplace learning is complex, contextual and conflictual. As a consequence, the final chapter, by way of a conclusion, explores the limitations of evaluation as a tool, given the ways in which workplace learning defies simple procedures for measurement.

To return to our starting point, the workplace is enormously significant as a site of learning and for this reason it merits study. But it is also problematic. The issues explored in this book demonstrate that it can open up learning opportunities for workers and it can close them down. Learning can demotivate or motivate; it can debase or enrich the experience of work; it can be a vehicle for coercion or for emancipation. Above all else, workplace learning is a contested terrain.

Notes

1   Similar questions were raised in relation to the concept of social cohesion at a two-day seminar on 'Evolutions démographiques et le rôle de la protection sociale: le concept de la cohésion sociale' at the Université Libre de Bruxelles, 16–17 September 1999.
2   This point was made by Nancy Jackson at the conference 'Researching Work and Learning' at the University of Leeds, 10–12 September, 1999.

References

Ackers, P., Smith, C. and Smith, P. (eds) (1996) *The New Workplace and Trade Unionism. Critical Perspectives on Work and Organisation*, London and New York: Routledge.

Arulampalam, W. and Booth, A. (1998) 'Training and labour market flexibility: is there a trade-off?', *British Journal of Industrial Relations*, 36, 4, 521–536.

Ashton, D., (1998) 'Skill formation: redirecting the research agenda', in Coffield, F. (ed.), *Learning at Work*, University of Bristol: Policy Press.

Ashton, D., Davies, B., Felstead, A. and Green, F. (1999) *Work Skills in Britain*, Research Centre on Skills, Knowledge and Organisational Performance (SKOPE), Universities of Oxford and Warwick.

Brown, P. (1995) 'Cultural capital and social exclusion: some observations on recent trends in education, employment and the labour market', *Work, Employment and Society*, 9, 1, 29–51.

Cockburn, C. (1983) *Brothers. Male Dominance and Technological Change*, London: Pluto Press.

Cully, M., O'Reilly, A., Millward, N. and Forth, J. (1998) *Workplace Employee Relations Survey. Preliminary Findings*, London: HMSO.

Eraut, M., Alderton, J., Cole, G. and Senker, P. (1998) 'Learning from other people at work', in Coffield, F. (ed.), *Learning at Work*, University of Bristol: Policy Press.

European Commission (1997) *Partnership for a New Organisation of Work*, Luxembourg: Office for Official Publications of the European Communities.

Gallie, D., 'Introduction' in Gallie, D. (ed.) (1988) *Employment in Britain*, Oxford: Basil Blackwell.

Hyman, R., 'Flexible specialisation: miracle or myth?', in Hyman, R. and Streeck, W. (eds) (1988) *New Technology and Industrial Relations*, Oxford: Basil Blackwell.

IRRU (1997) *Comments on the European Commission's Green Paper 'Partnership for a New Organisation of Work'*, mimeo, Coventry: University of Warwick, November.

Jackson, N. and Jordan, S. (1999) 'Skills training. Who benefits?', paper presented to the conference 'Researching Work and Learning', University of Leeds, 10–12 September.

Keep, E., 'Vocational education and training for the young', in Sisson, K. (ed.) (1994) *Personnel Management in Britain*, 1st edn, Oxford: Basil Blackwell.

Keep. E. and Huddleston, P. (1998) 'What do employers want from education? Questions more easily asked than answered. The question revisited', paper presented to the 4th International Partnership Conference, Trondheim, Norway, July.

Keep, E. and Mayhew, K. (1996) 'Evaluating the assumptions that underlie training policy', in Booth, A. and Snower, D. (eds), *Acquiring Skills: Market Failures, Their Symptoms and Policy Responses*, Cambridge: Cambridge University Press.

Keep, E. and Rainbird, H., 'Towards the learning organisation?', in Bach, S. and Sisson, K. (eds) (2000) *Personnel Management in Britain*, 3rd edn, Oxford: Basil Blackwell.

Lave, J. and Wenger, E. (1991) *Situated Learning. Legitimate Peripheral Participation*, Cambridge: Cambridge University Press.

Maurice, M., Sellier, F. and Silvestre, J. J. (1986) *The Social Foundations of Industrial Power. A Comparison of France and Germany*, Translation of *Politiques d'Education et Organisation Industrielle en France et en Allemagne*. Cambridge, Mass., and London: MIT Press.

McGivney, V. (1997) 'Adult participation in learning: can we change the pattern?', in Coffield, F. (ed.), *A National Strategy for Lifelong Learning*, Newcastle: University of Newcastle, 127–41.

Perlmutter, H. (1965) 'L'enterprise internationale, trois conceptions', *Revue Economique et Sociale*, 4, 1, 9–18.

Pollert, A. (ed.) (1991) *Farewell to Flexibility?*, Oxford: Basil Blackwell.

Purcell, K. (1998) 'Gender and the experience of employment', in Gallie, D. (ed.), *Employment in Britain*, Oxford: Basil Blackwell.

Rainbird, H. (1994) 'The changing role of the training function: a test for the integration of Human Resource and business strategies?', *Human Resource Management Journal*, 5, 1, 72–89.

Rainbird, H. (1997) 'The social construction of skill', in Jobert, A., Marry, C., Tanguy, L. and Rainbird, H. (eds), *Education and Work in Great Britain, Germany and Italy*, London and New York: Routledge.

Rainbird, H., Munro, A., Holly, L. and Leisten, R. (1999) *The Future of Work in the Public Sector. Learning and Workplace Inequality*, University of Leeds, Future of Work Programme, discussion paper no. 2.

Senge, P. (1990) *The Fifth Discipline. The Art and Practice of the Learning Organisation*, New York: Doubleday.

Streeck, W. (1989) 'Skills and the limits to neo-liberalism: the enterprise of the future as a place of learning', *Work, Employment and Society*, 3, 1, 89–104.

Sutherland, J. (1998) *Workplace Learning for the Twenty First Century. Report of the Workplace Learning Task Group*, London: Unison, March.

Thompson, P. (1983) *The Nature of Work. An Introduction to Debates on the Labour Process*, London: Macmillan.

CHAPTER 2

The organisation of the training function in large firms

Sonia Carey

Introduction

This examination of the training function is contextualised within that section of the Human Resource Management literature which positions training as a central element of company strategy (Guest, 1987). The structure of the training function, determined by its status and remit, may be said to reflect a company's commitment to its employees' long-term development and, within this paradigm, training is claimed to be a key determinant of competitive success (Bennet, Ketchen and Blanton Schultz, 1998). The training function, furthermore, may play an important socialisation role to reinforce company culture through company-specific programmes, promoting the general HRM goals of commitment, flexibility, quality and strategic integration (Guest, 1987). These general suppositions are reviewed in this chapter within a framework which seeks to identify how the structure and strategies of large organisations may promote, compromise or militate against that achievement.

Organisational strategy is necessarily conditioned by the external environment, the size of the organisation, products and the nature and complexity of its production technology. Company training policies are shaped by political, social, economic, technological and demographic conditions and can be developed or constrained by the educational, vocational and financial market systems. Within multinationals, the perceived increasing dissociation in the UK of state education and training provision from the needs of the enterprise, and the education system's inability to produce appropriately skilled individuals, has given rise to the development of organisation-wide standards of competence, development and education programmes. Companies may thereby address the shortcomings of the external environment directly through their own programmes. Since common international product standards have given rise to similar operational requirements in management policies across countries, training may be increasingly directed towards organisational- or project-based programmes on a global pattern. Arguably, training strategy could thus directly enhance the competitive advantage of those organisations. This potential clearly has significant implications for the training function.

The widely documented factors fostering the development of HRM focus largely on those product markets where organisational survival is equated with competitive advantage (Guest, 1987). Competitive pressures compelled many companies to develop mechanisms to manage changes associated with technological innovations and consequent market developments. Thus radical approaches are more likely to be introduced at board level when competitive pressures compel them to do so (Wright *et al.*, 1998).

The term HRM can be applied to a set of managerial initiatives designed to facilitate such changes. These initiatives have the specific aim of securing the organisation's competitive advantage through greater employment efficiency. The means to achieve this aim have profound implications for base levels of competence within the workforce and any long-term commitment to training and development. Where competitive advantage has been pursued through the provision of high-quality goods and services, employees become a valuable resource, and hence the concept of Human Resources Management becomes a strategic consideration. The term HRM, then, may be viewed as a strategy which adopts an integrated programme of matching particular organisational activities to the environment in which it operates. The development of such an all-embracing strategy requires structural changes and developed systems for it to be effectively carried forward. This chapter, therefore, is concerned with the resultant structures designed to administer organisational strategies.

The organisation of the training function and training activity should reflect company policy and strategic direction. This sets a number of challenges to the training function. It should not be assumed, for example, that organisations with declared HRM policies have developed and are developing training operations at all levels, adapted and able to respond to a dynamic environment. There is only limited evidence that this is the case, yet it crucially affects training personnel's ability or capacity to react effectively to the demands made of them (Ashton, 1998). The extent to which this is an association with a tradition or image of Taylorist modes of instruction, based only on the acquisition of a set of competencies necessary for the performance of given tasks, is considered later. At this juncture, it is sufficient simply to note that within such models, training is regarded as a cost rather than a core function and is therefore not a strategic consideration and is susceptible to cutbacks. Moreover, it belies the range of activities subsumed under the title of training, from the satisfactory completion of a single task, through interpersonal skills and organisational socialisation, to the analysis and application of complex technical data. It may be argued, then, that unless training becomes a core activity, with training personnel as core workers, the 'contract of complacency' (Stone, 1991) between employers and employees will continue to hinder the much vaunted 'training culture' sought by many organisations.

This chapter first examines the features of HRM and discusses to what degree it has been incorporated into corporate strategic thinking with reference to several studies. HRM is then discussed in the context of organisational structure and the extent to which the structure of a corporation, itself determined by strategy, inhibits the development of HRM in general and training in particular. The relationship between the training function and corporate structure is then questioned, together with the role of training in the delivery of corporate strategy. Finally, the conclusion suggests that traditional roles of trainers and training functions must be abandoned (or developed) if strategic HRM is to contribute to the success of corporations.

Features of Human Resource Management

HRM may be defined as a set of managerial initiatives which have the specific aim of securing the organisation's competitive advantage by utilising the labour resource more effectively. These initiatives are a coordinated organisational response to external market pressures. Where training is directly linked to competitiveness, then, these initiatives are more likely to be promoted at corporate level and become a strategic rather than operational issue. However, the development of such a strategy requires structural adjustments to provide a mechanism capable of translating strategic objectives into practice at all levels in the company, both vertically and horizontally.

Barney and Wright (1998) propose the use of the VRIO framework (value, rareness, imitability and organisation) to examine the role that the HR function plays in developing sustainable competitive advantage. They conclude that HR should provide the firm with resources that are rare, provide value and cannot easily be imitated by others.

Since the notion of HRM is derived from the uncertainties associated with rapid technological change, each component of HRM is designed to be a specific response to external economic and social conditions. Training plays a vital role, not only in retraining for process development but also in securing the corporate goals of commitment, flexibility and quality. It therefore becomes crucial to integrate the training function into mainstream business activity rather than maintain it as a peripheral activity. Thus the principal policy goal of HRM is considered here to be the concept of strategic integration. It requires cohesion vertically and horizontally, and is thus particularly difficult to achieve in multibusiness companies where the diversity of products and production methods inhibit lateral integration. It requires greater emphasis to be placed on the identification of training needs and the organisation of training. However, a large number of studies suggest that the strategic integration of training has not generally been achieved. The Price Waterhouse Cranfield Project, for example, identified a high proportion of European organisations, (60–90 per cent in the countries studied) which systematically analysed their training requirements. Nevertheless, the survey concluded that the consistency and coherence of training policies, and indeed their human resource strategy as a whole, were often too poor to underpin the corporate objectives they were designed to support (Syrett, 1990).

This may be due to a range of factors. The existing training personnel may not have sufficient status in the company to develop their function; production managers may not be committed to corporate objectives and therefore fail to promote training strategies; or there may be a general unwillingness to increase corporate funding for training purposes which inhibits the development of the function beyond established parameters.

Schuller argues that the devolution of responsibility to line managers and the encouragement of employee participation enhances worker commitment, the second policy goal of HRM (1991). If employees are involved directly or indirectly in company affairs, at whatever level, he continues, they will be more committed to the effective implementation of decisions than if such decisions are unilaterally imposed. More generally, their effort and enthusiasm will be greater, with consequent benefits for efficiency. Workers with costly transferable skills in whom the company has invested high training costs require personal training and development plans to secure their commitment to the company and thus reduce labour turnover. This places new demands on trainers at all levels, and broadens the responsibility of line managers who play a pivotal role within the human resources management model, and who occupy a central position in the implementation of training policy. However, initiatives can be heavily diluted by line managers who tend to concentrate on day-to-day operational affairs rather than corporate goals.

Both behavioural commitment to pursue agreed goals and attitudinal commitment reflected in a strong identification with the enterprise have not been universally secured even at management level. Thomas (1990), for example, draws attention to research which indicates that the aspirations and values of British management are changing, in that they are seeking careers which mirror their own personal values rather than those of the organisation.

The goal of employee commitment is thus based on the assumption that committed employees will be more satisfied, more productive and more adaptable. This adaptability or flexibility is an essential component of HRM and constitutes the third policy goal. At an organisational level this involves a need for delegation of control to avoid rigid hierarchical bureaucratic structures and demarcations among groups of workers or individual functions. At an individual level, new patterns of working allow a broad and flexible utilisation of the workforce across boundaries between production and technical work. Workers need to be trained in a range of tasks and be prepared to move between these as the production schedule demands. But being trained in a range of tasks does not necessarily imply the development of higher-level skills and, in high-volume production, this may be regarded as little more than 'flexible Taylorism' (Thompson, 1989).

The goal of quality relates to features of management behaviour which include the management of, and investment in, highly-skilled employees in order to produce high-quality goods and services. This goal necessitates a major investment in training and development programmes, as well as greater attention to recruitment and selection procedures.

There is clear evidence that such developments towards these goals have taken place. Indeed, studies of 'excellence' have formed the core around which models of HRM have been further developed. There is, however, a dearth of evidence to support the notion that the training function itself has undergone fundamental review. Thus the quantity of training may have increased, budgets may have been increased, but there may not necessarily be a corresponding qualitative improvement. Hendry (1991) for example, remarks that often the training only happens as an afterthought and even without the alignment of other HRM practices. Kinnie (1991) notes that long-standing obstacles to the effectiveness of training are still apparent. Often there is little thought as to what type of training is required and a tendency to use tried and tested methods and trainers. In other studies, the idea of human resource development (HRD) being a key element in the firm's corporate strategy did not find support (Storey, 1991). Recent research (Ashton, 1998) contrasts the role of training with the experience of learning, suggesting that in some cases companies can be unaware of barriers placed before employees because the process of learning itself is contentious.

The effectiveness of HRM depends on its alignment with the organisation's stage of development and its ability to balance corporate direction with customer-focused business units. Paradoxically, the principles of strategic HRM, which promote responsible autonomy, may be undermined by the rationale for decentralisation which focuses on 'professional entrepreneurship', possibly at the expense of wider HRM policies. This inherent contradiction creates tensions between central and local management and has important implications for the training function.

HRM and organisational structure

If, as Chandler (1991) suggests, structure follows strategy, the organisation of the training function will, to a significant degree, reflect the importance of training in corporate strategy. Since policy goals are designed to integrate with organisational structures to achieve the desired outcomes, one may consider the commitment to HRM by companies in terms of their structural ability to facilitate coordinated, integrated systems. Many case studies of organisations which have led to models of 'good practice' assume a broadly common organisational form where HRM strategies are supported by appropriate structures and systems at every level. Indeed, HRM has been defined in terms of whatever organisations regarded as 'models of excellence' do. On closer analysis, as Guest (1990) points out, there is often little similarity between the organisations save financial success.

Strategic HRM is a systems approach. Organisational change limited to single components has a limited impact at best (Useem and Gottlieb, 1990). Such changes not only render some of the organisational structures inappropriate but may also reduce, rather than enhance, their potential for efficiency.

The decision by companies to expand their portfolios through diversification and internationalisation, which occurred particularly in the 1960s, resulted in the evolution of organisations competing in a range of often unrelated product markets. In such circumstances, effective decision-making and entrepreneurial behaviour at business unit level could only be achieved through devolved decision-making structures. The need for greater flexibility in production patterns, working methods and increased employee motivation also supported the rationale for decentralisation. In some organisations, the accompanying restructuring was designed to incorporate HRM policies and systems. In others, the strategic decision to decentralise and the means by which the desired goals could be achieved are reflected in quite different organisational structures, styles of management and HRM.

By focusing on the role and structure of the training function in an organisational context, it may be possible to distinguish between those companies committed to the strategic integration of training within an HRM model, those whose structures inhibit central coordination or development of training standards and the organisations which positively discourage lateral integration. One may then consider the extent to which organisations have the capacity to develop an effective training function with a commitment to enhancing the training capability of the organisation. Since an HRM strategy in a large organisation must co-exist with a degree of decentralisation, it is necessary to address the inevitable tensions which arise as the balance of influence shifts between the 'professional entrepreneurs' within the business units and the specialist corporate functions, and how this affects the advantages, if any, of a central training function to coordinate organisation-wide training.

Much of the research on strategic HRM uses the Miles and Snow view of 'strategic typology' (Bennett, Ketchen and Blanton Schultz 1998). This proposes three types of organisation: those which search for new product/market opportunities; those which defend and maintain only a subset of potential product/market domains; and those which are a hybrid of the two approaches. Bennett, Ketchen and Blanton Schultz propose that only the hybrid type of organisation (the 'analysers') will have more integration between the HRM function and strategic decision-making.

In order to consider the level of influence afforded to training personnel and policies, Goold and Campbell's (1987) classification of organisations in terms of the centre's influence over business unit strategies is a productive framework for analysing the terms and structures within which managers propose and implement these strategies. They classify firms as strategically- or financially-oriented. Chandler (1991) suggests that Goold and Campbell's three styles of organisation, strategic planning, strategic control and financial control, result from different paths of growth and therefore from different patterns of investment and from different sets of organisational capabilities. These capabilities, in turn, reflect the different characteristics of the businesses in which the firms operate.

An outline of the different types of organisation, using Goold and Campbell's classification, provides a broad indication of the organisation and status of the training function. These are summarised in Table 2.1.

Financial control

Despite having the best profit performance and the largest growth in the 1980s, financial control companies in Britain grew almost wholly by acquisition rather than direct internal investment. Some of these companies were 'pure' conglomerates, such as Hanson Trust and BTR. They owned, rather than managed, diverse businesses.

The corporate office is generally small with almost no functional executives except in finance and public relations. The role of the corporate headquarters is essentially administrative or loss preventative, reviewing the financial performance of business units and adjusting the portfolio accordingly. Human resources are an accountancy matter. As training is not a strategic management issue, business units pursue individual human resource strategies. These costs are deemed budget items and are therefore likely to become the target of cost-reduction activities. The main skills required at corporate level are accountancy-related.

Divisional managers play a 'linking and surveillance' role between the units and the centre (Chandler, 1991), as business units define strategies. Since the

Table 2.1 Organisational styles and training implications

	Financial control	Structure Strategic control	Strategic planning
Strategy			
Portfolio	Unrelated businesses. Ownership rather than management.	Diversified businesses with common strategic characteristics.	Small number of core businesses. Related resource and skills.
Structure of accountability	Short lines of communication.	Bureaucratic planning process.	Bureaucratic procedures and decision-making.
Relatedness	Management skills. No technological synergies.	Technological linkages, some synergies.	Resources, technologies.
Growth	Acquisition.	Internal investment/acquisition.	Largely organic.
Focus	Capital budgeting process. Efficient use of corporate assets. Short term.	Long-term strategic thinking but short-run constraints.	Long-term product development.
Technology	Mature. Low R&D, low complexity.	R&D requirement for particular technologies.	Related technologies.
Value	Attached to share price, tangible physical resources.	Attached to share price/market share product development.	Product/market share and intellectual resources.
Skill	Acquisition and restructuring of underperforming businesses. Resource allocation.	Project management. Identifying technological synergies.	Potential synergistic relationships.
Markets	Stable/mature.	Mix.	Competitive/new.
Likely HRM features			
Aim	Efficient use of human resources and numerical flexibility. Non-economic decisions delegated.	Decentralised HRM. Autonomous business units.	Strategic integration of training into wider business planning.
Objective	Operating efficiency.	Devolved strategy. Balance strategic and financial controls.	Resource generation.
HRM representation	No corporate representation. Different employee relations policies at BU.	Low corporate representation. Higher status at local level.	Corporate. Coordinated HR policies.
Culture	No corporate culture.	Scope for subculture to develop because of customer rather than corporate focus.	Corporate culture and tradition.
Training	Peripheral to the achievement of corporate objectives. Low status/low profile.	Status depends upon individual businesses.	Strategically important. High profile. High status
Training budgets	A current discretionary expense.	Long-term investments. Vulnerable.	Long-term investment.
Focus on training	Business knowledge. No corporate mechanism to support HRM policies.	Disparate training requirements as skill levels differ between divisions. Mixture of training priorities. Limited corporate support.	Core competencies and capabilities a corporate resource. Organisation-wide planning.
Socialisation	HR policies an operational matter.	Decentralised HRM therefore limited.	An integral part of the training process.
Training personnel.	Training outsourced. In-house instructors. No financial logic in developing internal training function.	Internal specialists for technologically complex fields. Some outsourcing.	Internal training function.
Response to skills shortages	Increasing wages/poaching/contracting and temporary workers. Reliance on state provision of competence training.	Mix.	Training a long-term remedy to labour scarcity. Career planning. Less reliance on state provision.

BU = business unit

R & D = research and development

budgets of each unit are unrelated, these companies have the lowest linkages between divisions and the lowest overlap between units and within divisions. The centre focuses on budgets and concentrates on a rapid payback on capital expenditure rather than long-term plans. Current financial performance, then, is the critical measure of achievement. Weak businesses experience a management change or are divested. Clear standards and incentives are set by the centre for businesses to achieve.

British companies in this group have avoided acquiring businesses in technologically complex, capital-intensive industries where both process and product innovations require risky long-term investment or research and development (R&D) capability (*Financial Times*, 11 September 1992). Hanson Trust, for instance, remained successful because it concentrated on mature, low-technology, short-cycle businesses which were not very capital-intensive. BTR was similar with consequent implications for skills levels. Profit margins are enhanced by reducing manpower and decreasing investment, particularly in people. There is an unambiguous priority on enhancing shareholder value.

Financial control companies are characterised as having no overall corporate strategy other than portfolio management. The corporate plan is merely a collection of the business unit plans. Centralised strategic planning would have little benefit because planning is more closely integrated with the operation level. This, argues Hall, is an inseparable (and perhaps the most important) part of a general manager's job: 'It is a creative process founded on a deep understanding of the success factors of a particular business' (1987). Financial control companies which also included Trafalgar House (now owned by a finance company, HKL), Williams Holdings and Tomkins, were often criticised for their risk-averse, mechanical and unimaginative style; as well as for their failure to grow organically, for milking their businesses, asset stripping and failure to expand (*Sunday Times*, 2 May 1993).

Highly diversified firms have no need for interdependencies among business units, therefore there is no need for resource-sharing. Indeed, seeking such linkages might subvert the efficiency of capital allocation and performance monitoring. Human resource policies, therefore, are an operational rather than corporate responsibility. Tradition is not a feature of holding companies (Purcell, 1991).

As services may be bought from efficient outside suppliers, there is a greater dependence on the state and other bodies to provide appropriately skilled workers. Such companies respond to labour scarcities by increasing wages without adjustments in other human resource areas such as training. As Doeringer and Piore note, such compensation strategies produce an inflationary wage spiral without relieving much of the underlying scarcity of labour in the short run (1971).

Although businesses within financial control companies may pursue the goal of strategic integration, there is no corporate mechanism to support HRM policies. The essence of the financial control style remains its ability to improve performance in autonomous stand-alone businesses; it is less suited to a portfolio of 'core' businesses or those requiring coordination (Goold, Campbell and Luchs, 1993a). Since training tends to be regarded as an operational issue, corporate support for training initiatives is unlikely, as is enhancing the organisation's training capability. Human resource issues such as remuneration are fixed more by external market conditions because of the lack of intra-company progression and career structure.

Hall suggests that business unit managers require 'an intellectual framework on which their knowledge of the business and its environment can be arranged' (1987:86). Since corporate staff cannot get to know individual businesses, the focus of training is on business knowledge, markets and product knowledge for business unit managers. An organisation-wide knowledge base is not required, although a group identity is necessary for shareholders and therefore a strong centralised public relations function is often present.

Strategic planning

In contrast, strategic planning companies tend to be the least diversified, largely concentrating on related products and product markets. They have the most connections between divisions and the greatest overlap between business units within divisions. They are similar in nature to Rumelt's classification of 'related constrained' firms. This he takes to mean firms that are diversified around some single core resource, which can be tangible (a distribution system) or intangible (a technology or marketing ability).

Within these companies the centre actively develops a strategy with business unit managers and may also have a corporate strategy coordinating developments across the business units. Resource-sharing may be enhanced through the creation of administrative systems and cultural 'norms' (Rumelt, 1974). Performance targets are set in the context of broad, strategic terms and annual financial targets are perceived to be less important than strategic objectives.

Strategic planning companies, which include BOC, Cadbury-Schweppes, BP and the former UB, are most likely to have stated long-term aims and objectives, and seek to present a corporate character across businesses. Guest (1991) has suggested that only strategic planning companies have the capacity and rationale to develop HRM.

Quality of goods or services, as well as the behavioural and educational credentials of the workforce (identified as a major policy goal of HRM), can be best developed and monitored in strategic planning companies. Selection, promotion and development policies encourage high-ability employees to remain with the company. Unilever, one of the most homogenised forms of organisation, has a world-wide job evaluation scheme for posts at graduate recruitment level and above.

Within these companies, training is most likely to be represented at corporate level. The particular advantages of in-house training specialists, given the economies of scale of large organisations, are related to company-specificity of programmes. In addition, there are opportunities for training personnel to compensate for public sector educational or vocational deficiencies by building up an internal resource and offering remedial education programmes. Within strategic planning companies, in-house development programmes reflect and reinforce organisational values and norms, although this may not be an explicit aim.

Due to the inter-relationship between businesses, the opportunity for an inappropriate match between organisational needs and the content of training courses may be reduced, thereby arguably providing a higher return on the investment in training. Corporate training functions may monitor the quality of training provided internally and by external agencies. It is possible for preferred supplier lists of external training agencies to be developed and maintained for business units identifying similar training needs with a database incorporating a range of open learning packages and information systems to inform and update training personnel.

Where training is represented at corporate level, it necessarily has a higher profile and is more likely to be included in broader policy decisions which, in turn, enhances its status. Training personnel as part of the HRM function can exert considerable influence because they manage ports of entry and career ladders which influence potential mobility.

In companies with a highly-developed internal labour market, the wage competition model often present in financial control companies is replaced by the job competition model (King, 1994). Excess demand for a particular skill is less likely to induce increases in relative earnings which would create an imbalance in the internal wage structure. In this model, the company initially aims to increase the effort level and hence the productivity of its existing labour force. Vacancies are filled largely through internal promotions, with any necessary training provided internally. The internal wage structure offers sufficient incentive for workers to seek promotion, thereby reducing interfirm mobility. The reliance on the external labour market is therefore restricted to skill levels at the lower ports of entry. Deficiencies in literacy, numeracy or technological knowledge have to be remedied by developing 'core competencies' (Prahalad and Hamel, 1990) or 'core capabilities' (Stalk, Evans and Shulman 1992). Investment in this general training is based on the expectation that employees remain with the company.

Strategic planning companies have been criticised for their overanalytical, bureaucratic and time-consuming planning process. The case studies in Goold and Campbell's work (1987) indicated that, as a consequence, general management capability at business unit level was less developed. Although managers appeared to identify with the companies' ambitions for core businesses, a lack of autonomy, bureaucracy and unclear performance targets resulted in a degree of frustration. The structure and systems, then, allow control over standards of training at plant level but constrain innovation and are less responsive to adverse market and labour force conditions.

Human resource development plans, which are by their nature long-term investments, are not included in analysts' assessments of the share value of companies, making such policies a 'risk' on the part of the company in terms of short-term market valuation. Managers who opt for a more creative strategy of developing products and markets internationally, which promises more employment, are penalised by 'a stock-market conditioned to short-term earnings growth by the management style of Hanson and his imitators' (*Sunday Times*, 2 May 1993b). Consequently, strategic planning companies do less well in the capital markets and are prey to takeover bids.

Strategic Control

Strategic control companies tend to operate more businesses and have fewer overlaps and interrelationships between divisions and business units than strategic planning types. They are characterised by low planning influence and tight strategic controls. Business unit managers initiate the development plans; targets are set for strategic objectives such as market share, as well as financial targets which are expected to be met. This type of company was characterised in the later 1980s and early 1990s by takeovers, threats of takeovers and demergers (Goold, Campbell and Luchs, 1993b).

The decentralisation philosophy, it is claimed, has been welcomed by more capable and aggressive business level managements. Such companies diversified into often unrelated products and product markets. Goold and Campbell suggest that these types of company exhibit better financial performance; portfolio rationalisation; systematic, structured and analytically-based planning processes; and business unit motivation and capability for strategic thinking. Tighter controls have pushed up margins and reduced costs in many businesses. Low profitability or a perceived lack of strategic portfolio fit often result in closure or divestment decisions. However, they argue that within these organisations, which include the former ICI, Vickers and, at the time, Plessey, long-term strategic thinking and short-term control is hard to maintain, with the consequent problem of short-term and financial targets taking precedence over long-term strategy (1987). As Useem and Gottlieb observe, although strategic business units can develop autonomy, so that the focus is away from the parent company, ultimately financial controls will prevail when particular services can be supplied internally at a lower cost (1990).

Devolved responsibility for strategic development can distance the centre from the issues in each business. This may have an adverse effect on major strategic initiatives that require corporate sponsorship. Managers are able to think more strategically, have greater autonomy and clearer responsibility for performance, but potential cross-divisional interrelationships may be missed and the centre may be perceived as 'distant'.

Within such a framework, a corporate training function, if one exists, has fewer direct advantages. Organisation-wide programmes may appear irrelevant to business unit managers whose perceptions and expectations relate more closely to those of the customer than those of divisional or corporate personnel. Their own training personnel may be better able to determine and deliver business-oriented training within particular product groups in the organisation. Alternatively, training may be considered a support service and thus outsourced. As a support service rather than a core activity, it is more susceptible to cuts. If there is no comprehensive training infrastructure, disparate, uncoordinated training policies are pursued without an overarching organisational context. Thus Purcell argues that the 'worst position for the multidivisional company is to ignore the issue of style and culture by hiding behind the philosophy of decentralisation, so that no standards are set and confusion and inconsistency is mistaken for healthy diversity' (1986:40).

In a political and economic climate where the needs of the capital market take preference over the product market, the maintenance of stock market values by stringent financial measures may remain a feature of British industry. This may hinder the development of organic growth and perpetuate the charge of *ad hoc* corporate decision-making (Storey, 1991). Whereas the uncertainty in product markets has promoted the development of HRM, it has been hindered by the uncertainty in financial markets.

Decentralisation and strategic integration

In theory, as Nordhaug (1990) argues, decentralisation can only succeed if the capacity of decision-making in lower levels of the organisation is being developed through training programmes. This is true, he says, of both operationally-oriented training (technical) and training which aims to promote interrelationships between local decisions and the strategic goals of the organisation (personal and professional development and socialisation).

In practice, decentralisation and accompanying autonomy within business units may create tensions between them and the centre. The notion of strategic integration assumes that all organisations are or should be structured in a particular way, with a single set of goals which can be applied across product ranges and without reference to industry conditions. To minimise the possibility of departments or units pursuing their own goals in ways that conflict with the company's corporate objectives, a certain minimum level of knowledge may be needed. The process, therefore, is often linked with behavioural and attitudinal 'commitment'.

It cannot be assumed that senior management in an organisation will support new initiatives, or that they can be unambiguously translated into practice at plant level. In most decentralised organisations, directives may usually be circumvented if there is no support for them. As Harvey Jones observed, 'No form of instruction can be sufficiently detailed that it cannot be evaded by someone who is determined not to follow it' (Ansoff, 1987:8).

If the centre develops a disproportionate control over business unit planning, it may result in inappropriate strategies which do not reflect local realities and which reduce the ability of local management to respond effectively to specific opportunities and threats. If local management has a very high degree of autonomy, the centre has a reduced ability to make radical changes when these are perceived to be necessary and business units may develop objectives and norms fundamentally incompatible with those of corporate management.

Conventional wisdom says that cultural and institutional differences between countries and acquired/merged companies outweigh the forces for strategic convergence (Jain, Lawler and Morishimon 1998). However, the authors believe this is changing through a combination of the straightforward diffusion of best practices from parent to affiliate or 'reverse diffusion', where best practices from affiliates are adopted. The movement between strategic control and strategic planning styles may precipitate tensions as local managers develop a high degree of autonomy and develop strategic plans, only to see this eroded when central functions expand their influence; or, conversely, they are expected to develop strategic plans without the appropriate skills to facilitate their new role. It may be argued that moves to extend the centre's influence over business unit policy may be linked to the inadequate or narrowly defined training received by senior and general managers at business unit level. As a consequence, they are ill-equipped to develop effective strategic policy within the corporate framework. In practice, there is little evidence that at business unit level training is necessarily aligned with other HRM practices, or that it is a main component of corporate strategy (Hendry and Pettigrew, 1986).

Goold and Campbell suggest that strategic control companies are moving in the direction of strategic planning to overcome the problem of the 'distant' centre, but are maintaining devolved responsibility. Thus it may also be seen as a response to the ambiguities of the strategic control style which exhibits more pragmatic decision-making in response to financial market pressures and also part of a fluidity of movement between strategic control and strategic planning styles.

It is not possible both to provide strong leadership from the centre and to encourage entrepreneurial freedom for business unit managers. Corporate management cannot both impose sanctions for failure to reach targets and expect innovative strategies. Purcell (1989) sees the trend towards diversification and decentralisation as a major inhibitor of HRM. Indeed, he considers strategic business units (SBUs) and corporate HRM as incompatible.

Even within strategic planning companies, Goold and Campbell argue, long periods of style stability appear to be the exception. Periods of looser control are followed by a tightening-up, and strong central influence is followed by more delegation. Changes are more readily accepted when financial stress reinforces the challenge to 'old' ways of doing things.

Human Resources Management, corporate structure and the training function

The impetus for organisational change and the possibility of addressing market challenges, remedying knowledge and skill deficiencies, and developing organisation-wide bases of competence and human resource development, depend crucially on the operation of an efficient and developed training function. Models of corporate strategy and structure within financial control and strategic control companies in general preclude a central role for training. If human resource development is not afforded a central role, strategic choices in developing training policy are limited and the training function remains an add-on or periphery activity, so that its position in relation to the hierarchy of the organisation is more difficult to identify.

The devolution of training policy to operational level without corporate representation reduces the possibility of developing an integrated, coordinated and proactive training strategy. Decentralisation has not diminished the centre's power base. Indeed, as Alvesson (1991) comments, it has retained and reinforced control over critical investment decisions (although not necessarily human capital investments), thus strengthening its influence. A parallel development is the enlargement of the line manager's role requiring the development of broader managerial skills, and an understanding of corporate objectives and the associated attitudinal changes which the new and unfamiliar role requires (Sunderland, 1991). There is little published evidence to suggest that the emphasis on developing the skill base and levels of managerial competence have necessarily been mirrored in the development of the training function. A lack of in-house expertise and of coordinated training strategies has led to disparate training policies within some organisations, and an increasing use of external consultants without an effective evaluation of their quality and suitability.

Where investment was focused on capital stock rather than human capital in the production of low-cost standardised products, proven ability or even literacy were not prerequisites for employment. This was associated with the development of Taylorist principles of scientific management in the workplace and is still, in certain markets, a feature of British industrial training where the emphasis does not extend beyond technical competence. The training function, therefore, was concerned primarily with the acquisition of basic technical competencies. As a low-priority activity, it had low status and generally no career structure.

Within an HRM model, training is a high-profile activity but arguably remains a low-status function because of its historical associations and the lack of investment in the development of trainers. Training for technical competence is confined to specific operationally-orientated tasks. Labour productivity is increased by the transmission, through instruction, of information directly significant to the range of tasks associated with a particular occupation. New production methods may necessitate a broader range of competences, or a change in skill requirements, but not necessarily at a higher level than before. As Hyman comments, 'an expanded portfolio of competences does not necessarily equal enhanced skill, although the individuals will be of greater value to the employer' (1987).

The trainee is a largely passive recipient of instruction, regulated by the demands of the production schedule, customer requirements for increased and consistent quality, or legislation. Often groups of workers receive very little formal training and that is usually tied to some specific occasion or event, or to instruction regarding the use of new machinery. The employees who are most likely to need training are the least likely to get it: for example, young adults for whom training might be a powerful motivator. In Stone's US study (1991), for example, two-thirds of the total corporate training budget was spent on 'college-educated' men and women.

Training and retraining are responses to particular operational needs and therefore largely reactive and are determined by market demand, rather than being focused on transferable skills. Such training policies may be developed at business unit level without forming part of an organisation-wide training strategy. Where the focus of training is on technical competence, this is more likely to be reflected in low-status training personnel. As Pettigrew, Sparrow and Hendry (1988) remark, 'apart from the likely competence of training personnel this critically affects the image its activities have'. Thus the more the firm develops the training function within a production logic, the more the contents of trainer training will remain technical and contain few pedagogical or relational features (CEDEFOP, 1990). 'Unless the training specialist can avail himself of a complete analysis of a company's mechanics ... training functions will only revolve around mechanistic techniques and fail in the objective of developing human resources in line with a company's corporate policy' (Jaap and Watson, 1970).

Where the production process requires only technical competence, there is no financial advantage for the firm in investing in the human capital of workers. Development or education plans are considered inappropriate for workers whose long-term commitment may not be required and, since the nature of the work necessitates little initial training, the selection of employees can be easily made from the pool of unemployed with few vocational qualifications or work skills. Eraut (1997) proposes a definition of learning which should be narrowed to include only 'significant changes in competencies or understanding' and not include simple communication and understanding of information. Development refers to the transmission of competences that are less technical or task-specific and relate to the development of analytical capacities, problem-solving skills, communication skills and the ability to cope with change (Nordhaug, 1990).

As the principal rationale for decentralisation was the encouragement of more effective decision-making and entrepreneurial behaviour at business unit level, development programmes were important measures to achieve this as, hitherto, line managers were primarily concerned with operational affairs rather than strategic objectives.

The existence of a well developed training function impacts on the perceptions and expectations of the workforce. Employees' capacity and readiness to continue learning, and the acknowledgement by employers that this is increasingly important for organisational survival in core businesses, has led to educational initiatives in industry. A few companies provide in-house basic skills programmes. Some, for example, Ford and Rover, have taken steps to institutionalise educational activities as a means of securing organisational commitment and as part of a development of a 'learning culture'. The introduction of non-firm-specific education is a significant step in motivating individuals to pursue further formal and informal training. Evidence from case studies (Ashton, 1998) suggests that this form of learning is on the increase. As a result, in some cases, on-the-job training has been transferred to line management or is outsourced. The trainer's role has become more of a consultant to line management on techniques and courses available. 'Training is more highly focussed on improving company performance and the business objectives' (Ashton, 1998).

In companies committed to an HRM strategy because they have recognised the benefit of developing all employees, training must be seem to be an important and long-term strategic function. Hence, as in other functions of such importance, the trainers themselves must be of the highest quality and the training function must have a career development structure and be recognised as a core function with prospects which attract high calibre personnel, from which managers can be drawn to fill senior positions.

The multinational or large company espousing HRM which fully recognises the role and value of the training function should therefore develop a strategy which establishes a level of quality of achievement in the training of all its personnel. Because the strategy is universally applied to all business units irrespective of location, and because training personnel are themselves familiar with corporate strategy, the differences in quality and availability of national and local state-funded education and training resources then merely determine the level of resource which the company allocates to training in each business unit. Hence a multinational committed to HRM principles could have large training departments in one territory, while in another it merely takes advantage of public or private sector facilities, and this would be consistent with strategic aims.

Conclusion

The combination of external market pressures and tensions arising from changing organisation structures and styles focuses attention on HRM issues, the balance of attention being affected by the strategic priorities determined by the organisation. Employment efficiency in the internal labour market is the common theme, achieved by measures to increase motivation, commitment, flexibility and an emphasis on quality; but the means of achieving these varies. As industries become increasingly knowledge-based, companies need to develop a training infrastructure offering broad-based qualifications. Where there is a commitment to HRM through the strategic integration of training, organisational structures must be adapted and developed to facilitate and enhance training capacity and quality. Where training is represented at corporate level, organisation-wide standards may be set for all employees, moving the focus of training from technical competence to development and education. This involves removing the differential focus between those who currently undertake development programmes (generally managers and core employees), and those whose training has been restricted to technical competence.

Highly diversified corporations whose structures inhibit central coordination or development of a training standard, or conglomerates and companies which positively discourage lateral integration, are likely to exhibit a range of policies, at times contradictory, reflecting responses to market conditions which may affect some business units more adversely than others. In such organisations, disparate training needs are required for a wide range of skills, occupations and processes and hence a mixed pattern of training emerges to accommodate this.

With no organisation-wide standards or central direction for training or trainers, these companies are more likely to concentrate development programmes on employees in core businesses. This results in a divergence of intra-organisational policy objectives for training personnel whose qualifications and aspirations relate to the nature of the production process and customer requirements in the business unit, rather than national or international organisational standards.

Within companies where training has only an operational input, those employed in the training function may have a personal commitment to developing employee- rather than organisation-oriented programmes, but may be unable to do so within existing structures. They are therefore constrained from developing strategic objectives.

The role of the designated trainer or instructor with its emphasis on initial training for craft skills does not easily fit into the HRM model, and it is likely that the status of such personnel will differ from their colleagues in other sectors of the company, with consequent disadvantages for career advancement. By using external training companies for technical instruction, company training personnel can concentrate on broader responsibilities without being affected by market fluctuations which vary the amount of training activity in some sectors.

Raising the status of training involves developing the training function within organisations and investing further in the development of trainers. This necessitates a rejection of Taylorist modes of training policy and, perhaps more importantly, Taylorist attitudes towards training.

Information systems can be developed company-wide to inform line managers and training personnel internationally of legislative, production or organisational changes. Such systems can also feed product or customer information through the network from personnel in business units, thus reducing the 'distance' between central and local managers which hitherto had been a constraining factor. Such systems require a standard of capability among trainers in all markets.

The provision of educational programmes for all employees could help break down the institutionalised barriers to learning after the statutory school-leaving age. The benefits of continual learning, and the self-confidence which it develops, can feed back into the school system. Mechanisms may be created for trainees to play an active role and exercise control over their own development. None of this is possible without a commitment by senior management to employee development, and the structures, systems and personnel to develop an innovative international training function. It crucially requires a substantial shift in attitude in boardrooms towards the nature and role of the training function.

References

Alvesson, M. (1991) 'Corporate culture and corporatism at the company level. A case study', *Economic and Industry Democracy*, 12, 3 August, 347–9.

Ansoff, I. (1987) *Corporate Strategy*, Harmondsworth: Penguin Business Library.

Ashton, D. (1998) 'Skill formation: redirecting the research agenda', in Coffield, F. (ed.), *Learning at Work*, Bristol: Policy Press.

Barney, J. B. and Wright, P. M. (1998) 'On becoming a strategic partner; the role of human resources in gaining competitive advantage', *Human Resource Management*, 37, 1, 31–46 (Spring).

Bennett, N., Ketchen Jr, D. J. and Blanton Schultz, E. (1998) 'An examination of factors associated with the integration of human resource management and strategic decision making', *Human Resource Management*, 37, 1, 13–16 (Spring).

CEDEFOP Synthesis Report (1990) *The Training of Young People in Enterprises*, Berlin: CEDEFOP.

Chandler, A. D. (1991) 'The functions of the HQ unit in the multi business firm', *Strategic Management Journal*, 12.

Doeringer, P. B. and Piore, M. J. (1985) *Internal Labour Markets and Manpower Analysis*, New York: M. E. Sharpe, 2nd edn (first published 1971).

Eraut, M. (1997) 'Perspectives on defining "The Learning Society", for the ESRC Learning Society Programme', Brighton: Institute of Education, University of Sussex.

Goold, M. and Campbell, A. (1987) *Strategies and Styles: The Role of the Centre in Managing Diversified Corporations*, Oxford: Basil Blackwell.

Goold, M., Campbell, A. and Luchs, K. (1993a) 'Strategies and styles revisited: strategic planning and financial control', *Long Range Planning*, 26, 5, 49–60.

Goold, M., Campbell, A. and Luchs, K. (1993b) 'Strategies and styles revisted: strategic control – is it tenable?', *Long Range Planning*, 26, 6, 54–61.

Guest, D. (1987) 'Human resource management and industrial relations', *Journal of Management Studies*, 24, 503–21 (September).

Guest, D., (1990) 'Human Resource Development. Conditions for Growth', *Employment Gazette*, December.

Guest, D. (1991) 'HRM its implications for industrial relations and trade unions', in Storey, J. (ed.), *New Perspectives on Human Resource Management*, London: Routledge.

Hall, G. A. (1987) 'Reflections on running a diversified company', *Harvard Business Review*, 84–92, Jan.–Feb.

Hendry, C. (1991) 'Corporate strategy and training', in Stevens, J. and Mackay, R. (eds), *Training and Competitiveness*, London: NEDO.

Hendry, C. and Pettigrew, A. (1986) 'The practice of strategic HRM', in *Personnel Review*, 15, 5, 3–8.

Hyman, R. (1987) 'Flexible specialisation: miracle or myth?', in Hyman, R. and Streeck, W., *Industrial Relations and New Technology*, Oxford: Basil Blackwell.

Jaap, T. and Watson J. A. (1970) 'A conceptual approach to training', in *Personnel Management*, 31 September.

Jain, H. C., Lawler, J. J. and Morishimon, M. (1998) 'Multinational corporations, human resource management and host country nationals', *The International Journal of Human Resource Management*, 9, 4 (August), 553–66.

King, J. E. (1994) *Labour Economics*, London: Macmillan.

Kinnie, N. (1991) 'Human resource management and changes in management control systems', in Storey, J. (ed.), *New Perspectives on Human Resource Management*, London: Routledge.

Nordhaug, O. (1990) 'Human resource provision and transformation: the role of training and development', in *Human Resource Management Journal*, 1, 2, 19–20.

Pettigrew, A., Sparrow, P. and Hendry, C. (1988) 'The forces that trigger training', *Personnel Management*, December, 32.

Prahalad, C. K. and Hamel, G. (1990) 'The core competencies of the corporation', *Harvard Business Review*, March/April, 79–91.

Purcell, J. (1986) 'Employee relations autonomy within a corporate culture', in *Personnel Management*, February, 38–40.

Purcell, J. (1989) 'Corporate Strategy and the management of employee relations in the multi-divisional company', *British Journal of Industrial Relations*, 23, 3, 38–40.

Purcell, J. (1991) 'The impact of corporate strategy on human resource management', in Storey, J. (ed.), *New Perspectives on Human Resource Management*, London: Routledge.

Rumelt, R. P. (1974) *Strategy, Structure and Economic Performance*, Cambridge, Mass: Harvard University Press.

Schuller, T. (1991) 'Financial participation', in Storey J., (ed.) *New Perspectives on Human Resource Management*, London: Routledge.

Stalk, G., Evans, P. and Shulman, L. E. (1992) 'Competing on capabilities: the new rules of corporate strategy', *Harvard Business Review*, March–April, 57–69.

Stone, N., 'Does Business have any Business in Education?', *Harvard Business Review*, March–April, 54 (1991).

Storey, J. (1991) 'From personnel management to human resource management', in J. Storey, (ed.), *New Perspectives in Human Resource Management*, London: Routledge,.

Sunderland, R. (1991) 'Vanishing middle managers', *Investors Chronicle*, 14 June, 14–15.

Syrett, M. (1990) 'Have British employers responded to the training challenge?', *Industrial Society Magazine*, September, 16–18.

Thomas, M. A. (1990) 'What is a human resource strategy?', *Employee Relations*, 12, 3, 13.

Thompson, P. (1989) *The Nature of Work*, London: Macmillan.

Useem M. and Gottlieb, M. M. (1990) 'Corporate restructuring, ownership-disciplined alignment, and the reorganisation of management', *Human Resource Management*, Fall, 285–303.

Wright, P. M., McMahan, G. C., McCormick, B. and Sherman, W. S. (1998) 'Strategy, core competence, and HR involvement as determinants of HR effectiveness and refinery performance', *Human Resource Management*, 37, 1 (Spring), 17–27.

CHAPTER 3

Reconciling individual and organisational development: issues in the retail banking sector

Elena P. Antonacopoulou

Introduction

The on-going debate about the significance of human capital to an organisation's continuous improvement and prosperity has encouraged an increasing focus on the relationship between individual development and organisational development. The proposition that organisational development is shaped by the development of human resources has resulted in a renewed interest in developing the capacity and potential of individuals as a means of fulfilling organisational goals (Fombrum, Tichy and Devanna, 1984; Beer *et al.*, 1985). This view has been further reflected in the efforts by organisations to apply the HRD philosophy as evidenced by the introduction of initiatives such as the competencies framework, self-development, learning contracts, peer review and so on (Boak and Stephenson, 1987a, 1987b; Schuler and Jackson, 1987; Redman and Snape, 1992; Bones, 1994), which have sought to facilitate the process of communicating the expected standards of performance and skills, encourage self-reliance and build a more coherent approach to the mutual development of the organisation and the individual.

The emphasis on the interdependence between individual and organisational input in the process of development has led to the assumption that there is a strong link between individual development and organisational development. Although there may be a strong commonality of interests on the part of both the organisation and the individual in development activities, striking a balance between the competing priorities of the organisation and those of the individual is not at all easy, not least because any potential arbitration would have to address the asymmetry of power and control and the inequality in knowledge and experiences (in terms of information available). The asymmetry of power and knowledge between the individual and the organisation is a source of tension between rhetoric and reality in the way HRD activities are applied within organisations. This gap between philosophy and praxis in the development of human resources within organisations has led commentators to argue that individuals are exploited, their abilities homogenised so that they match the strategic contingencies of the organisation, and instead of winning 'true' commitment organisational practices are manufacturing consent and compliance (Legge, 1989; Townley, 1994; Storey, 1995).

These criticisms raise a series of additional questions such as the extent to which HRD activities are a proactive response to the changing requirements of the organisation for human resources, and indeed, whether it has allowed more flexibility and easier adaptability which are perceived as key drivers for organisational development and a source of competitive advantage (Hendry and Pettigrew, 1990). Organisational changes in response to external pressures (for example, competition) offer a very useful context for understanding the complexity of managing the differences in the perspective maintained by the individual and the organisation and the way these influence the expectations and attitudes of each party towards any attempt at reconciliation.

This chapter takes a critical look at the relationship between individual and organisational development. The discussion will consider if individual development and organisational development are the same, and whether the corresponding needs of the individual can be reconciled with those of the organisation. The discussion about individual development focuses on managers in particular. The choice to focus on managers as the unit of analysis when referring to individual development is based on the recognition that managers are a vulnerable group within changing organisations, in that they are frequently charged with the responsibility to mediate between the organisation (top management) and employees (at lower levels) in order to support the strategic direction set by the organisation (Brooks, 1980). Moreover, although managers are frequently considered to be more powerful and more in control of their development than the general employee population, it is not uncommon to find (as the findings reported in this chapter will also show) that managers perceive themselves to be as insecure about their development as other employees. Although the focus on individual managers limits the generalisability of the analysis to the wider notion of individuals within organisations, it provides a useful ground for exploring the dynamics embedded in the process of balancing personal against organisational development.

These dynamics are discussed in the chapter with reference to the HRD practices of three retail banks. The retail banking sector provides an interesting example of an industry that has undergone a process of reconstruction which demanded fast responsiveness to change and a high need for learning. Unlike any other period in the history of banking in the UK, the years 1980–95 have probably witnessed one of the most turbulent eras. The main changes have been triggered both by external and internal forces. The external forces arise from the trends in the world economy, whereas internal forces within the sector arise from changes in the market, the intensification of competition and the continuous developments in information technology which have forced a new era of efficiency on the sector and have triggered a new orientation towards the basic principles of banking.

The various internal and external changes are fundamentally transforming the role that staff are expected to play within the organisation. A critical concern for banks during the 1990s is the ability of the workforce to change and to manage the new technology. Banks realise that it is necessary to develop policies which will ensure that once skilled people are in position, they are retained and grown to meet the future needs of the business. Banks have recognised that decisions about human resources are at the cutting edge of the business, because unless people are carefully invested in, there is a real possibility of commercial failure. As a result, banks find themselves with an expanding mix of inter-related HRD problems to manage. Two of the most significant HRD processes of particular relevance to the present discussion are management training and development, and career development.

Traditionally, banks recruited school-leavers, who were trained through a formal, disciplined classroom approach and had to pass professional qualifications (for example, the ACIB Diploma) in order to meet the immediate needs of the bank. Given the rate of change and the degree of uncertainty in the sector, it is difficult to be clear as to the precise shape of future jobs and managerial responsibilities. This uncertainty has disrupted the traditional model of manpower planning and career development in banking and has had an impact on the system of rewards in many organisations in the sector (Hague, 1986; Thomas and Tilston, 1987). In the past, banks could structure their manpower needs because of the comparatively consistent growth in their business. Recent changes make planning staff numbers very difficult, and with the increasing cost-consciousness and resulting staff redundancies, many organisations find it difficult to coordinate the development of their existing staff. Moreover, as a result of the recent changes, the nature of managerial jobs has been substantially transformed from managing money and people to 'selling'. The criteria for career progression are no longer age and experience, but customer service and performance in meeting sales targets (Banking Information Service, 1991). In the light of all these changes banks can no longer maintain their paternalistic approach to staff development. Clearly, the psychological contract in banking careers is changing and it is no longer based on loyalty, commitment and lifelong employment (Herriot, Pemberton and Hawtin 1996). The new deal that is being struck between the bank and its future employees will shape the behaviours that managers will be expected to demonstrate.

The implications of these changes for individual and organisational development are discussed with reference to the approach adopted by three banks. The diverse responses of individual managers to different organisational policies and practices in relation to development are presented to illustrate the dynamic interaction between individual and organisational development. Moreover, the analysis highlights the conditions which affect whether a reconciliation between individual and organisational development is possible.

The relationship between organisation development and individual/management development

The assumption that the needs of the individual are (or should be) compatible with the needs of the organisation has dominated much of the management literature for decades. For example, in the training and development field there has been consistent reference to the importance of reconciling management development (MD) and organisation development (OD): (Frizell and Gellermann, 1988; Margulies and Raia, 1988). One finds that the assumption that individual development (ID) and OD are strongly interconnected is heavily influenced by the strategic role of MD. Many researchers (Annadale, 1986; Sadler, 1988; Papalexandris, 1988; McBeath, 1990; Wille, 1990) have argued that MD is a strategic function (that is, it is a key element in corporate strategy development) which contributes to the management of human resources by coordinating HRD activities (for example, recruitment, appraisal, career development, and so on). This approach towards MD has given rise to multiple models (Ashton and Easterby-Smith, 1979; Burgoyne, 1988; Kilcourse, 1988; Miller, 1991) which explore the connection and interaction between the key elements. A central principle of these models is that any attempt to develop managers in isolation from their context will be futile, because individual development and the development of the organisation have to be promoted in parallel.

The interdependence between OD and MD is also consistent with descriptions of OD which suggest that it is a means of adapting to new technologies and market challenges. According to Bennis (1970:1–15), OD is a 'complex educational strategy' which is intended to change the beliefs, attitudes, values and structures of organisations so that they can better adapt to the internal and external pressures exercised upon them. OD as an exchange of knowledge within and outside the organisation is perceived to be the result of conscious and unconscious educational practices and constant social interactions (Mirvis and Berg, 1977). OD described in these terms leads commentators (Lippitt, 1969; Lievegoed, 1980; Lessem, 1990; McBeath, 1990) to conclude that OD and MD are inseparable (in terms of the process). The justification they provide is one which accepts OD as an activity which focuses on behavioural rather than structural aspects of organisation, and looks for progress away from hierarchical structures to participative management styles and flexible forms of organisation. The significance of level of authority gives way, therefore, to the level of knowledge as the key influence in decision-making. This inseparation of OD from MD is also supported by Frizell and Gellermann (1988), who point out that it is not possible to do the one without doing the other as well at the same time. OD and MD, they suggest, entail the alignment of values, beliefs, vision and mission. Therefore, the current organisational changes demand a carefully planned and designed process relevant to the needs of the business and able to excite the participating managers.

According to Porter and McKibbin (1988), viewed from the organisation's objectives, MD is not some blunt instrument to be wielded indiscriminately, but rather is to be thought of more as a precise tool to be tailored to the particular needs that the organisation has for a given manager related to where that person is located both functionally and by level of management. On the other hand, viewed from the individual manager's perspective, the need for MD will also vary with the person's career stage. This leads the authors to conclude that there is a strong commonality of interests on the part of both the organisation and the individual manager in MD activities. Therefore, both OD and MD aim at utilising most fully and humanely the potential capabilities of an organisation's human resources.

Pedler, Burgoyne and Boydell (1986) raise the same point as being the philosophy and fundamental premise of their book (*A Manager's Guide to Self-Development*). They claim that 'any effective system for MD must increase the manager's capacity and willingness to take control over and responsibility for events and particularly for himself and his own learning'. This view is held by Williams (1987) as well, who appreciates that the organisation, the superior and the management development specialist are not responsible for the development of individual managers; rather, the responsibility lies completely with individual managers. The organisation's responsibility as reflected in the superior's behaviour should be one that restricts itself to providing encouragement, support and 'facilitation' during the self-development process. The organisation's role, therefore, is principally one of helping managers to help themselves to develop and become more effective. The same author reaches the conclusion that MD means self-development, a conscious response on the part of the individual to deal with what he or she recognises to be a developmental need. Real development can only take place when the individuals see for themselves the need to modify their behaviour, change their attitude, develop new skills, acquire new knowledge, improve their performance or prepare themselves for a different role. According to Lewis and Kelly (1986), this makes MD a challenging and rewarding process: challenging, because it requires managers to question their level of competence and effectiveness in relation to what is expected of them; and at the same time rewarding because it can create substantial improvements in performance which become a source of personal satisfaction and bring recognition and reward from the organisation.

The above overview makes it imperative that MD is an element of planning and essentially central to the strategic policy of an organisation at all levels (Wille, 1990). Miller (1991) shares the same view and suggests that 'if the organisation cannot articulate its strategy, how can MD programmes be put together which match it? "Development for what?" would be an appropriate question.' The same author proposes the development of a model which makes the required connections and interactions between the three key elements: namely, the level of strategy in the organisation, the strategy content and the hierarchical location. The author points out the need to remain sceptical about the difficulty involved with the separation of individual development needs from those of the organisation, as well as the close relationship it calls for between the HRM function (personnel specialists) and the decisions/actions taken in the process of developing the organisation strategy. Burgoyne (1988) recognises these and other related problems and introduces his model in the form of a 'ladder' or hierarchy to show the different steps an organisation has to go through in its journey to reach MD maturity. He describes maturity to be the state in which 'the organisation's corporate policy acts as the search for and realisation of corporate identity, and MD as the search for and realisation of individual identity'. The two 'feed' each other in a mutually beneficial developing process. The same idea is held by Kilcourse (1988), whose model addresses a summary of the above issues in what he calls 'parallel development' of the organisation and the individual. The key principle upon which his model rests is the mere fact that any attempt to develop managers in isolation from their context will be futile, therefore individual development, and the development of the organisational climate and structure, has to be promoted in parallel. This point is echoed by Herriot (1992:112), who says: 'development by the organisation without reference to the individual, and development by the individual without reference to the organisation, are both dead ends'.

In summary, the link between OD and ID appears to be strong when one takes the perspective of the organisation and assumes that development activities, designed for individuals, are tools that can be tailored to the particular needs that the organisation has in relation to its staff. The underlying issue, however, remains to what extent it is possible to achieve a mutually beneficial development by building a common identity for the individual and the organisation. Therefore any process which sets out to reconcile the needs of the individual and the organisation at minimum would need to address the priorities within each party as the starting point for understanding the expectations and perceived 'obligations' in the development of the organisation and the individual manager.

To pursue this question, a longitudinal study[1] was conducted comparing the approach adopted in three banks in their efforts to drive organisational change through the development of managers. The analysis focuses on three levels: the first level is that of the individual manager, and the second level is that of the organisational systems, while the third level aims to establish an understanding of the interaction between personal and organisational factors in the context of change. The interaction between individual and organisational factors is intended to explain, in the context of this analysis, the relationship between the development of the individual and the organisation, and to highlight the factors which underpin any attempt at reconciliation.

The HRD practices across three retail banks

As a result of the changes in the financial services sector, the three banks in this study (Bank A, Bank B and Bank C) have been undergoing numerous operational and strategic changes over the last few years. One of the most significant changes however, has been the cultural shift from being operational to becoming more sales-oriented. This shift has caused a reconsideration of their HRD strategy with an emphasis on management training and development. In some of the banks this meant a redefinition of the banks' training policies, the introduction of new appraisal systems and other reporting procedures.

A common strategy promoted by all three banks has been a greater focus on learner-centred strategies for the development of staff, and in particular the emphasis on a more active involvement by staff in their development. Self-development in particular is seen by the three banks as an appropriate strategy for developing staff in the light of the present uncertainties, because it allows the necessary flexibility and self-direction in the development process and facilitates a more immediate response to the changing needs of individuals and the organisation (Pedler, 1988; Stewart, 1991). Each bank has addressed this issue in a different way. In Bank A the philosophy underpinning the approach to staff development is a 'Do-it-yourself' (DIY) one. In Bank B the approach is making personal development part of assessment, while in Bank C the approach is on based on development reviewing which seeks to separate development from assessment. Each of these approaches is discussed in more detail in the sections which follow, alongside the reactions of individual managers to the new policies.

The 'do-it-yourself' approach: Bank A

Despite the numerous changes in the sector, Bank A has remained highly centralised in its human resources philosophy, and the approach to management training and development continues to be focused primarily on the needs of the organisation. The introduction of self-development in the bank's vocabulary has been relatively recent by comparison with the other banks. This bank believes that self-development, as an approach to management training and development, is less costly and more efficient, because the responsibility for development is transferred from the organisation to the individual. This removes some of the associated costs (in time and other financial resources) in setting up mechanisms which cater for managers' needs. A senior training manager made the following comments in relation to this issue. He said:

> more and more training will have to be done by members of staff in their own time and at their own expense in order to continue to qualify for their job ... the organisation will not be able to afford the sort of money that it has been to train for the future.

From the perspective of individual managers however, it is interesting to note that encouragement for self-development is closely associated by some managers with the level of seniority, and consequently the relative level of power and authority. In other words, managers point out that the level of control an individual can exercise in relation to personal development is limited by his or her level of seniority in the organisational hierarchy: the more senior, the more the control over personal development. Therefore, although the organisation may advocate personal responsibility, managers' experiences suggest that this is hardly the case. Moreover, managers argue that the encouragement for self-development is available only 'if individuals push for it actively'. As one manager put it: 'it forces you to do something, because if you don't develop yourself nothing happens'. According to managers, the bank's support for self-development is evident in certain specific procedures, such as the performance appraisal which, according to managers, 'provides guidance on the areas managers need to develop'. During the performance appraisal, managers are expected to report on the activities they have been involved in to develop themselves. Managers claim that this approach forces them to 'come up with something'. In other words, managers may make up a self-development story so that their progress is not affected. If managers are not seen as developing themselves they may get a 'black mark' which may limit their future prospects in the organisation. In the light of the recent redundancies within this and other banks, managers are keen to ensure that they are seen to be developing themselves in line with the requirements of the organisation. Essentially, managers' descriptions of the self-development approach within Bank A are characterised by fear and anxiety to follow the rules set by the organisation. In other words, managers' perceptions of the organisation's encouragement is defined primarily in relation to the way the bank expects individuals to behave. This observation shows a strong level of dependence by individual managers on the organisation and limited personal initiative.

Making personal development part of assessment: Bank B

A unique feature of the management training and development process within Bank B is the emphasis placed on learning. This is a recent change in training orientation within this bank which has resulted from survey findings, conducted within the organisation, which suggested that 60 per cent of the bank's population feel that 'training is attending courses'. These results encouraged the organisation to reconsider the training methods employed up to that point, and to introduce a wider range of flexible training methods. The bank expected that a shift to more flexible training methods would encourage staff at all levels to explore other learning opportunities and not rely on training courses alone in order to learn. This approach is intended to support the bank's objective 'to move away from a "push" strategy towards a "pull" strategy'. In other words, instead of sending people on training courses because their line manager believes they need it, individuals will be more proactive regarding their self-development and will take responsibility for it. To use the words of a senior training manager: 'The challenge for us is to move to a situation where it is not the business training the staff, but it is the business providing opportunities within which the staff can learn and grow.'

The recent changes in training philosophy within Bank B have sought to create a triangular partnership between the individual, the line manager and the training and development department. The training policy states explicitly that: 'The responsibility of line managers is to guide individuals in how best to equip themselves for their current and future roles. They are also responsible for ensuring that appropriate action takes place … The prime responsibility for learning rests with individuals in partnership with their line manager.' Although the emphasis on self-development, as a new approach to management development, appears to be similar to Bank A, in this bank the interest in introducing self-development is not purely the improvement of the financial performance of the organisation, but a concern with changing individual attitudes towards training and learning. The transition towards more self-directed learning approaches is recognised by training managers as a cultural change for the bank, because 'managers are not used to taking responsibility for their self-development'. One of the mechanisms which aims to assist this transition is the introduction of Personal Development Plans (PDPs) and specialist development programmes designed to cultivate responsibility for self-development at all levels. These initiatives have resulted in a revised statement of the bank's training and development policy statement which indicates that: 'Learning is not just about going on courses, it is about consciously using your work activities to develop yourself ... . Making the most of other support and learning resources now available. Taking responsibility for your own learning means you will be able to fulfil your development needs.'

The intensity in the message of the organisation seems to have reached individual managers who on the whole appear to acknowledge self-development as one of the key themes that the organisation is promoting. Although managers acknowledge the emphasis of the organisation for self-development, they perceive it as less of an encouragement and more of an *expectation*. A senior manager said: 'You're not encouraged, you're expected to take responsibility. You're expected to know things ... you do it for your own protection.' Managers pointed out that despite the emphasis on learning and self-development and the introduction of systems (such as PDPs) to support them, these initiatives have not provided them with a wider personal choice. As in Bank A, managers in Bank B explained that the annual appraisal process *assesses* individuals on their personal development activities and the learning they claim they have undertaken. Through their PDPs managers must demonstrate that they recognise their strengths and weaknesses and are clear about what they need to do in order to improve themselves. A manager made the following remarks: 'In the performance management system, individuals are asked to identify personal development initiatives. In some respects it forces you to think of something.' Another manager explained that, because of the link between self-development and performance appraisal, 'You have to show you do something, otherwise you are scored low and your salary is affected'. Therefore the position taken by the organisation regarding individual development signals what the bank values, which gives managers clues about what they are expected to do in order to progress. In essence, even though a much larger proportion of managers in Bank B, by comparison to Bank A, claim to be encouraged to develop themselves, a common characteristic is that managers in both banks develop themselves because the organisation expects them to do so, rather than because they personally value it.

Separating development reviewing from assessment: Bank C

In Bank C recent changes have provided a clearer focus for management training and development (in relation to the identified 'competencies' of the organisation) and a wider set of learning resources with an emphasis on individual differences in learning needs and styles. Training managers argue that the purpose of training is 'to develop generalists and not specialists and to provide a broad range of skills'. As with the other two banks, the identification of individuals' training needs is achieved through the performance appraisal process and other informal mechanisms (for example, dialogue with line manager, self-perception of development need and so on). Unlike the other banks, however, training managers place a lot more emphasis on clarifying the nature of the development need before deciding how to pursue it. Moreover, training managers strongly emphasise the diversity of training and development methods employed by the organisation, which aim to 'encourage individuals to take responsibility for their self-development'.

A unique characteristic of the approach of this bank is the 'Training and Development Review', which takes place every two to three years and is initiated by the individual. This review is intended to reflect the commitment of the organisation to staff development, by setting time aside specifically for reviewing the development needs of the individual. According to training managers, this approach 'enables managers to be actively involved in all the stages of the development process'. A significant objective underlying this approach is the organisation's belief that individuals should not associate training and development with assessment. Therefore this approach sets out to overcome some of the contradictory priorities in the appraisal process (Beer, 1981) and to communicate the emphasis placed by the bank on personal responsibility for development at all levels of the organisational hierarchy.

A central theme of the bank's training strategy, as is also the case in the other banks, is the responsibility of the individual for self-development and the close relationship between the individual, the line manager and the training department. Unlike the other banks, however, this theme has been central to the training strategy of the bank for a much longer period of time (since the late 1980s), and has been strengthened by various practical approaches which have demonstrated the bank's commitment. For example, a unique characteristic of the management training and development approach within Bank C has been the introduction of an internal library (LEAP) of training and development resources. The aim of this library has been to facilitate a positive attitude towards self-development. Established since 1988, LEAP is a comprehensive library consisting of books, audio tapes and video cassettes on 40 different subjects and around 850 different titles. Material can be borrowed by all employees and it is free of charge; according to the training managers, 'at least 60 per cent of the bank's staff use this facility'. A help line is also available for any queries on items included in the library.

This and other initiatives (for example, learning centres initiated during 1993 and modular programmes in collaboration with established business schools) aim to demonstrate the bank's commitment to investing in its employees' development and training and to reinforce the importance attached by the organisation to individuals taking responsibility for their development. Training managers emphasised that Bank C is 'moving away from instructor-led courses towards facilitator-led training'. All these initiatives by the bank have had a marked impact on managers' perceptions. By comparison to managers in the other banks, managers in Bank C unanimously agree that the organisation is very supportive of individuals taking personal responsibility for their development and progress. With reference to LEAP, a manager said: 'it's a first class library, a self-development package ... the organisation would love you to do something for yourself, and not to tell you what to do.' Managers point out that the emphasis on ownership has been a central feature of the bank's education strategy and the message of the bank has been consistent. It appears that managers in this bank see the value of personal development as part of their personal growth as very important in the light of the current changes in the sector and the organisation, and not merely as part of the organisation's policy. As one manager pointed out: 'Personal development is instigated by the personal need to have something to strive for.' Another manager added: 'I would develop myself regardless of the organisation policy. I would do it for myself, for personal satisfaction.' Having said that, there is limited evidence to suggest that managers in this bank are not influenced in their approach to self-development by the guidelines of the organisation. For example, some managers explained that they abandoned pursuing a professional qualification (the ACIB Diploma) as soon as they realised that the bank no longer valued it. This observation suggests that personal development in this bank, as with Banks A and B, is aligned to the requirements of the organisation. A key issue that arises from this observation is whether the fact that managers align their development to the requirements of the organisation means that their development needs are identical to the needs of the organisation.

The tensions between individual and organisational development

The preceding paragraphs show that all three banks have been responding to the recent changes in the sector by refocusing their attention on their human resources as a vital component of their survival. The similarities and differences across the three banks in relation to staff development indicate that the motives underpinning the present strategies, although superficially they appear to be promoting active involvement and participation by the individuals, in essence are driven by the needs of the organisation for flexibility. It is clear that the recent changes in the sector have disrupted the familiar way of doing things, particularly in the way banks plan and deliver their HRD strategy. The underlying motives of the organisation in encouraging individuals to pursue self-directed approaches to personal growth suggest some contradictions. Although each of the three banks introduced several mechanisms in support of self-development – some more structured than others – all are characterised by an element of *control* to different degrees. In encouraging managers to become responsible for their self-development, these organisations indirectly expect managers to develop themselves mainly in relation to areas which are relevant to the context of their organisation and the industry at large. There is little indication that these banks (possibly with the exception of Bank C) are encouraging self-development with a view to broadening individuals' perspective and consequently their wider employability. Instead, the emphasis on self-development is driven by the development needs of the bank. As a result the explicit and implicit messages of the various policies introduced by the three banks are often contradictory, thus creating more confusion for individuals. This confusion is reflected in individuals managers' perceptions of the extent to which their organisation encourages them to take responsibility for their development, which suggests that encouragement is frequently interpreted as an expectation. In other words, managers in the three banks do not appear to be pursuing self-development as part of a personal initiative. Instead, managers are developing themselves because this is what the organisation signals they should be doing. This point also suggests that individual managers in the three banks are essentially identifying themselves closely with the needs and requirements of the organisation, so that their personal development is driven by the development needs of the organisation. This point would also suggest that individual needs should be reconciled with the needs of the organisation.

Can organisational and individual development be reconciled?

The evidence from the three banks suggest that the characteristics of the sector, and the bureaucratic culture and structure of the banks themselves, have had an impact on the way individual managers perceive their development in relation to the development of the organisation. The characteristics of the retail banking sector, as discussed earlier, reflect a paternalistic approach to development with an emphasis on providing internally most of the skills required in the sector, thus creating a remarkable degree of loyalty and *esprit de corps* (Jones, 1991). Therefore an underlying assumption of the perspective that these banks take in relation to management training and development is that organisational and individual needs are the same; consequently, the development of individuals must be in line with the development needs of the organisation. It is not surprising that one finds that individual managers appear to share this view.

Managers across the three banks were asked whether they feel that a reconciliation between personal and organisational development needs is possible.

The findings show clearly that a very high proportion of managers across the three banks (Bank A: 83 per cent, Bank B: 81 per cent, Bank C: 69 per cent) believe that the needs of the individual can be reconciled with those of the organisation. Comparing managers' views on this issue across the three banks, it is evident that in A and B a much bigger proportion of the managers interviewed believe that 'individual and organisational needs are naturally related'. Managers who support this view point out that:

> personal and organisational needs go hand in hand, because the bank expects the individual to fulfil the corporate goals and provides the training for it. (Manager, Bank A)

> Personal development should lead to organisational development. People realise that by benefiting themselves they benefit the organisation and by benefiting the organisation they benefit themselves. (Manager, Bank B)

The view expressed by managers, who believe that individual and organisational development can be reconciled, shows that their perceptions and attitudes to development are shaped by their socialisation into the organisation's agenda which influences them to accept passively what they are being offered without questioning. It appears that managers' perceptions are based on the assumption that the organisation will look after them and their best interests. This assumption is based on the old psychological contract in the banking sector which no longer exists, yet managers' responses reflect their attempt to maintain their sense of security in the light of the current uncertainty in the sector. One possible explanation evident from the different approaches adopted between the three banks is that in banks A and B the emphasis on self-development has been more recently introduced and it is significantly different from what managers have been accustomed to so far. More importantly, however, the notion of self-development as adopted in banks A and B suggests a conflict of interests for the banks. Essentially the banks advocate personal responsibility for development, while at the same time they control to a large extent the development opportunities available and the areas in which individuals should be developing themselves. The latter point in particular indicates that self-development as adopted in these banks is a more sophisticated way of directing individual development in areas which are relevant and appropriate for the needs of the organisation. Overall, the approach of the organisation, coupled with the long history of paternalistic practices which managers are more accustomed to, result in the perceived reconciliation of individual and organisation development.

This reconciliation, however, is superficial and is primarily based on the control exercised by the organisation over individuals' development and the exploitation of individuals' development for organisational development. As a result of this approach to management training and development, the organisation imposes its definitions and priorities on individuals and creates a level of dependence on the part of the individual over the resources and direction provided by the organisation. The significance of this point is that it reveals how organisational development supersedes individual development and in some instances forces managers to believe that their needs are the same as those of the organisation (Rainbird and Maguire, 1993). A manager in Bank B makes the point, aptly saying: 'Personal and organisational development are interdependent, but the problem is that you usually get swallowed by the organisation's needs.'

This observation becomes more clear when one considers the views expressed by managers in Bank C. Even though managers in bank C in principle share the views of managers in banks A and B, unlike managers in the other two banks they appear to be more sceptical. In other words, managers feel that it is not easy to reconcile individual and organisational needs and for such a reconciliation to take place it requires a great deal of effort from both parties. Some of the comments made by managers in this bank included:

> in principle there should be a reconciliation; however, reaching a balance between business priorities and personal commitment to development, that's when it becomes difficult.

> a reconciliation may be possible providing the organisation knows your needs and you know the organisation. In the main the bank provides adequate training for future development, but individuals may require something else. Individuals should be left with the decision to undertake them or not.

> the organisation must give explanations of what is expected ... sometimes people tell the organisation what they think it expects to hear.

It is important to note that a much bigger proportion (31 per cent) of managers in Bank C believe that a reconciliation between individual and organisational needs can not be achieved. Managers who support this view argue that the diversity of individual development needs makes it impossible for the organisation to address this area. In relation to this issue a manager said: 'The bank is trying to be all things to all people, but it is not possible to do. People have different expectations.' Another manager added: 'we will always struggle to do that. Not many individuals have the foresight to develop themselves for the good of the organisation. There is a natural imbalance between individual aspirations and organisational commitment.'

Managers' comments only make it more clear that the reconciliation between individual and organisational development is an ideal than a reality. The relationship between individual development and the development of the organisation is characterised by tension, disagreement, asymmetrical power and control and inequality in knowledge and experiences (in terms of information available). In fact the organisation (as the more powerful actor in the relationship) enforces its own perspective on individuals' perceptions. This evidence provides no support for claims in the existing literature (such as those of Lippitt, 1969; Lievegoed, 1980, Frizell and Gellermann, 1988; Lessem, 1990; McBeath, 1990; and others) that OD and ID are strongly interconnected, or indeed that personal and organisational needs are compatible. This analysis shows that individuals are regulated and indoctrinated to pursue organisational goals as their own, thus passively accepting that what the organisation expects is what they should be doing. However, when managers are given more choice and freedom to pursue their development (as is to some extent the approach in Bank C) managers are more sceptical and critical of organisational expectations and more inclined to recognise the difficulties of reconciling their development needs with those of the organisation.

Despite the fact that both the individual and the organisation depend on each other to achieve their own objectives, the superiority of the organisation (in terms of power and information) creates an imbalance in the interaction which often results in the individual becoming more dependent on the organisation. The imbalance in this relationship increases the organisation's capacity to manipulate and exploit the individual in the direction which best fits its own concerns and priorities. From the perspective of the individual, this unequal relationship with the organisation creates a sense of helplessness and insecurity which often results in the employees giving up their personal goals and deriving their identity from the goals of the organisation to which they subscribe. This analysis demonstrates that the employment relationship is not unproblematic and the inequalities of power and control are exacerbated to the extent that individuals' development is driven by the development of the organisation.

Conclusion

This chapter critically examined the assumption in the existing literature that individual development is compatible with organisational development. The analysis and empirical evidence presented in this chapter illustrate the fact that the relationship between individual and organisational development is characterised by inequality in power and information, which creates an imbalance in the interaction between the two parties with the less powerful becoming more dependent. In the context of change the power of the organisation increases, intensifying the dependency of the individual on the organisation as the individual becomes more vulnerable and insecure about the lack of control over the outcomes and resources in relation to development. The findings show that the employment relationship is not unproblematic. What may on the surface appear to be a reconciliation of individual and organisational development is in fact a subordination of the needs of the individual in line with organisational expectations. Under these circumstances individuals are more inclined to demonstrate the behaviours which are in line with the social and cultural norms of the organisation. This observation highlights more clearly the political nature of the relationship between individual and organisational development, and shows that despite the fact that individual development is shaped by the development needs of the organisation, the development needs of the individual and those of the organisation are rarely the same.

Notes

1   The key focus of the study is the way individual managers learn and adapt during periods of change, and the extent to which organisational systems (specifically training and development) facilitate or inhibit such processes. The main strand of the field research was the qualitative interview (semi-structured), while observation, questionnaires and the critical incident technique were supplementary data collection methods employed. The managerial sample (78) in the three retail banks was randomly selected, incorporating managers across a broad spread of age, seniority, specialisation, gender and background. Managers classed as fast-track (who experienced different educational opportunities) were included in the sample and compared with non fast-track managers. In order to obtain the organisation's perspective apart from organisational records and archive material, a series of interviews were conducted with senior HRD managers. A total of six to eight HRD managers was interviewed within each bank to obtain data from the perspective of the organisation. A detailed account of the research design and strategy for collecting and analysing the data can be found in Antonacopoulou, (1996).

References

Annadale, S. (1986) 'The four faces of management development', *Personnel Management*, July, 34–7.

Antonacopoulou, E. P. (1996) 'A Study of Interrelationships: The Way Individuals Learn and Adapt and the Contribution of Training towards this Process', unpublished PhD, Warwick Business School, University of Warwick.

Ashton, D. and Easterby-Smith, M. (1979) *Management Development in the Organisation*, London: Macmillan.

Banking Information Service (1991) *A Future in Banking: the Branch Network*, London: Banking Information Service.

Beer, M. (1981) 'Performance appraisal: dilemmas and possibilities', *Organisational Dynamics*, Winter, 24–36.

Beer, M., Spector, B., Lawrence, P., Mills, D. and Walton, R. (1985) *Human Resources Management: A General Manager's Perspective*, New York: Free Press.

Bennis, W. G. (1970) *Organisation Development – Its Nature, Origins and Prospects*, Reading, Mass.: Addison-Wesley.

Boak, G. and Stephenson, M. (1987a) 'Management learning contract: from theory to practice, part 1 theory', *Journal of European Industrial Training*, 11, 4, 4–6.

Boak, G. and Stephenson, M. (1987b) 'Management learning contract: from theory to practice, part 2 practice', *Journal of European Industrial Training*, 11, 6, 17–20.

Bones, C. (1994) *The Self-Reliant Manager*, London: Routledge.

Brooks, E. (1980) *Organisational Change: The Managerial Dilemma*, London: Macmillan Press.

Burgoyne, J. (1988) 'Management development for the individual and the organisation', *Personnel Management*, June, 40–4.

Fombrum, C., Tichy, N. M. and Devanna, M. A. (1984) *Strategic Human Resource Management*, Chichester: John Wiley.

Frizell, N. and Gellermann, W. (1988) 'Integrating the human and business dimension of management and organisation change', in Mailick, S., Hoberman S. and Wall, S. J. (eds), *The Practice of Management Development*, New York: Praeger, 1–30.

Hague, H. (1986) 'Midland Bank staff offered flat-rate rise', *Financial Times*, 21 March, 16.

Hendry, C. and Pettigrew, A. M. (1990) 'Human resource management: An agenda for the 1990s', *International Journal of Human Resource Management*, 1, 1, 1–25.

Herriot, P. (1992) *The Career Management Challenge*, London: Sage.

Herriot, P., Pemberton, C. and Hawtin, E. (1996) 'The career attitudes and intentions of managers in the finance sector', *British Journal of Management*, 7, 2, 181–90.

Jones, C. (1991) 'A look into the crystal ball', *The Banker*, 141, 781 (March), 8–11.

Kilcourse, T. (1988) 'Making management development a co-operative venture', *Personnel Management*, August, 35–9.

Legge, K. (1989) 'Human Resource Management, a Critical Analysis', in Storey, J. (ed.), *New Perspectives on Human Resource Management*, London: Routledge, 19–40.

Lessem, R. (1990) 'From management development to developmental management', *European Management Development Journal*, 3, 14–17.

Lewis, M. and Kelly, G. (1986) *20 Activities for Developing Managerial Effectiveness*, London: Gower.

Lievegoed, B. C. (1980) *The Developing Organisation*, San Francisco, California: Celestial Arts.

Lippitt, G. L. (1969) *Organisational Renewal*, NewYork: Appleton-Century-Crofts.

McBeath, G. (1990) *Practical Management Development: Strategies for Management Resourcing and Development in the 1990s*, Oxford: Basil Blackwell.

Margulies, N. and Raia, A. (1988) 'The significance of core values on the practice of organisation development', *Journal of Organisational Change Management*, 1, 1, 6–17.

Miller, P. (1991) 'A strategic look at management development', *Personnel Management*, August, 45–7.

Mirvis, P. H. and Berg, D. N. (1977) *Failures in Organisation Development and Change*, New York: John Wiley.

Papalexandris, N. (1988) 'Measuring the effectiveness of an external management training seminar in Greece', *Management Education and Development*, 19, 1, 22–9.

Pedler, M., 'Self-development and work organisations', in Pedler, M., Burgoyne, J. and Boydell, T. (eds) (1988) *Applying Self-Development in Organisations*, London: Prentice-Hall, 1–19.

Pedler, M., Burgoyne, J. and Boydell, T. (1986) *A Manager's Guide to Self-Development*, 2nd edn, London: McGraw-Hill.

Porter, L. W. and McKibbin, L. E. (1988) *The Management Education and Development: Drift or Thrust into the 21st Century*, New York: McGraw-Hill.

Rainbird, H. and Maguire, M. (1993) 'When corporate need supersedes employee development', *Personnel Management*, February, 34–7.

Redman, T. and Snape, E. (1992) 'Upward and onward: can staff appraise their managers?', *Personnel Review*, 21, 7, 32–46.

Sadler, P. (1988) *Managerial Leadership in the Post-Industrial Society*, London: Gower.

Schuler, R. S. and Jackson, S. E. (1987) 'Linking competitive strategies with human resource management practices', *Academy of Management Executive*, 1, 3, 207–19.

Stewart, J. (1991) *Managing Change through Training and Development*, New York: Pfeiffer.

Storey, J. (ed.) (1995) *Human Resource Management: A Critical Text*, London: Routledge.

Thomas, M. and Tilston, D. (1987) *Human Resources Strategy in the Retail Financial Services Sector*, London: P.A. Management Consultants.

Townley, B. (1994) *Reframing Human Resource Management: Power, Ethics and the Subject at Work*, London: Sage.

Wille, E. (1990) 'Should management development be just for managers?', *Personnel Management*, August, 34–7.

Williams, M. (1987) 'Management self-development', in Steward, D. M. (ed.), *Handbook of Management Skills*, London: Gower, 5–28.

CHAPTER 4

Performance management and training

Bitten Hansen

Introduction

Performance management has been the topic of considerable academic and practitioner debate since the mid 1980s. There is no single way of defining the practices of performance management, but in general the concept is about managing performance at and between various levels within an organisation including individual, team and business unit level, and the concept therefore relates to employment relations as a field of study. Storey and Sisson (1993) emphasise that performance management has to be understood in the context of an increasing interest in HRM in general and with the individualisation of the employment relationship in particular. Performance management can therefore be understood as constituting an element in the wider political and economic context of neo-liberal policies associated with industrialised economies such as the UK and the USA during the 1980s and 1990s.

Within the substantial academic and practitioner literature on performance management, two extreme meanings of the concept can be identified. Performance management can be understood as an all-inclusive concept which refers to most of the human resource practices organisations engage in, including planning, training, coaching, remuneration, quality management and customer service. Performance management is also sometimes used virtually synonymously with individual performance related pay (PRP): (see Storey and Sisson, 1993). Performance management understood as an all-inclusive managerial strategy includes training as an essential and integral component. In most textbook examples of performance management systems, training is understood as an important outcome of the performance appraisal process. These textbook approaches assert that training needs are identified during the appraisal process, are implemented, and result in enhanced individual and organisational performance (Fowler, 1990; Bevan and Thompson, 1991; Fletcher and Williams, 1992a, 1992b; Armstrong and Baron, 1998; Williams, 1998).

This chapter argues that the nature of the relationship between performance management and training is problematic and conditional rather than simple and unambiguous. The complex relationship can be delineated into three factors. First, tensions arise due to the internal processes of operationalising performance management in organisational contexts. Second, there is a conflicting emphasis on workplace priorities in terms of the timescales and resources in relation to the introduction of performance management systems and training strategies. Third, there are pressures between performance management and training in terms of managerial priorities and concerns to connect human resource strategies and policies to the competitive strategy of the organisation.

This chapter provides a review and an examination of the meaning and rationale of performance management and analyses the implications of performance management for training and, in particular, a strategic approach to training. The chapter is structured in the following way. The first section describes the historical antecedents of performance management and examines the underlying reasons for a focus on the concept of managing performance. This is followed, in the second section, by an analysis of different perspectives on performance management and PRP. The third section provides an overview of performance management in action in the UK, and the fourth section discusses various critical themes related to performance management. The final section examines the relationship between performance management and training.

The historical antecedents of performance management

The management of performance as an idea is by no means new. Since the emergence of scientific management at the beginning of the twentieth century (Taylor, 1911), the maximisation of employee and organisation performance has been a central concern of management (Thompson and McHugh, 1990; Grint, 1991; Brown, 1992; Legge, 1995). Different approaches to managing performance have included the Human Relations movement with its emphasis on social relations and dynamics (Mayo, 1933), the recording of critical incidents (Flanagan, 1954) and the systems approach to individual and organisational activity (Scott, Banks and Lupton, 1956). The contemporary term 'performance

management', and the concerns of human resource management, can therefore be understood as a recent attempt to enhance individual and organisational performance through the alignment of previously disparate management techniques.

Formal monitoring and evaluation of employee and organisation performance have taken various forms throughout the twentieth century.[1] Research
conducted during the First and Second World Wars into the psychological
problems of service personnel and officer selection was reconfigured during
the 1950s and 1960s into merit rating techniques, with a focus upon individual
personality and traits. The Management by Objectives (MBO) movement
(Drucker, 1955), which became prominent in the 1960s and 1970s, claimed to
overcome some of the problems of trait rating such as subjective judgement
and a failure to link objectives to the organisational context. Management by
Objectives proposed an integrative approach to achieving organisational
goals through managing objectives, although subsequent criticisms of the
movement included the assertion that it still lacked an integrative link to the
corporate goals of the organisation. Other criticisms included its top-down
implementation process, an emphasis on individual managers and not all
employees within an organisation, and its focus on purely measurable elements of work. During the 1970s a form of performance appraisal became
widespread in which individual objectives were related to ratings of organisational performance. As with previous attempts to manage performance there
were substantial criticisms of the way in which appraisal schemes operated in
practice. The concept of performance management originated in the USA in
the mid-1980s as a new approach to managing performance, and by the end of
the 1980s and beginning of the 1990s performance management had entered
the vocabulary of human resource management in the UK (Fowler, 1990;
Armstrong and Baron, 1998).

Since the beginning of the 1990s, a number of factors can be identified as
stimulating UK organisations' interest in the phenomena of performance management. Storey and Sisson (1993) outline the contextual and organisational
imperatives for developing and implementing performance management.
First, increased domestic and international market competition has demanded
that organisations pay closer attention to the efficiency and effectiveness of
work organisation systems. Second, governmental pressure towards the public sector has been profound with implications for an emphasis on accountability, measuring activity and demands for increased efficiency and effectiveness. State enterprises, hospitals, schools and local government have come
under scrutiny by governments which pursued a broad-based neo-liberal
political agenda and implemented legislative reform (The Local Government
Management Board, 1994; Lane, 1995). Third, organisational restructuring has
been introduced in many organisational contexts with the aim of decentralis-
ing responsibility and accountability to devolved management levels and different business units within an organisation. Performance management sys-

tems, as 'tight-loose' structures, have become a crucial component in achieving devolved responsibility while maintaining centralised coordination and control. Performance management cannot therefore be understood merely as a consequence of changing organisational structures, but rather performance management constitutes a key means to restructure an organisation. Such developments have meant that line and business managers have an essential role in the implementation of performance management systems. Fourth, performance management provides organisations with a means of individualising the employment relationship and reducing the importance of collective employment rules and terms and conditions.

Perspectives on performance management

There are various approaches to understanding the focus and components of performance management. Williams (1998) discerns three main perspectives or types of performance management models which are useful as a starting point in providing an overview of the different ways in which performance management is interpreted. First, performance management is seen as a system for managing organisational performance in relation to organisational strategy (Rogers, 1990; Bredrup, 1995). According to this perspective, the focus is on an organisation having an integrated approach to planning, implementing, improving and reviewing performance. During the planning stage an organisation-wide vision and strategy are formulated and performance is defined in the context of the operational and/or service activity. The implementation of performance management systems is often accompanied by other techniques for improving organisational performance such as Business Process Re-engineering (BPR) and Total Quality Management (TQM). In the final stage, organisational performance is reviewed and evaluated.

Second, performance management is understood as a system for managing employee performance with a focus on the individual (Torrington and Hall, 1995; Ainsworth and Smith, 1993). It is, as in organisational performance systems, often represented as a cycle with a three-step process: planning, staffing and appraising (Williams, 1998). Third, performance management is conceptualised as a system for integrating the management of organisational and employee performance. This approach attempts to overcome the limitations of an emphasis on the organisation or individual by either integrating and making more explicit the relationship between organisational and individual performance or by giving organisational and individual performance equal importance. Storey and Sisson (1993) provide an example of a model which attempts to integrate organisational and individual performance through a top-down approach to performance management. This comprises setting clear objectives for individual employees derived from the organisation's strategy, a formal monitoring and review of progress towards meeting objectives, and utilisation of the outcomes of the review process to reinforce desired behaviour through rewards and/or to identify training and development needs. Bevan and Thompson (1991) describe a 'textbook' performance management system in which organisational and individual performance targets are simultaneously defined. Such a performance management system has the following characteristics:

- the organisation has a shared vision of objectives, or a mission statement, which is communicated to all employees
- the organisation sets individual performance management targets which are related both to operating units and wider organisational objectives
- regular and formal reviews of progress are conducted in relation to targets
- the review process is used to identify training, development and reward outcomes
- the effectiveness of the whole process and the contributions to overall organisational performance are evaluated to allow for change and improvements to be made.

The integration of human resource management components with business strategies and objectives is the essential and distinguishing characteristic of performance management compared with other mechanisms for managing performance. For Bevan and Thompson (1991), the integration process can be 'reward-driven' and/or 'development-driven'. The former approach concentrates on the role of performance payment systems in changing organisational behaviour and tends to place less emphasis on the range of human resource policies that can also be used to pursue performance objectives. The latter approach stresses the importance of ensuring that appropriate training and development activities are in place to meet the long-term objectives of the organisation and to ensure that business needs and training strategy are coordinated.

Performance related pay

PRP, as a form of reward management, can be defined as the existence of an explicit link between individual, team or business unit performance and a financial reward. The specific form of a performance related pay scheme depends on a combination of factors such as who is covered by the scheme, how the performance is measured and the particular way in which the reward is linked to the performance. With the development of performance management in the UK there has been renewed interest in pay systems which relate to individual performance. Individual performance schemes can be based upon an assessment of specific individual objectives (performance related pay), an assessment of certain behavioural traits (merit performance pay), or a combination of the two.[2]

Kessler (1994) provides a comprehensive review of the development of individual performance related and merit-based pay schemes. During the 1980s and early 1990s there was a substantial growth in the use of individual performance and merit-based schemes throughout the private and public sector, covering various management and employee levels. The new performance pay systems focused primarily on white-collar employees, as opposed to previous payment systems which were based on bonuses and piecework-based schemes for blue-collar employees.

Performance management in practice in the UK

The empirical evidence relating to performance management in a UK context is comprised of large-scale survey studies and several qualitative case studies. Large-scale postal surveys were undertaken in 1991 and 1997 by the Institute of Manpower Studies (IMS, now Institute for Employment Studies, IES) for the Institute of Personnel Management (IPM, now the Institute of Personnel and Development, IPD).[3] Both surveys aimed at exploring why, how and which organisations had adopted performance management in the UK (Fletcher and Williams, 1992a).[4] The 1997 survey also attempted to examine how performance management had developed in the UK since the beginning of the 1990s, although it did not have an identical sample of organisations (Armstrong and Baron, 1998).[5]

The first survey provided several explanatory factors for the introduction of policies to manage employee performance. The highest-ranked factor was to improve the effectiveness of the organisation. Other factors included motivating employees, improving training and development, and linking pay to performance. The survey also found that although a majority of organisations had general policies to improve employee performance, less than 20 per cent of organisations had a formal performance management programme which would include a formal appraisal system (Fletcher and Williams, 1992a).

The second survey provided evidence that there had been a considerable increase in the adoption of formal performance management processes, with 69 per cent of organisations stating that they operated formal processes to manage performance. This survey also provided information on specific components of organisations' performance systems. The most common feature was objective-setting and review which was conducted by 85 per cent of organisations, and annual appraisals which were undertaken by 83 per cent of responding organisations. A substantial feature of the 1997 survey, which was not reported in the first survey, was that 68 per cent of organisations had personal development plans.

The second survey reported that 43 per cent of organisations had performance related pay compared to 74 per cent of organisations in 1991.[6] Armstrong and Baron (1998:120) claim that the most significant difference between the two periods 'was the shift in emphasis from pay to development. Although pay was a feature in a significant number of performance-management schemes we studied, the overwhelming majority said that their processes were development-led and that a key issue was to identify and fill development needs.' The follow-up case studies for the 1997 research, however, provided substantially different evidence compared with the survey's evidence about the implementation of performance related pay. The case studies revealed that 82 per cent of organisations operated some form of performance or competence related pay. Armstrong and Baron (1998) suggest that the discrepancy may be partly due to the sampling differences between the survey and the case studies. It can, however, be argued that the discrepancy may be attributed to companies' interest in portraying their performance management systems as being development-led, which is done more easily through surveys as opposed to case studies. The promotion of employee development, a skilled workforce and organisational learning are becoming important factors in long-term organisational prosperity, particularly as markets become increasingly competitive.

Discussion about performance management

Conflicting and competing purposes

There are various rationales behind organisations developing and introducing performance management systems with different consequences for training, depending on whether training is seen as a key tool for improving individual performance or merely as an outcome of the process in terms of identifying training needs. Rationales for introducing performance management systems include factors external to an organisation comprising economic and political pressures for change, as well as internal factors within an organisation such as restructuring and changing work organisation processes. Case study research in a UK-based insurance company[7] during the mid-1990s illustrated that the development of performance management within the organisation was influenced by externally induced competitive pressures to become more efficient and to become more business and customer-focused (Hansen, 1994). These factors, together with a related demand for greater attention to the financial 'bottom line', were the impetus for substantial organisational reform. The introduction of an organisation-wide performance management system was understood by senior management as a lever for changing the company culture throughout all parts of the organisation. Such initiatives are based upon the assumption that culture is something that can be managed from senior levels in an organisation like a component in an integrated system. Industrial relations actors within the company provided one example of a competing perspective on performance management. For trade union officials and industrial relations managers, performance management and performance related pay was about the negotiation and boundaries of power between the company and the trade union in relation to decisions about wages and employment relations.

Barlow (1989:499) provides an argument relating to the rationale of performance when he asserts that 'organisations consequently experience pressure to incorporate management appraisal systems within their formal structures in order to maintain legitimacy and to avoid any suggestion of deviancy: failure to incorporate such conventional elements of structure is to risk being judged capricious, negligent and irrational'. Performance management, according to this perspective, can be seen to fulfil a function of defending the institutional status quo and legitimating managerial prerogative and self-interest, by virtue of the system's existence and apparent fairness, largely irrespective of how effectively it operates or what outcomes it achieves. Performance management systems can, in other words, be understood as having contested, multidimensional and multipurpose origins, and the success or failure of the systems needs therefore to be related to the particular, and competing, rationales for introducing such systems.

The underlying premises of many performance management systems are that they will improve internal communication of both the organisation's vision and objectives, increase employee involvement and motivation, and ameliorate individual performance, which will result in enhanced organisational performance. These outcomes are based upon the assumption that it is possible to measure and quantify improvements in communication, commitment, image and performance which may in fact be very problematic. It is also assumed that organisations do monitor and evaluate the effects of performance management systems. Empirical evidence illustrates that workplace reality may be quite different. Both the 1991 and 1997 UK surveys about performance management found that only about half of the organisations stated that they undertook or had mechanisms for monitoring and evaluation (Fletcher and Williams, 1992a; Armstrong and Baron, 1998).

These points highlight problematic assumptions about the approach to managing performance portrayed in prescriptive literature on performance management. The management of performance is understood to be a straightforward, linear and orderly process comprising development, implementation, appraisal and evaluation of performance objectives. It neglects the nature of implementation processes whereby new systems and policies are negotiated and changed within a particular organisational context. It also assumes that performance management systems are an unproblematic catalyst for enhanced individual motivation and skills and organisational performance. This conceptualisation of strategy formation is based upon a classical rationalistic approach to management (Porter, 1980, 1985), with the assertion that managing is a rational planning and implementation process. This perspective has come under substantial criticism from those who suggest that managing organisations is characterised, at least in a UK context, as much by short-term financial concerns, muddling-through strategies and politics and power as it is long-term planning, goal setting and reviewing (Whittington, 1993; Legge, 1995).

Ownership

Performance management systems are primarily developed by senior managements in conjunction with internal organisational development and personnel departments, and often with input from external consultants. An essential characteristic of performance management systems is devolved responsibility for implementation and administration of the systems to line or business managers (Guest, 1987). Gallie *et al.* (1998) reiterate the trend towards the increasing importance of line management supervision.[8] This also emphasises the important and problematic issue of the 'ownership' of such systems. Fletcher and Williams (1992a) point out that if line managers are not committed to or have ownership of a performance management system because it has been introduced in a top-down way, it is likely to be viewed as a troublesome administrative chore and not given sufficient resources.

The role of line managers in administering performance management systems has to be understood in relation to their increasing responsibility for work organisation and employment issues, including the development and motivation of their staff. In this context it is important to consider how line managers give priority to various tasks and to what extent they have autonomy or are constrained in allocating financial and time resources. This has considerable consequences for training and a strategic approach to training. Pettigrew, Sparrow and Hendry (1988) argue that the weak link in the implementation of training plans is line management. They comment that this is because of the overwhelming hidden 'time-cost' problem of releasing staff for training. Such time-cost issues become increasingly relevant as organisational restructuring moves towards flatter organisational hierarchies, fewer layers of middle management and increased pressure to meet performance targets. Time-cost problems are likely to be intensified in such organisations because of the reduced possibilities for internal progression. Without routes for internal career progression, managers may not emphasise training and development. Organisations that have a flat structure and do train and develop their employees may also find that other organisations poach their employees.

Winstanley and Stuart-Smith (1996) argue that employees' views should be considered during the design phase of performance management systems. They suggest that organisations should adopt a stakeholder perspective in which all organisational actors have the opportunity to contribute to the development process. Winstanley and Stuart-Smith (1996:71) claim that 'Performance management is still something which is largely "done to" the individual.' The idea of 'stakeholder synthesis' is presented as going beyond an analysis of the interests of all stakeholders within and around the organisation. Such an approach would, they propose, take account of all actors' views about business strategy and incorporate these views into a performance management system. As actors with legitimate concerns, employees could, for example, demand long-term development activities, such as a structured training programme. Legge (1998:26) provides a critical account of the stakeholder approach to managing competing organisational objectives. She argues that managements always have the possibility of introducing changes which have immediate detrimental consequences for employees – such as redundancy or termination of development and training activities – because it can be 'justified in terms of the short-term survival of the organisation' (1998:26). Such arguments provide a sceptical perspective on the possibility of organisational synthesis and mutuality.

Mutuality and unity

Performance management systems usually presuppose the co-existence of development and evaluation. The premise is that managers can evaluate and rate employee performance, thereby affecting future promotion opportunities and remuneration, while simultaneously coaching employees. Newton and Finlay cast doubt upon a priori assumptions about the outcome of appraisals and contend that 'it seems unlikely that an appraisee will view appraisal as a purely helping/counselling exercise where they may "confide" their job difficulties and anxieties, when there is often the possibility (even if not stated) that the appraisal "data" will be used in assessing promotion, transfer "or even a demotion" ' (1996:43). Such assumptions become even more complicated when the appraisal process is used both to identify developmental needs and possibilities for promotion as well as affecting performance related pay.

Newton and Finlay (1996) contend that prescriptive ideas about appraisal systems are influenced by the assumptions and methods of neo-human relations such as those developed by McGregor (1957). The proponents of neo-human relations assume that employment relations in general, and appraisal relations more specifically, are based upon a unitarist approach to managing in which employee and employer share common interests. Appraisal is a joint activity in which individual and organisational objectives can be integrated through individuals realising their potential, or self-actualisation as McGregor described it, through achieving organisational goals. He argues that a participative approach to appraisal would overcome potential judge/counsellor conflicts by providing the appraisee with the opportunity to influence the appraisal process through involvement in setting objectives and suggesting ways of achieving them. Grint provides a critical perspective on neo-human relations in stating that '[o]nly if employees' goals coincide with managerial goals can they legitimately be pursued within the context of the organisation' (1991:129). This highlights the way in which issues relating to power and conflicting interests in the appraisal process are often ignored.

The devolved appraisal process may also introduce new difficulties into manager and employee relations at the workplace. Carlton and Sloman (1992) found from a case study of a bank appraisal system that managers were hostile to its introduction because it was understood to be a bureaucratic form-filling exercise. Stiles *et al.* (1997) echo these sentiments about the perceived bureaucracy of appraisal systems. They argue that such systems divert managers from other managerial responsibilities, such as meeting customer service and production targets. Managers were also concerned about the effects the performance ratings would have on employees in terms of both motivation and demotivation.

Line or business managers may also find difficulty in undertaking performance appraisals of employees they have to work together with on a daily basis. Rating employees' performance may well intensify workplace pressures, between managers and employees and between employees, and help undermine existing bases of cooperation. Such outcomes would be intensified if managers have not been given sufficient training in conducting appraisals, especially because the appraisals form part of employees' long-term written personnel records. Managerial ambivalence towards performance management systems would also be exacerbated if managers viewed the system as having been imposed from senior levels in the organisation. According to Stiles *et al.* (1997), managerial apathy and scepticism in undertaking appraisals was also due to the lack of positive outcomes for development and remuneration. This resulted in a defensive use of appraisals by line managers through which the ratings of employees would not range across the whole spectrum of rating categories, but tend to converge towards average or above average ratings.

Politics and power

Many prescriptive accounts of the appraisal process, as a key part of a performance management system, consider the appraisal process to be more or less straightforward and unproblematic (Armstrong, 1992; Fletcher and Williams, 1992a, 1992b; Hartle, 1995; Armstrong and Baron, 1998). Other writers, including some of those mentioned previously, provide a more critical perspective of the appraisal process which foregrounds issues of politics and power and how appraisal systems are substantially undermined by their implicit and inherent subjectivity. It is apparent that when we consider concepts such as politics and power in relation to performance appraisal, training becomes an issue of lesser importance.

Longenecker, Sims and Gioia (1987) argue that rather than objective performance evaluation the main concern for managers when rating employees is how the rating affects themselves and how they can use it to their own advantage. This could take the form of maintaining their own performance rating and personal career aspirations, legitimating extra organisational resources and mediating local workplace conflicts. A further perspective on the political drama of performance appraisal is the resulting 'impression management' techniques adopted by employees as a result of the introduction of such systems (Goffman, 1959) which impacts on the ability of line managers to identify employees' training and development needs. According to Bowles and Coates (1993), this illustrates the inevitable exercise of social influences in the appraisal process, and this may lead to a shift from a concern with performance to a concern with conveying an appropriate image of how work is carried out.

Townley (1989) makes a related point about power relations. She describes the emergence of performance appraisal in terms of the changing locus of control in employer–employee relations. This is related to the way in which managers attempt to change organisational culture through the establishment of new shared norms, values and beliefs with the intention of facilitating greater organisational commitment and integration. Townley (1989:94) comments that these systems 'emphasise shifts from formal rules as to how the work is to be done, to implicit expectations as to how it should be done', and in doing so highlight the renegotiation of work power relations within an organisation. Drawing substantially upon a Foucauldian account of knowledge, Townley (1994) asserts that performance management systems can be understood as an attempt to renegotiate power/knowledge relations. Conveying implicit expectations is achieved through the exercise of tighter control and increased supervision across an organisation.

Other radical critiques of performance management systems include those suggested from labour process theory (Braverman, 1974; Rose, 1975; Littler, 1982). Fox (1974) provides an analysis which goes beyond pluralist accounts of employment relations.[9] For Fox (1974), pluralist accounts remain within a normatively consensus-based framework. According to this approach, conceptions of employment relations and managerial initiatives such as performance management systems misrepresent fundamental and structural inequalities in conditions, opportunities and the subordination of employees. From this perspective appraisals would be seen to constitute a depoliticising and normative mechanism through which management control may be enhanced, whilst simultaneously appearing to disperse it. Performance management systems, including appraisals, can be regarded as a system through which management achieves employee compliance with organisational concerns and obscures social and collective elements of work (Offe, 1976).

Setting objectives and related consequences

A central element in performance management systems is the process of setting employee objectives. Difficulties arise from organisational attempts to set meaningful objectives that are easily measurable and observable. The problem of setting employee objectives has implications for the type of training and development required in the sense that easily definable objectives are likely to demand specific training, whereas more complex objectives call for enhanced general development and training. Endeavours to set objectives are further complicated when qualitative or intangible aspects of organisational activity – such as, for example, customer service, communication and teamworking skills – are set as activities to be reflected in performance objectives. Bacal (1999:55) summarises the dilemma when he states that 'The less important the job task, the easier it will be to measure it exactly and objectively. The more important the job task (and the more complex), the more difficult it will be to measure it.' In other words, it is easy to measure the quantifiable and trivial, and harder to measure the important aspects of a job.

Bacal (1999) also discusses objective-setting in relation to the impact it has for producing conflicting objectives and confusing signals for individuals, teams and organisations. He asserts that a performance management system conveys to the employees how work should be performed and what values and culture the organisation favours. Performance management systems have, he argues, considerable consequences for organisations in terms of encouraging purely individualistic and competitive behaviour across an organisation. Performance management systems that focus upon individual responsibility and accountability reduce the incentives for teamwork, knowledge sharing and group learning, and for undertaking tasks which do not directly benefit an organisational actor. In such a context the introduction of team-based performance systems would also not overcome such pressures, but would be likely to add to the ambiguity of performance criteria systems, rather than clarifying or unifying objectives throughout an organisation.

Tendencies towards individualisation in the workplace may also encourage managers and employees to act not only in their own self-interest, but also in ways which prevent other organisational actors from achieving certain performance targets. Winstanley and Stuart-Smith (1996) echo such sentiments in asserting that individuals' interest in obtaining performance rewards, whether in terms of promotion, performance related pay or training, may override concerns for the business unit or organisational performance. However, such individualising effects may also occur simultaneously, with a reduction in the perception of individual contribution to performance targets, especially if combined with coaching by a line manager. Gallie *et al.* (1998:279) contend that if 'coaching by the supervisor raises general standards of work quality in a work group, this makes it more difficult for any one individual to shine relative to others'. Performance management systems, with their reliance upon a close line manager–employee relationship, may increase individual performance criteria while at the same time leaving less scope for autonomy and for claiming individual accreditation. The extent to which individualisation takes place will depend upon a range of internal and external organisational contexts. It is possible to assert, though, that the more successful a performance management system is, in terms of reconfiguring social relations in the organisation around individually defined goals, the more likely it is to undermine, and redefine, the existing basis of cooperation within the organisation around new criteria.

Contexts and problematics surrounding performance related pay

Storey and Sisson (1993:143) argue that 'individual PRP is being introduced for largely ideological reasons' in order to individualise the employment relationship. This individualisation, as an essential component of human resource management strategies, takes place through direct communication with employees and by minimising the role of trade unions. Smith (1992) contextualises such trends within a UK competitive business environment. Responses to competitive pressures are characterised by short-term muddling-through strategies concentrating on output, with changes driven by financial demands and cost-cutting imperatives. Smith (1992) draws upon Nolan (1989) to argue that performance related pay is as much about minimising labour costs as it is about increasing labour productivity. This takes the form of a low wage policy which, together with a reduction in the payouts from remuneration systems for high performance, is a means of maintaining UK companies' competitive position. As Smith states, 'only by depressing wages *relative to* other economies' has the UK economy remained internationally competitive (1992:179, emphasis in original).

Smith (1992) also describes the particularity of performance related pay to the UK. This can be characterised by the emphasis upon a direct link between individual performance and individual pay, rather than on the integration of the reward system to the organisation's human resource management strategy. Smith (1992:171) argues that although human resource management and performance management originated in the USA, performance related pay in the USA is 'not [based] on some crude link between pay and performance but rather on a much wider set of motivational issues including attraction, retention, expectancy, skill development, culture and reinforcement of organisation structure'. In this way, US companies attempt to integrate rewards with business strategies by providing other benefits, such as training opportunities for high performing individuals. It also illustrates how performance related pay in the UK has been adopted and designed around a particular economic context.[10]

The operationalisation of performance related pay in connection with individual performance is also problematic. The achievement of objectives in performance management systems, including an element of performance related pay, rests on the possibility of establishing a clear and effective link between performance and pay. Kessler (1994) discusses various ways in which this link may become distorted. First, it can become distorted because of the mechanics of the scheme, which are based on a straightforward link in which a certain rating of performance gives rise to a specific increase in pay. It can also be based on a more complicated mechanism whereby the link involves the position on a job scale and/or the pay in accordance with a particular salary range. Second, distortion can arise from the financial constraints under which many schemes operate. The budget available for individual performance related pay may not be sufficient for the extra remuneration to make a substantial difference, in which case it has consequences for pay as an incentive. Some organisations have developed guidelines for the distribution of performance ratings and pay to individuals within a particular team, department or business unit. The consequence of such distributions is that a certain rating for an individual may be amended at a later stage if the aggregated ratings exceed those provided by the organisation's pay distribution curve. This has effects in terms of undermining trust, commitment and motivation in the performance system and managerial competence.

The extent to which pay in and of itself constitutes a motivator for improved and increased performance has been subject to intense discussion (Brown and Walsh, 1994; Campbell, Campbell and Chia, 1998).[11] Inasmuch as most commentators agree that pay is an important factor for employees, the issue of whether pay is an extrinsic motivator is a more contentious issue. Brown and

Walsh claim that 'pay is only a part of the motivational package' (1994:461) and they emphasise the importance of guarding against pay as a demotivator rather than promoting pay as a motivator. Campbell, Campbell and Chia (1998) suggest that pay is more likely to be an incentive for employees if they experience the performance rating to be fair and there are clear and consistent links between ratings and performance pay.

The relationship between performance management and training

The focus so far has been on problematics associated with performance management and the implications of performance management for training, with only limited attention given to the ambiguous concept of training itself and, in particular, a strategic approach to training (see Chapter 2). A strategic approach to training can in general be characterised by a long-term perspective about why and how training is designed and implemented in the short- and long-term. Harrison (1992) explains how a strategic approach to the management of training must operate effectively at corporate, business unit/divisional and operational level, with the training at the operational level integrated into daily routines and procedures. For training to become strategic in this three-fold sense the training function must have a 'good fit' with the business, employ experts in training who can develop and provide effective management of training and link the training function to line management. In order to fulfil these criteria, Harrison (1992) claims it is necessary that the training strategy be developed at board level as an integral part of the overall strategy of the organisation. Hendry and Pettigrew (1986) also make the point that for the training function to be 'strategic' there must be an overall integrative approach which aligns human resource development to the business strategy of the organisation. This is in accordance with what the softer forms of human resource management literature prescribe (Keep, 1989).

The implication of organisations taking a strategic approach to training is that the training strategy is developed centrally within the organisation, with training needs identified and relayed from line management and training implemented by line management at the operational level and/or by the training/human resource department. Holden and Livian (1992) highlight problems between line managers' decentralised role as interpreters of organisation-wide personnel/human resource initiatives, and a centralised training function which creates and disseminates human resource strategies. The implementation of performance management and the development of a strategic approach to training are, in other words, brought into existence at different levels within an organisation. This has consequences for line managers within organisations, who have simultaneous responsibility for the operation of performance management systems and for identifying and implementing training.

Hansen (1994) examines the relationship between performance management and training, and, in particular, training strategy. She argues that the tensions in levels between performance management and training emanate from different time-frames and from the respective emphasis given by the company to performance management and training. The case study research revealed that the implementation of a performance management system into the company was directed towards achieving short-term performance objectives. Even though the performance management system aimed at being both development- and reward-driven, this was seen to be highly problematic. The focus on short-term performance objectives and rewards had consequences for the limited importance, time and resources allocated to training at operational level by line management. This highlighted the conflicting and competing objectives of the performance management system and the different time-frames which performance management and training implied. The emphasis was on short-term performance goals, which were output related and sacrificed long-term needs (such as training), which were productivity related. It was also related to the all-pervasive emphasis given to performance management above the needs for training and development and to the general lack of company-wide support for training.

The existence of a training strategy implies, according to Harrison (1992) and Hendry and Pettigrew (1986), the existence of a business strategy which is known by all managers and employees. Hansen (1994) found that the company she studied did not have an explicit long-term business strategy and this had consequences for its competitive strategy. The company responded in a reactive way to market changes and legislative requirements and this led to the development of efficiency and cost effectiveness measures, of which the performance management system was an important component. Such findings are consistent with generalisable characteristics of UK companies' competitive strategies across the economy. Competitive advantage is based upon cost competition allied with a voluntaristic company-based, rather than state-led, approach to training and development (Noble, 1998).

The relationship between performance management and training strategy can be characterised by its inherent tensions in terms of timescales and importance given to the two components. This does not, however, mean that these tensions will be of a similar extent at all times and in all organisational contexts. Whittington *et al.* (1999) utilise the notion of complementarities in order to understand the possibility of coherent and interlinked changes which help companies improve their performance. Complementarity theory proposes that by combining a number of practices at the same time the complete system of practices is much greater than the sum of its parts. Applying the notion of complementarities to the relationship between performance management and training strategy, it can be argued that performance management and training strategy can come together to improve business performance when, for example, recruitment policies and practices complement the performance of individuals, and when development and training are emphasised in the appraisal process, as opposed to reward outcomes. Edwards, Collinson and Rees (1998) remain sceptical of the possibility of such holistically integrated and implicitly unitary strategies whilst acknowledging that organisations do differ in their relative success or failure in implementing new practices, such as performance management. Contextual variables such as the trade union–management relationship, job security and the role of the training department in relation to general workplace practices will have effects on the relationship between performance management and training strategy.

Conclusion

This chapter has reviewed the emergence of performance management in a context of organisational responses to external economic and political pressures for effective and efficient processes. Performance management has also constituted a main component in the increasing interest in HRM with internal reorganisation processes comprising devolved responsibility and accountability to line management levels and a general individualisation of the employment relationship. Employers have regarded performance management as providing organisations with improved mechanisms of aligning organisational objectives for enhanced performance with objectives for individual performance. The development, implementation and outcome of performance management systems are, however, rarely without substantial problems. For Grint, the discrepancy between the rhetoric and reality of performance management systems can be summed up as: '[r]arely in the history of business can such a system have promised so much and delivered so little' (1993:64).

There are multiple and interlinked factors which account for the problems associated with performance management. These have been analysed in terms of the conflicting and competing purposes of performance management systems in relation to improving individual performance, performance related pay and identifying training and development needs. Problems were related to the ownership of performance management systems between line managers and senior managers, and how this became a particular problem for line managers in relation to other operational and managerial responsibilities. Additionally, the introduction of performance management systems is based on an underlying assumption of mutuality and unity and this ignores issues to do with the politics in the workplace and the changing power relations in organisations. Performance management systems also encounter the dilemma of developing measurable yet meaningful objectives in terms of establishing individual objectives and rewards, with consequences for individualistic behaviour.

The relationship between performance management systems and training has also been explored, especially within a UK context. The achievement of performance targets implies a short-term timescale which is at odds with the long-term nature of training and development strategies. The former is reflected in UK competitive business strategies based upon demands for short-term returns, competition on price and cost cutting. For organisations operating in markets based upon quantity rather than quality, maintaining a low-skilled labour force, minimum training and development may in fact be a strategic choice, at least in the short term. Yet as markets become increasingly competitive and technological innovations change workplace practices, companies are required to adapt to new business environments and changing contexts. Organisations that are successful in the long term are likely to be those that develop their managers' and employees' broad and unspecific skills with an understanding that such skills will be useful in various contexts, some of which may not yet exist. All organisations in fact face a tension between short term returns and long term change and adaptability, although this will depend upon the complex relations between organisational, sectoral and national contexts and in this sense it may not be useful to understand the short-term and the long-term as completely separate.

Notes

1 Armstrong and Baron (1998:29–48) provide a useful short history of performance management.

2 Competence based pay, as opposed to performance related or merit based pay, is based upon an agreed framework of future capabilities and not on the achievement of specific and past results.

3 For other sources of information about performance management in practice in the UK see The Industrial Society (1994), which also carried out a survey, and Incomes Data Services (1992, 1997).

4 The questionnaire was answered by 856 private and public organisations of varying sizes and industrial sector. Follow-up in-depth case studies were also carried out.

5 The questionnaire was based on answers from 562 organisations. In addition to the survey, visits to a limited number of organisations were conducted, and attitude surveys and focus groups were also undertaken.

6 For a comprehensive review of the practice of performance related pay in the UK with evidence from surveys and case studies, see Kessler (1994).

7 The research was based on an intensive qualitative case study methodology. Materials were derived from semi-structured interviews, attending and observation of meetings and internal documentary resources from the company. Twenty interviews were conducted over a two-week period with senior managers, line managers, administration staff, sales consultants and trade union officers from the training department, the personnel department, head office administration, branches and the trade union. Two meetings at the training department were attended as an observer.

8 This research finding forms part of the national *Employment in Britain* survey. See Gallie *et al.* (1998) for other results of this large-scale survey.

9 A pluralist account of organisations contends that conflict may be endemic to organisational activity (Fox, 1966), but it is possible to achieve consensus on particular issues and as such the employment relationship cannot only be understood purely as a zero-sum power relationship. Such ambivalences in the employer–employee relationship mean that there is explicit employee interest and power in maintaining the on-going survival of the organisation.

10 See Fox (1998) for an elaboration of the UK business environment, particularly the chapters that deal with UK management and human resource management, vocational education and training, and industrial relations.

11 Since the Hawthorne experiments in the late 1920s the debate about motivation and the role of economic rewards has been an intensely contested issue. See Brown (1992) for an overview.

References

Ainsworth, M. and Smith, N. (1993) *Making it Happen: Managing Performance at Work*, Sydney: Prentice-Hall.

Armstrong, M. (1992) *Human Resource Management. Strategy and Action*, London: Kogan Page.

Armstrong, M. and Baron, A. (1998) *Performance Management. The New Realities*, London: Institute of Personnel and Development.

Bacal, R. (1999) *Performance Management*, New York: McGraw-Hill.

Barlow, G. (1989) 'Deficiencies and the perpetuation of power: latent functions in management appraisal', *Journal of Management Studies*, 26, 5, 499–516.

Bevan, S. and Thompson, M. (1991) 'Performance management at the crossroads', *Personnel Management*, November, 37–9.

Bowles, M. L. and Coates, G. (1993) 'Image and substance the management of performance as rhetoric or reality?', *Personnel Review*, 22, 2, 3–21.

Braverman, H. (1974) *Labor and Monopoly Capital*, New York: Monthly Review Press.

Bredrup, H. 'Background for performance management'in Rolstadås, A. (ed.) (1995) *Performance Management: A Business Process Benchmarking Approach*, London: Chapman & Hall.

Brown, R. K. (1992) *Understanding Industrial Organisations. Theoretical Perspectives in Industrial Sociology*, London: Routledge.

Brown, W. and Walsh, J. (1994) 'Managing pay in Britain', in Sisson, K. (ed.), *Personnel Management. A Comprehensive Guide to Theory and Practice in Britain*, Oxford: Basil Blackwell.

Campbell, D. J., Campbell, K. M. and Chia, H. (1998) 'Merit pay, performance appraisal, and individual motivation: an analysis and alternative', *Human Resource Management*, 37, 2 (Summer) 131–46.

Carlton, I. and Sloman, M. (1992) 'Performance appraisal in practice', *Human Resource Management Journal*, 2, 3 (Spring) 80–94.

Drucker, P. (1955) *The Practice of Management*, London: Heinemann.

Edwards, P., Collinson, M. and Rees, C. (1998) 'The determinants of employee responses to total quality management: six case studies', *Organization Studies*, 19, 3, 449–75.

Flanagan, J. C. (1954) 'The critical incident technique', *Psychological Bulletin*, 51, 327–58.

Fletcher, C. and Williams, R. (1992a) *Performance Management in the UK. An Analysis of the Issues*, London: Institute of Personnel Management.

Fletcher, C. and Williams, R. (1992b) 'The route to performance management', *Personnel Management*, October, 42–7.

Fowler, A. (1990) 'Performance management. The MBO of the '90s?', *Personnel Management*, July, 47–51.

Fox, A. (1966) 'Industrial sociology and industrial relations', *Royal Commission on Trade Unions and Employers' Associations*, Research Paper, 3, London: HMSO.

Fox, A. (1974) *Beyond Contract: Work, Power and Trust Relations*, London: Faber & Faber.

Fox, S. (ed.) (1998) *The European Business Environment: UK*, London: International Thomson Business Press.

Gallie, D., White, M., Cheng, Y. and Tomlinson, M. (1998) *Restructuring the Employment Relationship*, Oxford: Clarendon Press.

Goffman, E. (1959) *The Presentation of Self in Everyday Life*, New York: Penguin.

Grint, K. (1991) *The Sociology of Work. An Introduction*, Cambridge: Polity Press.

Grint, K. (1993) 'What's wrong with performance appraisals? A critique and a suggestion', *Human Resource Management Journal*, 3, 3, 61–77.

Guest, D. E. (1987) 'Human resource management and industrial relations', *Journal of Management Studies*, 24, 5, 503–21.

Hansen, B. (1994) 'The Missing Link – Performance Management and Training Strategy at Spire Insurance', unpublished Master's dissertation in Industrial Relations, Warwick Business School, University of Warwick, September.

Harrison, R. (1992) *Employee Development*, London: Institute of Personnel Management.

Hartle, F. (1995) *Transforming the Performance Management Process*, London: Kogan Page.

Hendry, C. and Pettigrew, A. (1986) 'The practice of strategic human resource management', *Personnel Review*, 15, 5, 3–8.

Holden, L. and Livian, Y. (1992) 'Does strategic training policy exist? Some evidence from ten European countries', *Personnel Review*, 21, 1, 12–23.

Incomes Data Services (1992) *Performance Management*, IDS Study 518, November, London: Incomes Data Services.

Incomes Data Services (1997) *Performance Management*, IDS Study 626, May, London: Incomes Data Services.

Industrial Society (1994) *Performance Management*, London: Industrial Society.

Keep, E. (1989) 'Corporate training stategies: the vital component?' in J. Storey, (ed.), *New Perspectives of Human Resource Management*, London: Routledge.

Kessler, I. (1994) 'Performance pay', in Sisson, K. (ed.), *Personnel Management. A Comprehensive Guide to Theory and Practice in Britain*, Oxford: Basil Blackwell.

Lane, J. E. (1995) *The Public Sector. Concepts, Models and Approaches*, London: Sage.

Legge, K. (1995) *Human Resource Management. Rhetorics and Realities*, London: Macmillan.

Legge, K. (1998) 'The morality of HRM', in Mabey, C., Salaman, G. and Storey, J. (eds), *Strategic Human Resource Management*, London: Sage.

Littler, C. R. (1982) *The Development of the Labour Process in Capitalist Societies*, London: Heinemann.

Local Government Management Board (1994) *Performance Management and Performance Related Pay*, London: The Local Government Management Board.

Longenecker, C. O., Sims, H. P. and Gioia, D. A. (1987) 'Behind the mask: the politics of employee appraisal', *Academy of Management Executive*, 1, 3, 183–93.

McGregor, D. (1957) 'An uneasy look at performance appraisal', *Harvard Business Review*, 35, 89–94.

Mayo, E. (1933) *The Human Problems of an Industrial Civilization*, New York: Macmillan.

Newton, T. and Finlay, P. (1996) 'Playing God? The performance of appraisal', *Human Resource Management Journal*, 6, 3, 42–58.

Noble, C. (1998) 'International comparisons of training policies', in Maybey, C., Salaman, G. and Storey, J. (eds), *Strategic Human Resource Management. A Reader*, London: Sage.

Nolan, P. (1989) 'Walking on water? Performance and industrial relations under Thatcher', *Industrial Relations Journal*, 20, 2, 81–92.

Offe, C. (1976) *Industry and Inequality*, London: Edward Arnold.

Pettigrew, A., Sparrow, P. and Hendry, C. (1988) 'The forces that trigger training', *Personnel Management*, December, 28–32.

Porter, M. E. (1980) *Competitive Strategies: Technologies for Analyzing Industries and Firms*, New York: Free Press.

Porter, M. E. (1985) *Competitive Advantage: Creating and Sustaining Superior Performance*, New York: Free Press.

Rogers, S. (1990) *Performance Management in Local Government*, Essex: Longman.

Rose, M. (1975) *Industrial Behaviour. Theoretical Development since Taylor*, London: Allen Lane.

Scott, W. H., Banks, J. A. and Lupton, T. (1956) *Technical Change and Industrial Relations. A Study of the Relations between Technical Change and the Social Structure of a Large Steelworks*, Liverpool: Liverpool University Press.

Smith, I. (1992) 'Reward management and HRM', in Blyton, P. and Turnbull, P. (eds), *Reassessing Human Resource Management*, London: Sage.

Stiles, P., Gratton, L., Truss, C., Hope-Hailey, J. and McGovern, P. (1997) 'Performance management and the psychological contract', *Human Resource Management Journal*, 2, 1, 57–66.

Storey, J. and Sisson, K. (1993) *Managing Human Resources and Industrial Relations*, Buckingham: Open University Press.

Taylor, F. W. (1911) *Principles of Scientific Management*, New York: Harper & Row.

Thompson, P. and McHugh, D. (1990) *Work Organisations. A Critical Introduction*, London: Macmillan.

Torrington, D. and Hall, L. (1995) *Personnel Management: HRM in Action*, 3rd edn., Hemel Hempstead: Prentice Hall

Townley, B. (1989) 'Selection and appraisal: reconstituting "social relations" ', in Storey, J. (ed.), *New Perspectives on Human Resource Management*, London: Routledge.

Townley, B. (1994) *Reframing Human Resource Management. Power, Ethics and the Subject at Work*, London: Sage.

Whittington, R. (1993) *What is Strategy and Does it Matter?*, London: Routledge.

Whittington, R., Pettigrew, A., Peck, S., Fenton, E. and Conyon, M. (1999) 'Change and complementarities in the new competitive landscape: a European study, 1992–1996', *Organization Science*, 10, 5, 583–600 (September).

Williams, R. S. (1998) *Performance Management. Perspectives on Employee Performance*, London: International Thomson Business Press.

Winstanley, D. and Stuart-Smith, K. (1996) 'Policing performance: the ethics of performance management', *Personnel Review*, 25, 6, 66–84.

CHAPTER 5

Multinational companies: innovators or adaptors?*

Paul Marginson

Introduction

MNCs dominate the international economy and are instrumental in driving forward processes of globalisation. Estimates of the number of multinationals world-wide rose from 37 000, owning 265 000 foreign subsidiaries in 1994, to over 53 000 with 448 000 subsidiaries overseas in 1998 (UN, 1994, 1998). In 1993, flows of foreign direct investment displaced conventional trade in goods and services as the most important form of international economic exchange (UN, 1993). Their contribution to trade is substantial too: Dicken (1998:43) reports that approximately one-third of world trade was accounted for by intra-firm transfers of goods and services across borders. Not surprisingly, multinationals employ a significant proportion of the workforce, particularly in the industrialised economies. The most recent figures available estimate that MNCs directly employ a total of 73 million people world-wide, 61 million in the industrialised economies (of which 44 million are employed in operations in the home country and 17 million in overseas operations), and 12 million in the developing countries. In total, MNCs' direct employment accounts for some 20 per cent of the workforce in the industrialised countries, to which can be added a further equivalent proportion employed in local supplier

---

* This chapter revises and updates an article first published in *Human Resource Management Journal*, 4, 4 (Summer 1994). In writing this new version, I am grateful for comments from Tony Edwards.

companies (UN, 1994). MNCs have long been seen to play an important role in shaping changes in industrial relations structures and practice (Marginson and Sisson, 1996), including the diffusion of innovative practices across national borders. The types of activity MNCs engage in, and their decisions on where, across countries and regions, to locate different kinds of operation have important implications for skill requirements and training in national and local economies.

Three-quarters of foreign direct investment flows are between the industrialised economies, involving two-way flows between countries within and between the three major economic blocs (North America, western Europe and Japan and East Asia): the so-called 'Triad' (UN, 1998). Amongst the industrialised economies, some countries are primarily hosts to flows of inward investment, whereas others are primarily the source of flows of outward investment and a third group are characterised by both significant outflows and inflows. Australia, Ireland, Portugal and Spain fall amongst the first group, Germany, Japan and the Netherlands amongst the second, and France, Italy, the UK and the USA amongst the third. Accordingly the share of employment accounted for by multinationals, and whether it is due primarily to overseas- or indigenously-based multinationals or to both, varies considerably between countries.

For example, approaching 45 per cent of Ireland's total manufacturing employment is accounted for by foreign-owned multinationals, but only a small proportion by multinationals based in Ireland. In contrast, whereas foreign-owned MNCs account for 15 per cent of total manufacturing employment in the UK, indigenously-based multinationals account for 45 per cent of the total (UN, 1988, 1994). Further, whereas around one-quarter of the employment of UK- and US-based MNCs is overseas, the proportion for their Japanese-based counterparts is almost 40 per cent. Conversely, affiliates of overseas-owned MNCs account for just 1 per cent of total manufacturing employment in Japan (UN, 1994:185). There is considerable variation between sectors too, with the dominance of multinationals being greatest in the petroleum, chemicals, automotive and electrical engineering industries and least in the service sectors (Dunning, 1993), although the 1990s have seen rapid increases in foreign direct investment in services (Dicken, 1998:50).

An indication of how far these transnational investment flows are resulting in companies which are global in scale can be gleaned from data on the largest 100 multinational companies ranked according to total assets. Employment in overseas operations account for more than three-quarters of total employment in a little over one-in-five of these, and for more than 50 per cent and up to three-quarters in a further three-in-five (calculated from table II.1, UN, 1998). In total, then, just one-half of the very largest multinational companies have a majority of their employment outside their home countries (most of these are based in small economies such as the Netherlands, Sweden and Switzerland). Thus whilst multinational companies are an increasingly dominant force in

private sector employment across the industrialised world, only a small number of individual companies can be said to be truly international employers.

The impact of MNCs on the quality and volume of employment and on
labour practice in the industrialised economies has been the subject of extensive debate. Some see multinationals as a source of significant employment
creation often in relatively advanced industries, and hence of innovations in
labour practice and demand for a well-trained workforce and for new skills.
Others see MNCs as undermining employment security through their ability
to switch production to other, lower-cost locations, an ability which also
enables them to progressively drive down the terms and conditions of labour.
Yet others see multinationals as adapting to and further shaping a division of
labour between national economies within each of the regional economic blocs
that comprise the Triad, which serves to reinforce existing differences in labour
skills, labour productivity and labour costs between national systems. Each of
these contesting perspectives is addressed in the course of the chapter.

The chapter focuses on the impact of MNCs in the industrialised economies,
and in particular on the highly internationalised UK economy which, more
than any other large industrialised country, represents an economy dominated
by multinational companies. The next section considers contrasting implications of the activities of multinationals for employment and labour practice.
The following two sections explore factors underlying the considerable variation evident in the employment and labour practices of MNCs. Thus the third
section examines the likely consequences for employment and labour practice
of alternative motivations for companies to become multinational in scope,
whilst the fourth section highlights the important role of differences in management style and organisation. The fifth section looks at the case of Britain,
and considers the implications of the economy's role in the growing European
(and global) division of labour being shaped by MNCs for employment and
labour practice.

Employment and labour practice effects

The activities of multinational companies have generated particular concerns
in terms of their effects on (i) employment and (ii) the terms and conditions of
labour, which are distinct from those associated with nationally-based companies. But benefits in terms of both employment and the terms and conditions
of labour have also been associated with multinational activity. The following
discussion is structured around a consideration of these differing 'employment' and 'labour practice' effects.

In terms of employment effects, three sources of concern can be identified.
The first, from the perspective of the source nation, is a loss of employment at

home as multinationals extend their overseas operations at the expense of domestically-based activity. This has been a matter of long-established concern in Britain and the USA, which until recently provided the strongest evidence for job loss amongst major source nations (Ramsay, 1990). Surveying 58 large British-owned multinationals in the manufacturing sector, Stopford and Turner (1985) reported that these companies had cut their total employment in Britain by 600 000 in the period 1972–83 whilst increasing their employment overseas by a total of 200 000. Ferner (1997b) cites a study by Woodall (1994) reporting a similar trend amongst US-based MNCs in the years 1977–89. More recently such concern has extended to France and Germany, in the shape of growing debate over the process of *délocalisation* in the former and the future of 'Standort Deutschland' in the latter (Ferner, 1997b).

The other two concerns relate to the host nation, the first of these being the alleged footloose nature of (some) multinational activity. Because multinationals can switch locations according to prevailing economic, political and fiscal circumstances, it is argued that employment is relatively insecure. Examples include the well publicised decision by Renault to close its plant at Vilvoorde in Belgium and transfer production to its operations in Spain, despite the favourable performance of its Vilvoorde plant as compared to some of its operations in France (EIRO, 1997), and the recent announcement by Levi-Strauss of retrenchments in its European operations amidst concerns that production is being transferred to sites in developing countries (European Works Council Bulletin, 1998). A third source of concern is the type of skills associated with the operations of overseas-owned multinationals. Operations are said to be typically relatively routine in terms of the production process, requiring at best a semi-skilled workforce. Research and development activities are rarely located outside the source country, leading to what Dicken (1998:262) describes as 'truncation' of industrial activity in host economies. Where overseas multinationals are associated with the displacement, or acquisition, of indigenous producers – as has been the case in the automotive and other consumer goods industries in Britain – the problem of associated skill loss appears to be particularly acute. Young, Hood and Hamill (1988:94), reporting on a study of the chemicals, mechanical and electrical engineering industries, find that overseas-owned firms employ significantly fewer staff on managerial and professional grades, and significantly more at operative level, than their UK-owned counterparts.

On the benefit side, from the perspective of host nations overseas-owned companies can be a significant source of increased employment. In the 1990s, inward investment by North American-, Japanese- and other East Asian-based multinationals concerned to establish operations within the EU's single market, together with substantial investments by German- and French-based companies, have had beneficial effects on levels of employment in Britain. Official figures report the creation of 46 000 new jobs during 1996 and 1997 (*Financial Times*, 21 January 1998). Insofar as these companies source components and services from the local economy, these beneficial employment effects can spill over into the wider economy.

Turning to 'labour practice effects', the main source of concern lies in the enhanced bargaining power possessed by multinationals in relation to their workforces as compared with nationally-based firms. Their enhanced bargaining power stems from their ability to 'divide and rule' amongst workforces located in different countries, for whom there are considerable difficulties of organisation, communication and differences of interest in developing a common position across borders (Cowling and Sugden, 1987). The advantages accruing to multinational companies manifest themselves in a variety of ways: the ability to switch production from one location to another (or to credibly threaten to do so); dual sourcing of products and services from locations in different countries, enabling multinationals to minimise the disruption caused by local (nationally-based) industrial disputes; the remoteness of corporate decision-makers from trade union negotiators, left to deal with local managers negotiating to a mandate determined in another country; the sheer scale of the financial resources behind multinationals and the lack of financial transparency in decisions on the future of local operations.

Certainly there are examples of these factors at work. The initial decision of companies, such as Mercedes-Benz, to locate production facilities outside their home country provides management with an additional bargaining lever over its domestic workforce: threats to relocate overseas can no longer be seen as empty (Mueller, 1996). The practice of dual sourcing is illustrated by Ford's decision to transfer part of its proposed investment in new capacity in engine manufacture from South Wales to Cologne, stimulated by concern at becoming too reliant on the Bridgend plant for engine supply (*Financial Times*, 10 April 1990). The large automobile multinationals have routinely exercised 'coercive comparisons' (Mueller and Purcell, 1992) of workforce performance across sites in different countries, involving threats to switch production away from poorly performing sites and promises to direct new investment to those with superior performance, so as to extract concessions in working practices from local workforces (see Mueller and Purcell's 1992 study of engine manufacture). In the food industry, Coller (1996) describes how the competition for production allocations between the European plants of the ice cream business of a large multinational rests in part on comparisons of workforce performance. The scope to exercise such threats to switch production, and thereby extract concessions in working practices, are progressively enhanced as multinationals organise production on an international scale.

Hoover's 1993 decision to relocate production of a particular business line from France to Scotland was explicitly linked to substantial concessions obtained from the Scottish workforce ('The Hoover affair and social dumping', 1993). It also vividly illustrated the fact that employees in both countries lacked any rights of representation and influence at the transnational level where the decision was taken. The EU's 1994 directive requiring multinational companies to establish European Works Councils (EWCs) to inform and consult with employee representatives on transnational matters starts to address this gap. Even so, Renault announced its decision to close its Vilvoorde plant in Belgium without consulting the EWC, although the closure was subsequently delayed by judgements in the French courts and the EWC was successful in organising widespread protest action, including a stoppage of work across the company's operations in all European countries (EIRO, 1997).

All these considerations might suggest that multinationals are able to drive a 'hard bargain' with their workforces, exerting a negative impact on the terms and conditions of workers in the countries in which they operate. Yet the evidence on pay and other benefits is overwhelmingly to the contrary. Across the industrialised economies, average earnings at establishments with foreign parents are above those of their indigenously-owned counterparts (UN, 1994:197). In Britain, establishments belonging to multinationals, whether they are overseas- or UK-owned, pay higher wages and provide more comprehensive fringe benefits than do locally-based companies (Buckley and Enderwick, 1985; Weber-Fahr and Edwards, 1994). If multinational companies are associated with the payment of better terms and conditions, they are also said to employ advanced management techniques which bring with them innovatory labour practices. Surveying large companies in the UK, Purcell *et al.* (1987) found that overseas-owned enterprises were more likely to employ sophisticated forms of employee involvement and participation than British-owned companies, a finding confirmed by their subsequent survey (Marginson *et al.*, 1993). Similarly, interest in Japanese employment practices stems from the innovatory forms of production and management organisation that Japanese-owned multinationals are introducing into their plants in Britain (Oliver and Wilkinson, 1992).

Clearly all these employment and labour practice effects, both detrimental and beneficial, are unlikely to operate simultaneously within particular multinationals. Put another way, reaching an aggregate assessment is likely to conceal as much as it uncovers. Different employment and labour practice effects will be found in differing mixes in different multinationals. The next two sections explore how differences in the labour practices of multinationals can be accounted for by considering, first, companies' motivations for becoming multinational and, second, their management approach and organisation.

Motivations for going multinational

In considering the differing motivations lying behind company decisions to become multinational in scope, it is helpful to distinguish between explanations concerned with factor supply and those concerned with competitive strategies in the product market. A second distinction can also be made between explanations rooted in the concept of economic efficiency and those focusing on the exercise of economic power. The discussion below indicates how alternative explanations have differing implications for the terms and conditions of labour.

Considerations of factor supply principally relate to the securing of raw materials and of labour supply. The first can be dealt with briefly, as the implications for the labour practices of multinationals concerned are not clear cut. Securing control over key raw materials might be the motivation for companies to become multinational in their scope. Where there are limited sources of supply upstream, companies are exposed to the risk of being 'held to ransom' by local companies controlling supply. Alternatively, if supply remains in the hands of local companies, problems of quality control may be experienced in the supply of raw materials. In either case there are clear incentives for companies to acquire upstream suppliers and in so doing become multinational (see Teece, 1986). Indeed, this was the origin of many early British-based multinationals such as Dunlop, Cadbury, Brooke Bond, Unilever and Shell. The oil and mining sectors provide major contemporary examples. Where such multinationals are also able to establish themselves as monopsony purchasers of labour in particular localities, then scope exists to drive a particularly harsh bargain with their workforces over pay and conditions.

Explanations rooted in the conditions of labour supply find their clearest expression in the literature on the 'new international division of labour'. Thus Froebel, Heinrichs and Kreye (1980) argued that technological advances in communications, innovations in production organisation and management technique, plus the growing availability of pools of un- and underemployed labour in urban areas in developing countries, have made it feasible for companies to service the markets of the advanced industrialised countries from production sites in the Third World. These are characterised by cheap wages, poor conditions and low labour standards. Hours of work are long and there is strong labour discipline. Recent evidence is available from the textiles and clothing and electronics industries (Dicken, 1998).

Even as a cost-minimisation strategy, the 'new international division of labour' literature has been the subject of extensive criticism. By focusing on wage costs it overlooks the substantial productivity differentials that can and do exist between workforces in developing and developed countries, due to factors such as education and training, absenteeism and employee motivation, which can make for lower unit labour costs at sites in industrialised economies (Cho, 1985). Also neglected is the potential for restructuring production at sites in developed countries in order to reduce (unit labour) costs. In separate studies of two British-based multinationals in textiles – a sector for which there is some supportive evidence for a new international division of labour – both Elson (1986) and Walsh (1989) show how the companies concerned secured significant cost reductions in their British-based operations through the application of new technologies and production rationalisation across sites. The extent to which aspects of production can be decoupled and relocated is also open to question: the introduction of 'just-in-time' (JIT) production systems increase the importance of spatial proximity amongst different production activities controlled by an enterprise. The broader implication of these criticisms is that production is only likely to be relocated to cheap labour locations overseas in particular circumstances, when there is no scope for technological advancement or other forms of organisational change.

Yet perhaps the greatest shortcoming of the 'new international division of labour' literature is its failure to account for the dominant pattern of multinational investment flows. These primarily remain amongst the advanced industrialised economies rather than between them and developing countries. Whilst figures on investment flows indicate some slight re-orientation towards developing countries, three-quarters of all new overseas investment by companies continues to be amongst industrialised nations (Dicken, 1998:45–7). Explaining the interpenetration of the industrialised economies by each other's capital (the simultaneous existence and growth, for example, of the presence of US multinationals in Britain and British multinationals in the USA) points to the importance of market-orientated motivations for companies to become multinationals. It is to these that we now turn.

There are two main strands of market-orientated explanation of the motivation to become multinational in scope: the first underlines the efficiency benefits of internalising international trade within the firm (Buckley and Casson, 1976; Teece 1986); the second stresses the exercise of market power in overseas markets (Hymer, 1976; Cowling and Sugden, 1987). Efficiency explanations, known as 'internalisation theory', are based on the idea that companies have a competitive or strategic advantage which is not tradeable in the market. The advantage might be a tangible asset such as a technology or particular product brand. In the case of a technology, the alternative of licensing may require the disclosure of information to a local producer that enables the technology to be copied. A similar argument applies to particular brands (think, for example, of the consequences of disclosing the ingredients of Coca Cola). In either case, establishing local production and thereby becoming multinational facilitates expansion. Evidence of concern to exploit technological advantage is indicated by the high proportion of multinationals in manufacturing which employ continuous flow or assembly line technologies (Dunning, 1993). These technologies tend to be associated with particular patterns of labour practice, associated with the payment of relatively high wages and good conditions of employment, because of the potential costs of disruption. Such costs arise out of the capital-intensive nature of continuous flow production and the high degree of interdependency within assembly line production.

Alternatively the competitive or strategic advantage may be an intangible asset, such as the ability to innovate, the ability to market or a particular management system. Such advantages cannot be traded in the market, and hence it is argued that companies can only exploit them in overseas markets by establishing operations there. In terms of management systems, part of a company's strategic advantage may lie in its approach to managing the workforce. During the 1960s and 1970s, part of the competitive advantage enjoyed by US multinationals in Europe was seen to lie in the bureaucratic employment systems developed as adjuncts to mass production methods. Latterly, by integrating their labour management policies with their longer-term business strategy through the adoption of human resource management approaches, a second group of US-based multinationals has been seen to possess a competitive advantage. The connections between 'just-in-time' production, total quality production and the employment systems said to be characteristic of Japanese-based multinationals have been seen to be a source of, if anything, even greater competitive advantage (Oliver and Wilkinson, 1992).

The emphasis in this line of analysis is on multinationals as innovators or leaders in labour practices, which may in turn involve the acquisition of new skills by local workforces. A further implication is that the commitment of companies to markets is likely to be longer term, reflected in a relatively high degree of employment security.

Explanations for multinationality focusing on the exercise of (a degree of monopoly) power in the product market also take as their point of departure the possession by companies of a strategic advantage and the existence of imperfections in markets (Hymer, 1976). However, unlike internalisation theory, the prime motivation for entering overseas markets is viewed in terms of companies' potential ability to exercise a degree of control over that market. In turn, it is argued that this is related to the ability to differentiate products and services according to local tastes. But overseas producers are seen as 'foreign' in the eyes of local customers and are therefore at a disadvantage compared to local producers. The establishment of local operations enables overseas-based companies to overcome this. In this light, 'localness' becomes one dimension of product differentiation and thereby the ability to secure an element of monopoly profit. Moreover, since there are advantages accruing to being a local producer, rival multinationals are expected to follow each other into local markets (Cowling and Sugden, 1987).

'Localness' can also be politically defined, in the sense that companies servicing markets from overseas can have tariffs or quotas imposed on them. Amongst the industrialised economies such tariff and non-tariff walls increasingly operate at the level of the regional blocs which comprise the Triad rather than at the level of individual nation states. As the process of economic integration within the EU has moved from the creation of the Single European Market in 1993 to the launch of the single currency in 1999, this has been a major motivation lying behind the establishment by Japanese, and further North American multinationals of (additional) production operations in Europe (Ramsay, 1995). (It does not, however, explain why they should be overwhelmingly located in Britain.)

Since, according to these arguments, companies' commitment to particular product markets is likely to be long term, concerns about employment insecurity are unlikely to be realised. Turning to labour practices, securing the advantage of being seen to be a local producer might lead multinationals into adopting, or adapting to, local practice. Multinationals might also be concerned to be viewed as 'good employers' locally, leading them to provide better pay and conditions than the local average. The emphasis here is on multinationals as adaptors rather than innovators.

In sum, viewed in terms of alternative motivations for companies to become multinational in scope, the implications for employment security and labour practice are very different. If the motive for multinationality is a strategic advantage in a particular management system or technique, then multinationals may act as innovators in terms of labour practice; whereas, if local market servicing is the prime motivation, multinationals are more likely to be adaptors. In both instances, the implications for employment point towards relative security rather than insecurity. If, however, securing cheap labour is a prime motivation, employment will be insecure and pay and labour conditions poor. Yet cheapness is just one amongst a number of factors determining unit labour costs that may influence companies' decisions. Factors promoting productivity (such as skills and reliability) are also of central importance. Hence multinationals tend to segment and stratify their operations across different locations according to the differing kinds of labour supply available in different countries, reflecting their need for relatively skilled, high-productivity labour in some operations but semi-skilled, routinised labour in others. As growing integration in the regional blocs of the Triad widens the scope of final product markets to continental dimensions, the scope for such segmentation and stratification of operations according to labour requirements correspondingly increases (this theme will be returned to in the section analysing Britain's role in the multinational division of labour).

Management style and organisation: towards the global company?

A second, and cross-cutting, way of accounting for differences in labour practice between multinationals is to differentiate between them in terms of their management style and organisation. Discussion of the influence of management style dates back to Perlmutter's (1965) classification of multinational companies according to the cultural influences acting on management. Perlmutter distinguished between companies which are 'ethnocentric', 'polycentric' and 'geocentric' in their management approach. In companies which are ethnocentric in their approach, overseas subsidiaries are wholly-owned and are managed as a cultural extension of the parent by managers from the source country. Polycentric enterprises are characterised by local participation in ownership, and a management style which is locally determined and implemented by locally recruited managers. Over time, Perlmutter expected multinationals to move from either an ethnocentric or a polycentric approach to a geocentric approach, where management practice is shaped much more by the nature of particular businesses than by the practices associated with either the source or host countries.

Implications for labour practice are reasonably clear: ethnocentric multinationals can be expected to (try to) introduce labour practices from the source country in their overseas operations, in other words to be innovators, whereas polycentric multinationals can be expected to adopt local labour practices, or to be adaptors. Research evidence suggests that US-, and more recently Japanese-, owned multinationals tend towards an ethnocentric approach, whereas British-owned multinationals appear to be more polycentric in their approach (Ferner, 1997a). Aside from differences according to source nation, an important consideration influencing management approach will be the means by which overseas operations were established: greenfield sites lend themselves to an ethnocentric approach whereas acquisition of existing local producers lends itself to a polycentric approach. In the case of geocentric multinationals, companies can be expected to diffuse examples of 'best' labour practice, in the light of production and business requirements, between operations in different countries. Unlike ethnocentric multinationals, 'best' or innovatory labour practices may originate in subsidiaries in host countries and flow back to the source country, as well as flowing from the source country to overseas subsidiaries (Edwards, 1998). Coller (1996) provides examples of such two-way flow diffusion in a large European food multinational.

In terms of management organisation, the international business literature has generated a number of taxonomies to account for the differing business strategies and internal structures of multinational companies. Typically these locate companies according to a matrix which reflects the relative strength of global pressures towards coordination and centralisation on the one hand, and local pressures towards devolution and local autonomy on the other, operating on the dual logics of marketing and production (see, for example, Bartlett and Ghoshal, 1992). Porter's (1986) distinction between companies operating in 'multi-domestic' industries, where competition is nationally bound, and those operating in industries which are 'global' in scope has been particularly influential. Amongst multinationals in 'multi-domestic' industries, national operations in terms of both production and marketing are relatively stand alone, and national boundaries form the prime axis of internal management organisation in the shape of the national subsidiary. In 'global' industries, both markets and the organisation of production are international in scope and the primary axis of internal management organisation becomes the individual (international) businesses. Intermediate forms of organisation are found in industries which lend themselves to internationally centralised production but local marketing, and vice versa (Bartlett and Ghoshal, 1992).

Internationalisation of markets, a process which multinationals themselves are playing a central role in driving forward, is leading more and more multinationals to internationalise production and service provision, and, correspondingly, to shift from the nationally-based forms of organisation associated with 'multi-domestic' business strategies to the international forms of organisation required to compete in 'global' industries (Marginson *et al.*, 1995). These transnational forms of multinational organisation increasingly differentiate between global regions as well as distinct international businesses within a single multinational company. Moreover, whereas in the past the headquarters functions and research and development activities of multinationals tended to be concentrated in the source country, with nationally-based subsidiaries being essentially production and sales facilities, evidence suggests that some multinationals are spreading the headquarters functions and research and development activities of their different international businesses across countries too (Forsgren, Holm and Johanson 1992).

This process of internationalisation has led writers such as Ohmae (1990) to argue that multinationals are becoming 'stateless' organisations on a global scale, increasingly detached from the societies in which they are originated. However, Hu (1992) has questioned how far companies are becoming truly geocentric or global in their approach, arguing that many multinationals remain essentially ethnocentric. Ferner and Quintanilla (1998) show how pressures to internationalise are leading MNCs based in Germany to adopt a range of management practices characteristic of the management approaches of US- and UK-based multinationals. But they conclude that such a process of 'Anglo-Saxonisation' is occurring in a distinctively German manner, whilst Ruigrok and van Tulder (1995) show the extent to which even many of the largest multinationals remain nationally based in terms of concentration of employment and sales in the home country, the dominance of the board by home country nationals and sources of finance.

None the less, the spread of more international forms of management structure amongst a growing number of multinationals has significant implications for labour practice. Companies increasingly have the potential to implement common policies and practices across borders and, as noted above, to diffuse 'best' or innovatory practices across operations in different countries from wherever they are identified (Edwards, 1998). In addition, the adoption of international systems of performance control means that companies are able to compare the labour performance of sites in different countries (as well as financial and sales indicators) and, as Mueller and Purcell (1992) argue, to deploy these comparisons in business decisions on investments and restructuring, and to secure concessions from workforces deemed to be performing poorly.

Overall, although the deepening of international forms of management organisation amongst MNCs means that diffusion of innovatory labour practices across borders (from host to source as well as source to host countries) is likely to intensify, differences between multinationals, in terms of the balance of innovation and adaptation, will persist. This is because labour practices are shaped by contrasting styles of management approach, the mode by which overseas operations are established, the business strategy and internal structure of multinationals and characteristics of the industrial relations systems of the different nation states in which multinationals operate. Moreover, as MNCs become more internationalised in the scope and organisation of their operations, decisions on the location of production and service operations, of research and development activities and of headquarters functions within their internationally integrated businesses are having enormous repercussions for the division of labour between national economies. As activities become increasingly segmented and stratified across countries, nations are finding themselves 'the host of specialised facilities which are mere cogs in the [European and world-wide] strategies of giant firms' (Auerbach, 1989:266).

The next section examines the labour market implications of these processes for the British economy, in the context of the growing possibilities for a continental division of labour that are accompanying economic and market integration within the EU.

Britain's role in the multinational division of labour

Of the major industrialised economies, the UK and US economies are distinguished by the extent to which they are both the source and the recipient of substantial stocks and flows of foreign direct investment (UN, 1998). Within Europe, 'the UK is in a unique position of being both a major location for and source of foreign acquisitions' (Hamill, 1992:138). Home- and overseas-based multinational companies dominate the UK's output, trade and employment, especially in the manufacturing sector, accounting for an estimated two-thirds of manufacturing output, 60 per cent of manufacturing employment and 80 per cent of manufacturing exports (Marginson, 1994, Dicken, 1998). Amongst European-owned multinationals, British-owned companies are distinctive in the extent to which their overseas investments are located in North America as well as elsewhere in Europe (Ruigrok and van Tulder, 1995). Even so, growing economic integration within Europe during the 1990s has been reflected in a growing proportion of UK overseas investment going to other European countries. At the same time, the UK has been the most important recipient of flows of inward investment within Europe, particularly from multinationals headquartered in North America and East Asia (Barrell and

Pain, 1997; Dicken, 1998). Also, amongst European-owned multinationals, UK companies have been the most active (in terms of both predators and targets) in cross-border mergers and acquisitions within the EU, and in North America in recent years (Edwards, 1999).

A second feature of Britain's role in the multinational division of labour is its industrial and technological dimension. There is a marked difference in the sectoral concentration of British-owned multinationals, as compared with their German- and French-owned counterparts. British-owned companies are heavily weighted towards non-manufacturing (largely service) activities, French-owned companies less so. In contrast, the majority of German-owned multinationals are in manufacturing (Sisson, Waddington and Whitston, 1992). The largest number of British-owned manufacturers are in food, drink and tobacco, and more generally British-owned multinationals remain concentrated in relatively low-technology industries, pharmaceuticals and aerospace being notable exceptions (Stopford and Turner, 1985). Correspondingly, inward investment into Britain appears also to be concentrated in relatively low-technology sectors (Barrell and Pain, 1997).

Britain's success in attracting substantial flows of inward investment during the 1980s and 1990s was attributed by Conservative governments up until 1997 to successful policies to deregulate labour markets, constrain trade union organisation and activity and therefore restrain labour costs (Pain, 1997). Favourable comparisons were drawn with labour market conditions in continental Europe, said to be characterised by excessive regulation and higher labour costs. According to inward investors themselves, the advantages of the UK as an investment location for projects which are potentially mobile within western Europe are several, of which labour market factors are one. First, the UK provides an open, deregulated business environment (including ready availability of suitable new sites); second, it represents a major market and some inward investors wish to be close to customers; third, there is the strength of the UK's infrastructure in business and financial services to consider; fourth, the importance of the English language; fifth, the quality of the pool of labour available in terms of training and skills; and sixth, the deregulated nature of the labour market, facilitating the use of flexible labour practices and involving relatively low labour costs (*Financial Times*, 24 October 1995; Industrial Relations Services, 1996).

An indication of the relative importance of labour factors in the location decisions of multinationals, and which labour considerations are more salient, is provided by findings from a 1992 survey (Marginson *et al.*, 1996:195–8). Of 65 multinationals reporting investments at new sites within Europe, three-quarters reported labour considerations to be of 'some' or 'considerable' importance, including one-quarter reporting them to be of 'considerable importance'. And two-thirds of all 104 multinationals responding to the survey reported labour considerations to be of 'some' or 'considerable' importance in decisions on locating capital investment at existing sites. For each instance where at least some account was taken of labour considerations in investment decisions within Europe, respondents were asked what kinds of factor were taken into account (Marginson *et al.*, 1996:195–8). In the case of greenfield site investments, four out of every five respondents cited skills and labour force qualifications, and wage and non-wage costs as factors which had attracted them to a particular location; whereas two out of every five respondents cited statutory employment rights as a factor deterring investment at a particular location. In the case of capital investment programmes at existing sites, by far the most commonly cited factor was labour force skills and qualifications (mentioned by 9 out of 10 respondents). Confirming earlier argument, considerations of labour force skills and qualifications would appear to be at least as important, if not more so, than labour costs. Similar conclusions are drawn by Cooke (1998) from his study of the labour factors determining the location of US foreign direct investment across nineteen Organisation for Economic Co-operation and Development (OECD) countries.

Such evidence returns us to the question of the kind of inward investment that has been attracted by Britain's increasingly de-regulated labour market. A variety of further research data throws light on the respective importance of labour costs, the conditions of labour and skills and qualifications in determining Britain's role in the multinational division of labour. Compared with other industrialised economies, Britain is indeed a low labour-cost country. Hourly wage costs in Britain are noticeably lower than those in the USA, Japan, France and Germany (Nolan and Walsh, 1995; Agarwal, 1997). When 'on costs' (covering things such as social welfare, training and holidays) are taken into account, Britain emerges with a distinct cost advantage as compared with all other major industrialised nations. However, because productivity in Britain lags behind that of the other main industrialised economies (Barrell and Pain, 1997), unit labour costs in Britain are no lower than those elsewhere (Adnett, 1995). Within the EU, Austria, Italy, the Benelux and Nordic countries, as well as France and Germany, all have higher levels of productivity, offsetting higher labour costs, than the UK. Moreover, Britain's relative position in terms of both labour costs and productivity within the EU has remained unchanged since the early 1980s (Commission of the European Communities, or CEC, 1993, 1997). This suggests that Britain's competitive advantage lies in low-wage, labour-intensive, low-skill and therefore relatively low-productivity sectors.

Turning to the 'conditions of labour', companies based in Britain are subject to fewer statutory constraints as to how they deploy and manage their workforces than in the other major economies within the EU (Cooke, 1998). Restrictions on the use of atypical forms of employment, such as fixed-term and temporary workers, are less stringent in Britain, and so too are the regulations governing redundancy. And Britain, along with Ireland, is alone amongst EU countries in not having a mandatory system of works councils or similar within the enterprise. Until recently, workers in Britain did not enjoy the protection of minimum pay or working time found elsewhere in Europe. Moreover, employers perceive the UK as having the weakest employment protection regulations within the EU (CEC, 1993). Aside from the potential benefits to companies in terms of costs and the exercise of managerial prerogative, a further observation is important: by placing fewer statutory constraints on employers, or employees and their trade unions, as to labour practice there is correspondingly greater scope for innovatory practices in Britain compared with, say, Germany. This, too, may be attractive to multinationals keen to transfer labour practices which are considered to be an essential part of their production and management systems. Yet the absence of statutory regulation can also have a downside. Ferner (1997b) argues that, faced with the need to restructure, multinationals may be more prone to close an operation in the UK than in, say, France or Germany, because the costs of 'exit' are low in Britain.

Claims about the skills available to inward investors have to be seen in the context of the activities that multinationals are actually choosing to locate in Britain. It has long been observed that these tend to be relatively low-skilled assembly, and subassembly, operations involving routinised and standardised production methods (Young, Hood and Hamill, 1988). There are few signs that this pattern is changing, and rather more that it is being reinforced (Barrell and Pain, 1997). Research and development expenditure in UK subsidiaries of overseas-owned MNCs is lower than elsewhere in Europe, implying that there is relatively less demand for research-based skills. The car industry in Britain illustrates the point. The demise of the British-based manufacturers has been accompanied by the downgrading by overseas-owned manufacturers of their British facilities in terms of research and development activity and their centrality to their wider European operations (Nolan and Walsh, 1995).

A final key to understanding the character of the investments overseas-owned multinationals have located, and will continue to locate, in Britain lies in the nature of the activities that British-based multinationals are engaged in. As has already been noted, these are primarily low technology and low skill in character, being concentrated in sectors such as food, drink, tobacco, paper and textiles in manufacturing and in hotels, leisure and finance in services. Such sectors are not research-intensive. Exceptions are the presence of British-based multinationals in the capital- and research-intensive aerospace and pharmaceuticals sectors. In the case of pharmaceuticals, the presence of strong British-based companies in a research-intensive sector is reflected in the extent to which overseas-owned multinationals have established research and development facilities in Britain.

In sum, the UK economy has a distinctive position within the multinational division of labour as an outward base and inward location for relatively low-technology, labour-intensive and low-skill kinds of industrial activity. Given the low level of research activity amongst many British-based multinationals and the relative lack of demand for associated skilled labour, few overseas-based multinationals are likely to be drawn to Britain as a research and development, and therefore high-skill, location.

Conclusion

To an ever-increasing extent, levels of employment, the structure of employment, skills and training required, labour practices, labour conditions and industrial relations in particular national economies are being shaped by the decisions of multinational companies organised and integrated on a transnational scale. Within Europe, this process is being accelerated as market integration is driven further forward by Economic and Monetary Union. This ongoing process of internationalisation will result in further diffusion of labour, employment and other practices deemed as instances of 'best' practice to and from the operations in different countries within MNCs, providing an impetus to associated training and skill acquisition. At the same time, the tendency of MNCs to segment and stratify the constituent activities within internationalised operations according to the varying characteristics of the wage, productivity, training and industrial relations regimes of different national economies will act to constrain the extent of this first dynamic. Thus, both innovation stemming from diffusion of new practices and adaptation to practices embedded in particular national systems will continue to be evident.

In Britain, the present government aspires to create a high-skill economy, attractive to a particular type of inward investor (*Financial Times*, 24 July 1997). The evidence presented in this chapter does indeed demonstrate that within Europe multinationals are as concerned with the quality and productivity of labour as they are with wage and non-wage costs, if not more. Yet realising such a policy objective, given the role of the UK economy in the multinational division of labour within Europe as a location offering the advantages of an available, relatively cheap, unprotected and semi-skilled labour supply, would require a radical transformation.

References

Adnett, N. (1995) 'Social dumping and European economic integration', *Journal of European Social Policy*, 5, 1, 2–12.

Agarwal, J. (1997) 'European integration and German FDI', *National Institute Economic Review*, 160 (April), 100–11.

Auerbach, P. (1989) 'Multinationals and the British economy', in Green, F. (ed.), *The Restructuring of the British Economy*, London: Harvester.

Barrell, R. and Pain, N. (1997) 'The growth of foreign direct investment in Europe', *National Institute Economic Review*, 160 (April), 63–75.

Bartlett, C. and Ghoshal, S. (1992) *Managing Across Borders: The Transnational Solution*, London: Century Business.

Buckley, P. and Casson, M. (1976) *The Future of the Multinational Enterprise*, London: Macmillan.

Buckley, P. and Enderwick, P. (1985) *The Industrial Relations Practices of Foreign-Owned Firms in Britain*, London: Macmillan.

CEC (1993) *Employment in Europe: 1993*, Luxembourg: CEC, Office for Official Publications of the European Communities.

CEC (1997) *Employment in Europe: 1997*, Luxembourg: CEC, Office for Official Publications of the European Communities.

Cho, S. K. (1985) 'The labour process and capital mobility', *Politics and Society*, 14, 2, 185–222.

Coller, X. (1996) 'Managing flexibility in the food industry: a cross-national comparative case study in European MNCs', *European Journal of Industrial Relations*, 2, 2, 153–72.

Cooke, W. (1998) 'The influence of industrial relations factors on US foreign direct investment abroad', *Industrial and Labor Relations Review*, 51, 1, 3–17.

Cowling, K. and Sugden, R. (1987) *Transnational Monopoly Capitalism*, Brighton: Wheatsheaf.

Dicken, P. (1998) *Global Shift: Transforming the World Economy*, London: Paul Chapman.

Dunning, J. (1993) *Multinational Enterprises and the Global Economy*, New York: Addison-Wesley.

Edwards, T. (1998) 'Multinationals, labour management and the process of reverse diffusion', *International Journal of Human Resource Management*, 9, 4, 698–709.

Edwards, T. (1999) 'Cross-border mergers and acquisitions: the implications for Labour', *Transfer*, 5, 2.

EIRO (1997) 'The Renault case and the future of social Europe', *EIR Observer Update*, 2/97, 2–3.

Elson, D. (1986) 'The new international division of labour in the textile and garment industry', *International Journal of Social Policy*.

European Works Council Bulletin (1998) 'Levi-Strauss factory closures – "the next Renault affair"?', *European Works Councils Bulletin*, 18, 2 (November/December).

Ferner, A. (1997a) 'Country of origin effects and HRM in multinational companies', *Human Resource Management Journal*, 7, 1, 19–37.

Ferner, A. (1997b) 'Multinationals, "relocation" and employment in Europe', in Gual, J. (ed.), *Job Creation: The Role of Labour Market Institutions*, Aldershot: Edward Elgar.

Ferner, A. and Quintanilla, J. (1998) 'Multinationals, national identity and the management of HRM: "Anglo-Saxonisation" and its limits', *International Journal of Human Resource Management*, 9, 4, 710–31.

Forsgren, M., Holm, U. and Johanson, J. (1992) 'Internationalisation of the second degree: the emergence of European-based centres in Swedish firms', in Young, S. and Hamill, J. (eds), *Europe and the Multinationals*, Aldershot: Edward Elgar.

Froebel, F., Heinrichs, J. and Kreye, O. (1980) *The New International Division of Labour*, Cambridge: Cambridge University Press.

Hamill, J. (1992) 'Cross border mergers, acquisitions and alliances in Europe', in Young, S. and Hamill, J. (eds), *Europe and the Multinationals*, Aldershot: Edward Elgar.

Hu, Y. (1992) 'Global or stateless corporations are national firms with international operations', *California Management Review*, 34, 2, 107–26.

Hymer, S. (1976) *The International Operations of National Firms: A Study of Direct Foreign Investment*, Cambridge, Mass: MIT Press.

Industrial Relations Services (1996) 'From overseas to over here – the employment policies and practices of inward investors', *IRS Employment Trends*, 617 (October), 5–11.

Marginson, P. (1994) 'Multinational Britain: employment and work in an internationalised economy', *Human Resource Management Journal*, 4, 4, 63–80.

Marginson, P., Armstrong, P., Edwards, P. and Purcell, J., with Hubbard, N. (1993) 'The control of industrial relations in large companies', *Warwick Papers in Industrial Relations*, 45, IRRU: University of Warwick, December.

Marginson, P., Armstrong, P., Edwards, P. and Purcell, J. (1995) 'Extending beyond borders: multinational companies and the international management of Labour', *International Journal of Human Resource Management*, 6, 3, 702–19.

Marginson, P., Armstrong, P., Edwards, P. and Purcell, J. (1996) 'Facing the multinational challenge', in Leisink, P. van Leemput, J. and Vilrokx, J. (eds), *The Challenges to Trade Unions in Europe*, Aldershot: Edward Elgar.

Marginson, P. and Sisson, K. (1996) 'Multinational companies and the future of collective bargaining', *European Journal of Industrial Relations*, 2, 2, 173–98.

Mueller, F. (1996) 'National stakeholders in the global contest for corporate investment', *European Journal of Industrial Relations*, 2, 3, 345–68.

Mueller, F. and Purcell, J. (1992) 'The Europeanisation of manufacturing and the decentralisation of bargaining', *International Journal of Human Resource Management*, 3, 1, 15–24.

Nolan, P. and Walsh, J. (1995) 'The structure of the economy and Labour market', in Edwards, P. (ed.), *Industrial Relations: Theory and Practice in Britain*, Oxford: Basil Blackwell.

Ohmae, K. (1990) *The Borderless World: Power and Strategy in the Interlinked Economy*, New York: Free Press.

Oliver, N. and Wilkinson, B. (1992). *The Japanisation of British Industry*, Oxford: Basil Blackwell

Pain, N. (1997) 'Continental drift: European integration and the location of UK foreign direct investment', *The Manchester School Supplement*, 65, 94–117.

Perlmutter, H. (1965) 'L'enterprise internationale, trois conceptions', *Revue Economique et Sociale*, 4, 1, 9–18.

Porter, M. (ed.) (1986) *Competition in Global Industries*, Boston, Mass.: Harvard Business Press.

Purcell, J., Edwards, P., Marginson, P. and Sisson, K. (1987) 'The industrial relations practices of multi-plant foreign owned firms', *Industrial Relations Journal*, 18, 2, 130–7.

Ramsay, H. (1990) '1992: the year of the multinational?', *Warwick Papers in Industrial Relations*, 35, November.

Ramsay, H. (1995) 'Le défi Européen', in Amin, A. and Tomaney, J. (eds), *Behind the Myth of the European Union*, London: Routledge.

Ruigrok, W. and van Tulder, R. (1995) *The Logic of International Restructuring*, London: Routledge.

Sisson, K., Waddington, J. and Whitston, C. (1992) 'The structure of capital in the European community: the size of companies and the implications for industrial relations', *Warwick Papers in Industrial Relations*, 38, Coventry: University of Warwick, IRRU, February.

Stopford, J. and Turner, L. (1985) *Britain and the Multinationals*, Chichester: Wiley.

Teece, D. (1986) 'Transactions cost economics and the multinational enterprise', *Journal of Economic Behavior and Organization*, 7, 1, 21–45.

'The Hoover affair and social dumping', *European Industrial Relations Review*, March, 14–19 (1993).

UN (1988) *Transnational Corporations in World Development*, New York: UN Centre for Transnational Corporations.

UN (1993) 'Transnational corporations and integrated international Investment', *World Investment Report 1993*, Geneva: UNCTAD.

UN (1994) 'Transnational corporations, employment and the workplace', *World Investment Report 1994*, Geneva: UNCTAD.

UN (1998) 'Trends and determinants', *World Investment Report 1998*, Geneva: UNCTAD.

Walsh, J. (1989) 'Capital restructuring and technological change', in Tailby, S. and Whitston, C. (eds), *Manufacturing Change*, Oxford: Basil Blackwell.

Weber-Fahr, M. and Edwards, T. (1994) 'Regional integration and labour markets: the role of multinational enterprises', Report for the OECD, Coventry: University of Warwick, IRRU.

Woodall, P. (1994) 'You ain't seen nothing yet: the biggest threat to workers is not from imports, but from a mass migration of investment', *The Economist*, 1 October.

Young, S., Hood, N. and Hamill, J. (1988) *Foreign Multinationals and the British Economy*, London: Croom Helm.

CHAPTER 6

Training in greenfield sites

Helen Newell

Introduction

Greenfield sites have been heralded by many academics and practitioners alike as a panacea for the problems besetting manufacturing industry because they offer exceptional opportunities for change. It is argued that in a greenfield site the implementation of innovative working practices, such as human resource management, will be much easier than in an existing site, since there are no pre-existing expectations or assumptions about the way in which work should be organised. This potential for change has important implications for corporate training policies. For example, Keep (1992) has argued that the adoption by companies of a strategic approach towards the training and development of their workforce represents a vital component of any meaningful form of HRM, but that in order to develop this kind of strategic approach the integration of training and development into wider business planning is crucial, although rarely achieved. Even though managers may wish to develop a strategic approach to HRM they are often constrained by existing policy and practice, by history and by the difficulty of managing the kinds of change required without costly upheavals. As a result, many of the basic processes and procedures that ought to underpin HRM are simply not widespread amongst British employers. Much more common, even within organisations that are attempting to formalise their employment management systems, is that such processes and procedures operate, at best, in a very piecemeal way.

Academics and practitioners alike have seen 'greenfield' sites as one possible solution to this dilemma of how to develop a truly integrated and strategic approach to HRM. This is because greenfield sites are seen to provide exceptional opportunities, the opportunity to start with a clean slate and to get 'everything right first time'. Lawler, for example, argues that such sites 'simply have a number of advantages ... . They can start with a congruent total system; ... . it is possible to do the whole organisation at once ...' (1986:307). Similarly Clark (1995) notes that greenfield sites offer opportunity structures for innovation, experiment and new philosophies. In other words, it is in greenfield sites that we should see the most innovative employee policies, state of the art technology and flexible working practices and, in support of these policies, the most advanced and comprehensive employee training initiatives.

We should note, however, that this does not mean that every company opening a new plant will take the opportunity to adopt what might be described as a 'soft' HRM approach (Storey, 1992) with an emphasis on fully developing the potential of the company's human resource. As Leopold and Hallier comment, even in new plants:

> if management believe that the competitiveness of the business requires commitment, flexibility and non-union working, then senior managers might find a strategic HR approach desirable. But if it is felt the product market is relatively stable, then the routineness and predictability of a more traditional personnel management approach might seem more appropriate. (1997:73)

If it is true that greenfield sites offer exceptional opportunities, we should be especially concerned to ask whether the implementation of such innovative employment policies has been successful, for if it has not been possible in what seem to be very favourable conditions what then is the likelihood of the adoption of such strategies in existing plants where the majority of manufacturing is concentrated?

This chapter considers the extent to which the claims made about greenfield sites are true, focusing in particular upon training provision, by examining the available research evidence. It begins by examining the concept of a greenfield site and analysing why we might expect to see good training practice on such sites. It then looks at the relevant survey and case study evidence which suggests that greenfield sites do not provide substantially more training than other plants and that employees working in greenfield sites are not satisfied with the levels of training provided, before examining the reasons which lie behind these findings.

What is a greenfield site?

So what is special about a greenfield site, and what is it that offers employers such wonderful opportunities? Definitions of what constitutes a greenfield site vary greatly; however, a review of the relevant literature suggests that the following are key features of an 'ideal' greenfield site.

New location and building

Typically the choice of a new location serves to isolate the new site from existing plants of the same company, as well as from other plants in the same industry. The aim here is to emphasise the 'discreteness' of the new plant, keeping it quite separate from any others and so avoiding any possibility of 'contamination' of the new management approach, and the policies and practices which stem from it. However, location is also heavily influenced by government financial incentives, the availability of large tracts of relatively cheap land and access to transport routes. Baird, commenting on greenfield sites in Australia, points out that 'as a consequence of earlier spatial development, the choice of location for greenfield sites often coincides with areas of low industrialisation, high unemployment and moderate to low union activity, thus increasing the attraction of the location to management' (1994:1).

Some people argue that locating plants in areas of high unemployment will provide both a large labour pool and a compliant workforce, grateful for their jobs and thus willing to accept whatever policies and practices management decide upon. This overlooks the important issue of skill requirements. A large labour pool does not necessarily overcome problems of skill shortages, and those with higher skills are likely to be sought after by other employers in the area and are thus unlikely to be particularly compliant.

Along with the new location there is often a brand new building, purpose-built to create exactly the right environment, not only for the new technology that it will house, but also to nurture the new philosophy, policies and practices. In a study of the top 21 American non-union companies Foulkes emphasised the importance of what he called 'situational factors' in both 'fostering an effective personnel program and encouraging a climate of trust and confidence' (1981:91). This included choosing rural rather than suburban sites and limiting the size of facilities, as well as careful landscaping.

New work organisation

New or 'state of the art' technology is often a feature of greenfield sites. They allow organisations considering the introduction of advanced technological change to design, lay out and equip a site according to current and future business requirements, rather than working within the constraints of an existing building. In these cases employers often express the view that what they need to operate this new technology are highly-skilled employees, often expressed in terms of the best available. In some sites, however, the approach is not to adopt new technology but to use existing technology in a different way. Where innovations in technology are limited, pressures to become more competitive may result in solutions born out of work re-organisation. As a result, new work organisation is probably more important than new technology *per se*. Greenfield sites provide an ideal environment for such developments because there are no existing social relations or custom and practice.

New employees

Often referred to as 'green' labour, the new plant's employees will not necessarily be starting their first job, but typically they will not have worked for that company before and generally will not have worked in the same industry before. As a result, employees will not have pre-conceived ideas about 'how things should be done around here' and can be relatively 'easily moulded into an homogenous group fitting the different organisations' cultures with relative ease' (Reitsberger, 1986:51). In other words, employees have not yet been socialised into particular patterns of behaviour at work (Delbridge and Turnbull, 1992; Garrahan and Stewart, 1992).

Recruitment and selection are thus key activities for greenfield sites, the aim being to select a new workforce which will meet the requirements of the company. In this respect the concept of 'fitting in' is an important selection criterion and acceptability is likely to be seen to be as (if not more) important as ability. Townley (1989) has argued that there appears to be a growing trend in the use of more systematic selection and appraisal procedures. She believes that this is linked to an increasing emphasis placed on the 'attitudinal and behavioural characteristics of employees', factors which readily lend themselves to monitoring through selection and performance review (1989:92). Furthermore, this monitoring is seen to be necessary as greater discretion is devolved to the individual and/or work group, as direct or technical supervision of work is replaced by greater employee flexibility and autonomy. Such moves, Townley argues, are integral to HRM and contrast sharply, with the concern for behavioural and attitudinal characteristics of employees shown, for example, by the early Quaker employers or even some 'American welfare capitalists' (Townley, 1989:92).

Similarly, in their study of Japanese subsidiaries in the UK, White and Trevor argue that the approach taken to the issue of recruitment and selection 'is one of the most significant aspects of Japanese thinking about personnel' (1983:124). They also comment that attitude was more important than technical competence, the emphasis being on people who would 'fit in'. Similar evidence is supplied by Wickens (1987) about Nissan.

This aspect of recruitment and selection is particularly important when a desire to attract 'the best' employees is coupled with the contagious enthusiasm of greenfield site managers. As Lawler (1978) noted from his research into 'new design' plants in the USA, the type of selection processes that were used often created high expectations amongst recruits about what it would be like to work in the new plant. The innovative employee selection processes used in many of these plants stressed that the work would be challenging and different, that working would be more flexible and that training would be given. Employees not unrealistically concluded, therefore, that things would be totally different from the way that they are in a typical plant. Training plays a key role, too, not only in attracting potential employees to the firm, but also in encouraging them to stay. As Sisson (1989) argues, training plays an important role in retaining employees in that it demonstrates that the company values them.

New management philosophy

Sisson has attempted to draw together the key features of those greenfield site companies adopting 'soft' HRM policies and practices. Whilst he recognises that these may vary from site to site, he says that typically they have the following type of features:

> a commitment to an explicit philosophy or style of management; flexibility of working; single status; integrated salary structures; continuous training and the payment for skills acquired; direct communication with the workforce through regular meetings; a joint consultative council, together with (in some cases) the exclusive recognition of a single union; 'no strike' provisions which rule out industrial action even as a last resort; and pendulum arbitration. (1994:23)

Two features of the policies and practices that Sisson describes are of special interest in relation to training: (i) the notion of flexible working; (ii) the development of an internal labour market where pay and promotion are governed by reference to internal bureaucratic procedures, rather than to external market mechanisms. Each of these features merits closer examination.

One Incomes Data Services study claimed that 'full flexibility remains almost entirely confined to greenfield sites' (1990:5). The emphasis here is on functional rather than numerical flexibility, in order to end job demarcations both within particular groups of workers and between different groups of workers. The International Labour Office (ILO) defines functional flexibility as 'the readiness and ability of employees to adapt to the changing contents of their jobs' (Sisson, 1995:1). The picture which is often drawn of greenfield sites is of a small, multiskilled and highly flexible workforce in capital-intensive manufacturing industry, where flexibility is either 'implied' or even 'required' by the introduction of new 'state of the art' technology.

We should, however, be wary of thinking that full flexibility is common in greenfield sites, since this is not always borne out by the available evidence. A number of case studies suggest that despite having the perfect opportunity to introduce full functional flexibility, many greenfield sites neither want it nor use it. For example, in his study of Venture Pressing's greenfield site, Preece notes that 'production staff have *had* to be flexible because they have been waiting for work to come in – hence they've been sweeping up, tending plants, etc. whereas tool room staff have been pre-occupied with preparing the tooling etc. for production – doing their specialist job as it were' (1993:33). Similarly, Clark in his study of a greenfield site found that even under conditions which were highly favourable to full flexibility, it had been not actually been used. He highlights six reasons why management sought limited rather than full flexibility:

- many employees were more suited to, and more interested in, certain tasks than others – *horses for courses*;
- there were significant advantages in having employees who were specialists in one area – *specialist knowledge*;
- giving employees responsibility for a particular area worked to the benefit of both managers and employees, in that employees were more likely to be committed to the achievement of high quality work – *ownership*;
- requirements for on-the-job training for new recruits meant that some existing employees needed to act as trainers and therefore needed to be fully up-to-date and knowledgeable about their own machine processes – *trainers*;
- unless employees were given a regular opportunity to practise their skills they could not retain them. The opportunity to practise regularly on a wide range of machine processes was not feasible in practice – *skill retention*;
- flexibility was limited by tight staffing levels. In the administration area tight staffing levels meant that staff could not be spared for training in a different area – *staffing levels*.

(Clark, 1993:126–7)

Thus, whilst we can say that *if* functional flexibility is in place it carries with it a requirement for widespread and continuous training, we cannot rely on it being the main or sole trigger for training in greenfield sites. So what other factors might lead greenfield site companies to use the opportunity to develop a strategic approach towards training and development?

As indicated above, the second area of policy and practice identified by Sisson (1989) as being important in relation to training provision is the attempt to create an internal labour market. This is particularly true where training is provided in company-specific skills which are not easily transferable to another company. In addition, recruitment of new employees is restricted to a limited number of lower levels within the firm and is linked to clearly defined career ladders within the organisation, with the result that recruitment at higher levels becomes unnecessary. Systematic and comprehensive payment systems are designed to support the overall aims of the plant and also serve to further isolate the firm from the external labour market, by paying according to performance or seniority rather than according to market rates.

The research evidence

So do the opportunities provided by greenfield sites actually result in the successful adoption of the type of training and development activities that are likely to maximise the potential of the company's human resources? Is there widespread and comprehensive training in greenfield sites and has this been successfully integrated into the company's wider business planning? What are the factors which affect training in greenfield sites? These questions are crucial, because if this has not been achieved in greenfield sites, can we realistically expect to see it happen anywhere else?

Guest and Hoque (1994) carried out a survey which compared HRM in establishments which employed 50 or more staff, 97 of which they described as 'pure' greenfield sites (new premises built at a location where no previous employment existed) and 154 as 'refurbished' sites, including some that were shut down and completely refurbished before re-opening under new ownership as well as some that had undergone less dramatic change. They found that in relation to training 68 per cent of greenfield sites, as compared to 54 per cent of refurbished sites, claimed to have deliberately developed a 'learning organisation', although the difference between the two results was not statistically significant. In contrast, only a small minority of establishments had specified an annual minimum training requirement and, although greenfield sites were more likely to have done this than refurbished sites, again the results were not statistically significant.

It is difficult to draw any strong conclusions from these results. In the first place, the data represent only management claims and there is no attempt to see how far management rhetoric is actually matched by practice (for example, by seeking employee views). We know from other research that management and employee views about what constitutes training can differ dramatically: for example, from their case study research Rainbird and Maguire concluded that much of the training reported by companies was carried out for the purposes of organisational rather than individual development. This suggested that 'many employees would not regard the training they receive as training at all, since it neither imparts transferable skills nor contributes to personal and educational development' (1993:37).

Second, it is difficult to infer anything about particular training policies or anything about levels of training from the questions that were asked. There is enormous ambiguity surrounding what constitutes a 'learning organisation' and the steps necessary to become one. Furthermore, the failure to set minimum training standards could mean either at one extreme that training was perceived to be of little or no importance so that minimum standards were deemed unnecessary or, at the other extreme, that training was taken so seriously that no minimum limits were necessary. The only clear outcome of this survey, as far as training is concerned, is that there does not appear to be any significant difference between greenfield and refurbished sites in the adoption of HRM policies in relation to training and development.

Three greenfield site case studies

The empirical research data presented in this chapter provides an unusually detailed insight into employment practices at greenfield sites in the UK and suggests a variety of factors which influence whether the rhetoric surrounding training in greenfield sites is actually translated into practice. The data come from case studies of three greenfield site companies. Four principal methods of data collection were used for the research: a study of written company documentation (including company working papers, minutes of meetings and copies of visual aids used by managers in presentations to other parts of the company); unstructured interviews with a number of key people involved in the establishment of the new sites; a series of semi-structured interviews with senior, middle and junior plant managers; and a structured survey of a larger number of employees, administered on a one-to-one basis, which provided the opportunity to follow up the survey questions with more probing questions. In all, 105 interviews were undertaken in the three plants, including 38 managers and 67 employees (which represented more than 12 per cent of the non-managerial employees working in the plants). The sample was stratified to reflect the proportion of different skill groups to the workforce as a whole, and within each skill group the sample was chosen on a numerically random basis. (For a more detailed discussion of the research method, the survey used and the research findings, see Newell, 1991, 1993.)

From this research it is clear that a large proportion of the greenfield site employees were dissatisfied with the amount of training they received. Employees were asked whether they had *the right amount of training to do [their] jobs*. While 60 per cent of the greenfield site respondents said yes, 40 per cent (a substantial minority) felt that they did not receive sufficient training to do their jobs, let alone to help improve performance, allow them to progress through the organisation or obtain promotion. This certainly suggests a lack of systematic and comprehensive training programmes in greenfield sites, but what are the factors which are likely to influence training provision, and why do the results appear to be relatively poor?

In order to understand the choices made by companies about business and personnel or human resource strategies, an understanding of the context within which the companies are operating is important. Therefore an outline sketch of each site is provided, giving information about the organisation of work, the skill requirements and the projected training needs for each site, before the key factors influencing training are analysed.

Brewco

In 1979 Brewco owned a total of 17 breweries and 56 bottling/ distribution depots, which have subsequently been rationalised down to six breweries and 29 bottling/distribution depots. In recent years, Brewco has diversified away from the core beer business towards both the international spirit market and the development of retailing beyond the pub, suggesting that its long-term future lies not in brewing but in retailing. Retail profits already dwarf those made though production and distribution.

Three important factors influenced the company's decision to establish a greenfield site: competition in the brewing industry, a perceived need to introduce new technology resulting from this increased competition, and factors relating to distribution. Traditionally breweries had been built around large volume production of a limited number of products. However, beer sales began to fall and consumer taste switched towards lager and wine, with much more emphasis on speciality products and 'take-home packs' and less on consumption on licensed premises. The new plant was designed to cope with this 'lager boom'. The prospect of a new site in South Wales was attractive not only because of the financial assistance available in the form of government grants for development areas, but also in terms of communications. Furthermore, there was a plentiful supply of labour which was used to working in process industries in general, although not in brewing in particular.

The basic aim was to create a 'high productivity environment' using as much new technology as possible. The key to the plant's success was seen to depend upon three things: communication, training and single status. The structure for the new plant would be simple. There were to be only two grades of manual worker. 'Generic' job descriptions were drafted according to responsibilities rather than duties, and people were to be trained to ensure that they were competent to do all the jobs within a particular area of the plant. The flexibility envisaged was horizontal rather than vertical: it was within rather than across functions. The Transport & General Workers Union (TGWU) district officer was involved throughout the training courses and policy development process.

Employee attitudes towards training

Approximately half of the employees interviewed at Brewco said that they were happy with the amount of training that they received. However, of that 48 per cent many people also commented that this related only to their induction training. Once the induction training had been completed there was no programme of on-going training. Indeed, even where new machinery had subsequently been introduced (especially in the canning department), the feeling was that 'you have to teach yourself as you go along', since no further training programmes were available.

As a result, one particular area of concern for employees was promotion. Whilst almost two-thirds of those interviewed expressed a desire to be promoted, many interviewees also commented that 'promotion is very difficult, you need qualifications. Years ago you wouldn't have needed the paper.' Whereas it would once have been possible to progress from a craftsman role into management ranks through appropriate in-house training, for the new plant you needed formal educational qualifications (generally a degree). This view was shared by many of the managers:

> The opportunities for promotion have moved, the goal posts have moved, because of the need to get highly skilled people in; the trigger point has moved, it now depends upon qualifications. I'm recruiting managers now who need to have a degree at first line level, but once upon a time that role would have been covered by one of the good technicians or craftsmen. The craftsmen have usually only got ONC or HNC which to some extent precludes them from taking that step. (Block Manager)

Highly skilled for this company increasingly meant formal educational qualifications, rather than vocational training and qualifications.

Cableco

Cableco, an electrical cable business, is part of a diversified multinational company, with 135 plants in 16 countries throughout the world, employing some 69 000 people. By 1987, turnover stood at nearly £135 million and the workforce at approximately 2200 employees. Cableco operates on the basis of supplying a range of different cables that might be required by one customer for a single project. The cables differ not only in terms of their physical size but also in terms of their technical complexity, and range from high voltage

electrical cables used for power transmission to optical fibre telecommunica-
tion cables. In 1984 it was decided that the company's survival required a fundamental change in technology. This involved closing down the existing plant
and undertaking a programme of capital investment worth some £20 million,
including the building of a new plant to house the latest in computer integrated manufacturing (CIM) systems. It was hoped that the CIM approach
would enable the company to take full advantage of a reduction in labour,
materials and work-in-progress, as well as helping to maintain quality standards and to improve customer service by responding quickly to changes in
customer demand, particularly regarding quantity and colour of the cable's
plastic coating.

Given the adoption of the 'latest and best' in technology, it was also decided
that the plant should have the 'latest and best' in employee relations policies.
They would 'complement the unit's advanced technology ... flexible, computerised production needs flexible, computer literate employees' (in-house publication). The company recognised that the CIM system they had chosen had certain implications for the employees who would use it. The type of skills which
were required would be diagnostic rather than motor-related with only a limited degree of manual skill necessary (such as in the setting-up of machinery,
threading the machines, or possibly some welding). Although the process itself
was not going to be high speed it would require constant operator attention
since it was based upon a highly deterministic process control system requiring
the application of detailed production schedules as set out on the computer
screen. The input of the correct data was crucial given the nature of system.

Another fundamental consideration was the need for flexibility. This was
thought to be necessary to cope not only with unexpected circumstances, but
also to allow for individual preferences and development, whilst still maintaining a degree of specialisation sufficient to achieve levels of competence
that were adequate to meet production targets. Employees would be able to
opt to move from operations to programming or into the sales section, for
example. It was also considered important that operators be made aware of
the activities taking place in other areas.

The recruitment process included the assessment of personality profiles and
computer aptitude testing – with help from the local college of further education – as well as conventional interviewing techniques. The emphasis, however, was not merely on recruiting employees with the right technical skills but
on recruiting employees that would fit the ethos of the new plant: in other
words, 'on recruiting employees with good interpersonal skills, with the right
attitudes towards flexibility, adaptability and team working and ... a general
interest in the new ideas that the plant was based upon' rather than those with
existing technological skills (Corporate Personnel Manager).

The provision of a thorough and on-going training scheme was thought to
be fundamental to the success of the package of employee policies. The aim
therefore was to compile 'detailed and comprehensive training programmes'

for all employees in the plant, not only to enhance the more traditional skills, but also to 'develop teambuilding and teamworking skills' (internal company memorandum). It was intended that training be provided both on-the-job and off-the-job, and for this purpose a computerised training system, the Plant Operation Emulation System or POEMS, requiring an investment of some £100 000, was developed to enable employees to be trained in all aspects of the plant's computer operations. In addition, it was decided that the assistance of the local technical college should be sought.

The selection of additional skill modules was to be determined by Cableco's managers, 'taking into account both the operational requirements of the new plant as well as the abilities and aspirations of the employee' (Working Party Report). Such requirements, aspirations and abilities were to be discussed at an annual meeting with each employee. Employees would be provided with the appropriate training for further skill modules at a maximum rate of two per year until a 'grade ceiling' was reached. It was decided that a total of six additional skill modules per individual employee would be the maximum that the plant's management would be able to use effectively within the foreseeable stages of the plant's development. Employees would also be expected to maintain their skills and undergo any necessary conversion training without acquiring any wholly new skill modules.

Employee attitudes towards training

Eighteen months after the plant opened only half the employees who were interviewed were happy with the training they were receiving and less than half were happy with the arrangements that had been made for training. In fact, since virtually no training was being provided it is surprising that any employees were happy with the situation. Where training was happening it was being done on an *ad hoc* basis in order to train someone to operate a particular machine. Many people thought that the idea behind skill modules was a good one, but the way the scheme was operating in practice was the source of a lot of dissatisfaction:

> As an idea skill modules are good, we can understand management's side of it. Everyone being trained up to a certain standard, but we've heard nothing from them ... Everyone must get a chance at all the skill modules. There are people now who've been here for nearly two years without moving round at all. (Operator)

> I've been here for 3 months. The person who's training me has only been here a couple of weeks longer. (Operator)

In other words, unhappiness stemmed from two factors: first, there simply was not enough training being provided and, second, any training that did take place was aimed at meeting immediate employer needs and bore no relationship to the sophisticated training programmes that had been discussed as part of the skill module package. In addition, none of the employees interviewed mentioned having been given training in interpersonal or communication skills or in team-building. As a result there was limited movement across different parts of the process as the managers quickly came to value having 'experts' running the machines. Often these experts, by default, became trainers themselves.

The failure of the skill module system also had consequences for the payment system since without the opportunity to acquire new skills there was no opportunity to increase pay: 'Basically, because skill modules are not in place we are training to do the jobs, without getting the financial rewards that go with them' (Operator). Bearing in mind that the base rate which Cableco's employees were getting was only slightly higher than average local pay rates, the fact that skill module increments were not available for the first twelve months led to difficult wage negotiations. It took almost two months before a solution to the problem was agreed: employees who had been employed for 12 months or over would be given a nominal skill module (and hence an increase in salary). In the minds of the Cableco employees, it suggested that skill modules were more closely associated with pay increases than with flexible working practices and training. When asked on what basis they were paid, less than half of the interviewees said that they were paid according to skills acquired. Nearly half said that they were all paid according to the same rate for the job, and over 10 per cent that they did not know on what basis they were being paid.

As in Brewco, most employees also felt that without qualifications promotion was going to be very difficult, largely because 'there's nowhere to go. There are only three main jobs, shift manager, factory manager and business manager. They're out of the shop floor league' (Operator). The producers and maintainers clearly saw that while it might have been possible to get promotion 'pay-wise' had the skill module system been in place, promotion 'status-wise' was out of the question. This was the subject of some resentment since just under three-quarters of those who were interviewed commented that they wanted to be promoted and had believed when they took the job that their prospects of promotion were good because the plant was small and likely to expand quickly.

Grimco

The fibres division of the parent company is comprised of two subdivisions, cellulosics and acrylics, and Grimco falls within the cellulosics (woodpulp-based or organic fibres) sector. At one time 20 factories operated in the UK making man-made fibres, but that has now been reduced to only four, with a subsequent reduction in workforce from 120 000 in the mid-1970s to around 45 000 in the 1990s.

In 1981 the company's chemists developed a new way of dissolving cellulose and technologists converted the substance into a new fibre, a solvent-spun cellulosic cotton substitute, but of much higher quality than other alternatives. A decision was taken to invest £9 million in a plant to produce the new product. The size of the plant was to be relatively small, intended only to prime possible markets. The plant was to be a 'semi-technical company': that is, it was not expected to be immediately completely commercially viable, but it was to be run on commercial lines. It was envisaged that the plant would require approximately 45 people. The manufacturing process would run for 50 weeks per year, 24 hours a day, on a three-shift system.

Each shift would have five people – one senior process technician and four shift process technicians – who would undertake all the jobs associated with running the line, including minor engineering duties. These would form a team with the senior process technician as team leader. The four process technicians would move round each day to a new part of the process. In addition, there would be a team of one senior engineer and four multiskilled engineers – each of whom would have a different core trade, such as instruments, electrical or mechanical – who would work flexibly across all areas. There would be a day technician responsible for handling all the raw materials, the baling of the finished fibres, lower level engineering and some maintenance, such as cleaning the jets and the filters. Day-to-day operations would be run by the manufacturing manager, who would have control of both engineering and production.

Employees also were given extensive training at the research laboratories where the new process had been pioneered. There was a close working relationship between the development chemists, the technicians, the new managers and the process technicians throughout the recruitment, start-up and commissioning stages, including the recruitment of some members of the development team to the new company. Careful steps were taken in the development stages of the new plant, with new staff being recruited many months before operations commenced, so that training could take place and teamworking could be established at an early stage.

Employee attitudes towards training

Grimco employees were very happy with the training they had received, but only up until the time when the plant was fully commissioned. During the commissioning phase, every employee was given individual training on the simulation line at the research laboratories for several months before the new plant was opened. Operators had the opportunity to learn about all the different processes and the work was interesting and varied. Employees were involved in designing their new working practices. Furthermore, during this period great efforts were taken to treat the employees as 'staff': for example, by making sure that they stayed in good accommodation and treating them as a valuable part of the new team. This training was supplemented by site presentations and question-and-answer sessions about the new work process and practices. Comments included: 'We did very well, we got lots of training.' (Operator); 'I spent two months working on the job with the others, on every part of the process, I have no complaints about that' (Operator).

However, once the commissioning phase was over and the plant became operational the emphasis shifted from preparation and improvement to production and steady state. Training was no longer carried out at the laboratories, and employees were now expected to carry out the practices and routines they had designed, and not to spend time on trying to improve them any further. In contrast to the months spent in the commissioning stage, the work became routine and repetitive: 'We need more [training], once you get to know the process you can always go on making improvements' (Operator); There's only been one new person since we started up. He wasn't sent away for training at all, he's just been broken in gently' (Operator).

In terms of flexibility, there was evidence of shift process technicians carrying out day-to-day maintenance, although with potentially disastrous results. Following the maintenance and cleaning of part of the machinery, a valve was replaced the wrong way round, later leading to an 'exotherm' or explosion, which brought the whole process to a halt for more than three days. Whether this resulted from insufficient training is difficult to say, but it does raise questions about the safety of the operation of the new plant.

The factors which influence training

The failure to establish an internal labour market

Despite attempts by these greenfield sites to construct strong internal labour markets through the use of comprehensive training in company-specific skills, by linking payment systems to internal rules rather than the external labour market, and by providing advancement within the company, these attempts were not successful. In Brewco, while respondents believed that promotion was not impossible, it was not seen to be a likely prospect. Many employees commented that promotion was very difficult and that 'it is just possible' rather than probable. This view was shared by managers, who believed that in reality there was little opportunity for promotion because of the gap that had opened up between first line manager level, where a university degree was deemed necessary, and operator levels.

Similarly, Cableco failed to develop policies which would isolate it from the external labour market (which might have been achieved through offering higher wages than other companies in the area or by providing their own training programmes) and thus protect itself from the growing shortage of skilled labour. This led to particular problems of recruitment and retention in the maintenance department and the consequent distortion of the company's systems as attempts were made to react to these problems. The plant's development engineer confirmed the importance of the impact of a tight external labour market:

> The job that I left vacant in the steel works 18 months ago is still vacant. Wages have to go up and I think they will start to spiral quite rapidly. I think that's going to create more problems here. We've already lost 6 good guys. We're still only a baby of a plant really and we've already lost all those good guys to Fords and other places. Pay is important in that.

This was as a result of other companies, including Ford, Bosch and Hitachi, moving to the same area in search of the same type of skilled labour. The company's response, which was to create new structural levels within the maintenance department, had the effects of distorting the payment system which caused feelings of resentment, particularly amongst the production workers. The belief that companies can effectively insulate themselves from the external labour market was ill-founded. If several companies decide to move at the same time and to the same place in search of the same type of labour, then the effect of their moving substantially alters the existing business environment.

This is reminiscent of the problems suffered by Cadbury at their Chirk plant, following the company's decision to use their position of strength in the local labour market to set pay levels at a lower level than in their other plants, despite the fact that this decision carried with it 'the future seeds of discontent' (Whitaker, 1986:668). As Whitaker reports, there was significant pressure to justify the investment at Chirk and 'higher starting rates would not have helped this' (Whitaker, 1986:668). Furthermore, as Purcell points out: 'organisation-based employment systems work best from an employer's perspective when the external labour market pressures are largely benign' (1991:40): that is, when the firm is not recruiting and when labour turnover is low. In South Wales, many companies shared Cableco's enthusiasm for the establishment of a greenfield site in the development area. What had been an area of high unemployment quickly suffered an extreme shortage of skilled labour. In such circumstances the labour market pressures were hardly likely to remain benign.

The importance of a training 'champion'

Two of the greenfield sites, Brewco and Grimco, invested in training programmes for all new employees, managers and non-managers alike. In particular, in Grimco, this investment was substantial. However, both companies, whilst providing initial training, failed to follow this through with the provision of on-going training. Why was this?

Pettigrew *et al.* (1988:28) argue that two types of factor will influence companies to provide training, and the first of these they call 'business strategic' factors. These refer to the extent to which an organisation's environment is changing: for example, technological or product market changes which signal a skills gap or the need to alter the company culture. If the skills that are needed are not available in the labour market then companies are likely to introduce their own training programmes to remedy the resulting skills gap. A second set of factors relates to the recognition of the contribution that training can make to an organisation's performance. Some of these factors relate to the politics and personalities of the organisation.

In terms of providing a 'vision' and ensuring that the values comprised in that vision are truly implanted into a new organisation and that they are reproduced over time, leading to a sustainable 'management style', the role of the 'founding father' has long been recognised by writers on organisations. As Purcell (1989:88) points out:

> It is important to note that the well-known examples of sophisticated human resource management embedded in corporate strategy (IBM, Hewlett Packard, Marks & Spencer) are exceptions which prove the rule. In these companies the values and approach of the founders of the company are much in evidence (as is the case with Matsushita) and they tend not to deviate much from their core business.

Whilst in greenfield sites we may not be able to talk about 'founding fathers', it is clear from the case study evidence that unless someone takes on the role of human resources champion, to advise and monitor human resource developments, people issues, such as training, can all too easily be forgotten in the stress of the new plant start-up.

Trevor (1988), writing about Toshiba, claimed that 'vision' and 'leadership' were the two crucial elements of success of their greenfield site and attributed these to one particular individual, Geoffrey Deith. Similarly Preece (1993) showed how at VPL Anthony O'Leary, the Human Resources manager, played a central and leading role, with the HR function making important contributions to the design of the organisation, its culture, policies and procedures. From this research it is clear that in Grimco the careful recruitment and induction of the management team, who already shared many of the values underlying a management philosophy which emphasised the importance of training and development, led successfully to all the managers taking responsibility for ensuring that HR goals were achieved during the start-up period, but this did not continue once the operations were in steady state. Perhaps this was due in part to the lack of any individual with responsibility for personnel or human resource issues.

In Cableco the general manager was described as charismatic and as being responsible for developing a vision of the sort of plant and personnel policies that would be pursued. However, the departure of the personnel manager only four months after the plant had been opened, and the failure to replace him for a further seven months, clearly resulted in the neglect of personnel issues and the failure to implement policies relating to training, skill-based pay and monitoring employee performance, when line managers were already overburdened with getting the new plant up and running. Indeed, a common theme in the greenfield site literature is the importance of the transfer from start-up or commissioning phase into steady state production, and the lack of planning for it. As Leopold and Hallier comment:

> During this period ... there is a buzz of excitement in the workplace, a common sense of euphoria and a willingness to work beyond the call of contract and duty. However, this phase must come to an end and is followed by a period of consolidation... Surprisingly most of our companies stumbled on this recognition, rather than planned for it. (1997:82)

Training as part of an integrated package

Where there is a closely integrated package of human resource policies, then failure in one area can have serious knock-on effects for other areas, especially where the plant is going through a start-up phase where pressure is considerable. The series of events in Cableco where personnel policies were intimately bound up with state of the art technology are an excellent example of this. There were significant problems with the automated machinery which led not only to delayed delivery dates, but also meant that even when it was delivered much of the machinery could not be used. Such problems led to a number of other consequences. Without machinery that worked, training could not take place; and even where machines were working there was no systematic way in which training programmes within one functional area could be developed. Some training did of necessity take place, but the trainers were still discovering how the machines worked and training often amounted to little more than trial and error. Certainly no skill modules could be compiled, for no one could assess the combination of skills and knowledge required (for a particular skill module) until the machinery was working.

The role of trade unions

It is clear from Guest and Hoque's survey (1994) that trade union recognition is limited in greenfield sites. Their research showed that only 20 per cent of greenfield sites recognised a trade union compared to 42 per cent of refurbished sites. This suggests that we are unlikely to find trade unions acting as advocates for employee training in most greenfield sites. Indeed, of those 20 per cent of greenfield sites that did recognise unions, more than 80 per cent took the form of a single union agreement. Given that in many instances of single union agreements it is the employer that chooses the union they would prefer to work with before any employees are recruited to the plant, this type of union agreement has often been criticised for producing weak unions at the beck and call of management rather than protecting their members' interests.

This was a view confirmed in the case study research. Although all three plants recognised trade unions for the purpose of collective bargaining and 85 per cent of the greenfield respondents were trade union members, interviews with employees revealed that the unions had little power or influence over managers. Among the comments made were these: 'I don't think a lot of them. They're not forthcoming with the information. You only know what they want you to know'; 'It's only a channel for information coming down'; and 'I don't talk to the union much because there's nothing to talk about.'

When asked what were the advantages of being a trade union member, 41 per cent of respondents said that it would provide help in case of accidents and 35 per cent that it would provide final protection against the employer. Only 6 per cent felt that the unions provided any voice in the company. Furthermore, only 17 per cent of respondents felt that their union performed quite or very well in their organisation.

It is particularly interesting to look at Cableco, where there was a single union agreement governing trade union recognition which contained a clause placing an obligation on the company to provide training for employees, as well as an undertaking by employees to undergo training. An issue which arose consistently during the employee interviews was the failure of the union to influence the training situation. The reason most employees gave for this was that: 'It's really a management choice union. Terms and conditions were agreed upon before any employee was even taken on here.' Another said, '[The managers] have the best of all worlds, they can point to the fact that there is a union here knowing that it's a tame union.'

The level of union membership in the plant was 84 per cent but over 80 per cent of the interviewees thought that the managers had either some or a lot of influence over the union. In addition, only 8 per cent of the respondents thought that the union performed very well, 30 per cent believing that it performed quite well or so-so and 25 per cent assessing its performance as bad. Typical comments were: 'It performs as well as it can'; 'We only saw them when they came to sign on'; and 'It doesn't have the strength it should have.'

The importance of business strategy

The picture which is often drawn of greenfield sites is of a small, multiskilled and highly flexible workforce in a capital-intensive manufacturing industry, where flexibility is either 'implied' or even 'required' by the introduction of new 'state of the art' technology. All three of the greenfield site companies studied here were seeking to introduce new technology and, in terms of recruiting new employees, all the companies talked about having the 'best available', the *best* meaning the most highly skilled (almost regardless of the role they were to carry out), those who were prepared to be flexible, and those who expected to be able to improve and develop their skills. However, there was to some extent a gap between the rhetoric of flexibility and skill acquisition and the reality of life in the plant, particularly as the start-up process was left behind and the plants moved into steady state operation.

In Brewco, during the two years that it took to see the plant through building and start-up, the situation in the brewing industry had changed quite substantially due to the recession, and what had been an urgent demand for increased lager production had decreased considerably by the time the new plant was opened. This had a particular effect on training. Whilst many interviewees commented that there had initially been a lot of training, this was largely induction training which had not been followed up. Similarly, in Grimco employees complained that since the business had moved into steady state there had been no new training. In Cableco, the practical difficulties of moving employees around different areas of the plant in order to offer training on a variety of different machines and in different skills proved to outweigh any perceived advantage. The company soon found it was more effective to keep an employee who demonstrated particular skill on a machine on that same machine. It seemed pointless, 'As soon as we get someone who can virtually run the machine and is experienced, [to move] them away and then go through the pain of the process deteriorating with someone who's totally green again' as a shift manager said; a producer's view was that: 'I've been here for 18 months and I've only got one skill module. I'm now experienced on the machine and I'm being used as a trainer. I've been on one section for 12 months instead of 3.' Furthermore, in Brewco, over a longer time period and following product market changes, steps were taken to reduce the skill levels required in some areas of the plant by mechanising processes that were previously done by operators, in order to save costs.

Following the work of Burns and Stalker (1966) the ideal-typical greenfield site can be classified as an organic system (for example, little organisational hierarchy, broadly defined jobs, lateral consultation rather than vertical command, and generalised task commitment) rather than a mechanistic system (hierarchy of authority and control, detailed job specifications, vertical command communication). The work of the Boston Consulting Group (1970) and the work of the contingency theorists suggest that the organic (greenfield-type) organisation is normally associated with the embryonic organisation operating in a market with little market share, but potential for high market growth.

In the case studies discussed in this chapter, whilst the technology in each plant was both state of the art and new to each organisation, once in place it was not expected to change rapidly. The investment was seen as a long-term, one-off investment for the future. Furthermore, the reason behind choosing technology 'at the frontier' was largely to find a way to protect the company's position in a mature market of which the company already had a large share. Once in steady state production the emphasis was rather different: at Brewco the lager market changed substantially, rendering the plans for the new plant largely redundant, and the whole exercise very expensive. In Cableco, the failure of the new technology meant that the time period for commissioning and full production was extended more than once, involving substantial costs since this meant a delay of more than 18 months in closing the old plant. As time went on, managers became increasingly desperate to have the new plant operational and, more importantly, to make money. In Grimco, the plant was experimental and a few months after commissioning the company took the decision not to open full-scale production in the UK, but to do this in the USA where there was the promise of greater market opportunities and lower production costs, because of savings on the importation of raw materials.

These changes represent a significant alteration in business strategy. Whilst initially, therefore, each of the plants might have been classified according to Schuler and Jackson's typology (1987) as pursuing quality enhancement strategies, by the time they reached the commissioning stage the most accurate description of business strategy was probably one of cost reduction. From Schuler and Jackson's point of view this change in business strategy has significant implications for choices about personnel policies and practices. They argue that a business quality enhancement strategy is best supported by a set of policies which encourage, amongst other things, high levels of employee involvement in work tasks and extensive and continuous training. In contrast, a cost reduction strategy would be best supported by employee policies that are characterised by a short-term focus, minimal levels of employee training and relatively fixed and explicit job descriptions that allowed little room for ambiguity or freedom.

Conclusion

It is clear from the above discussion that whilst there may be a great deal of publicity surrounding greenfield sites, there is little empirical evidence available to support the idea that greenfield sites in practice have substantially superior training provision compared with non-greenfield or so-called brownfield sites. To what extent, then, can we say that the problems faced by these two types of organisations, greenfield and brownfield sites, are similar or different? Are the key factors which influence training provision in greenfield sites – the failure to establish an internal labour market; the importance of a training 'champion'; training as part of an integrated package; the role of trade unions; and importance of business strategy – substantially different from those which influence training in brownfield sites?

In many ways these problems are quite common aspects of managing the employment relationship and do not depend upon a plant being brownfield or greenfield. For example, the failure to establish an internal labour market in Brewco arose from the decision to adopt a very flat organisational structure, which meant that career progression was effectively halted. This is common in many organisations which have undergone de-layering and 'down-sizing' as a result of organisation re-structuring. Similarly, Cableco's decision to set relatively low wages which failed to insulate them from the external labour market was driven by the desire to keep costs to a minimum, another common behaviour for brownfield as well as greenfield companies. In terms of having a 'training champion', we know from the work of authors such as Storey (1992) and Tyson and Fell (1986) that the power and influence of personnel managers varies from organisation to organisation, and in general so called 'change-makers' or 'architects' are more likely to have an impact on personnel and HRM policies than 'hand maidens' or 'clerks of works'. We should not therefore be surprised that individuals play similar roles in greenfield site settings.

In relation to the role of trade unions, perhaps one might argue that the relative lack of power of the trade unions in greenfield sites, given the predominance of non-union or single union arrangements, is likely to exaggerate the effect of this factor, but not substantially alter its general features. However, the remaining two factors, the need for an integrated set of policies and the importance of business strategy, do help us to understand some of the major differences between brownfield and greenfield sites. A common theme that emerges from the case study evidence on greenfield sites is the inability of managers to consider the sustainability of their approaches once the plant has progressed through the commission stage and into steady state production (Newell, 1991; Leopold and Hallier, 1997).

There is a great deal of evidence to suggest that companies have taken steps to develop what appear, at least initially, to be highly integrated and appropriate policies and practices for the new plant. But these policies and practices tend to be relevant only to the start-up and early development of the plant, obscuring any potential problems with consolidation. Promises are made to employees, and then not kept; attempts to develop an employment relationship based upon consensus and employee commitment give way to a return to more 'traditional' ways of managing in the face of the pressure to produce. Leopold and Hallier argue that: 'this is explained by the fact that senior management believed they had introduced an inclusive and robust HR approach which would not require adaptation to either external or internal factors, and should therefore be capable of sustaining the organisation through change' (1997:2).

This suggests that, far from being easy to innovate in greenfield sites, difficult problems are often encountered where sites move into steady state production, and the companies' main concerns are about greater formalisation and increasing production volume. Problems of consolidation and market instability once the start-up phase is over often bring with them new pressures, requiring the adaptation of policy and practice. The original opportunity structures for innovation, new ideas and experimentation tend not to last into maturity, and senior managers' commitment to HRM in general and training provision in particular may well alter when subjected to market pressure and changes in leadership. Perhaps the real problems lie not in whether or not plants can be described as greenfield or brownfield, but in the failure to understand that there is no 'one best way solution' to manage human resources. The test of managerial ability is perhaps the extent to which the implications of a chosen policy have been thought through and the response to possible outcomes anticipated, rather than the ability to design and implement the 'ideal plan'.

References

Baird, M. (1994) 'Greenfield sites and workplace change', paper presented to the 8th Conference of the Association of Industrial Relations Academics of Australia and New Zealand, February.

Boston Consulting Group (1970) *The Product Portfolio Concept*, Perspective No. 66, Boston, Mass.: Boston Consulting Group.

Burns, T. and Stalker, G. M. (1966) *The Management of Innovation*, London: Tavistock.

Clark, J. (ed.) (1993) *Human Resource Management and Technical Change*, London: Sage.

Clark, J. (1995) *Managing Innovation and Change, People, Technology and Strategy*, London: Sage.

Delbridge, R. and Turnbull, P. (1992) 'The management of labour under the JIT manufacturing systems', in Blyton, P. and Turnbull, P. (eds), *Reassessing HRM*, London: Sage.

Foulkes, F. (1981) 'How top non-union companies manage employees', *Harvard Business Review*, September/October, 86–95.

Garrahan, P. and Stewart, P. (1992) *The Nissan Enigma*, London: Mansell.

Guest, D. and Hoque, K. (1994) *Human Resource Management in Greenfield Sites: Preliminary Survey Results*, CEP Working Paper No. 530, London: London School of Economics.

Incomes Data Services (1990) *Flexibilty At Work*, IDS Study no. 454, March.

Keep, E. (1992) 'Corporate training strategies: the vital component?' in Salaman, G. (ed.), *Human Resource Strategies*, London: Sage, 320–36.

Lawler, E. (1978) 'The new plant revolution', *Organisational Dynamics*, Winter, 3–12.

Lawler, E. (1986) *High Involvement Management: Participative Strategies for Improving Organisational Effectiveness*, San Francisco: Jossey Bass.

Leopold, J. and Hallier, J. (1997) 'Start-up and ageing in greenfield sites', *Human Resource Management Journal*, 7, 2, 72–91.

Newell, H. (1991) 'Fields of dreams: Evidence of 'new' employee relations in greenfield sites', unpublished thesis, Oxford University, Oxford.

Newell, H. (1993) 'Exploding the Myth of Greenfield Sites', *Personnel Management*, January, 20–3.

Pettigrew, A., Sparrow, P. and Hendry, C. (1988) 'The forces that trigger training', *Personnel Management*, December, 28–32.

Preece, D. (1993) 'Human resource specialists and technical change in greenfield sites', in Clark, J., (ed.), *Human Resource Management and Technical Change*, London: Sage.

Purcell, J. (1989) 'The impact of corporate strategy on human resource management', in Storey, J. (ed.), *New Perspectives on Human Resource Management*, London: Routledge.

Purcell, J. (1991) 'The rediscovery of the management prerogative: the management of Labour relations in the 1980s', *Oxford Review of Economic Policy*, 7, 1, 38–48.

Rainbird, H. and Maguire, M. (1993) 'When corporate needs supersedes employee development', *Personnel Management*, February, 34–7.

Reitsberger, W. D. (1986) 'British employees: responding to Japanese management philosophy', *Journal of Management Studies*, 23, 5 (September), 50–9.

Schuler, R. and Jackson, S. (1987) 'Organisational strategy and organisatonial level as determinants of human resource management practices', *Human Resource Planning*, 10, 3, 209–13.

Sisson, K. (1989) *Personnel Management in Britain*, 1st edition, Oxford: Basil Blackwell.

Sisson, K. (1994) *Personnel Management in Britain: A Comprehensive Guide to Theory and Practice in Britain*, 2nd edition, Oxford: Basil Blackwell.

Sisson, K. (1995) 'Functional Flexibility: The Need For A Re-Appraisal?' Briefing Paper prepared for the ILO's World Employment Report, IRRU.

Storey, J. (1992) *Developments in the Management of Human Resources*, Oxford: Basil Blackwell.

Townley, B. (1989) 'Selection and appraisal: reconstituting "social relations"?' in Storey, J. (ed.), *New Perspectives on Human Resource Management*, London: Routledge.

Trevor, M. (1988) *Toshiba's New British Company – Competitiveness through Innovation in Industry*, London: Policy Studies Institute.

Tyson, S. and Fell, A. (1986) *Evaluating the Personnel Function*, London: Hutchinson.

Whitaker, A. (1986) 'Managerial strategy and industrial relations: a case study of plant relocation', *Journal of Management Studies*, 23, 6 (November),.

White, M. and Trevor, M. (1983) *Under Japanese Management: The Experience of British Workers*, London: Heinemann.

Wickens, P. (1987) *The Road to Nissan*, London: Macmillan.

CHAPTER 7

Training and new forms of work organisation

Chris Rees

Introduction

There has been much concern in recent years with the development and introduction of new ways of organising work which facilitate flexibility and improved quality, and which encompass and accommodate new technologies. What are these new forms of work organisation? And what are their implications for workplace training?

This chapter is concerned with examining the links between workplace training and work organisation, and advances the central argument that focused training is one of the necessary conditions for success in introducing new forms of work organisation. It begins with a brief overview of developments in work organisation through the twentieth century, before turning to a consideration of recent developments in job design which have been aimed at improving employee flexibility, satisfaction and commitment. Here, particular emphasis is given to TQM initiatives, and data are presented from two recent studies of TQM, both of which serve to highlight the contribution of targeted training to employee commitment.

Whilst targeted training may be a prerequisite for successful work organisation, it remains only one factor. The chapter thus moves on to put training in the context of other issues which are considered to be necessary requirements. These are discussed in the context of the European Commission's recent Green

Paper, *Partnership for a New Organisation of Work*, and the chapter ends by drawing out some of the wider policy implications of these debates.

Developments in work organisation

Following Buchanan (1994), approaches to the design of work systems can be seen as having progressed through three broad phases during the twentieth century. In the first of these three phases, from 1900 to 1950, approaches to work design were dominated by the principles of 'scientific management', based upon task fragmentation and the clear division between manual or clerical work on the one hand, and management responsibilities on the other. A particular form of production system and work organisation is often presumed to have dominated American and European economies during this period. This system is characterised by mass production and is often referred to as 'Fordism' (after Henry Ford, the automobile manufacturer), with the underlying principles owing much to the work of F. W. Taylor (1911), and frequently referred to collectively as 'Taylorism'.

Taylor developed the means whereby the labour process could be designed and organised to facilitate the mass production of standardised products. This was achieved through the design and fragmentation of work into a large number of small tasks, each of which required very little skill and was performed by workers on a repetitive basis. Responsibility for the design, planning, organising and control of the process of production was to be divorced from the labour engaged in the production process, and where possible the machine – the technology – was to control the pace of production; as labour became more and more proficient, the speed of the machine could be increased and the rate of production enhanced.

Under a system such as this, the training requirements are virtually nil, since jobs are broken down and simplified into a number of small tasks which can be performed repetitively by unskilled labour: 'workers do not need to be given expensive and time-consuming training. Those who leave or who prove to be unreliable can be replaced quickly. Management is not dependent on potentially scarce skills and knowledge to guarantee the continuity of production' (Buchanan, 1994:87). The second phase in work organisation, broadly from 1950 to 1980, saw the development of the 'quality of working life' (QWL) movement, which advanced a range of techniques as antidotes to scientific management. Fordist systems tended to result in bored and alienated labour forces which posed both motivational and control problems, and this led to a number of experiments in job design that were driven by alternative views of motivation, and which were concerned to ally employee satisfaction with productive efficiency, competitiveness and profitability. As management in

Western industrialised countries became increasingly aware of the 'hidden' costs of monotonous work and dissatisfied workers, researchers at the Tavistock Institute of Human Relations in London argued that Taylor had gone too far with the fragmentation of work and that productivity could be improved by enlarging jobs (Trist *et al.*, 1963). 'Job enlargement' involves the recombination of tasks separated by scientific management techniques. Subsequent developments in work design techniques beyond job enlargement and job rotation were influenced by the 'humanistic' psychology of Maslow (1943) and Herzberg (1966, 1968), both of whom emphasised that human beings have innate needs, organised in a loose hierarchy.

Translating Maslow's expression of human needs into work design principles, the Tavistock consultants were responsible for the concept of the 'composite autonomous work group' or 'self-managing multi-skilled team', and confirmed the social and economic advantages of self-managing work groups with 'responsible autonomy'. In the case of autonomous (or semi-autonomous) teams, the principles of both enlargement and enrichment are extended and applied at a group level, and a group of employees become collectively responsible for a wider range of tasks – for example, a complete car rather than just a part – and also for the kind of roles that were previously performed by supervisors, such as the scheduling of the work and the pace at which the work is performed. Sweden is usually acknowledged as the country in which modern attempts at the design of effective autonomous teams originated, and companies such as Saab and Volvo are perceived to have been at the forefront of these developments.

A third broad phase in work organisation is discernible from 1980 onwards, since when a variety of methods has been used to extend the concept of the autonomous group, primarily to address competitive pressures by increasing organisational flexibility and responsiveness. The talk now is of 'high performance work systems' which utilise team-based approaches to work and organisational design in so-called 'new design plants'. While the goals underpinning the QWL movement in the 1960s and 1970s concerned the costs of labour turnover and absenteeism, and other costs arising from boredom and apathy, the objectives of work design in the late 1980s and the 1990s concern the need for quality, flexibility and responsiveness in meeting customer requirements in an increasingly competitive climate. Whitfield and Poole sum up the change as follows:

> The key element in this change is seen to be the emergence of holistic systems of work practices which are introduced strategically as a package rather than in a piecemeal manner... Recent years have witnessed an intensified interest by management throughout the industrialised world in the question of organising employment to enhance organisational performance... The main aim of employers in introducing such innovations has been to attain/retain competitive advantage in increasingly complex product markets. (1997:745)

The term 'flexible specialisation' (Piore and Sabel, 1984) is commonly used to refer to a particular model of production that includes the following elements: functional flexibility; higher levels of responsibility and autonomy on the part of the workforce; a degree of overlap between skills and specialisms; and a degree of judgement and skill on the part of labour. By the early 1980s these developments, allied to changes in the political and regulatory environments, had encouraged a new approach to the organisation of work and the demand for labour. This was summed up in the model of the 'flexible firm', devised by Atkinson (1984), which distinguishes between the 'external' and 'internal' labour markets, 'core' and 'peripheral' workers, and the various dimensions of flexibility ('functional', 'numerical' and 'temporal').

The requirements that these so-called 'post-Fordist' production systems make of the labour resource can be seen in many of the 'softer' HRM models which refer to the desirability of quality, flexibility, commitment and cost-effectiveness (Beer *et al.*, 1984; Guest, 1987; Singh, 1992). As regards the implications for training, the demand for large quantities of relatively unskilled labour – characteristic of Fordist systems – has been replaced by a demand for labour that is 'multi-skilled' and flexible, that does not need external supervision, and that is both familiar and comfortable with the new technologies. As Whitfield and Poole (1997) report, more innovative work systems typically involve the linking of formal training programmes to employee involvement in decision-making, some form of contingent pay, careful attention to job design and selection procedures, and extensive quality control (Appelbaum and Batt, 1994; Osterman, 1994; Dyer and Reeves, 1995). As we will see later in this chapter, the view that these new forms of work organisation are not only economically efficient but also have the potential to encourage greater employee involvement and enhanced employee satisfaction is one that underlies the assertions and exhortations made in the European Commission Green Paper on *Partnership for a New Organisation of Work* (1997).

During this 'third phase' in the development of work organisation, many organisations have sought to copy others who appear to have been more successful in confronting the challenges of the global economy and changing product markets. In the UK this has often involved studying the methods of Japanese organisations, in which the emphasis upon quality and employee involvement and commitment have commonly been seen as sources of competitive advantage. As a result, we have seen organisations experimenting with a wide range of methods such as quality circles, cellular manufacturing, teamworking, *kaizen* or continuous improvement processes, and JIT production systems. The popularity of initiatives such as quality circles has waned in recent years, perhaps in part because organisations have introduced more comprehensive approaches, such as TQM. The next section considers case study evidence on the nature of workplace training across a range of TQM organisations.

Total quality management and training

Evidence suggests that throughout the 1980s increasing numbers of companies were attempting to integrate training strategies with business objectives and to assess the effectiveness of their training investment on a more systematic basis (Rainbird, 1994). One of the major ways in which business strategies and training were integrated was through the development of total quality management techniques and customer care initiatives (Incomes Data Services, 1990) as a means of facilitating organisational and culture changes.

Despite these trends having continued apace throughout the 1990s, the literature on continuing training at the workplace level is fairly limited because very little information has been collected on company training on a systematic basis. Case study evidence can therefore make a useful contribution. The author has recently been involved in two studies (Rees, 1996, 1998) of quality management initiatives, covering a total of ten organisations. In the first of these (Rees, 1996) four organisations were studied: 'Auto Components', 'Office Tech', 'New Bank' and 'Hotel Co'. In a second, related study (Collinson *et al.*, 1998; Edwards, Collinson and Rees, 1998) a further six named organisations were studied: Severn Trent Water, Halifax Building Society, Lewisham Borough Council, South Warwickshire NHS Trust, British Steel (Shotton works) and Philips Domestic Appliances (Hastings plant).

In the first study (1996), the evidence clearly showed that where management gave serious attention to training as a key element of the process of introducing and sustaining TQM, this was reflected in widespread employee commitment. However, despite this headline finding, an emphasis on training is not a sufficient prerequisite for employee commitment.

This latter point is best illustrated by the case of Auto Components, where relatively high levels of employee support for TQM appeared to have little to do with training. Despite their clear recognition of the amount of both on- and off-the-job training having increased markedly since TQM was first introduced, only 8 per cent chose to describe the training they received as 'more than adequate', with over half describing it as either 'barely adequate' or 'not at all adequate'. The main criticism was that production requirements too often meant that training got sidelined. This is reflected strongly in many of the comments made on the questionnaire returns, such as:

> Getting parts out the door is seen as more important than training, and this gets in the way of commitment to training.

> It's all production here, and they don't want you to switch the machines off and take time out for training, which is a false economy in the end.

Management tell customers what great training there is all the time, when really we're doing it all off our own backs.

The TQM programme at Auto Components has involved the company in making a heavy investment in training for those in the 'new shop'. Employees are sent on team-building exercises and on specialist manufacturing technology courses. And at the end of a two-year training period, each multi-skilled worker takes a 'skills test', a practical on-the-job assessment, and has a final interview with the Production Manager and the Personnel Manager. This is part of the move towards more formal assessment of employees' competencies, and after successful completion of the training each employee is issued with a 'multi-skill certificate'. Despite the stress which management at Auto Components put on training as a key element of TQM, employees can see the reality of lack of management commitment to it. In saying that there will be an emphasis on training, management may have raised the expectations of those in the new factory, and if those expectations are not met, resentment may set in.

As noted, employee commitment to TQM is generally strong at this company. This suggests, first, that training is an important but not a determining influence upon employee commitment, and, second, that the factors influencing employee acceptance of TQM work in combination, so that in this case employee dissatisfaction with training is not sufficient to detract from the generally positive attitudes towards other aspects of management strategy.

Managers at Office Tech have far more limited espoused training ideals. Training is restricted to basic on-the-job issues and reflects the need to maintain consistency in product quality. It is notable that employees appear to be far more satisfied; one-third described the training as 'more than adequate' (and the other two-thirds as 'adequate but nothing more'). This is not to say that Office Tech employees were not critical (many questioned the competence and commitment of the trainers themselves), but in general they know what the training is for, they see it being delivered as described, and they consequently have less cause for complaint. The training programme may be less ambitious than at Auto Components, but at least it would appear to meet its more limited objectives.

Training at New Bank aims to equip employees with the skills considered necessary to improve customer service and find sales opportunities. Branches have regular training days, and longer courses are held at a national training centre. Much emphasis is placed on examining ways of finding sales opportunities, and employees also receive regular training on new technology. A significant proportion of employees was critical of the training for being too idealistic and a 'management fad', and many actually reported that their 'real' training had decreased. Some said that training was 'not frequent enough' or was 'too basic and idealistic', as reflected in the following comments:

A certain idealism pervades outside training courses, which does not reflect the actuality of branch life.

Training appears to be given to support statistics rather than need, i.e. [so management can say that] *x* amount of staff will have seen this video, or *x* amount of training has been done within a given period.

Unfortunately, monitoring of the benefits of training is non-existent, and staff have little time to practise what they have learned due to every-day working pressures.

Training appears to be most clearly connected to TQM at Hotel Co. There is a lengthy induction programme for all new staff, and the scope and limits of 'empowerment' are spelled out clearly to each employee in a practical way; in the words of an Assistant General Manager, it is 'drummed into them that this is something we are committed to'. Following this, regular training days are held in all hotels. It would appear that Hotel Co delivers on its training promises far more than Auto Components, and the attitudes of employees towards training are the most positive from across the four companies. In general, then, Hotel Co employees have a high opinion of the training they receive, and appear to appreciate the more targeted format that it takes. Across the four companies, most employees perceived the main reason for training to be adding further skills to their basic job. But at Hotel Co, 'developing team spirit' was seen as a key reason for training and, perhaps more significantly, virtually all employees at Hotel Co selected 'achieving higher quality standards' as one of the reasons for the training.

The clear inference from this data is that employees prefer straightforward targeted training (as at Hotel Co and, to a lesser extent, Office Tech), rather than training which is either felt to be too idealistic and have little or no relevance to the reality of everyday work (as at New Bank), or sidelined when production needs take over (as at Auto Components). Where management pays insufficient attention to training, it is likely to play little part in contributing to feelings of commitment. But where there is greater attention given to relating training to specific TQM issues, and where these promises are followed through in practice, then employee commitment may as a result be significantly enhanced.

This emphasis on the 'context-dependent' nature of employee commitment also comes through from the second study, which found a strong tendency for employees most favourable to quality programmes to be those who said that they had been trained specifically in quality ideas or in teamwork principles. By contrast, other forms of training, and the total amount of training, had no effect.

Reported amounts of training were substantial across all six organisations. Eighty-five per cent of respondents reported some training, and 65 per cent put the level at one week or more per annum. Given that a number of the six organisations (notably British Steel) are seen as 'training organisations', this is perhaps not surprising. However, the study sought to discover whether this training covered merely basic skills or whether it involved something new, be it use of new methods or equipment or specifically quality-related activities. Basic training was, not surprisingly, mentioned most often but the use of new equipment ran it a close second. About half of the respondents, and as many as two-thirds at Halifax and British Steel, felt that teamworking or quality was a component of their training. However, only around a quarter specified this as the main purpose. As the study's Report notes: 'This is potentially a point of some importance. Given the weight given to quality in all six organisations, it is notable that approaching half the respondents did not feel that they had received any specific training in quality initiatives, and few thought that this was the main purpose' (Collinson *et al.*, 1998:52).

Of those who felt that training was no more than adequate or worse (65 per cent of the sample), an open-ended question sought out the reasons form this. Comments included the poor quality of the training itself and a lack of resourcing, that training was of a reasonable quality but insufficient time was given to it, that it was unspecific or irrelevant to their work needs, that it was divorced from day-to-day duties, and that pressure of work prevented training being used in practice. The overall evaluation of training was reasonably good, but there were a number of substantial areas of concern. The number of respondents making criticisms of training was just over half the total number in the survey, and there were plainly some important reservations as to what training was achieving.

Of particular interest are the connections between training and attitudes to quality. The study focused on whether or not teamworking or improved quality standards were felt to be among the purposes of training (as distinct from being its main purpose). Overall 55 per cent of non-managerial employees cited one of these purposes (the proportion ranged from 40 per cent in Philips to 69 per cent in British Steel). When the links between this measure and attitudes to quality were examined, some clear associations emerged. For example, there was a very strong link with perceived influence over quality; of those specifying this form of training, 71 per cent said that they had a significant influence over quality, as against 50 per cent lacking this training. Moreover, the researchers also created variables indexing the presence of training in basic skills and in the use of new technology and equipment. Neither of these measures had a significant relationship with attitudes to quality, suggesting that it is specifically training in teamworking and quality initiatives which is crucial. To quote from the Report once more, 'it was not the case that those receiving training in quality were concentrated in certain organisations in which attitudes to quality were particularly favourable.... In short, forms of training were linked to attitudes to quality' (Collinson *et al.*, 1998:53). So, the inference from this data is that training has a key role in sustaining employee commitment to new forms of work organisation. This means not training in general, for we have seen that the overall amount of training seemed unrelated to views on quality, but specific targeting at quality or at teamworking. In the organisations reported here, it was experience of this kind of targeted training that was important in generating favourable employee attitudes towards quality. The chapter now moves on to put these case study findings in context by considering some of the wider debates concerning the link between training and work organisation.

The European work organisation agenda

Until recently the EU has had relatively little involvement in work organisation issues, but this is now changing as various internal interests press the argument that enhanced flexibility and new forms of work organisation are integral to the achievement of enhanced competitiveness and employment. Recent documents and agreements have emphasised the importance of flexibility to the pursuit of high employment, such as the European Commission report on *Employment in Europe in 1996* (1996) and the *Title on Employment* agreed at the Amsterdam Inter-Governmental Conference in 1997. Further impetus has been given to the debate by the publication by the European Commission of a Green (Consultative) Paper, entitled *Partnership for a New Organisation of Work* (1997). This defines work organisation as:

> the way in which the production of goods and services is organised at the workplace. The focus is on a new organisation of work... This concept implies, in particular, the replacement of hierarchical and rigid structures by more innovative and flexible structures based on high skill, high trust and increased involvement of employees. (European Commission, 1997:1).

The introduction to this consultative document makes clear the three central aims which the authors of the Green Paper believe are achievable simultaneously:

> While much has been written about the need for flexibility of the labour market and its regulation, much less has been said about the need for flexibility and security in the organisation of work at the workplace... An improved organisation of work ... can make a valuable contribution ... to the competitiveness of European firms ... the improvement of the quality of working life and the employability of the workforce'. (European Commission, 1997:1)

The challenge is no less than the development of a 'new paradigm' that can contribute to enhanced competitiveness, safeguard employment and at the same time improve 'quality of working life'. This emphasis reflects much of the practice of work design, which assumes that it is possible to 'discover the elusive common ground for the simultaneous satisfaction of human and organisational goals through the judicious manipulation of job characteristics' (Buchanan, 1994:86).

Given the context-dependent nature of the effects of changes in work organisation, these objectives will clearly not be realised through the top-down application of normative models and consultancy-style 'blueprints for change'. What is needed is case study-based evidence, such as that presented in the previous section, which highlights the conditions for the success or failure of particular organisational initiatives, combined with an awareness of the contingent nature of such developments. There remains no 'one best way' and no easy route to any 'new paradigm'. As such, if new forms of work organisation are to be promoted on a Europe-wide basis, what is required is 'horizontal co-operation, based on departing from existing differences in approaches to work organisation... In this way the issue of work organisation can be given a European profile based on differences, as distinct from the Japanese or North American profiles that are based on cultural non-difference' (Ennals and Gustavsen, 1998:160). There are a number of factors which need to be addressed in combination if this 'new agenda' for work organisation is to bear fruit, not the least of which is the need to strike a balance between flexibility and security. A number of organisations have begun to recognise this, and a key feature of recent agreements has been an explicit trade-off between internal flexibility on the part of employees in return for a measure of employment security (Scarbrough and Terry, 1996; Industrial Relations Review and Report 1997). This section of the chapter stresses two of the other key factors, before the next section takes up some of the difficulties with the analysis and prescriptions contained in the 'new agenda' approach.

The importance of training

Evidently, changes to production technologies and working practices will have education and training implications. There is an emerging consensus that changes in production processes and in the nature of product markets require a more highly trained workforce, and continuing training is increasingly recognised as contributing to productivity and to the management of change through the adaptation and extension of skills on the one hand, and in facilitating new patterns of work on the other (Rainbird, 1994). Dunlop (1992) has argued that effective training policies are fundamental to economic growth and productivity, and in a major survey of Western European nations (Hilb, 1992), 'human resource development' was found to be the most important personnel function in all the countries concerned. The more recent EPOC study (European Foundation, 1997) also stressed the importance of training, finding that the higher the qualification of employees and the more substantial the training for direct participation, the greater were the effects of direct participation.

The case study evidence presented in this chapter highlights above all the need for the provision of focused training. As reported in the previous section, there was a strong tendency for employees most favourably disposed to quality programmes to be those who said that they had been trained specifically in quality ideas and teamwork; by contrast, other forms of training, and the total amount of training, had little or no effect. It is also generally recognised that training provision is at the heart of the development of so-called 'high-performance work systems'. Once again, the key issue is not so much the quantity of training but its orientation. Such systems require workers not only with highly-developed core skills, but also technical skills which cut across traditional functional areas, as well as the ability to change their skill-base frequently during their working lives. All this will evidently require a more flexible training system than has been experienced to date.

The importance of partnership

The authors of the Green Paper are keen to emphasise the importance of 'partnership' between employees and employer to the high-skill, high-trust and adaptive workforce which, they argue, is necessary to facilitate and take full advantage of the new forms of work organisation that are considered to be the key to the achievement of competitiveness in the new global marketplace. The authors talk of inviting 'the social partners and public authorities to seek to build a partnership for the development of a new framework for the modernisation of work. Such a partnership could make a significant contribution to achieving the objective of a productive, learning and participative organisation of work' (European Commission, 1997:ii).

The previously mentioned need to balance flexibility and security certainly requires high trust relations at the workplace level. Partnership at the workplace level requires a recognition by management of employees as key stakeholders, in return for their contribution to quality, and a move away from adversarial industrial relations. In the UK, the need to develop a new culture of partnership is also seen by the Trades Union Congress (TUC) as an essential element of the so-called 'new unionism' (TUC, 1996). It requires a constructive dialogue about good practice in order to balance increased productivity and growth on the one hand, with QWL requirements and increased employment on the other.

There is a growing body of evidence to support this emphasis on the importance of partnership, grounded in employee representation, in bringing about the modernisation of work organisation. This evidence suggests that 'direct' and 'indirect' employee participation mechanisms are mutually reinforcing as opposed to conflictual (European Foundation, 1997; Sako, 1998). For instance, the EPOC study shows that the greater the involvement of employee representatives in the introduction of direct participation, the greater the reported effects on a range of key indicators of business and labour market performance. Furthermore, in the study by Collinson *et al.* (1998) reported earlier, all six organisations were unionised. Two were characterised by a strong management–union relationship, two by the marginalisation of unions, and two by a more anti-union stance. The researchers found that the success of TQM declined across these three categories. This and other evidence (Scott, 1994; Glover and Fitzgerald-Moore, 1998; Wright and Edwards, 1998) suggests that the existence of strong cooperative relationships with relevant trade unions can ease the acceptance of changes in work organisation, while the absence of a good working relationship between the management and the union makes it harder to win the trust of individual employees. And as Warhurst and Thompson (1998:21) argue, if reforming governments need examples of how to reward innovation and partnership in the workplace, these are available from Sweden (the Swedish Work Environment Fund) or Australia (the Australian Productivity Commission), both of which have encouraged collaboration on workplace innovation between employers, unions and researchers. Evidence from the USA (Bluestone and Bluestone, 1992; Levine, 1995) also demonstrates the success of stakeholding firms, with strong unions and a 'mutual gains' agenda, and with a vested interest in ensuring competitiveness through investment in skills and equipment. As Keep and Rainbird point out, trade union involvement in the introduction of new forms of work organisation is also likely to stimulate 'employability':

> Since union members' interests are best served through the development of skills which have wide recognition in the labour market, as opposed to the task- and firm-specific requirements of employers, the incorporation of unions is conducive to driving the training system towards meeting long-term skill requirements rather than employers' immediate needs. (1995:516)

Of course, the effect of unions is likely to be complex. While some have supported new work organisation innovations, others have been hostile to them, often perceiving them as posing a threat to collective representation (Guest, 1995; Ackers, Smith and Smith, 1996). If partnership is the way forward, ways must be found of reconciling 'representation' with the process of management, and of finding 'institutions that bring representation and participation together in a reciprocal relationship ... [This] requires new social structures at the workplace level ... [and] a need to cultivate these emerging trends as a tool for change' (Garibaldo, 1997:8).

Problems with the 'New Agenda' approach

The previous section outlined briefly some of the latest thinking on work organisation, as well as some of the necessary requirements for these ideas to succeed. The chapter now turns to consider some of the difficulties with these arguments.

In the broadest sense, the main weakness of the arguments in the Green Paper stems from the uncritical acceptance of the 'transformation thesis' of work organisation. While there are undoubtedly fundamental changes occurring in industrial society which are leading to a questioning of traditional forms of work organisation, as outlined at the beginning of the chapter, it does not necessarily follow that there has been a genuine, sustained and irreversible shift in management thinking. It is too easy to optimistically assume that new forms of work organisation allow for a positive-sum game in which workers benefit from enhanced autonomy and discretion while employers gain higher productivity. Many who witness changes in work organisation have also assumed that they signal a decisive break with the principles of Taylorism and Fordism, as reflected in the concepts of 'post-Fordism' and 'flexible specialisation' (Piore and Sabel, 1984), 'new production concepts' (Kern and Schuman, 1984), 'neo-Fordism' (Boyer, 1988) and 'lean production' (Womack, Jones and Roos, 1990), as well as the more popular management notions of 'excellent' companies (Peters, 1987) and the 'post-modern factory' (Drucker, 1990). While this plethora of new labels suggests genuine concern and change, there is a need for caution here. As Hyman notes,'there is little warrant for the argument that Fordism or Taylorism was ever a general and hegemonic basis for the organisation of work; or that a decisive, global transformation has occurred, or is occurring' (1997:352).

To begin with, the evidence shows that many of the initiatives upon which the 'transformation thesis' is based are not nearly as common or extensive as its proponents would have us believe. For instance, the EPOC study (European Foundation, 1997) shows that new forms of work organisation are very much a minority movement. Starkly, the proportion of workplaces with semi-autonomous group work approximating to the 'Scandinavian' model (that is, extensive delegation plus high qualification plus high training intensity) was less than 2 per cent. Moreover, only about one in ten workplaces might be said to have been 'skills-oriented' inasmuch as the level of qualification required was high or very high and there was fairly intensive training of managers and workers for direct participation.

Furthermore, even where change is taking place we need to remember that new approaches to work organisation frequently combine elements of more established practices. As Warhurst and Thompson put it, 'continuity is as pervasive as change, if for no other reason than because new ideas and practices are by definition built on the legacy of the old' (1998:19). This is evident in the case of banks, who are introducing business centres with a customer care focus, new technology and new skills at the same time as back office jobs are shifted to 'call centres' and 'office factories' under Taylorist forms of organisation. It is also evident in recent analyses of Japanese car assembly methods such as 'Toyotaism', which reveal many similarities with traditional Taylorism (see Delbridge, 1998). We thus need to remember in all the talk of 'new paradigms' and 'win–win situations' that Taylorism, with its associated adverse effects on labour as summarised earlier in the chapter, is far from dead and buried. Indeed, 'Taylor's ideas have become a central feature of the taken-for-granted organisational recipe that many managers still apply to the design and redesign of work without serious question or challenge' (Buchanan, 1994:88). We should also bear in mind that changes in work organisation are invariably motivated by the desire to compete more effectively, and the driving force behind change is likely to be profit. This too has not changed. Management interest in work organisation remains primarily a financial interest, and 'flexibility' is more often than not perceived by managements almost exclusively in terms of reducing labour costs.

What these points indicate is that the more progressive or 'enlightened' approach that the Green Paper exhorts organisations to adopt is only one among a series of options. This point is well made by Regini (1995), who found a wide range of competitive and production strategies being adopted by managements in Europe, by no means all of which were consistent with notions of 'post-Fordism' or 'flexible specialisation'. Five ideal types of strategy were identified: 'diversified quality production', 'flexible mass production', 'flexible specialisation', 'neo-Fordist' and 'traditional small firm'. The key implication for training requirements is that each of these strategies embodies a different pattern of human resource utilisation in terms of types, levels and mixes of skill, and only some require labour that is functionally flexible. Work organisation thus has different trajectories:

> Each of these trajectories ... starts from the same point – the questioning of traditional forms of work organisation in the light of intensifying competition. In each case, however, the outcome is very different reflecting specific products and services, market position, cost pressures, technology, and management frames of reference... The great mistake is to assume that the new forms of work organisation supposedly emerging are inevitable and universal in their application. (IRRU, 1997:7–6)

Not only are there weaknesses in the analysis which informs the arguments in the Green Paper, but there is also a tendency to underestimate the problems that organisations have in introducing the kinds of work organisation practices now assumed to be in the ascendancy. It is now well established that innovative employment practices work best if introduced in internally consistent 'bundles' rather than on an individual basis, the logic being that such practices have combined effects which are greater than the sum of their individual effects (Dyer and Reeves, 1995; MacDuffie, 1995). However, there is a strong temptation for managements to prefer an *ad hoc* or incremental path to change rather than bundles, since thoroughgoing change is considered expensive and the benefits unknown. In doing so 'organisations come up against the problem of "complementarities" or integration... Inevitably, the danger of the incremental approach is that individual practices are tried and rejected because they appear to be unsuccessful in themselves' (IRRU, 1997:9).

Linked to this, even if it can be proved that new forms of work organisation lead to significantly superior outcomes than more traditional methods, they might still be perceived by managements as less cost-effective. They typically involve high costs during their set-up periods, and thus need to yield higher returns to justify their existence. The evidence in any case suggests that the link between new forms of work organisation and organisational performance is both complex and variable, and that the context in which they are situated is a crucial determinant of their success.

It may also be the case that positive associations between new forms of work organisation and organisational performance reflect the fact that more successful firms use their competitive success to develop more innovative human resource policies, irrespective of their effects on future performance. A similar point is made by Shackleton *et al.* (1995), who suggest that a degree of reverse causality may be at work. In other words, high value-adding firms may have additional resources which they choose to devote to training and education, regardless of whether or not this produces increased productivity or financial performance. As Morris points out, 'investment in training and education may be necessary in specific circumstances to promote economic growth, but it is rarely sufficient and frequently follows on from, rather than leads to, the creation of high value adding jobs' (1999).

In the UK, many of these problems are exacerbated by the voluntarist system of training provision, which has the effect of discouraging human capital investment as an organisational strategy by enabling firms to externalise adjustment costs. The continuing training of employees is generally perceived as the responsibility of the employer on the one hand, and the individual employee on the other. However, individual employers, acting on a rational basis, will not invest in training since they find it cheaper to recruit skilled labour from other employers, and there is considerable evidence to demonstrate that existing patterns of labour market segmentation are consequently reinforced:

> Those employed in small firms, part-time workers, the less well-educated and qualified, the self-employed, older workers, and manual workers are all less likely to receive training. Because certain groups of people are more frequently concentrated in certain types of employment – for example, women in part-time employment – disadvantage in access to training disproportionately affects some sections of the

working population... A market-driven training system reinforces existing patterns of discrimination in access to training. (Keep and Rainbird, 1995:531)

The restructuring of work may thus generate losers as well as winners, and there is likely to be growing polarisation in the workforce. While members of the 'core' group may well benefit from some security of employment and demand for the skills that they possess, and the organisation might thus be prepared to invest in their training and development, working outside the core may be characterised by uncertainty and high levels of anxiety and stress. There tend to be unequal outcomes in other respects, too. The distribution of 'lifelong learning' is unbalanced, with those who are already well-educated participating to a much wider extent. Individuals with education of a university standard are two to three times as likely to participate in job-related training as those who have not completed upper secondary education. Older workers, too, tend to be disadvantaged. And it goes almost without saying that the unemployed and those outside the labour market and education system generally have little opportunity of participating in job-relevant learning (McKenzie and Wurzburg, 1997/8).

The policy challenges

The chapter has suggested some of the promise of new forms of work organisation, as well as highlighting some of the pitfalls. In the light of this analysis, what kinds of policy changes are required if the promise is to be realised and the pitfalls avoided?

The first set of issues relates to the spread and dissemination of innovations in work organisation. The UK remains one of the few countries in Northern Europe to lack a coherent national policy framework and institutional structure for the promotion of these issues. There is a need to resource change in individual companies, but dissemination of new forms of work organisation and the skills required to make them succeed are lagging behind the pressures for change generated by global competition. The Directorate General V-initiated 'European Work and Technology Consortium', whose report *Work Organisation, Competitiveness and Employment: The European Approach* was launched as the background paper to the UK Presidency Conference on Work Organisation in April 1998, points out that 'business support organisations, consultants, trainers, employers' associations and trade unions lack detailed knowledge of the nature and potential of new forms of work organisation' (Totterdill, 1998:4). Under intense competitive pressure from global markets, many UK companies may well be seeking to move towards a focus on increased teamworking, multi-skilling and employee involvement. However, as the Green Paper accepts, firms have often found it difficult to access appropriate knowledge, experience, skills and learning materials to resource this process of change.

A second set of issues relates to the evidence pointing to there being losers as well as winners as a result of the introduction of new forms of work organisation. There consequently needs to be an active role for policy-makers not just in terms of encouraging organisations to modernise, but also in terms of maintaining and developing a safety net of minimum standards available to individual workers who may be unlikely to benefit from the changes. One wide-ranging analysis of the Green Paper (IRRU, 1997) summarises a number of the changes considered necessary in this respect. These include: a set of universal individual employment rights (to continuing education and training, information and consultation, participation in the planning of work, and representation at work); the enshrining of these rights in higher level agreements and/or legislation to give the clearest indications of the direction in which organisations are expected to go; and an active labour market policy to help deal with the potential mismatch between the education of the workforce and the type of jobs available.

The consequences of the weak system of institutional regulation of training in the UK were documented in the previous section. More highly regulated training systems are found in other European countries, which ensure higher levels of investment in training. However, the examples of France and Germany demonstrate that, even in more regulated training systems, access to continuing training is restricted and tends to favour those employees who already have the highest levels of qualification (Rainbird, 1994). Shackleton *et al.* (1995) also demonstrate that there are significant variations across the five wealthiest G7 countries – the USA, UK, Germany, France and Japan – in the amount of education and training received by men and women, young and older workers and the employees of large and small organisations. It has become fashionable in policy-making circles to argue that the main route to organisational and national economic advantage is through increased investment in education and training (see Reich, 1991), but recent comparative evidence (Ashton and Green, 1996; Crouch, Finegold and Sako, 1999) suggests that at present there is far too little comparable data available for robust conclusions to be drawn about the incidence and effects of training in different countries.

Despite difficulties with cross-national comparisons, the voluntarist system in the UK remains particularly problematic. Faced with the 'externality' problem – that is, that it is not rational for organisations to invest in education and training from which they are not going to reap the benefits – the onus therefore falls on the individual to take responsibility for his or her career or, rather, to ensure that he or she is 'employable'. The Department for Education and Employment (DfEE) issued a Green Paper on lifelong learning which argues that greater responsibility for self-management, self-learning, more customer interface and greater clarity in staff roles and accountability are becoming pre-requisites for competitive success, redefining the skills required from man-agers, supervisors and shopfloor workers (DfEE, 1998). But this emphasis on self-learning is also fraught with difficulties, not least for the simple reason that 'the ability of the individual to influence their future organisation's use of skills is virtually non-existent' (IRRU, 1997:13). Policy suggestions have been advanced to tackle this problem. For instance, the expenses of lifelong learn-ing could be treated like a business cost for individuals, deductible from their taxable earned income (as is already the case for enterprises). This approach would strengthen the incentive for individuals to take on more of the costs themselves. Another way of strengthening the incentives for employers would be to persuade enterprises to treat training as an investment. Although there are formidable barriers to measuring and valuing skills acquired in training and reporting them in company balance sheets, it may be feasible for compa-nies to disclose information on the impact of training on company perfor-mance. This would allow investors in capital markets to identify more readily those companies who improve their performance though training, and thereby reduce their cost of capital. As McKenzie and Wurzburg (1997/8) note, there is strong support for investigating the feasibility of developing guide-lines on the disclosure of such information – analogous to financial accounting standards – that would ensure that it is transparent and comparable (see OECD, 1997). Spreading the practice of lifelong learning clearly depends on finding ways of assessing and recognising the learning that occurs outside for-mal educational institutions.

Conclusion

The implications of new forms of work organisation for workplace training are clearly substantial. Changes in work organisation require workers to be more flexible, and hence training needs to go beyond a narrow focus on a specific job in a specific work-setting. Skills learned also need to cut across a number of conventional boundaries, putting a premium on multi-skilling. Moreover, training has the biggest impact on enterprise performance when it is under-taken in connection with systematic, as opposed to isolated, changes in work organisation. Training, when linked to systematic technological innovation and organisational change, is consistently associated with increases in pro-ductivity of the order of 10–20 per cent (McKenzie and Wurzburg, 1997–8; Whitfield and Poole, 1997). This chapter has explored some of the issues surrounding the relationship between work organisation and training, and has considered some of the policy options available for the realisation of these benefits.

The need for organisational change is recognised more and more, and there is now a European policy significance to new forms of work organisation. Models for shaping company structures and organisational competencies have come to be recognised as one of the determining factors in the future competitiveness of European organisations. At the heart of these debates is the possibility of a convergence between competitiveness, employment and 'quality of working life'.

We have seen here that the achievement of these aims is far from straightforward. If there is an emerging European 'paradigm' that can meet these three criteria, its supporters need to remain cognisant of the highly contingent and complex nature of successful work organisation innovations. Among a range of policy issues, perhaps the most critical in the UK is the need to develop institutional structures which mitigate the 'poaching' or 'free rider' problem caused by the reluctance of firms to finance the acquisition of general skills due to the fear that non-training firms will recruit those trained at the end of the training period. Also important is the need to ensure that training provision is targeted around specific work organisation issues, and to promote 'social dialogue' and 'partnership' at the local level as the means to implement change.

References

Ackers, P., Smith, C. and Smith, P. (1996) *The New Workplace and Trade Unionism*, London: Routledge.

Appelbaum, E. and Batt, R. (1994) *The New American Workplace*, Ithaca, NY: ILR Press.

Ashton, D. and Green, F. (1996) *Education, Training and the Global Economy*, Cheltenham: Edward Elgar.

Atkinson, J. (1984) 'Manpower strategies for the flexible organisation', *Personnel Management*, August, 28–31.

Beer, M., Spector, B., Lawrence, P. R., Quinn, M. D. and Walton, R. (1984) *Managing Human Assets*, New York: Free Press.

Bluestone, B. and Bluestone, I. (1992) *Negotiating the Future: A Labor Perspective on American Business*, New York: Basic Books.

Boyer, R. (1988) *La Théorie de la Régulation: Une Analyse Critique*, Paris: Editions La Découverte.

Buchanan, D. A. (1994) in 'Principles and practice of work design', in Sisson, K. (ed.), *Personnel Management: A Comprehensive Guide to Theory and Practice in Britain*, Oxford: Basil Blackwell.

Collinson, M., Rees, C. and Edwards, P. K. with Inness, L. (1998) 'Involving employees in total quality management: employee attitudes and organisational context in unionised environments', *DTI Employment Relations Research Series* No. 1, London: Department of Trade and Industry.

Council of the European Union (1997) 'Intergovernmental Conference Draft Treaty', Office for the Official Publications of the European Communities.

Crouch, C., Finegold, D. and Sako, M. (1999) *Are Skills the Answer?: The Political Economy of Skill Creation in Advanced Industrial Countries*, Oxford: Oxford University Press.

Delbridge, R. (1998) *Life on the Line in Contemporary Manufacturing*, Oxford: Oxford University Press.

DfEE (1998) *The Learning Age: A Renaissance for a New Britain*, London: DfEE, CM 3790.

Drucker, P. F. (1990) 'The emerging theory of manufacturing', *Harvard Business Review*, 68, 3, 94–102.

Dunlop, J. (1992) 'The challenge of human resources development', *Industrial Relations*, 31, 50–5.

Dyer, L., and Reeves, T. (1995) 'Human resource strategies and firm performance: what do we know and where do we need to go?' *International Journal of Human Resource Management*, 6, 3, 656–70.

Edwards, P. K., Collinson, M., and Rees, C. (1998) 'The determinants of employee responses to total quality management: six case studies', *Organisation Studies*, 19, 3, 449–75.

Ennals, R. and Gustavsen, B. (1998) 'Work organisation and Europe as a development coalition', *Concepts and Transformation*, 3, 1/2, 153–62.

European Commission (1996) *Employment in Europe 1996*, European Commission.

European Commission (1997) *Partnership for a New Organisation of Work*, European Commission, COM (97) 128.

European Foundation (1997) *New Forms of Work Organisation – Can Europe Realise its Potential?: Results of a Survey of Direct Employee Participation in Europe*, Luxembourg: Office for Official Publications of the European Communities.

Garibaldo, F. (1997) 'Knowledge, competition and employment', paper presented to Work and Technology Consortium Conference on 'Real Change in Organisations', Bologna, 9–10 June.

Glover, L. and Fitzgerald-Moore, D. (1998) 'Total quality management: shop floor perspectives', in Mabey, C., Skinner, D. and Clark, T. (eds), *Experiencing Human Resource Management*, London: Sage.

Guest, D. (1987) 'Human resource management and industrial relations', *Journal of Management Studies*, 24, 5, 503–21.

Guest, D. (1995) 'Human resource management, trade unions and industrial relations' in Storey, J. (ed.), *Human Resource Management: A Critical Text*, London: Routledge.

Herzberg, F. (1966) *Work and the Nature of Man*, London: Staples Press.

Herzberg, F.(1968) 'One more time: how do you motivate employees?', *Harvard Business Review*, 46, 1, 53–62.

Hilb, M. (1992) 'The challenge of management development in Western Europe in the 1990s', *International Journal of Human Resource Management*, 3, 575–84.

Hyman, R. (1997) 'Review of Littek, W., and Charles T. (eds) "The new division of labour: emerging forms of work organisation in international perspective" ', *Organisation Studies*, 18, 2, 350–2.

Incomes Data Services (1990) 'Training strategies', IDS Study No. 460.

Industrial Relations Review and Report (1997) 'Cementing a new partnership at Blue Circle', *Employment Trends*, 638, August.

IRRU (1997) 'Comments on the European Commission's green paper "Partnership for a new organisation of work" ', mimeo, Coventry: IRRU.

Keep, E., and Rainbird, H. (1995) 'Training', in Edwards, P. K. (ed.), *Industrial Relations: Theory and Practice in Britain*, Oxford: Basil Blackwell.

Kern, H. and Schuman, M. (1984) *Das Ende der Arbeitsteilung?*, Munich: Beck .

Levine, D. (1995) *Reinventing the Workplace*, Washington, DC: The Brookings Institute.

MacDuffie, J. P. (1995) 'Human resource bundles and manufacturing performance: organisational logic and flexible production systems in the world auto industry', *Industrial and Labor Relations Review*, 48, 197–220.

McKenzie, P. and Warburg, G. (1997/8) 'Lifelong learning and employability', *The OECD Observer*, 209, 13–17.

Maslow, A. (1943) 'A theory of motivation', *Psychological Review*, 50, 4, 370–96.

Morris, H. (1999) 'Review article: does the learning society pass the test?', *Human Resource Development International*.

OECD (1997) *Enterprise Value in the Knowledge Economy: Measuring Performance in the Age of Intangibles*, Paris: OECD Publications/Boston, Mass.: Ernst & Young.

Osterman, P. (1994) 'How common is workplace transformation and who adopts it?', *Industrial and Labor Relations Review*, 47, 2, 173–88.

Peters, T. (1987) *Thriving on Chaos: Handbook for a Management Revolution*, London: Macmillan.

Piore, M. and Sabel, C. (1984) *The Second Industrial Divide: Possibilities for Prosperity*, New York: Basic Books.

Rainbird, H. (1994) 'Continuing training', in Sisson, K. (ed.), *Personnel Management: A Comprehensive Guide to Theory and Practice in Britain*, Oxford: Basil Blackwell.

Rees, C. (1996) 'Employee involvement in quality management strategies: a case study based analysis', unpublished PhD thesis, University of Warwick.

Rees, C. (1998) 'Empowerment through quality management: employee accounts from inside a bank, a hotel and two factories', in Mabey, C., Skinner, D. and Clark, T. (eds), *Experiencing Human Resource Management*, London: Sage.

Regini, M. (1995) 'Firms and institutions: the demand for skills and their social production in Europe', *European Journal of Industrial Relations*, 1, 2, 191–202.

Reich, R. (1991) *The Work of Nations: Preparing Ourselves for 21st Century Capitalism*, London: Simon & Schuster.

Sako, M. (1998) 'The nature and impact of employee "voice" in the European car components industry', *Human Resource Management Journal*, 8, 2, 5–13.

Scarbrough, H. and Terry, M. (1996) 'Industrial relations and the reorganisation of production in the UK motor vehicle industry: a case study of the Rover Group', *Warwick Papers in Industrial Relations*, No. 58, Coventry: IRRU.

Scott, A. (1994) *Willing Slaves?: British Workers Under Human Resource Management*, Cambridge: Cambridge University Press.

Shackleton, J. R., with Clarke, L., Lange, T. and Walsh, S. (1995) *Training for Employment in Western Europe and the United States*, Cheltenham: Edward Elgar.

Singh, R. (1992) 'Human resource management: a sceptical look', in Towers, B. (ed.), *The Handbook of Human Resource Management*, Oxford: Basil Blackwell.

Taylor, F. W. (1911) 'Principles of Scientific Management', New York: Harper and Row.

Totterdill, P. (1998) 'Britain's advantage?: Work organisation, innovation and employment', mimeo, Nottingham Trent University: UK Work Organisation Network.

Trist, E. L., Higgin, G. W., Murray, H. and Pollock, A. B. (1963) *Organisational Choice*, London: Tavistock.

TUC (1996) 'Partners for progress: next steps for the new unionism', London: TUC.

Warhurst, C. and Thompson, P. (1998) 'Hands, hearts and minds: changing work and workers at the end of the century', in Thompson, P. and Warhurst, C. (eds), *Workplaces of the Future*, London: Macmillan.

Whitfield, K., and Poole, M. (1997) 'Organising employment for high performance: theories, evidence and policy', *Organisation Studies*, 18, 5, 745–64.

Womack, J., Jones, D. and Roos, D. (1990) *The Machine that Changed the World*, New York: Rawson.

Wright, M. and Edwards, P. K. (1998) 'Does teamworking work, and if so, why?: a case study in the aluminium industry', *Economic and Industrial Democracy*, 19, 1, 59–90.

CHAPTER 8

Workplace industrial relations and training[1]

Jason Heyes

Introduction

It has become commonplace to emphasise the importance of VET to the future prosperity of organisations, workers and national economies. The adoption by firms of production methods based on flexible forms of work organisation and continuous improvement is said to require a concomitant up-grading of workers' skills. Training is seen as essential if firms are to develop the organisational resources they need to respond to intensified competition and product market uncertainty (Streeck, 1992a). Skill acquisition is also viewed as important in equipping workers with protection against employment instability (Finegold and Soskice, 1988). With the notion of a 'job for life' applying to a declining proportion of the workforce, policy-makers have sought to encourage workers to take more responsibility for training. The expectation is that training will enhance workers' ability to adjust to shifting employment opportunities.

Concerns such as these have encouraged commentators to explore training provision in different national contexts. Considerable attention has been devoted to comparisons of aggregate training data, state interventions and the regulatory frameworks that influence training activity (Campinos-Dubernet and Grando, 1988; Caillods, 1994). The workplace, by contrast, has received relatively little attention, despite it being at this level that skills are utilised and training decisions frequently taken. In particular, there has been insufficient consideration of the relationship between training provision and workplace industrial relations (Heyes, 1993). This issue is, however, increasingly recognised as being one of importance, particularly given the emphasis placed by UK trade unions on active participation in training decisions at the workplace (Rainbird, 1990:4).

This chapter provides a review of the extant literature on training and workplace industrial relations and explores the interests of managers, unions and workers as they relate to training. The discussion is organised in four sections. In the first section, which is primarily concerned with the issue of VET and competitive performance, the key themes of the chapter are established. Attention is drawn to how the economics and HRM literatures in this area have diverted academic enquiry away from the social dimension of skill formation. The remainder of the chapter exposes the damaging consequences of this neglect, showing how it has served to limit understanding of the industrial relations implications of training. The influence of employers and trade unions over training activity is explored in the second section. The third addresses the issue of 'social partnership' between trade unions and employers with respect to training, highlighting areas where possible conflicts of interest may emerge. The final section returns to issues of training and competitiveness and demonstrates the important role of production politics in determining the performance outcomes resulting from training activity.

Human Resource Management and human capital

The relationship between training and economic performance has formed the crux of the VET debate. Skills and knowledge of various kinds have been identified as key 'endogenous' determinants of economic growth (Romer, 1990; Grossman and Helpman, 1991; Gemmell, 1996). Training is believed to have a major influence on both labour productivity and the trading performance of industrialised nations (Oulton, 1993). The economic benefits of training are also emphasised by those who view it as a necessary accompaniment to emerging systems of production based on principles of quality and flexibility (for example, Streeck, 1992a; MacDuffie and Kochan, 1995; Kabst, Holt Larsen and Bramming, 1996).

The economic benefits of training are treated as axiomatic in the HRM literature. Attempts to identify the precise nature of the causal relationships involved tend to be both vague and speculative. Hyman (1992:258), for example, claims that training investments transform the 'performance potential of employees and managers', serving to constitute employees as strategic resources as opposed to disposable commodities. Willmott (1993:254) emphasises that training provides management with an opportunity to communicate and reinforce company values and expectations so as to encourage worker cooperation. In a similar vein, Keep (1989) argues that training acts as a signal to employees, demonstrating to them that they are valued by their employer. This is said to have the effect of increasing employee motivation.

Beyond assertions such as these, performance issues have tended to be neglected in the HRM literature. Systematic investigation of the impact of training on performance at the level of the workplace has largely been left to economists. Perhaps the most widely cited studies dealing directly with per-formance issues at the micro-level are those that have been conducted by the National Institute for Economic and Social Research (NIESR) in the UK. Based on international comparisons of matched samples of plants in industries such as clothing (Steedman and Wagner, 1989), engineering (Daly, Hitchens and Wagner, 1985), biscuits (Mason, Van Ark and Wagner, 1994) and hotels (Prais, Jarvis and Wagner, 1989), the studies examined the relationship between skill levels and performance, as measured in terms of productivity. Inadequately trained labour was found to be of fundamental importance in explaining the inferior performance of British plants when compared to those in economies such as Germany, France and the Netherlands. Although widely cited, this finding has rarely been subjected to critical scrutiny. An exception is Cutler (1992), who argued that the NIESR studies took insufficient account of differ-ences in capital equipment. Cutler also raised the possibility that the inferior performance of the British plants was a result of a lack of training for certain categories of employee as opposed to insufficient training *per se*.

Cutler's critique suggests the need for a more cautious assessment of the relationship between training and productivity. Yet most HRM commentators continue to assume the existence of a direct, positive relationship between skill formation and economic performance. Striking parallels exist between the treatment of training to be found in the HRM literature and that provided by mainstream economics. For neo-classical economists, training gives rise to capabilities – termed 'human capital'- which positively influence individuals' productivity and hence earnings potential (Mincer, 1958; Becker, 1962, 1975). Human capital is equivalent to physical capital, in the sense that it is an asset which provides a stream of productive services. The productivity of labour is dependent on investments made by individuals and firms in human capital. Human capital theory pays no attention to the question of how management extracts effort from workers. The implication is that skills are simply put to 'productive' use in the pursuit of management-defined goals. It follows that human capital theory treats as irrelevant issues of power and conflict, and dis-regards class-based antagonisms (Bowles and Gintis, 1975; Fine, 1998:58). Training is treated in strictly technical terms rather than as a social process involving groups with potentially conflicting interests.

The assumptions of the human capital approach are remarkably harmo-nious with those of HRM. Where human capital theory treats labour as an asset in which to invest, HRM views labour as a resource to be developed. Similarly, the neglect of power considerations in human capital theory is entirely consistent with the unitarist ethos of HRM. Furthermore, both the human capital approach and HRM assume that workers and employers have a joint interest in training. Human capital theory asserts that training provides benefits to employers in the form of productivity increases, while employees benefit from higher lifetime earnings. In the HRM literature, the benefits to employers take the form of a more committed, motivated and productive workforce, while employees experience psychological rewards associated with more interesting, varied and challenging work. Both human capital theory and HRM, therefore, present training activity as a 'positive-sum game'.

Employers, trade unions and training activity

The assumption of mutual gains has influenced which aspects of the training debate have been treated as problematical. Considerable attention has, for example, been devoted to comparative analyses of the factors that promote (or suppress) training activity at the workplace. Assessments are generally underpinned by an implicit belief that 'more is better'.[2] Comparisons typically make use of regularly available indices of skill formation, such as the incidence and duration of training, training expenditure and levels of qualifications held by workers (for example, Prais, 1993; Lynch, 1994). On this basis, the UK economy is commonly identified as suffering from serious structural deficiencies in its skills base when compared to other advanced industrialised nations (Green and Ashton, 1992). While commentators have not assumed uniform underprovision at the enterprise level, 'islands of excellence' (Streeck, 1989) are treated as exceptions to the rule (see Keep, 1993:106).

Various explanations have been advanced for the poor training record of UK employers. Finegold and Soskice (1988:22), for example, argue that employers' demands for more highly-skilled labour are suppressed by, among other things, the dysfunctional relationship between financial and industrial capital and the inadequacy of state-sponsored training programmes. For Streeck (1989), the critical factor has been that of market failure. He argues that organisations require skills that are simultaneously 'high', in the sense that they embody significant levels of technical competence, and 'broad' in that they facilitate flexible working and rapid adaptation. Yet rational employers are argued to lack incentives to invest in training leading to 'broad and high' skills. This is because such skills represent 'redundant capacities' in that they must exceed employers' present requirements if future flexibility is to be assured. 'Broad and high' skills also constitute 'collective goods' since they are of value to rival firms. If employees take up alternative employment opportunities once they have been trained, the investing firm will fail to capture a return on its investment. Streeck claims that given the absence of effective regulation in the UK, employers are encouraged to underinvest in training while attempting to resource their skills needs by poaching from rival firms. He contrasts this situation with that of Germany where a combination of factors, including coherent state initiatives with respect to VET, and cooperation by the social partners at various levels, are argued to have circumvented market failure.

Attention has also been given to the possible impact that trade unions might have on training investment decisions. Mincer (1983) argued that unions were likely to have had a depressive effect on 'general' training activity in US firms because of their role in promoting seniority rules. Seniority determines which workers will be promoted, and therefore receive training, in the event of higher level vacancies arising. Mincer argued that individual workers therefore face few incentives to undertake general training and that 'whatever training exists in union firms ... almost by definition all of it is specific to the firm' (1983:239). He suggested that higher levels of specific training activity might be expected in unionised firms when compared to non-unionised enterprises given that lower quit rates tend to be observed in the former. However, Mincer found the influence of unions on specific training to be insignificant and thus concluded that the net impact of unions on total training activity was negative.

Other accounts have emphasised the role of trade unions in pay bargaining. Human capital theory implies that the willingness of employers to provide training diminishes where trade unions are able to negotiate real wage increases for trainees. Explanations for the declining volume of apprenticeship training in the UK from the mid-1960s onwards have centred on unions' attempts to narrow the earnings gap between young trainees and skilled adult workers in the same job (Marsden and Ryan, 1991; Gospel, 1995). Union successes in this regard are said to have encouraged the emergence of inflexible wage structures and reduced the return employers received on training investments. Employers, in the face of declining profit levels, responded by reducing their investments in apprentice labour. The success of the German apprenticeship system, by contrast, is said to be the result of the relatively low wage costs associated with young trainees (Oulton and Steedman, 1994; Soskice, 1994).

Other commentators have suggested that trade unions may have a positive role to play in encouraging training activity within firms. First, trade unions may encourage job tenure by providing employees with a 'voice' as an alternative to expressing their grievances through 'exiting' (quitting) employment (Freeman and Medoff, 1984). Low labour turnover will increase the probability of employers being able to secure a return on investments in training and should in turn lead to an increase in their propensity to train. Second, as argued by Nolan (1996), unions may close off routes to competitiveness based on the intensive use of low-wage, low-skill labour. The implication is that employers will be encouraged to up-grade their production techniques and invest more heavily in the skills of their employees. Finally, Williamson (1985:254–6) has suggested that unions may play an important 'governance role' where workers possess firm-specific (or 'task-idiosyncratic') skills. Such skills are argued to provide workers with bargaining leverage and thus make possible 'opportunistic haggling' over rewards. The threat of haggling is argued to be particularly acute where rewards are individualised (Williamson, Wachter and Harris, 1975). Trade unions and collective agreements, by promoting collective interests over those of individual workers, reduce the scope for costly, opportunistic behaviour and thus serve as a positive force for efficiency. Although Williamson does not pursue the point, the implication is that employers will be more prepared to invest in workers' skills where trade unions are present.

Evidence for a positive association between training and trade union presence has been found for both the USA (Osterman, 1995) and the UK (Greenhalgh and Mavrotas, 1994; Arulampalam and Booth, 1998). Drawing on data from the 1991 Employers' Manpower and Skills Practices Survey (EMSPS) and the Labour Force Survey of Autumn 1993, Green, Machin and Williamson (1995, 1996) discovered that employees in workplaces where trade unions were recognised stood a significantly higher chance of receiving training than those in non-unionised workplaces. Unionised workplaces were also more likely to have training plans. In suggesting explanations for the positive association between unions and training activity, Green, Machin and Williamson emphasised the importance of union 'voice effects'. Further recent evidence is provided by the 1998 Workplace Employee Relations Survey which found that the availability of training opportunities, and number of days' training undertaken by employees, were positively associated with union recognition (Cully *et al.*, 1998:20). Sixty-two per cent of employees in workplaces where trade unions were recognised received training in the year prior to the survey, compared to 54 per cent of employees in workplaces where no union members were present.

Other findings suggest that training activity is further enhanced where, in addition to achieving recognition, trade unions are actively involved in training decisions. Based on a survey of 792 members of the Manufacturing Science and Finance union (MSF), Heyes and Stuart's (1998a) study found that members were more likely to receive training, have opportunities to train, achieve qualifications and enjoy a pay increase as a result of training where the MSF had an active role in training decisions. A positive association between trade union activity and training has also been found for Australia. Kennedy *et al*'s. (1994) study, which drew upon data from the 1989–90 Australian Workplace Industrial Relations Survey (AWIRS), found that trade unionism was associated with superior provision of formal training programmes. This was only the case, however, 'where unions [were] active within the workplace and not merely *de jure* representatives of the work-force' (Kennedy *et al.*, 1994:577).

Social partnership and training

The above findings reveal little about the means by which trade unions secure a role in training decisions, the nature of their role, how union representatives seek to mobilise members in support of training and so forth. Nevertheless, they suggest that trade unions may have a beneficial effect on training provision. A number of commentators have suggested that trade unions themselves have much to gain from encouraging employers to invest in training. As Streeck has notably argued:

> What wage bargaining was for distributional unionism, training may become for unions working on and through the production side of the economy and making their peace with it: an opportunity for conflictual cooperation, or cooperation through conflict; for redistribution in the general interest; and for deep involvement of unions in the management of an advanced industrial economy and society. (1992b:255)

Questions remain, however, about the tactics unions should adopt in pursuing a role in training and, by extension, the type of industrial relations environment that is most conducive to training activity. Streeck (1992b:263–5) argues that employers are most likely to adopt a high-skills strategy where trade unions are able to successfully prevent employers from basing their competitive strategy on low wages and low skills. Others place more emphasis on consensus. Mathews (1993), for example, claims that a joint approach by trade unions and management towards training necessitates that the 'traditional adversarial' agenda of industrial relations be completely transcended (by unions).

In the UK, trade union involvement in training has been particularly discussed in the context of 'partnership' approaches to lifelong learning (Fryer, 1997; DfEE, 1998). Ford and Watts (1998) have described the various parts that unions can play, such as developing learning guidance for members, encouraging members to make use of training opportunities, and facilitating the formation of linkages between employers and local communities. Enthusiasm for a 'partnership' approach to training has been expressed by significant sections of the trade union movement. Particularly important has been the 'new agenda' initiative, which has encouraged unions to attempt to extend joint regulation in order to enhance members' 'quality of life' at work. The TUC has been particularly active in promoting lifelong learning. As part of its 'Bargaining for Skills' campaign the TUC has pledged support for the National Targets for Education and Training. It has also entered into joint projects with Training and Enterprise Councils (TECs) designed to encourage unions to develop an active approach to training at the workplace. Social partnership has been emphasised as a means of ensuring a more equal distribution of skills while simultaneously bringing about a positive transformation in attitudes towards training and organisational change (TUC, 1995b:25). The TUC has asserted that trade unions can 'try to ensure that training is geared towards the long term needs of workers, as well as the business needs of employers' (TUC, 1995b:1). 'Employee development' represents more than a potential bargaining issue; it is also viewed as a vehicle for gaining influence over other issues normally characterised by managerial prerogative, such as restructuring and relocation plans and investment strategy (TUC, 1991:12).

There have been a number of well-publicised examples of apparently successful joint initiatives on education and training. Perhaps most notable is Ford's Employee Development and Assistance Programme (EDAP). The scheme, which was agreed by the company and the unions in 1987, provides employees with opportunities for personal development in areas that are not directly related to their jobs. Job-related training remains strictly within the province of separate company-specific arrangements. The implementation of the programme was intended to provide an opportunity for Ford's management and trade unions to develop a 'non-adversarial' mode of engagement, which management hoped would lead to 'improvements in the industrial relations climate of the Company at national and local level' (Mortimer, 1990:309). Another example of cooperation between unions and employers is provided by the Return to Learn programme initiated by Unison (Munro, Rainbird and Holly, 1997). This scheme provides educational opportunities for those previously disadvantaged in education.

Other successful cases have been publicised by the TUC (1996a), yet a number of observers have expressed scepticism about the prospects for widespread involvement by trade unions in training (see Claydon, 1993; Kelly, 1996; Heyes and Stuart, 1998b). These commentators have questioned whether employers are likely to concede a role to trade unions unless obliged to by legislation (as is the case in France, for example). Evidence suggests that training is rarely an issue for collective bargaining and that employee development is normally considered a managerial prerogative (Millward *et al.*, 1992:225; Payne, Forrester and Ward, 1993:27; Claydon and Green, 1994). Even where training provision is formally negotiated, unions face the challenge of ensuring that employers adhere to agreements. The difficulties that unions may encounter in this regard were brought to light in Stuart's (1994, 1996) study of the UK printing industry. Despite the implementation of a national agreement on 'recruitment, training and retraining' in the industry, Stuart found continuing diversity of practice at plant level. The agreement proved ineffective in ensuring that use was made of formal training programmes at the workplace. Moreover, despite expectations of union involvement through negotiated 'manpower plans', training decisions continued to be taken unilaterally by management. Stuart concluded that the likely benefits to trade unions and their members from adopting a cooperative approach over training have been overstated.

The optimistic scenario for trade union involvement turns on a somewhat arbitrary distinction between conflictual and non-conflictual issues. Finegold (1991:108), for example, while emphasising that terms and conditions of employment are 'subject to legitimate disagreement and conflictual bargaining between management and workers', argues that training holds out possibilities for 'working in tandem'. Yet the distinction between conflictual and non-conflictual issues is far from clear cut. As the TUC has noted: 'The more trade unions start to talk about employee development ... the more they will find themselves questioning "existing managerial prerogatives", and the financial advantages management have appropriated for themselves on this basis' (TUC, 1991:13). Although training may be considered a relatively non-conflictual issue where it is not directly job-related (as in the case of Ford's EDAP programme), 'traditional' issues are likely to come to the fore where the training in question is, for example, related to the re-organisation of work. At such times the issue of training will be enmeshed in a broader set of concerns relating to reward, effort and control over production.[3] The effect of treating training and development as distinct from other workplace industrial relations issues is, therefore, to under *politicise* skill formation. By way of injecting some social content into the analysis of training and development, the following section explores a number of areas where the interests of trade unions and employers with respect to skill formation are likely to be antagonistic, rather than complementary.

The production politics of training

TUC (1996b) guidance to negotiators involved in training emphasises the need to promote equality of opportunity. This is an important objective given that *in*equality of opportunity represents such a striking aspect of employer-provided training. Evidence suggests that employers deliberately differentiate between workers when providing access to training (Cordery, Mueller and Sevastos, 1992; Heyes and Stuart, 1996:13). As Hand, Gambles and Cooper, (1994) note, given that it is the employer who holds the information about available training opportunities, the 'power of choice [over courses and who may take them] resides primarily with the employer, sometimes leaving employees unaware of potential opportunities to learn'.

Training activity clearly varies according to hours worked. The findings from the 1998 *Workplace Employee Relations Survey* (Cully et al., 1998:19–20) suggested that full-time employees were more likely to receive training than those working part-time (62 per cent and 52 per cent respectively). Of those working less than ten hours a week, only 43 per cent had received any training in the year prior to the survey. Although female workers dominate part-time employment, access to training is more commonly available to male part-timers (McGivney, 1994:33; DfEE, 1997a:66). The disadvantaged position of women workers with respect to training is a commonly noted phenomenon (for example, Green, 1991) although there is evidence that the gender gap in the UK has shrunk in recent years (Gallie *et al.*, 1998:46). Evidence also suggests that temporary workers are less likely on average to receive training than those on permanent contracts. Mouriki's (1994) study of six organisations, for example, found that training opportunities were arranged to cater for full-time employees and that workers on non-standard contracts therefore tended to miss out. A further study, based on data from the British Household Panel Survey collected over the period 1991–5, estimated that male temporary workers were 16 per cent less likely to receive training than those on a permanent contract. The equivalent figure in the case of female employees was estimated at 12 per cent (Arulampalam and Booth, 1998).

The issue of access to training opportunities raises the question of how much say employees have in determining the training they receive. Formal appraisal schemes may offer a way for employees to achieve an input into decisions regarding their training. The number of appraisal schemes in operation has increased in recent years, particularly among Japanese- and American-owned companies and their UK subsidiaries (Townley, 1989, Gallie *et al.*, 1998:68). The coverage of appraisals has been extended beyond managerial grades so as to include white and blue-collar workers (Hyman and Mason, 1995:84). Yet the influence of appraisals on training generally appears to be quite limited in the UK. Just over half the respondents in the 1992 Employment in Britain survey stated that they experienced formal appraisals, yet only one in three employees claimed that appraisals affected their training and development (Gallie *et al.*, 1998:68). Moreover, joint assessment of training needs tends to be confined to non-manual employees (Tremlett and Park, 1995:14, Gallie *et al.*, 1998:68).

Possible reasons for employers' reluctance to provide employees with a 'voice' in determining training were suggested by a survey of 582 employers carried out in the early 1990s by the (then) Employment Department (Metcalf, Walling and Fogarty, 1994). Eighty-four per cent of the survey respondents believed that they should encourage their employees to participate in education and training throughout their adult lives. Eighty-eight per cent also felt that employees should be encouraged to take more responsibility for their training (Metcalf, Walling and Fogarty, 1994:60–2). However, employers also saw disadvantages in employees having a greater input into training decisions. Concerns were expressed about the cost implications and the risk that employees would demand 'inappropriate' training. Some employers believed that education and training distracted workers from their jobs and interfered with work routines.

An important consideration is the extent to which managers formally recognise new skills developed through training. Recognition is far from automatic and thus raises serious issues for employees and trade unions. As Rainbird has argued:

> Management may impose new skills on workers and resist acknowledging their existence if training is very short or informal and takes place outside the ambit of union control and initiatives ... the unions' ability to claim new skills and to obtain formal recognition for them will be fundamental to the redefinition of skilled work. (1988:176)

One way in which skills may be formally recognised is by linking training to financial rewards. Where training is job related, unions are likely to be concerned that members receive financial compensation for their training efforts and the skills they develop (Industrial Relations Review and Report, 1990:12). Active attempts to ensure that employers provide financial rewards clearly force trade unions to address distributional issues (Winterton and Winterton, 1994:7; Stuart, 1996:257). As such, the limits of cooperation may become rapidly exposed. Neither can inter-union cooperation at the workplace be taken for granted. The sectional interests that characterise multi-union environments may give rise to conflicting agendas with respect to training. Unions may experience difficulties in identifying common interests where training activity threatens established pay differentials and job demarcations.

Conversely, pay increases may become conditional upon skill acquisition. Skill-based payment systems have received attention from companies in the UK and USA (Incomes Data Services, 1992). The benefits that skill-based pay are thought to deliver include an improved skills base, enhanced employee flexibility, loyalty and motivation, and structured career paths for employees. A number of organisations have travelled further down this route and implemented 'competency frameworks' designed to relate employee attributes, such as skills, attitudes and experience, to organisational goals. Companies such as Thomas Cook and British Sugar encourage employees to progress through various levels of competency, with each successive level attracting a higher salary. These companies neither expect, nor desire, all employees to reach the highest level of competency. Those employees remaining at lower levels 'will not, however, receive salary increases apart from market-related adjustments' (Incomes Data Services, 1997:7). From the employee's point of view, not only are concerns with equality of access likely to be to the fore, but there may also be anxieties resulting from a perceived pressure to acquire skills. Those workers who have little inclination to undertake further training may fear that management will come to see them as 'underachievers'. In certain cases, therefore, workers' concerns may be less with obtaining access to training than with ensuring that a refusal to train does not result in their being penalised in some way (Heyes and Stuart, 1999).

The issue for trade unions, therefore, is how to protect the interests of those members who are reluctant or unwilling to voluntarily undertake training and development. There are clear tensions between trade unions' support for employer-provided training and goals such as greater equality in the labour market. Mahnkopf (1992) has explored this issue in the context of the adoption of 'skill-oriented' collective bargaining strategies by German trade unions. Mahnkopf suggests that traditionally disadvantaged (for example, female) workers who fail to benefit from further training may find themselves pushed into insecure, low-paid jobs as they compete against a highly qualified 'worker elite' (1992:77). An alliance between 'enlightened' employers and core workers could therefore operate to the detriment of employees in the periphery. The overall effect would be to reinforce labour market segmentation, an outcome Mathews (1993:605) refers to as 'incipient polarisation'. It is possible that the perception of such dangers by union members may prove a stumbling block in union efforts to stimulate grass roots enthusiasm for a 'skill-oriented strategy' (Mahnkopf, 1992:77).

Financial rewards are not the only way by which skills may be recognised. A key issue is whether training is linked to the achievement of externally recognised qualifications. Evidence suggests that trainees generally view certification of skills as important (Fuller and Saunders, 1990). As Forrester, James and Thorne (1995:61) note, certificates represent 'tangible "proof" that [workers] have gained new skills and knowledge'. The TUC has emphasised that in 'bargaining for skills', union negotiators should attempt to ensure that the training members receive is broad based, of good quality and linked to externally recognised qualifications (or credits which contribute towards such qualifications). Yet much employer-provided training is not linked to formal accreditation (DfEE, 1997b). One reason for this is that training is often of short duration, reflecting employers' short-term needs (Rainbird, 1994; DfEE, 1997a:67). Employers may also be reluctant to link training to recognised qualifications if they are concerned about the consequences for workers' inter-firm mobility. There may be a fear that education and training will raise employees' expectations and lead to increased turnover as upskilled employees seek more challenging work elsewhere (Tremlett and Park, 1995:10). If so, employers may choose to emphasise forms of training that are relatively narrow, firm-specific and uncertified. Yet the interests of employers will here conflict with the interests of those employees who wish to acquire transferable skills and qualifications. As Tremlett and Park observe, 'individual employees may well have much broader training requirements than those which their employers consider will directly benefit the organisation' (1995:8). Issues of quality are also clearly important. Felstead and Green (1996) note that training for qualifications (or credits towards them) has tended to expand, but they also emphasise that the expansion has coincided with an increased emphasis on short courses and thus conclude that the qualifications obtained may be of a low standard.

Finally, trade unions are forced to consider the relationship between training and labour utilisation. A key consideration, particularly where training accompanies work re-organisation, is whether workers are likely to experience greater autonomy and job enrichment, or alternatively an intensification of effort, as a result of training. In the industrial relations literature this question has been addressed in the context of initiatives designed to erode demarcations and encourage functional flexibility. A distinction is commonly made between multi-skilling and multi-tasking (Garrahan and Stewart, 1992; Legge, 1998:291). Both terms imply a horizontal and vertical expansion of job boundaries alongside an erosion of demarcations. But whereas the former is associated with 'genuine' skill formation, involving formal training programmes and recognised qualifications, the latter implies that functional flexibility is achieved via task enlargement and effort intensification. O'Reilly argues that analysis of functional flexibility initiatives therefore 'needs to distinguish where task expansion has led to up-skilling, as distinct from ad-hoc, piecemeal change with the repercussions of intensifying work' (1992:392).

One recent survey of over 4500 union activists attempted to do this by providing evidence on both multi-skilling and task flexibility (Waddington and Whitston, 1996). The survey found multi-skilling to be present at 16 per cent of workplaces while task flexibility was reported by 23 per cent of the survey respondents. Yet the distinction remains deficient in a number of respects. First, the empirical grounds for distinguishing multi-skilling from multi-tasking are insufficiently clear; second, the analytical value of the distinction remains obscure; and finally, the extent to which upskilling and work intensification may be compatible (or elements of deskilling and upskilling co-exist) tends to be overlooked. These complexities have been exposed by the 1992 Employment in Britain survey which found upskilling to be associated with higher levels of work effort as well as greater intrinsic job interest (Gallie *et al.*, 1998:42).

Perhaps more fundamentally, the distinction between multi-skilling and multi-tasking fails to capture the complex, dynamic processes of adjustment which result from training and the re-organisation of work and production. By locating training within an analysis of shifting patterns of labour utilisation, the social significance of training at the workplace can be made more apparent. Peck has argued in this regard that:

> The process of reconstituting skills as *flexible* skills is not just an issue of workplace organisation or efficiency, but has wider ramifications for the distribution of power within the labour market. Indeed, employers' desire to redistribute labour market power may be the motivation for many flexibility strategies. Reorganising skills means reorganising power relationships.
>
> (1996:135; emphasis in original)

Case study findings have pointed to some of the practical difficulties that can beset multi-skilling initiatives. Cordery, Mueller and Sevastos's (1992) examination of teamworking in a minerals processing plant in Australia found that the pace of skills acquisition by workers was relatively slow. Workers expressed concerns relating to the lack of financial inducements, the effort required to acquire skills, and the stress involved in taking on certain 'higher-skill' activities. At the same time, management failed to provide adequate resources for training, confined the scope of skills development to semi-skilled tasks, and closed off access to certain forms of training once a 'sufficient' number of workers had acquired the necessary skills. These developments resulted in workers questioning management's commitment to teamworking.

Cordery, Mueller and Sevastos also reported that multi-skilling resulted in workers achieving greater control over aspects of their work. This issue was the central focus of Heyes' (1996) study of a chemical plant in the UK. The study showed how multi-skilled workers employed their skills so as to exert collective influence over the pace of work and pursue goals that conflicted with those of management. The study further demonstrated how disparities between the earnings of team members, produced as a result of the redeployment of craft workers into processing work, created a reluctance on the part of process workers to perform maintenance tasks for which they had been trained. These findings echo other case study evidence which has demonstrated how discriminatory pay practices can conflict with established perceptions of fairness and equity and undermine the basis for cooperation in production (see Geary, 1992). Pay individualisation may therefore frustrate attempts to introduce working practices based around multi-skilled teams (MacInnes, 1987:120).

The tensions that might arise between skill formation and flexibility initiatives have been more readily recognised in the case of numerical flexibility. This term is commonly used to refer to the ability of employers to adjust the size of their workforce in line with production requirements. It implies an increased reliance on non-standard forms of employment (for example, temporary or self-employment). It is commonly claimed, however, that numerical flexibility may lead to difficulties associated with the supply and reproduction of skills (Rubery, 1989:169, Gough, 1992; Standing, 1997:22). Abraham and Houseman (1993:132), for example, contend that overreliance on the ability to lay workers off 'results in an unnecessary loss of firm-specific worker skills and a corresponding reduction in productivity' (cited in Buchele and Christiansen (1995:407). Evans' (1990) study of the UK construction industry highlighted how the growth in casual hiring and labour-only subcontracting (on a mainly self-employed basis) in the 1980s interacted with a neglect of training so as to constrain the scope for innovation. Evans also noted that uncoordinated wage bargaining in the industry exposed firms to competitive wage inflation, a problem that was exacerbated by recurring skills shortages. Economic upswings in industries such as construction may therefore serve to strengthen the individual bargaining position of those self-employed workers who possess scarce and highly valued skills (Jones, 1996:122).

Conclusion

Economic concerns have been central to the VET debate. They have also served to shape the debate in particular ways. Acceptance of the 'high skills–high productivity' equation has been widespread among policy-makers, employers, trade unions, and also academics. It is therefore tempting to assume a commonality of interest at the level of the workplace. Yet many of the studies reviewed in this chapter suggest that it is misleading to conceive of training as a positive-sum game in which all workplace actors automatically stand to gain.

Training provision involves more than technical questions about how skills are developed: it also has political implications. The character of training provision may reveal much about the prevailing balance of power at the workplace and how material interests are pursued. As Allen (1975:213) observed, skill is the medium through which power is exercised at the workplace. Workers use their skills as tactical resources in pursuing non-managerial goals. Management therefore faces a contradiction, for while the development of new skills may result in an increase in the productive potential of workers, it may also threaten new forms of job control premised on the ownership and utilisation of these skills. Prospects for the emergence of controls over effort may be particularly acute where training takes place in an on-the-job context. Under such circumstances, the knowledge transmitted by workers is likely to include established understandings about the frontier of control and norms relating to effort levels.

There is a need for a better understanding of the objectives that workplace actors seek to achieve as a result of training. To date, little work has been done on the social dynamics of partnership approaches to training. Investigation of apparently successful examples of cooperation is thus required. More needs to be discovered about the means by which trade unions secure a role in training decisions, the problems that partnership may pose for trade union representatives, and the nature and scale of any benefits received by members. Finally, far more has to be discovered about the impact of training activity on economic performance, and the relationship between industrial relations and competitiveness more generally (Nolan, 1993). It should be recognised that the consequences of training for performance will depend upon how, and in whose interests, skills are utilised. Management–worker relations at the point of production will therefore have an important influence on training activity and outcomes. A useful way of taking the empirical agenda forward would be for researchers to engage in intensive investigation of the workplace. Exploration at this level may encourage an analysis of training that is sensitive to production politics, and which treats the definition, acquisition and utilisation of skills as contested features of the employment relationship.

Notes

1   I am grateful for comments made by Helen Rainbird and Mark Stuart on an earlier draft of this chapter.
2   For an exception see Shackleton (1993).
3   Finegold (1991:107) recognises this but fails to fully engage with the implications.

References

Abraham, K. G. and Houseman, S. H. (1993) *Job Security in America: Lessons from Germany*, Washington, DC: Brookings.

Allen, V. L. (1975) *Social Analysis: A Marxist Critique and Alternative*, London: Longman.

Arulampalam, W. and Booth, A. (1998) 'Training and labour market flexibility: is there a trade-off?', *British Journal of Industrial Relations*, 36, 4, 521–36.

Becker, G. S. (1962) 'Investment in human capital: a theoretical analysis', *Journal of Political Economy*, 70, 9–49.

Becker, G. (1975) *Human Capital*, 2nd edn, New York: Columbia University Press.

Bowles, S. and Gintis, H. (1975) 'The problem with human capital theory – a Marxian critique', *American Economic Association*, 65, 2, 74–52.

Buchele, R. and Christiansen, J. (1995) 'Productivity, real wages and worker rights: a cross-national comparison', *Labour*, 9, 3, 405–22.

Caillods, F. (1994) 'Converging trends amidst diversity in vocational training systems', *International Labour Review*, 133, 2, 241–57.

Campinos-Dubernet, M. and Grando, J. (1988) 'Formation professionelle ouvrière: trois modèles européenes', *Formation/Emploi*, 22, 5–29.

Claydon, T. and Green, F. (1994) 'Can trade unions improve training in Britain?', *Personnel Review*, 23, 1, 37–51.

Cordery, J. L., Mueller, W. S. and Sevastos, P. P. (1992) 'Multi-skilling in practice: lessons from a minerals processing firm', *The Journal of Industrial Relations*, 268–83.

Cully, M., O'Reilly, A., Millward, N., Forth, J., Woodland, S., Dix, G. and Bryson, A. (1998) *The 1998 Workplace Employee Relations Survey: First Findings* ESRC/ACAS/PSI/DTI.

Cutler, T. (1992) 'Vocational training and British economic performance: a further instalment of the "British labour problem" ', *Work, Employment and Society*, 6, 2, 161–83.

Daly, A., Hitchens, D. M. W. N. and Wagner, K. (1985) 'Productivity, machinery and skills in a sample of British and German manufacturing plants', *National Institute Economic Review*, February, 48–61.

DfEE (1997a) *Labour Market and Skill Trends 1997/1998*.

DfEE (1997b) *Skills and Enterprise Executive*, 4/97.

DfEE (1998) *The Learning Age: A Renaissance for Britain*, London, The Stationery Office.

Evans, S. (1990) 'Free labour and economic performance: evidence from the construction industry', *Work, Employment and Society*, 4, 2, 239–52.

Felstead, A. and Green, F. (1996) 'Training implications of regulation compliance and business cycles', in Booth, A. L. and Snower, D. J. (eds), *Acquiring Skills: Market Failures, Their Symptoms and Policy Responses*, Cambridge: Cambridge University Press.

Fine, B. (1998) *Labour Market Theory: A Constructive Reassessment*, London: Routledge.

Finegold, D. (1991) 'Institutional incentives and skill creation: preconditions for a high skill equilibrium', in Ryan, P. (ed.), *International Comparisons of Vocational Education and Training for Intermediate Skills*, London: Falmer.

Finegold, D, and Soskice, D. (1988) 'The failure of training in Britain: analysis and prescription', *Oxford Review of Economic Policy*, 4, 3, 21–52.

Ford, G. and Watts, T. (1998) *Trade Unions and Lifelong Guidance*, National Institute for Careers Education and Counselling, London.

Forrester, K. P., James, J. and Thorne, C. (1995) *Training Matters: Vocational Education and Training in the Retail Sector*, Manchester: USDAW.

Freeman, R. B. and Medoff, J. L. (1984) *What Do Unions Do?*, New York: Basic Books.

Fryer, R. H. (1997) *Learning for the Twenty-First Century: First Report of the National Advisory Group for Continuing Education and Lifelong Learning*.

Fuller, A. and M. Saunders (1990) *The Potential Take-Up of Mass Training*, Lancaster: Institute for Research and Development in Post-Compulsory Education, Lancaster University.

Gallie, D., White, M., Cheng, Y. and Tomlinson, M. (1998) *Restructuring the Employment Relationship*, Oxford: Oxford University Press.

Garrahan, P. and Stewart, P. (1992) 'Management control and a new regime of subordination: post-fordism and the local economy', in Gilbert, N., Burrows, R. and Pollert, A. (eds), *Fordism and Flexibility: Divisions and Change*, London: Macmillan.

Geary, J. F. (1992) 'Pay, control and commitment: linking appraisal and reward', *Human Resource Management Journal*, 2, 4, 36–54.

Gemmell, N. (1996) 'Evaluating the impacts of human capital stocks and accumulation on economic growth: some new evidence', *Oxford Bulletin of Economics and Statistics*, 58, 1, 9–28.

Gospel, H. (1995) 'The decline of apprenticeship training in Britain', *Industrial Relations Journal*, 26, 1, 32–44.

Gough, J. (1992) 'Where's the value in "Post-Fordism"?', in Gilbert, N., Burrows, R. and Pollert, A. (eds), *Fordism and Flexibility: Divisions and Change*, London: Macmillan.

Green, F. (1991) 'Sex discrimination in job-related training', *British Journal of Industrial Relations*, 29, 295–304.

Green, F. and Ashton, D. (1992) 'Skill shortages and skill deficiency: a critique', *Work, Employment and Society*, 6, 2, 287–501.

Green, F., Machin, S. and Wilkinson, D. (1996) 'Trade unions and training practices in British workplaces', *Centre for Economic Performance*, Discussion Paper 278.

Greenhalgh, C. and Mavrotas, G. (1994) 'The role of career aspirations and financial constraints in individual access to vocational training', *Oxford Economic Papers*, 46, 579–604.

Grossman, G. M. and Helpman, E. (1991) 'Trade, knowledge spillovers, and growth', *European Economic Review*, 35, 517–26.

Hand, A., Gambles, J. and Cooper, E. (1994) *Individual Commitment to Learning: Individuals' Decision-making About 'Lifetime Learning'*, Employment Department Research Series, No. 42.

Heyes, J. (1993) 'Training provision and workplace institutions: an investigation', *Industrial Relations Journal*, 24, 4, 296–307.

Heyes, J. (1996) 'A formula for success? Training, reward and commitment in a chemicals plant', *British Journal of Industrial Relations*, 34, 3, 351–70.

Heyes, J. and Stuart, M. (1996) 'Does training matter? Employee experiences and attitudes', *Human Resource Management Journal*, 6, 3, 7–21.

Heyes, J. and Stuart, M. (1998a) 'Bargaining for skills: trade unions and training at the workplace', *British Journal of Industrial Relations*, 36, 3, 459–67.

Heyes, J. and Stuart, M. (1998b) 'Training and development: a role for trade unions?', *Centre for Industrial Policy and Performance Bulletin*, No. 12 (Spring) University of Leeds.

Heyes, J. and Stuart, M. (1999) 'Skills matrices, personal development and "business needs": evidence from the engineering sector', mimeo, Leeds University Business School.

Hyman, J. (1992) 'Training and development', in Towers, B. (ed.), *The Handbook of Human Resource Management*, Oxford: Basil Blackwell.

Hyman, J. and Mason, B. (1995) *Managing Employee Involvement and Participation*, London: Sage.

Incomes Data Services (1992) *Skilling Up*, IDS Study, No. 500, February.

Incomes Data Services (1997) *Developing Competency Frameworks*, IDS Study, No. 639, December.

Industrial Relations Review and Report (1990) 'Training – the union perspective', *IRS Employment Trends*, 475.

Jones, B. (1996) 'The social constitution of labour markets: why skills cannot be commodities', in Crompton, R., Gallie, D. and Purcell, K. (eds) *Changing Forms of Employment*, London: Routledge.

Kabst, R., Holt Larsen, H. and Bramming, P. (1996) 'How do lean management organisations behave regarding training and development', *The International Journal of Human Resource Management*, 7, 3, 618–39.

Keep, E. (1989) 'Corporate training strategies: the vital component?', in Storey, J. (ed.), *New Perspectives on Human Resource Management*, London: Routledge.

Keep, E. (1993) 'Missing presumed skilled: training policy in the UK', in Edwards, R., Sieminski, S. and Zeldin, D. (eds), *Adult Learners, Education and Training*, London: Routledge.

Kelly, J. (1996) 'Union militancy and social partnership', in Ackers, P., Smith, C. and Smith, P. (eds), *The New Workplace and Trade Unionism: Critical Perspectives on Work and Organization*, London: Routledge.

Kennedy, S., Drago, R., Sloan, J. and Wooden, M. (1994) 'The effects of trade unions on the provision of training: Australian evidence', *British Journal of Industrial Relations*, 32, 4, 565–80.

Legge, K. (1998) 'Flexibility: the gift-wrapping of employment degradation?', in Sparrow, P. and Marchington, M. (eds), *Human Resource Management: The New Agenda*, London: Financial Times.

Lynch, L. M., 'Introduction', in L. M. Lynch (ed.), *Training and the Private Sector: International Comparisons*, Chicago: University of Chicago Press 1994).

MacDuffie, J. P. and Kochan, T. A. (1995) 'Do US firms invest less in human resources? Training in the world auto industry', *Industrial Relations*, 34, 2, 147–68.

McGivney, V. (1994) *Wasted Potential: Training and Career Progression for Part-Time and Temporary Workers*, Leicester: The National Organisation for Adult Continuing Education.

MacInnes, J. (1987) *Thatcherism at Work: Industrial Relations and Economic Change*, Milton Keynes: Oxford University Press.

Mahnkopf, B. (1992) 'The "skill-oriented" strategies of German trade unions: their impact on efficiency and equality objectives', *British Journal of Industrial Relations*, 30, 1, 61–81.

Marsden, D. and Ryan, P. (1991) 'Initial training, labour market structure and public policy: intermediate skills in British and German industry', in Ryan, P. (ed.), *International Comparisons of Vocational Education and Training for Intermediate Skills*, London: Falmer.

Mason, G., Van Ark, B. and Wagner, K. (1994) 'Productivity, product quality and work-force skills: food processing in four European countries', *National Institute Economic Review*, 1, 62–83.

Mathews, J. (1993) 'The industrial relations of skill formation', *The International Journal of Human Resource Management*, 4, 3, 591–609.

Metcalf, H., Walling, A. and Fogarty, M. (1994) *Individual Commitment to Learning: Employers' Attitudes*, Employment Department Research Series, No. 40.

Millward, N., Stevens, M., Smart, D. and Hawes, W. R. (1992) *Workplace Industrial Relations in Transition*, Aldershot: Dartmouth.

Mincer, J. (1958) 'Investment in human capital and personal income distribution', *The Journal of Political Economy*, LXVI, 4, 281–302.

Mortimer, K. (1990) 'EDAP at Ford: a research note', *Industrial Relations Journal*, 21, 4, 309–14.

Mouriki, A. (1994) 'Flexible working: towards further degradation of work, or escaping from stereotypes', *Warwick Papers in Industrial Relations*, 49.

Munro, A., Rainbird, H. and Holly, L. (1997) *Partners in Workplace Learning: A Report on the Unison/Employer Learning and Development Programme*, London: Unison.

Nolan, P. (1993) 'The past strikes back: industrial relations and UK competitiveness', *University of Leeds Review*, 36, 195–210.

Nolan, P. (1996) 'Industrial relations and performance since 1945', in Beardwell, I. (ed.), *Contemporary Industrial Relations: A Critical Analysis*, Oxford: Oxford University Press.

O'Reilly, J. (1992) 'Where do you draw the line? Functional flexibility, training and skill in Britain and France', *Work, Employment and Society*, 6, 3, 369–96.

Osterman, P. (1995) 'Skill, training and work organization in American establishments', *Industrial Relations*, 34, 2, 125–46.

Oulton, N. (1993) *Workforce Skills and Export Competitiveness: An Anglo-German Comparison*, NIESR Discussion Paper (New Series) No. 47 (July).

Oulton, N., and Steedman, H. (1994) 'The British system of youth training: a comparison with Germany', in Lynch, L. M. (ed.), *Training and the Private Sector: International Comparisons*, Chicago: University of Chicago Press.

Payne, J., Forrester, K. and Ward, K. (1993) *Adult Learners at Work*, Department of Adult Continuing Education, University of Leeds.

Peck, J. (1996) *Work-Place: The Social Regulation of Labor Markets*, New York: The Guilford Press.

Prais, S. J. (1993) *Economic Performance and Education: The Nature of Britain's Deficiencies*, NIESR Discussion Paper Series, No. 52.

Prais, S. J., Jarvis, V. and Wagner, K. (1989) 'Productivity and vocational skills in services in Britain and Germany: hotels', *National Institute Economic Review*, 52–70, November.

Rainbird, H. (1988) 'New technology, training and union strategies', in Hyman, R. and Streeck, W. (eds), *New Technology and Industrial Relations*, Oxford: Basil Blackwell.

Rainbird, H. (1990) *Training Matters: Union Perspectives on Industrial Restructuring and Training*, Oxford: Blackwell.

Rainbird, H. (1994) 'Continuing Training', in Sisson, K. (ed.), *Personnel Management: A Comprehensive Guide to Theory and Practice in Britain*, 2nd edn.

Romer, P. M. (1990) 'Human capital and growth: theory and evidence', *Carnegie-Rochester Conference Series on Public Policy*, 32, 251–86.

Rubery, J. (1989) 'Labour market flexibility in Britain', in Green, F. (ed.), *The Restructuring of the UK Economy*, Hemel Hempstead: Harvester Wheatsheaf.

Soskice, D. (1994) 'Reconciling markets and institutions: the German apprenticeship system', in Lynch, L. M. (ed.), *Training and the Private Sector: International Comparisons*, Chicago: The University of Chicago Press.

Standing, G. (1997) 'Globalization, labour flexibility and insecurity: the era of market regulation', *European Journal of Industrial Relations*, 3,1, 7–37.

Steedman, H. and Wagner, K. (1989) 'Productivity, machinery and skills: clothing manufacture in Britain and Germany', *National Institute Economic Review*, May.

Streeck, W. (1989) 'Skills and the limits of neo-liberalism: the enterprise of the future as a place of learning', *Work, Employment and Society*, 3,1, 89–104.

Streeck, W. (1992a) 'Productive constraints: on the institutional conditions of diversified quality production', in Streeck, W., *Social Institutions and Economic Performance: Institutional Studies of Industrial Relations in Advanced Capitalist Economies*, London: Sage.

Streeck, W. (1992b) 'Training and the new industrial relations: a strategic role for unions?', in Regini, M. (ed.), *The Future of Labour Movements*, London: Sage.

Stuart, M. (1994) 'Training in the printing industry: an investigation into the recruitment, training and retraining agreement', *Human Resource Management Journal*, 4, 2, 62–78.

Stuart, M. (1996) 'The industrial relations of training: a reconsideration of training arrangements', *Industrial Relations Journal*, 27, 3, 253–65.

Tomaney, J. (1990) 'The reality of workplace flexibility', *Capital and Class*, 40, 29–55.

Townley, B. (1989) 'Selection and appraisal: reconstituting "social relation" ', in Storey, J. (ed.), *New perspectives on Human Resource Management*, London: Routledge.

Tremlett, N. and Park, A. (1995) *Individual Commitment to Learning: Comparative Findings for the Surveys of Individuals', Employers' and Providers' Attitudes*, DfEE, Research Series, No. 68.

TUC (1991) *Collective Bargaining Strategy for the 1990s*, London: TUC.

TUC (1995a) *Bargaining for Skills: Trade Unions and Training and Enterprise Councils Working in Partnership for Training*, London: TUC.

TUC (1995b) *Funding Lifelong Learning: A Strategy to Deliver the National Education and Training Targets*, London: TUC.

Waddington, J. and Whitston, C. (1996) 'Empowerment versus intensification: union perspectives of change at the workplace', in Ackers, P., Smith, C. and Smith, P. (eds), *The New Workplace and Trade Unionism: Critical Perspectives on Work and Organization*, London: Routledge.

Williamson, O. E. (1985) *The Economic Institutions of Capitalism: Firms, Markets, Relational Contracting*, New York: The Free Press.

Williamson, O. E., Wachter, M. L. and Harris, J. E. (1975) 'Understanding the employment relation: the analysis of idiosyncratic exchange', *The Bell Journal of Economics*, 6, 250–78.

Willmott, H. (1993) 'Strength is ignorance; slavery is freedom: managing culture in modern organizations', *Journal of Management Studies*, 30, 4, 515–52.

Winterton, J. and Winterton, R. (1994) *Collective Bargaining and Consultation over Continuing Vocational Training*, Sheffield: Employment Department.

CHAPTER 9

The worker basic skills 'crisis': some industrial relations implications

Susan Hoddinott

Introduction

Over the past decade and a half, on both sides of the Atlantic, the idea that workers' literacy or 'basic skills' levels[1] are significantly (and critically) deficient in relation to the requirements of their jobs has been aggressively promoted by sections of business, adult education, the state sector and even organised labour. Indeed, in both North America and UK, the promotion of this idea may be seen to have amounted to a *campaign*, the objective of which has been to persuade employers, policy-makers and the public – including workers themselves – of the seriousness of the putative problem and the urgency of the need for intervention.

One consequence of what may be called the 'workforce literacy campaigns' has been a generalised scapegoating of national workforces, as both company-level failures and national economic crises have been attributed to the quality of the labour supply. Another outcome has been the stigmatisation of workers whose educational credentials or facility with the language of the workplace may be relatively low, irrespective of their ability to do their jobs. In some cases, this has had direct negative consequences for workers as they have been subjected to increased scrutiny at their workplaces through observation, through testing, or through their performance in so-called workplace literacy/basic skills programmes.

This chapter provides a critical examination of the putative worker basic skills crisis and its impact on workers. It argues that the current consensus that workers' literacy skills are critically deficient in relation to the demands of their jobs has not arisen in response to a growing and manifest problem; on the contrary, it is a consensus which has needed to be constructed. For, though individual workers may indeed aspire to improve their educational credentials, there is little evidence to support the idea that workers' intellectual skills/educational qualifications are inadequate for the jobs they are doing; on the contrary, there is substantial evidence that workers in general possess qualifications beyond the requirements of their jobs.

A particular focus of the chapter is the industrial relations implications of the general acceptance of the 'fact' of widespread worker basic skills deficits and, in respect of this, the position of trade unions on the issue is examined. The chapter concludes that the impacts on workers stemming from an acceptance of the idea of a basic skills crisis – including increased scrutiny of literacy and language competencies of workers and the promotion and establishment of 'basic skills' programmes of questionable value in workplaces – ought to give cause for those unions which have endorsed claims of a 'crisis' and embraced the idea of workplace literacy programmes to re-evaluate their position. Such an evaluation, it is suggested, should be guided by an acknowledgement and reassessment of the principal worker issues involved: the educational needs or desires of formally undereducated workers on the one hand, and the training needs of low-paid and manual workers on the other hand. Some considerations with respect to reassessing these issues are presented and alternative approaches are proposed.

A 'crisis' of worker basic skills

By 1987 the movement to reform education in the USA had focused its attention squarely on the supposed impacts of education on the national economy and the role of the present (allegedly poorly educated) workforce in America's fall from global pre-eminence. The position was stated most succinctly in a report entitled *Workforce 2000: Work and Workers in the 21st Century*, prepared for the US Department of Labor by the conservative think tank, the Hudson Institute:

> Unconstrained by shortages of competent, well-educated workers, American industry would be able to expand and develop as rapidly as world markets would allow. Boosted by the productivity of [a] well-qualified workforce, US-based companies would reassert historic American leadership in old and new industries, and American workers would enjoy the rising standards of living they enjoyed in the 1950s and 1960s. (Johnston and Packer, 1987:116)

Workforce 2000 was a media hit in the USA; the 'crisis' it foretold was featured on the covers of all the nation's major newspapers and magazines.

The report's impact on the re-emerging adult literacy 'crisis' in the USA would be instantaneous. *Workforce 2000* lent both credibility and support to the process of transforming America's recurrent 'crisis' of adult illiteracy into a crisis of worker illiteracy, a process already well under way in most of the country in 1987. The 'crisis' of worker illiteracy would spill outside the USA's borders as well. In Canada, for example, two highly publicised surveys in this period reported that illiteracy among workers cost the country's industries billions of dollars annually (Creative Research Group, 1987; Canadian Business Task Force on Literacy, or CBTFL, 1988). And in the UK the central government agency for literacy, the Adult Literacy and Basic Skills Unit (ALBSU: since 1994, the Basic Skills Unit) commissioned a survey of employers in 1990 aimed at determining the costs of 'poor basic skills' to business and industry (Kempa, 1993). The survey report concluded that worker basic skills deficiencies cost UK industries £4.8 billion annually.

The OECD would also follow the trend established by the USA in its 1992 publication, *Adult Illiteracy and Economic Performance*, addressing the issue of literacy problems among workers in OECD countries. The report's starting position reflected the contemporary Canadian, American and UK analyses. Literacy levels in the years ahead, it asserted, would be 'intrinsically ... tied to the capacity of firms and nations to respond to economic challenges' (Benton and Noyelle, 1992:9).

In publications and reports such as these – of which there were literally hundreds produced in North America in the decade following *Workforce 2000* – literacy levels of the workforce (and education levels more generally) have been not only credited with determining the ability of nations to compete in the global economy; but they have also been used, in crude applications of human capital theory, to rationalise falling wages and benefits within nations. In the USA, for example, worker illiteracy has provided a 'natural' explanation for the dramatic decline in wages and fall in living standards experienced by the majority of the American workforce over the past two decades (see, for example, Reich, 1992).

Examining the 'crisis' and its impact on workers

Is there a crisis of worker basic skills? A critical examination of the evidence

In their attempts to make the problem of worker illiteracy 'real' in the public imagination, to impress on employers the impacts of the putative problem on company profits, and to persuade public policy-makers of its impacts on national competitiveness, those who have campaigned on the issue of workforce illiteracy on both sides of the Atlantic have tended to overstate any actual problem which may exist. They have also tended to distort both the nature and the potential impacts of literacy or language difficulties in the workplace.

It has been in Canada and UK that officially sponsored or government sanctioned 'documentation' of worker basic skills deficits has made the strongest claims to authoritativeness. The CBTFL, founded in 1985 for the purpose of promoting 'awareness' of worker illiteracy among employers, claimed, in a highly publicised 1988 report, that illiterate workers cost Canadian employers $4 billion annually through such effects of illiteracy as industrial accidents, low productivity and absenteeism (CBTFL, 1988). Though the CBTFL figures would pass for the first empirical account of the problem for Canada, they were based on nothing more than the 'estimates and educated guesses of [mainly American] experts' (CBTFL, 1988). Similarly, in the UK, the central government's ALBSU claimed, on the basis of a 1990 telephone survey of personnel and training managers, that problems associated with workers' basic skills deficits cost UK employers £4.8 billion annually (Kempa, 1993).

Surveys and reports such as these – all undertaken to encourage employers to support workplace basic skills programmes – have played an important role in the workforce literacy campaigns, providing the 'hard evidence' which those promoting such programmes at 'ground level' have used to generate regional, local and even firm-specific estimates of the extent of worker basic skills deficits. To a large extent, however, claims of significant worker basic skills deficits in all three countries have been made without any supporting evidence, even of the questionable kind provided by the surveys described above. Unsupported generalisations and unsubstantiated stories appear in the majority of accounts of the 'problem'. An article in a 1986 newsletter of the US Business Council for Effective Literacy (BCEL) like the CBTFL, a corporate foundation founded for the express purpose of waging a public campaign on the issue – illustrates well the casual attitude towards substantiation which has characterised most media accounts of the putative problem in North America. Indeed, though it presented the problem entirely through the presentation of undocumented 'cases' and apocryphal anecdotes, the article would become the cited source for many subsequent accounts of the issue by the media as well as many other participants in the workforce literacy campaigns (BCEL, No. 8, 1986:3). The article is also noteworthy for its presentation of the 'nature' of worker illiteracy, a presentation which employed all the stereotypical images of the adult illiterate as not only fundamentally illiterate, but also unintelligent, deceptive and, ultimately, very dangerous. Because, as noted, the images would be recycled in a range of campaign literature (including popular media accounts) over the decade, the BCEL article warrants particular attention here. The unnamed author of the article provided a number of 'profiles' of illiterate workers and, though some were given the stamp of authenticity through being identified with a well-known company, no source was given for the information. The profiles included a Ford Motor employee who had 'bluffed his way' through job application, memos, and instruction manuals (even his high school equivalency exam pass had been 'pure guess-work'), and a welder who had 'cheated his way through welding school' and whose inability to read the word *clockwise* had led him to install an industrial blower incorrectly, costing the company 'thousands of dollars'. The article also included a number of anecdotes, none of which were attributed and all of which had the distinct ring of 'urban myths'. They included the story of a feed-lot labourer who had killed a herd of cattle by accidentally feeding them bags of poison, and a steel-mill worker whose misordering of spare parts resulted in a $1 million cost to the company.

The contrary evidence: the underutilisation of workers' qualifications and skills

It is an irony that a crisis of worker literacy has been proclaimed at a time when general educational attainments on both sides of the Atlantic have reached unprecedented levels. In contrast to the types of subjective and spec-ulative 'evidence' put forward to support the thesis of a crisis of worker liter-acy, the evidence of rising educational attainment among workers in both North America and UK is clear and unequivocal. As early as 1970, 'overedu-cation' – in the sense of workers having both educational qualifications and skills which they were neither required nor entitled to bring to their employ-ment – was identified as a growing problem. The 'credential inflation' identi-fied by Berg (1970) continued unabated in both the USA and Canada through-out the 1970s and 1980s. In respect of the USA, Rumberger reported that the number of college graduates in the labour market had increased three-fold between 1960 and 1980, with the result that by 1980 almost 20 per cent of all US workers (and more than 25 per cent of young workers) had completed four years or more of college (1984:343). As he also documented, however, the growth in the number of highly-skilled jobs had not kept pace with rising edu-cational attainments and, as a consequence, it is estimated that 25–50 per cent of recent college graduates are overqualified for their current jobs. According to the US Bureau of Labor Statistics, there was an estimated surplus of 3.8 mil-lion college graduates in the American labour force in 1980 (Rumberger, 1984). In Canada, a similar pattern has been documented; citing 1989 Canadian data on the 'formal mismatch' between employees' educational attainments and the job-entry requirements established by employers, Livingstone noted that 'nearly a third of all employed university graduates had jobs that did not need a degree, over 40 per cent of those with college certificates had jobs which required less formal schooling, and about a third of the workers with high school diplomas had jobs that did not need those diplomas' (1996:80–1). Analysing data from a 1989 Canadian literacy survey, Boothby (1993) reported that a large majority of Canadian workers possess reading abilities greater than the reading requirements of their jobs as rated by the federal employment department's General Educational Development index.

Although extensive participation in higher education is a more recent phenomenon in the UK, a recent study by the Confederation of British Industry (CBI, 1994) indicates that the trend in that country is similar to the North American case. The study reports that, 'Many graduates are now entering first and second jobs which had traditionally been filled by schoolleavers', and that 'at least a quarter of private sector employers substituted graduates for non-graduates between 1985 and 1988' (quoted in Brown, 1994:612).

In spite of the strong evidence of significant overeducation (in relation to the demands of paid work), there remains considerable support for the argument that workers in general are *underprepared*. In large measure, claims of worker underpreparedness are sustained not in terms of current performance in existing jobs, but on the basis of assumptions about the changing nature of work. The conviction that work is in the process of radical overall 'upskilling', and that the pace of change in the skill composition of work will become even more rapid in the near future, underlies arguments for continuing high (individual) investments in higher education. And, as documented in the first section of this chapter, it is also the basis for much of the workforce illiteracy diagnosis.

Many analysts have challenged these assumptions. Mishel and Teixeira, for example, have provided a systematic critique of one of the most influential American 'upskilling' texts, *Workforce 2000*, a report which, as already noted, did much to boost the fledgeling American workforce literacy campaign. The report's analysis of future job skill requirements was based on an interpretation of forecasted occupational shifts (Johnston and Packer, 1987). The authors argued:

> the jobs created between 1987 and 2000 will be substantially different from those in existence today. A number of jobs in the least-skilled classes will disappear while high-skilled professions will grow rapidly. Overall, the skill mix of the economy will be moving rapidly upscale, with most new jobs demanding more education and higher levels of language, math and reasoning skills (1987:96)

Analysing the same data (from the Bureau of Labor Statistics) on which the authors of Workforce 2000 based their claims, Mishel and Teixeira (1991) take issue with both the claim that shifts in the distribution of jobs will result in overall upskilling and the contention that changes in the tasks required in given jobs will have the effect of increasing the skill composition of those jobs. With respect to the first claim, they note that there is 'much less change ... occurring in the overall distribution of jobs' than is generally believed

(1991:101). While they concede that the fastest occupational growth is in some of the most highly skilled occupational groups, they note that these groups are quite small to begin with and, even given relatively higher growth, net employment in these groups will remain small. They observe that the data in Workforce 2000 itself show that the five most highly skilled occupational groups (including the three fastest-growing groups) will constitute only 10.6 per cent of net new jobs between 1984 and 2000 and, by 2000, will still make up only 6.1 per cent of the overall job pool (1991).

Some impacts of the workforce literacy campaigns on workers

Clearly, there is scope for a variety of employer and state responses to widespread illiteracy among workers, whether imputed or real. Responses will be conditioned by the general political and economic environment, however. Employers' responses to the presumption of illiteracy among either their existing workforces or job applicants, for example, will reflect the price of labour as well as the degree of choice they may exercise in terms of the selection and retention/disposal of workers. These, in turn, will be influenced by the level of unemployment (either locally, regionally or nationally), the availability and level of benefits for the unemployed, the density and strength of worker organisation, the general labour relations environment, and the degree of state regulation of employment practices. Public policy responses will reflect, among other factors, the general political and economic goals of governing parties as well as their particular approaches to labour force development.

Notwithstanding the scope for variable response (and the real potential for punitive responses on the part of employers), many of those who have campaigned on the issue, including organised labour, have tended to take the optimistic view. Employers, it has been assumed, will either institute workplace programmes themselves or facilitate the establishment of programmes by other agencies if they can be persuaded that worker illiteracy threatens profitability. In fact, such views are not warranted in the current period, if, indeed, they ever are. On the contrary, the political and economic context of recent campaigns to create an issue of worker illiteracy has shaped both employer and public policy responses in ways which have further disadvantaged less formally qualified workers both in the labour market and in their workplaces. The campaigns – including efforts by educationalists as well as trade unions to promote the establishment of targeted basic skills programmes – have all potentially jeopardised the job security of workers and have contributed to creating an environment in which workers are more likely to be subjected to unwarranted scrutiny and in which a range of punitive employer and public policy measures may appear to be reasonable and legitimate responses to alleged basic skills deficits.

The problematising of workers' literacy/basic skills competencies described here has taken place in the context of increasing employment insecurity in both North America and England. Continuing high levels of unemployment in Canada and England, and periodic sharp rises in unemployment in the USA, have resulted in the permanent removal from the labour force of a significant proportion of those displaced from work over the past two decades. Many others have succeeded in retaining only the most tenuous connection to paid work, typically in temporary and part-time jobs with the minimum legislated conditions and benefits of employment (Schachter, 1995; Hughes, 1996). The 'filtering down' of workers with more formal qualifications has meant that those with fewer qualifications are disproportionately represented among both the unemployed and the underemployed (Atkinson, 1992; Kirsch, Jungeblut and Campbell, 1992; Statistics Canada, 1996). Furthermore, the relative decline of employment in manufacturing sectors in all three countries has had an especially pronounced impact on workers with less formal qualifications. At the same time as the pool of available jobs for the less formally qualified has shrunk, the trend towards 'credential inflation' has heightened. On both sides of the Atlantic, as noted above, increasing numbers have continued into post-secondary education and generally high rates of unemployment have allowed employers to increase entry requirements and recruit more formally qualified workers without additional cost (Brown, 1994; Gordon, 1996; Livingstone, 1996). In such a climate, the likelihood of an applicant with any degree of literacy (or language) difficulty being hired (or retained) is remote, *except where such competencies are not an issue for the employer*. In spite of this, however, the marketing of workplace literacy programmes in both North America and England has centred on the generalised problematising of workers with less formal qualifications for, though workforce literacy campaigners generally pay lip service to the notion that basic skills problems may be found throughout the employment hierarchy, it is invariably workers with low qualifications, low skills, low wages, and low English (and, in Canada, French) proficiency who are identified as likely to have problems and who are targeted by workplace literacy programmes (see, for example, Rees, 1990; Wellborn, 1990; Ioannou *et al.*, 1991).

The arguments put forward by those promoting workplace literacy programmes (including purely speculative claims about the extent of worker literacy deficit and the impacts of the supposed deficits in the workplace) have potentially lent support to the weeding-out of the less formally qualified; and by supporting the generalised raising of hiring criteria, they have also potentially furthered the marginalisation of all less formally qualified workers, both employed and unemployed. In Ontario, Canada, for example, a government publication advised employers to review their hiring, promotion and other human resource practices to ensure that they clearly specified prerequisite skills. It also advised them not to take the literacy skills of workers for granted, but to search for evidence of illiteracy (Ontario Ministry of Skills Development, undated). Similarly, the national employer survey conducted by the ALBSU in the UK strongly emphasised the potential losses to firms which neglected to screen job applicants for literacy competence. The report on the survey stated that the 'relatively large proportion of companies not testing specific skills, *especially at blue collar level*, could lead to the recruitment of staff inadequately skilled in reading, writing, numeracy and verbal communications' (Kempa, 1993:25; emphasis added).

The extension of employer prerogative and increased scrutiny of workers is justified

Those campaigning on the issue of worker basic skills deficits not only assume the establishment (and changing) of hiring criteria and the indiscriminate use of testing to be the undisputed prerogative of the employer; they also typically assume that employers are not making sufficient use of their prerogative to ensure the profitability or safety of their enterprises. Such assumptions are, of course, far from the truth; most trade unions would acknowledge the critical importance – to seniority and job security, for example – of limiting employers' prerogative in this respect. It is in the USA, however, where – in the context of the struggle over civil rights – employers' prerogative in respect of the selection and *de*selection of workers through either testing or the setting of hiring criteria has been most successfully contested and where legislated protections for workers have been gained. Because the US case illustrates so concretely the potential of the workforce literacy campaigns to influence regressive change in respect of these issues, it warrants particular attention here.

At issue has been Title VII of the Civil Rights Act of 1964 which prohibits the use of testing to influence any employment decision if it results in discrimination (Philippi, 1993). The act requires that, before a test can be used to influence an employment decision, it must be 'validated' for job-relatedness. This means that the employer must be able to demonstrate a high correlation between successful test performance and successful job performance. Further, unless job progression is likely within a 'reasonable period of time', employees can only be tested at or near the entry level for the position (BCEL, No. 17, 1988:6). The workforce literacy campaigns have presented employers with both a justification and a process for the broadening of 'job-relatedness', in the form of the 'literacy task analysis'. Widely used in the USA and Canada, literacy task analyses – as used by would-be programme deliverers to establish the need for their services – have purported to demonstrate that even the most menial and unskilled of jobs require the exercise of highly-developed cognitive abilities and advanced literacy and language skills. The implications for rendering a wider range of tests legally defensible in the context of the US legislation are clear. Thomas Sticht, the internationally renowned workplace literacy 'expert', advised American employers that, while general literacy tests would probably fail to meet the legal requirements imposed by Title VII, tests based on specific literacy analysis of the job could be shown to have 'content validity', and could thus be defended in the courts if necessary (quoted in BCEL, No. 22, 1990:6).

As Title VII also prohibits the use by the employer of educational requirements not warranted by the duties and responsibilities of the job, it is clear that employers have an interest in defining literacy (and thus educational) requirements of jobs as broadly as possible. As an article in the BCEL *Newsletter* noted, courts 'had often overturned high-school-diploma requirements for production, maintenance, and apprenticeship positions where the result is discriminatory. Lower and more specifically defined education level requirements have been approved for such relatively low-skilled jobs' (BCEL, No. 17, 1988:6–7). Again, because the literacy task analysis process typically ascribes literacy content to virtually all jobs – including those where workers themselves claim no reading and writing is required – its potential for the rationalisation of inflated job qualification requirements is clear.

Issues and problems associated with workplace literacy/basic skills programmes

Job security issues

Arguably the most problematic aspect of locating literacy/basic skills programmes at the workplace – or, indeed, of targeting particular workers for basic skills programming at the workplace or elsewhere – is the identification (either implicit or explicit) of literacy or basic skills deficiencies and the potentially negative impacts this may have on the job security or promotion prospects of the workers so identified. That the threat posed by so-called 'basic skills assessments' which typically precede the institution of a workplace programme – and, indeed, by participation in the programme itself – is real is evidenced in the responses of employers to questions on the issue. US executives surveyed in 1989, for example, reported that they would not expect workers to come forward for basic skills assessment or programmes for a number of reasons (Omega Group, 1989:17). One respondent cited the very real likelihood that any workers who did so 'would be stigmatised by the organisation ... and [their] progress within the company would suffer, both in terms of promotions and salary increases'. Another stated that a worker who 'comes forward with a literacy problem and is unable to successfully complete the program would be publicly known to have failed, and other job capabilities and his future potential would be questioned'.

There is substantial evidence in the reports on workplace literacy promotion that workers are, indeed, well aware of the potential for just such responses on the part of the employer. Various accounts of the institution of a workplace literacy programme in a north-west of England heating plant, for example, attest to the fact that not only the pre-programme 'basic skills assessment' but participation in the programme itself caused participants to feel vulnerable to punitive action including job loss (see, for example, Frank, 1990; Nieduszynska, 1992).

Another aspect of participation in workplace literacy/basic skills programmes which potentially compromises job security relates to the expectations which employers (and, indeed, workers themselves) may attach to that participation. Those who promote workplace literacy/basic programmes as the answer to alleged workforce literacy deficits generally make claims for the benefits which workers and employers can derive from such programmes out of all proportion to the capacity of the programmes to deliver. For, although workplace literacy/basic skills programmes are typically very time-limited (frequently providing only one or two hours a week of instruction and as few as 20 hours in total), programme deliverers may lead both the participating workers and their employers to believe that significant gains in literacy/language and/or numeracy skills can be achieved. Many go further, and claim that measurable impacts (of the improved literacy/language/numeracy skills) on productivity, safety, and service can be achieved. And many also make claims for the value of their programmes to the successful implementation of new work organisation or new management regimes (see, for example, Ioannou *et al.*, 1991; McIntyre, 1991; Workbase Training, undated).

In many cases, deliverers not only promise significant change but, in order to demonstrate the effectiveness of their programmes, they also provide post-programme assessments of participants or encourage and assist employers in carrying out their own assessments. In the USA, the most common method of evaluation is the use of standardised tests (of reading, mathematics, or English as a Second Language) before and after the programme (Schultz, 1992). This presents a potentially serious threat for the workers/participants who are expected to make measurable (and significant) literacy, numeracy or language gains – as defined by standardised tests – on the basis of instruction which is generally directly job-based and which is typically of less than 120 hours' duration. Failure to do so might reasonably be interpreted by the employer as a negative indication of the worker's ability and potential, since the programme deliverers have, through the employment of such tests, declared an expectation of measurable gains to be warranted. Other methods of evaluation which have been employed by US workplace literacy programme deliverers – and endorsed by the federal government's National Workplace Literacy Program – include establishing productivity ratings for individuals against which future gains may be measured, monitoring employees' safety records, assessing employees' attitudes and ('where the workers' abilities have a direct impact on company sales') measuring sales volumes (Evaluation Research, 1992:37–8).

Although there has not been extensive use of standardised testing in workplace literacy programmes in Canada and England, most deliverers either implicitly or explicitly promise improved job performance as a result of worker participation in their programmes (see, for example, Ioannou, *et al.*, 1991; Workbase Training, undated). In many cases, deliverers actually encourage employers to conduct assessments of worker performance and attitude after participation in programmes.

Quality of training opportunity is low

In general, the quality of learning opportunity offered to workers who enrol in workplace literacy/basic skills programmes is low. Among the principal reasons for this is that such programmes are not generally strongly supported by employers; in fact, the majority of workplace literacy programmes on both sides of the Atlantic have been 'one-off' ventures supported by state funding as 'demonstration' projects to persuade employers of their value. As such, they have tended to be experimental, generally eschewing established literacy or language curricula in order to be seen as 'relevant' to immediate workplace needs. In a number of cases, the prohibition of the use of 'traditional' methods or 'academic' curricula has been stipulated by the programme funders.[2] They have also, as noted above, tended to be of very short duration, with the instructional time dictated by the available funding (which, whether provided by the employer, the union or the state, is usually strictly limited) or by the employer's willingness to make the necessary accommodations including providing instructional space and time off work, for example. Pedagogical issues rarely, if ever, enter into considerations about programming arrangements.

In North America, quality of opportunity has been further compromised by the widespread use of both unqualified and unpaid labour in the delivery of workplace literacy programmes. Voluntary literacy organisations, educational institutions and trade unions have all endorsed the participation of volunteer tutors in the delivery of programmes. Indeed, in Canada, volunteer teaching by fellow union members has been adopted as the model of choice for workplace basic skills by the Canadian Labour Congress, and several member federations of the Congress have obtained state funding to organise programmes on this model.

Trade unions and the worker basic skills 'crisis': rethinking the issues

Union concurrence with workforce illiteracy diagnosis is problematic

Though trade unionists have in some cases disputed the notion of workers' culpability in company failure, economic decline, industrial accidents and the range of other supposed impacts of worker illiteracy, they have generally failed to counter the claim that worker illiteracy is widespread. On the contrary, they have in many instances been central to the promotion of worker illiteracy as a problem, including to their own members and their members' employers.[3] They have also been strong and influential advocates of specially targeted 'basic skills' programmes to address the 'problem', in many cases becoming the organisers or deliverers of such programmes.

The extent to which trade union leadership and shopfloor representatives believe that workers have significant literacy or basic skills problems is difficult to assess. There is evidence, however, that in many cases unions are adopting the opportunistic position which many professional educationalists have done with respect to the issue: if governments and business interests are arguing that a section of the workforce is underskilled, then this can only support unions' training objectives, whether in collective bargaining or in broader 'human resource' policy development. As expressed by the American Federation of Labor–Congress of Industrial Organizations (AFL–CIO), for example, 'The heightened public interest in workplace literacy gives a special timeliness to unions' initiatives in worker education. So does the widespread national concern about maintaining a skilled and competitive workforce in a changing economy' (Sarmiento and Kay, 1990:14).

Given the arguments which are generally used to support claims of worker illiteracy, the ways in which presumed illiterate workers are typically portrayed, and the very real potential for punitive employer measures in response to suspected or demonstrated illiteracy, trade union support for such claims, whether implicit or explicit, is problematic, both for their own membership and (arguably even more so) for workers in general. It must be borne in mind that the majority of workers likely to be suspected of basic skills deficits or subject to 'basic skills assessments' – workers in unskilled jobs, workers with low formal qualifications and workers who do not speak the language of the workplace as their first language – are not members of unions (Rainbird, 1994; Rubery, 1995). This is particularly true of the USA, where union density is among the lowest in the Western industrialised world and where, incidentally, the majority of workforce literacy campaigning has occurred. Where unskilled workers are unionised, it has not been common practice for their unions to negotiate for either initial or recurrent training for them. In all workplaces, whether unionised or not, the majority of training opportunities are provided for skilled sections of the workforce (craft, technical and professional workers) and management staff (Canadian Labour Market and Productivity Centre, or CLMPC, 1991; Rothwell, 1993). Indeed, as the preceding section argued, even in those cases where the rhetoric about worker literacy deficit (or the use of tests or 'basic skills assessments') is matched by the provision of workplace literacy/basic skills programmes, this may not be to the benefit of the workers involved.

The presumption by many unions that certain sections of their membership would be best served by workplace-based or worker-targeted 'basic skills' programmes has caused them to overlook other types of programme which may be both more useful in the context of the workplace and more suited to the parameters of workplace-based training. For the endorsement by trades unionists of short courses as an appropriate response to 'illiteracy' or so-called 'basic skills deficits' betrays a misunderstanding of the nature of adult illiteracy and adult undereducation. Courses of 100–200 hours' duration (and workplace programmes are typically much shorter) offer little opportunity for significant change in fundamental abilities. Furthermore, if workers are disadvantaged at the workplace because they lack educational credentials, then no amount of 'basic skills' tuition will ameliorate that disadvantage if it does not also provide formal and recognised credentials. Yet many of the workplace 'literacy' or 'basic skills' programmes which have received public funds are defined explicitly as alternatives to formal programme options which offer credentials.[4] Even where literacy programmes offer credentials (as they generally now do in the UK, for example), a 'basic skills' credential runs the real risk of serving merely as a marker of low attainment.

For workers who have actual literacy problems, workplace literacy programmes can offer little, if any, benefit. And, considering that they frequently involve the administration of standardised reading tests (both pre- and post-programming), they generally entail a certain amount of anxiety and a considerable degree of risk. Adults who have completed several years of schooling but remain unable to read and write with reasonable facility frequently manifest significant learning problems and require the attention of well-trained teachers and a variety of high quality learning resources. Many have identifiable learning disabilities which may require the intervention of learning specialists.

Need for a re-evaluation of issues involved

The nature of trade union involvement in supporting and/or delivering workplace basic skills or literacy programmes suggests the need for a re-evaluation of two separate issues. The first is that of access to training opportunities for those classes of workers typically excluded from employment-based skills training. The second relates to the needs of workers for whom literacy difficulties or lack of facility with the language of the workplace may either threaten employment security or present obstacles to mobility in internal labour markets or to the take-up of training opportunities. In many (and perhaps most) cases, the issues of access to training opportunities and literacy/language difficulties are not significantly related. It cannot be assumed that either literacy or language difficulties affect workers' competence to do their jobs; undereducated and limited English proficiency workers are seldom hired without the employer's knowledge, and the jobs they occupy are generally organised to minimise or eliminate the need for either literacy or language. Employment-based training for work which entails little or no reading or writing is also unlikely to require significant exercise of literacy competencies. Indeed, it may be argued that the assumption that any degree of educational, literacy or language deficit is necessarily reflected in diminished ability to perform at work or in training programmes has been one of the central misrepresentations of proponents of workplace literacy programmes.

If the motivation for trade union involvement in workplace basic skills and literacy programmes is to secure greater equality of access to training opportunities for all classes of workers, then there are obvious difficulties with the way in which the objective has been pursued. Promoting training on the basis of worker deficit – as such programmes typically are – can do little to advance the position of marginalised workers either in their workplaces or in external labour markets. If the objective of equal access to training were to be pursued meaningfully, it would first be necessary to determine what types of training would actually advantage the workers in question; it would then be necessary to plan for the delivery of training in a manner which would optimise the benefits which might accrue to participating workers. It is clear that the 'deficit' approach to training opportunities which has characterised the promotion of literacy/basic skills programmes has little possibility of positively affecting workers' earnings, promotion prospects or job security, except insofar as they function as selection sites and result in such gains for a select few. Since the majority of such programmes are premised on the assumption that workers are not fully competent to perform the jobs they are now in, it would seem the best they could offer workers would be the hope of keeping their current jobs and maintaining their present benefits. But, since in many cases expectations about what such programmes can achieve are unrealistically high and workers are apt to be assessed on the basis of expectations (as measured by standardised tests or workplace performance) rather than on the actual programme content, it is arguably just as likely that participation may actually jeopardise job security.

If unions were to approach bargaining for training for those in manual and low-paid work from the perspective of securing equality of training opportunity rather than from a perspective of deficit, it is unlikely that workplace 'basic skills' programmes would feature at the top of any priority list. More likely to be at the top of such a list would be those very necessary types of training which have direct and immediate impacts on the quality of working life but to which many manual and low-paid workers (both unionised and non-unionised) never gain access. These would include, for example, induction training and health and safety training, the content of which could fit within the time-frames usually negotiated for workplace basic skills programmes far better than the basic skills programmes themselves do.

Apart from the question of the content of training, unions also need to give priority consideration to the conditions under which training takes place. The method of delivery of programmes, the language in which training is delivered and the level at which it is pitched, the timing of programme delivery and arrangements for time off work: all of these are critical to whether a worker is able to either take up training opportunities or significantly benefit from them. In order to ensure that opportunities are both meaningful and equitable, unions will need to become strong advocates for training which is responsive to the needs of particular classes of workers. Workers who have been hired in the knowledge that they are not fluent in the language of the workplace, for example, should not be required to attain second-language fluency in order to gain access to necessary training. Similarly, training for jobs which require little or no exercise of literacy skills should not be pitched at a level (or delivered through a medium) which requires highly-developed literacy skills. Scheduling of training should ensure that shift workers are not excluded from training opportunities. And workers should not be required (or expected) to participate in work-related training outside their normal working hours; it needs to be recognised that, even where compensation is awarded for after-work participation, there are many workers (women, in particular) whose after-work responsibilities make it impossible for them to participate.

If a union's assessment of its members' training needs or aspirations indicates interest in (or need for) either basic education or language training, provision for such training would be best achieved through negotiating for paid educational leave. Since the admission of basic educational need generally presents the possibility of employers taking punitive action, workers would be well advised not to reveal such need at the workplace; and unions would best serve their membership by negotiating a general entitlement to paid leave to attend any formal educational or training programme of the worker's choice. There are models of such negotiated leave, where the focus is on entitlement rather than deficit, and where a degree of confidentiality is assured.

With respect to the issue of access to basic education and language services for workers, organised labour will need to recognise that such services properly fall, along with other basic education services, within the domain of the welfare state. This means that appropriate trade union responses ought to concentrate, first, on influencing the development of state adult basic education provision so that it more adequately reflects the level and type of need as well as the potential demand; and, second, on facilitating access to these state services for their members. The example of Italian trade unions' efforts to secure basic education services for their members, initially undertaken in 1972 by the metalworkers' union, and eventually influencing virtually all collective bargaining and ultimately the general state provision of basic education opportunities for adults in that country, illustrates the potential for organised labour to influence public policy on adult basic education in just such a broadly progressive way.[5]

Notes

1   The reader will note that the terms 'literacy' and 'basic skills' are used interchangeably throughout the chapter, and also the terms 'illiteracy' and 'basic skills deficits'. This reflects the interchangeability of the terms in the public discourse on the issue.

2   Such was the case, for example, with the US National Workplace Literacy Program and the Massachusetts statewide Workplace Education Initiative (Hikes, 1991; Evaluation Research, 1992).

3   In Canada and the USA, the major trade union federations – the Canadian Labour Congress and the AFL-CIO – and many of their affiliates have been participants in the public discourse on workforce illiteracy and have largely concurred with public policy-makers and business and industry interest groups on both the existence of widespread basic skills deficit in the workforce and the kinds of intervention which can appropriately address the problem (see, for example, Sarmiento and Kay, 1990; Turk and Unda, 1991). In these countries, trade unions have also developed and operated workplace literacy programmes both independently and as participants with employer representatives on programme management boards. Although labour has had less of a public role in the worker literacy issue in the UK, one of the main deliverers of workplace literacy programmes in that country and a principal promoter of the idea of worker basic skills deficits, Workbase

Training, has had the support of the TUC, as well as several member unions, from its inception as a project of the National Union of Public Employees in 1978.

4   This is true, for example, of the workplace basic skills programmes operated by member unions of the Canadian Labor Congress. It was also the case with programmes funded under the US National Workplace Literacy Program.

5   Meghnagi (1997) provides a full discussion of the '150 hours policy', including its broader societal impacts.

References

Atkinson, J. (1992) 'Swimming against the tide: literacy difficulties and the labour market', *Education and Training*, 34, 2, 11–17.

BCEL, *Newsletter*, various issues.

Benton, L. A. and Noyelle, T. (1992) *Adult Illiteracy and Economic Performance*, Paris: OECD.

Berg, I. (1970) *Education and Jobs: The Great Training Robbery*, Harmondsworth: Penguin.

Boothby, D. (1993) 'Schooling, literacy and the labour market: towards a "Literacy Shortage"?' *Canadian Public Policy – Analyse de Politiques*, xix, 1, 29–35.

Brown, P. (1994) 'Education, training and economic change', review article, *Work, Employment and Society*, 8, 4, 607–21.

CBI (1994) *Thinking Ahead: Ensuring the Expansion of Higher Education in the 21st Century*, London: CBI.

CBTFL (1988) *Measuring the Costs of Illiteracy in Canada*, Toronto: CBTFL.

CLMPC (1991) *National Training Survey*, Ottawa: CLMPC.

The Creative Research Group (1987) *Literacy in Canada: A Research Report*, Toronto: Southam Newspaper Group.

Evaluation Research (1992) *Workplace Education: Voices from the Field*, Washington, DC: US Department of Education.

Frank, F. (1990) 'Partnership in practice: an account of a basic skills training scheme at a heating engineering company in the north west of England', unpublished project for Open University Professional Diploma in Post Compulsory Education.

Gordon, D. M. (1996) 'Underpaid workers, bloated corporations: two pieces in the puzzle of US Economic decline', *Dissent*, Spring, 23–4.

Hikes, J. (1991) 'The Massachusetts workplace education program', *Basic Skills in the Workplace*, in Taylor, M. C., Lewe, G. R. and Draper, J. A. (eds), Toronto: Culture Concepts.

Hughes, J. (1996) 'Disappearing jobs, falling incomes', *European Labour Forum*, 17, 25–9.

Ioannou, M., Nore, G., Poulton, B. and Thompson, S. (1991) 'How to assess learners and build workplace literacy programs', *Basic Skills for the Workplace*, in Taylor, M. C., Lewe, G. R. and Draper, J. A. (eds), Toronto: Culture Concepts.

Johnston, W. B. and Packer, A. H. (1987) *Workforce 2000: Work and Workers for the Twenty-first Century*, Indianapolis: Hudson Institute.

Kempa, S. (1993) *The Cost to Industry: Basic Skills and the UK Workforce*, London: ALBSU.

Kirsch, I. S., Jungeblut, A. and Campbell, A. (1992) *Beyond the School Doors: The Literacy Needs of Job Seekers Served by the US Department of Labor*, Washington, DC: US Department of Labor.

Livingstone, D. W. (1996) 'Wasted education and withered work: reversing the "postindustrial" education-jobs optic', in Dunk, T., McBride, S. and Nelsen, R. W. (eds), *The Training Trap: Ideology, Training and the Labour Market*, Winnipeg/Halifax: Society for Socialist Studies/Fernwood Publishing.

McIntyre, M. (1991) *Promoting Workplace Literacy in Kingston: A Process Report*, Kingston, Ontario: Kingston Literacy.

Meghnagi, S. (1997) 'Connections between collective bargaining, job training and educational research in Italy', in Jobert, A., Marry, C., Tanguy, L. and Rainbird, H. (eds), *Education and Work in Great Britain, Germany and Italy*, London: Routledge.

Mishel L. and Teixeira, R. A. (1991) 'Behind the numbers: the myth of the coming labor shortage', *The American Prospect*, Fall, 98–103.

Nieduszynska, S. (1992) 'Work-place basic education', *RaPAL Bulletin*, 17, 1–5.

OECD (1992) *Adult Illiteracy and Economic Performance*, Paris: OECD.

Omega Group (1989) *Literacy in the Workplace: The Executive Perspective (A Qualitative Research Study)*, Haverford, PA: Omega Group.

Ontario Ministry of Skills Development (undated) *How to Set up Literacy and Basic Skills Training in the Workplace*, Toronto: Government of Ontario.

Philippi, J. (1993) *Legal Considerations Concerning Literacy Testing in the Workplace*, Springfield, VA: Performance Plus Learning Consultants.

Rainbird, H. (1994) 'Union policies towards the training of workers with a low level of qualification: a comparative analysis', *European Journal of Vocational Training*, 2, 55–61.

Rees, L. (1990) *Setting up Workplace Basic Skills Training: Guidelines for Practitioners*, London: ALBSU and Workbase Training.

Reich, R. B. (1992) 'Training a skilled work force: why US corporations neglect their workers', *Dissent*, 39, 1, 42–6.

Rothwell, S. (1993) 'Annual Review Article 1992', *British Journal of Industrial Relations*, 31, 1, 135–49.

Rubery, J. (1995) 'The low-paid and the unorganized', in Edwards, P. (ed.), *Industrial Relations: Theory and Practice in Britain*, Oxford: Basil Blackwell.

Rumberger, R. W. (1984) 'Growing imbalance between education and work', *Phi Delta Kappan*, 65, 5, 342–6.

Sarmiento, A. R. and Kay, A. (1990) *Worker-Centered Learning: A Union Guide to Workplace Literacy*, Washington, DC: AFL-CIO Human Resources Development Institute.

Schachter, H. (1995) 'The dispossessed', *Canadian Business*, May, 30–40.

Schultz, K. (1992) *Training for Basic Skills or Educating Workers?: Changing Conceptions of Workplace Education Programs*, Berkeley, CA: National Center for Research in Vocational Education, University of California at Berkeley.

Statistics Canada (1996) Human Resources Development Canada and National Literacy Secretariat, *Reading the Future: A Portrait of Literacy in Canada*, Ottawa: Ministry of Industry, Government of Canada.

Turk, J. and Unda, J. (1991) 'So We Can Make Our Voices Heard: The Ontario Federation of Labour's BEST Project on Worker Literacy', in Taylor, M. C., Lewe, G. R. and Draper, J. A. (eds), *Basic Skills for the Workplace*, Toronto: Culture Concepts.

Wellborn, R. (1990) 'Workplace education – an option for the 90s', *Literacy Works*, 1, 3, 6–7.

Workbase Training, 'An analysis of shop floor problems as a result of communications skills difficulties', *Implementing Training and Development for Employees and Supervisors*, (promotional pamphlet), London: Workbase Training (undated).

CHAPTER 10

Unions and workplace learning: conflict or cooperation with the employer?

Jim Sutherland and Helen Rainbird

Introduction

Strong, cooperative relations between trade unions and management have been seen as central to the work modernisation agenda, both in managing processes of change in the workplace and in contributing to workers' employability in the wider labour market (see Chapter 7 above). Although it is important not to overstate the extent of the transformation of work organisation and the development of more participative management styles, there are nevertheless significant policy developments (at European level and within EU member states) which are intended to develop approaches to workplace learning based on social partnership.[1] More generally, many EU member states have systems for involving the social partners in the management of the institutions of their vocational training systems as a means of devolving responsibility for the development and implementation of policy in this field. The EU itself has been instrumental in encouraging the use of collective agreements on continuing vocational training as a means of promoting social dialogue on training (Blanpain, Engels and Pellegrini, 1994; Heidemann *et al.*, 1994). Under the 1997 Treaty of Amsterdam member states are required to report annually on the achievement of the objectives in their Employment Action Plans which include the development of measures to promote employability and work modernisation through social partnership (Hall, 1998).

Trade unions have to respond to the work modernisation agenda and to employers' and governments' concerns with the development of a framework capable of responding to the challenges of competition in an increasingly glob-alised economy. Two German writers, in particular, have analysed the impli-cations of this for trade union strategies towards training. Mahnkopf (1991) has argued that the defence of 'Fordist achievements' – the wages and condi-tions of work associated with a routinised division of labour and forms of work organisation – is an insufficient response and that unions need to develop active modernisation policies. She identifies two options: price-ori-ented and skill-oriented strategies. The former involves focusing on interven-ing on wages, protecting the terms and conditions of the core workforce at the expense of peripheral workers and accepting the employers' strategy of price competition. Productivity growth is thus achieved through managerial control and worker compliance. In contrast, the skill-oriented strategy involves trade unions themselves supporting the spread of work modernisation and defend-ing wages and conditions, alongside access to continuing training and retrain-ing for all groups of workers. The latter involves them challenging the employers' prerogative as far as continuing training is concerned and devel-oping 'productivity coalitions' with them.[2]

Yet trade union cooperation with employers on skill formation raises well-founded concerns about its implications for their ability to negotiate effectively on other aspects of the employment relationship. Streeck argues that 'popular images of a harmonious "new industrial relations" based on common interests in high skills are dangerously simplistic – mixing truths and delusions, pro-found insights and business school rhetoric' (1992:251). He warns against mis-understanding the relationship between productive cooperation and distribu-tive conflict on the one hand, and between cooperative policy and adversarial politics on the other. Rather than signalling the end of adversarial conflict and the adoption of management's modernisation agenda, strategies towards skill formation and lifelong learning can provide trade unions with opportunities for the constructive and creative rethinking of policies. He argues:

> one can fully agree with the proposition that unions should embrace skill formation as the centre piece of a new cooperative, and productivistic strategy, *and at the same time insist* on unions' need for a strong independent power base giving them, just as in the past, a capacity to impose rules and obligations on employers which these would not voluntarily obey or accept. (1994:252)

In this chapter, we examine the opportunities and threats for trade unionists in developing strategies towards workplace learning. We do this by drawing on the issues confronting trade unionists in Great Britain where the experience of deregulation and voluntarism under the Conservative governments between 1979 and 1997 has left a particular legacy. Unlike other European countries which have sought to involve trade unionists in the institutions of training, the Conservative government progressively excluded them from a tripartite regime involving the state, employers and the unions, installing a neo-liberal regime whereby employers' interests were prioritised and state intervention was restricted to labour market programmes (King, 1993). It is now recognised that the experience of almost two decades of voluntarism has 'failed the economy, the interests of employers and the interests of working people ... alike' (Sutherland, 1998:3). Since the Labour government came to power in 1997, lifelong learning and skills development have been placed high on the list of government priorities and firmly on the industrial relations agenda. In particular, the government is seeking to encourage the concept of 'partnership in learning' through a number of initiatives, including the creation of a University for Industry (UfI), Individual Learning Accounts (ILAs) and the DfEE's Union Learning Fund (ULF) aimed at supporting trade union innovation in learning.[3]

These developments in the wider policy environment need to be set against the internal dynamics of trade unions and, in particular, the ways in which they adapt to the changing structure and composition of the workforce, the recruitment and retention of members, the defence of individual and collective interests and the building of organisational capacity. The development of trade union strategy towards workplace learning is centrally concerned with questions of organisational renewal. In particular, in the 1990s it has been linked to debates about the development of a 'new bargaining agenda', alongside issues such as equal opportunities, working hours, the environment and opportunities presented by the European Social Charter on workers' fundamental rights (Industrial Relations Review and Report, January, 1991:9; Rainbird and Vincent, 1996). It is also linked to debates about the extent to which trade unions have oriented their activities towards the servicing of members as individuals under the banner of 'the new unionism', and how far this involves continuity and change with traditional collectivist approaches to the defence of members' interests (see, for example, Heery and Kelly, 1994; Smith, 1995; Heery, 1996).

In this chapter we argue that the lifelong learning agenda opens up new opportunities for trade unions to develop strategies towards workplace learning which we define as 'that learning which derives its purpose from the context of employment' (Sutherland, 1998:5). In other words, it is not solely about job-related training, but also access to transferable skills and broader forms of employee development which may not be immediately work-related, but which may be accessed through the workplace. This is encapsulated in the concept of 'learning at, for and through the workplace'. It examines the extent to which such strategies can rely on the mechanisms of collective bargaining and whether the broadening of the scope on which unions represent their members' interests requires the development of new approaches and procedures. In particular, it explores the extent to which the development of partnerships with employers in this specific arena is compatible with maintaining the ability to mobilise independently around the traditional wage bargaining agenda. It is divided into four sections. First, it explores the rationale for trade union interest in workplace learning and areas of convergence and divergence with the interests of the other major stakeholders: employers and government. Second, it examines the scope for incorporating workplace learning into the collective bargaining agenda. Third, it examines some of the factors that need to underpin approaches to workplace learning based on social partnership. Finally, it concludes that although trade unions are developing approaches to workplace learning both through traditional collective bargaining and through partnerships with employers, there are limits to which these can be extended without a system of statutory rights and entitlements.

The rationale for trade union interest in workplace learning

Workplace learning enables individuals, employers and organisations to respond to the changing nature of economic activity; to contribute to improved efficiency and productivity; and to meet the personal and career development needs of individuals. The report of NAGCELL argues that

> If the workplace is to become a major location for learning, people will need to be able to learn there for a variety of reasons, some directly related to current work needs, others to future personal or organisational ones. For many the workplace is the only place where they will engage in formal learning and this calls for the adoption of a wide definition of workplace learning. (Fryer, 1997)

There are three major stakeholders in workplace: government, employers and individual employees represented by their trade unions. Each has a different rationale for engaging in workplace learning.

By and large, employers tend to be most interested in the competitiveness agenda. However, their interests in skill formation tend to be overshadowed by the problems of obtaining a return on their investment in a free market for labour. They therefore tend to prioritise job-specific and company-specific training, rather than investment in transferable skills which are widely recognised in the labour market because of the uncertainties of realising the benefits. They are least likely to invest in broader employee development opportunities for workers which can best equip them for changes within work and employability within the wider labour market. Streeck argues that the fundamental uncertainty about whether training expenses can be recovered results in chronic underinvestment in training, making market failure 'endemic and inevitable'

(1989). He criticises the deregulation of training, arguing for institutional mechanisms to allow the costs as well as the benefits of training to be spread amongst employers. In this way, social institutions can create incentives for investment in skill formation and contribute in a positive way to economic performance.

Governments are interested in promoting the competitiveness of the economy as a whole through an adequate supply of skills as a means of promoting a positive trade balance. This also means managing processes of industrial restructuring and, in particular, ensuring that workers made redundant from declining industries are equipped with the skills to find employment in expanding sectors of the economy through active labour market policies. There are a range of mechanisms which can be drawn on (for example, through the state's responsibility for general education and through rights and obligations established in law). In addition, governments can encourage or require companies to invest in training either through direct state intervention or more devolved forms of policy implementation through the delegation of responsibilities to different stakeholders (such as employers, the trade unions, educational interests). Although workplace learning is directly linked to industrial, economic and labour market policy, governments may also support learning as an end in itself as a means of promoting citizenship and a more inclusive and egalitarian society.

Trade unionists might be interested in workplace learning for a number of reasons. First, their members are recipients of training and other learning opportunities in the workplace and it is in their interests that they should have skills which enhance their bargaining power and employability rather than limit their choices in employment. Second, in some instances, members are employed in educational institutions as teachers and support staff or as trainers and instructors in other organisations. Third, there are broader citizenship issues which trade unionists need to address as members of society and parents. These are linked to the ways in which learning opportunities and widening participation can contribute to a more egalitarian society and to combating social exclusion. Finally, some unions are providers of learning opportunities themselves, for example, Unison, the Amalgamated Engineering and Electrical Union and various union initiatives developed through the DfEE's ULF since 1998. There are therefore a number of different trade union agendas.

The competitiveness agenda

Trade unionists have an interest in ensuring that the organisations they work for compete on the basis of the quality of goods and services rather than price, if they are to defend members' wages and conditions of employment. In Mahnkopf's terms, they have an interest in pursuing skill-oriented strategies which close off the possibilities for employers to engage in price-based competition and deskilling (1991). Although this applies primarily to the private sector because of the pressures of international competition, trade unions in the public sector also have an interest in supporting skill-based strategies to improve the quality of services as a means of retaining political support for public provision. This is not to argue that all employer investment in training benefits the employee. On the contrary (see Chapter 8 above) it can lead to work intensification and the legitimisation of new forms of work organisation. However, if trade unions are involved in decision-making processes about workplace training, there is greater potential to establish an independent trade union agenda (with benefits for employees as well as the employer) than if they have no voice at all. There is also scope to formulate proactive and preventative policies with a long-term perspective rather than incorporation into crisis management on the employer's terms.

The equality agenda

Class, race, gender and age have a significant bearing on access to learning opportunities both within the workplace and outside. The most highly qualified have greatest access to training and development in the workplace and are more likely to undertake learning activities outside work on their own initiative. A Gallup survey commissioned by the National Institute of Adult and Continuing Education found that 60 per cent of adults had not been engaged in any formal or informal learning activity in the previous three years, and that the highest participation rates were amongst younger adults and the higher socio-economic classes and lowest amongst older workers, especially skilled and unskilled manual workers and the unemployed (McGivney, 1997:129–30). Unions organising workers in manual and routine clerical grades may therefore have an interest in negotiating for access to workplace learning as part of a broader strategy towards equal opportunities in employment. For non-traditional learners, who might otherwise lack confidence to engage in learning, the trade union can play an important role in creating a collective framework for participation: for example, in negotiating for educational leave, access to support structures and other resources (Munro and Rainbird, 2000). Since the least skilled workers are most at risk from becoming unemployed, this can decrease the likelihood of social exclusion and contribute to mobility within employment.

The organising agenda

The development of a strategy towards workplace learning provides unions with opportunities to address the interests of different groups of members and potential members. The 'new bargaining agenda' has been developed partly in response to the perceived needs of women and more highly-qualified workers who are seen as less militant than the traditional manual membership base of the trade unions (Industrial Relations Review and Report, January, 1991). Its provision by trade unions either as a service to individual members or as a benefit of employment achieved through collective bargaining has been seen as creating recruitment incentives. Moreover, learning opportunities accessed through the union can also contribute to members' active participation in union branch structures and in their communities. Unison's experience with the Return to Learn programme, which provides a second chance of education, has shown that a proportion of students completing the course become more active in the union.[4] The union is developing a new role – that of the lifelong learning adviser – within the branch structure to recognise this new route into activism (Munro and Rainbird, 2000). In the same way, the workplace learning agenda provides new challenges for trade union education services more generally to prepare shop stewards and officers to represent members' interests on training and development issues.

If trade unions are to demonstrate their relevance to members and potential members in these new circumstances, they have to ensure that they have access to learning opportunities which not only satisfy the needs and interests of business and the economy but which also give individuals choices in employment and in their lives outside the workplace. The broader challenges of lifelong learning are substantial: a transformation of compulsory education to improve the acquisition of learning skills and an enthusiasm for learning; a huge expansion of learning opportunities for work and leisure; and the creation of workplaces as centres of innovative learning. In the following section we explore the extent to which trade unions can achieve this through traditional collective bargaining strategies.

Approaches based on collective bargaining

In developing a strategy towards workplace learning trade unionists need to address a number of key questions: should the initiation of learning strategies be left to management? Should trade unionists simply add learning opportunities to the list of periodic demands in the context of traditional collective bargaining and the annual pay round? If not, what might the role of trade unions be in the development of learning strategies and the identification and planning of learning needs? There appear to be advantages for both parties in leaving the initiation of strategy and provision to the employer and for trade unions to respond to these initiatives.

Locating demands for access to learning opportunities within the traditional structures of collective bargaining or within the context of the periodic pay round of negotiations has a certain logic for trade unions. Learning, or training provision, is an element of individual employee need within the context of the employment relationship, and trade unions will claim that all aspects of that relationship are negotiable and best dealt with across the bargaining table. Trained employees make a contribution to efficiency and productivity and therefore provide significant advantages to the employer. Consequently, it can be argued that employers should provide and pay for training in the same way as they should pay for all other aspects of terms and conditions of employment. For trade unions, this is a comfortable location, where they are used to making demands on employers and seek to negotiate the best deal. It has the advantage of enshrining rights to training within the framework of the contract of employment, as with other negotiated terms and conditions. By dealing with training in this location it avoids the establishment of competing sources of influence or power for trade union negotiators, which might occur if training issues were dealt with outside that framework. An example of this can be found in the concept of the 'safety representative', introduced by the 1974 Health and Safety at Work Act. Some unions saw this as the creation of a new representative in the workplace rather than the provision of new and better powers over health and safety for existing representatives. Rather than registering all shop stewards as health and safety representatives, an additional post was created. In some cases this created tensions where non-shop steward safety representatives preferred to resolve problems with management through consultation rather than through collective bargaining procedures, leading to conflict between the two forms of workplace representation.

Nevertheless, there are some significant disadvantages to an emphasis on collective bargaining as the principal or best vehicle for achieving strategies towards workplace learning. The 1998 *Workplace Employee Relations Survey* found that in 47 per cent of workplaces with more than 25 employees there were no union members at all, compared to 36 per cent in 1990. Union recognition for collective bargaining purposes was found in 45 per cent of workplaces, compared to 53 per cent in 1990 and 66 per cent in 1984 (Cully *et al.*, 1999). The association of trade union recognition with large workplaces and favourable employer attitudes may limit the extent to which best practices on training based on collective agreements can be extended to employees where there is no such recognition.

Locating access to learning opportunities within the context of collective agreements can also encourage the notion that learning is a cost similar to wages, holidays and overtime premia. It therefore encourages the offsetting of learning costs against pay and other benefits, rather than encouraging employers and trade unionists to see learning as an investment for the future. Moreover, by focusing on a monetary value it ignores other resources which can support workplace learning, such as entitlements to learning; to time off; to information, support, advice and encouragement provided through collectively negotiated structures; as well as opportunities for learning through experience (for example, through forms of internal job rotation, acting up and secondments within the workplace itself).

The use of collective bargaining as the main mechanism for dealing with training may also have the effect of focusing attention on the pay and conditions of trainees, at the expense of the learning process. Ryan reports that in the engineering industry between 1925 and 1964 trade union bargaining strategies towards training focused on apprentice pay rates, recognition to bargain on behalf of apprentices and ratios of trainees to qualified workers. He argues that the unions' focus on reducing pay differentials between youth and adult workers was one of a number of factors which contributed to the decline in apprentice numbers by the 1960s and 1970s, given the high cost of training (1999). Trade unions must address the wages and conditions of young workers if they are to demonstrate the relevance of trade union membership and organisation to them. However, if they are to develop strategies towards the learning process, this presupposes institutional structures which give them a formal representational role. The logical extension of Ryan's argument is not that trade unions should support low wage rates for young workers (compare this to the exemptions from the national minimum wage provisions for young workers), but that young workers should have access to structured learning opportunities, and trade unions, as their representatives, should be involved in overseeing their operation, along with other stakeholders such as employers.

A focus on collective bargaining may also have the tendency to build accredited or certificated learning into pay and salary structures. The use of job evaluated grading systems and the linking of earnings and qualifications in agreements may be difficult to unpick as change occurs. It therefore encourages management to limit learning opportunities to task- and job-related provision linked to the payment system and makes it more difficult for trade unions to widen the range of learning opportunities available. An example of this was the 'Purple Book' in local government covering, among other things, the salary structure for non-manual workers.[5] Many qualifications were built into the grading structure as requirements for additional salary increments, qualifications which, over time, related to defunct activities or were unnecessary as tasks were altered by technological developments. The task of up-dating was affected by the 'price' of the grading structure and management's interest in keeping the impact on salary costs down.

There is another sense in which strategies based on collective bargaining may contribute to restricted access to work-based qualifications. Employees in different occupational groups (and often different trade unions) may collude with management in attempting to limit access to learning opportunities in order to maintain pay and status differentials *vis-à-vis* other occupational groups. Cockburn's study of the printing industry examines the gender and inter-union dynamics (craft versus non-craft unions) of skill differentials based on different levels of access to apprenticeship. The knowledge and competence base of these differentials was undermined by the replacement of hot metal printing technology by desk-top publishing, even though pay differentials were retained (1983). The point here is that the nature of the production process, in combination with weak institutional regulation of vocational training and occupationally-based trade unions as opposed to industrial unions, created a situation in which scarce skills were at a premium. Skill scarcity thus contributed to workers' strategies of job regulation and control, but this was achieved at the expense of other groups of workers' access to work-based learning. Trade unions must defend their members' interests, but competition between trade unions, in combination with bargaining strategies based on differential pay, can militate against equality in access to workplace learning.

A further barrier to dealing effectively with learning through traditional forms of collective bargaining is that many employers see any employee or trade union involvement in policy formation and delivery as unnecessary and an encroachment on management's 'right to manage'. The retention of collective bargaining as the main mechanism for dealing with workplace learning reinforces the perception that it is the subject of conflicting interests, rather than an arena in which there are some areas of joint interest. Paradoxically, it is, of course, true that in attempting to extend the scope of issues on which they represent their members' interests, trade unions are encroaching on an area of management prerogative, but in other respects it is opening up new possibilities for workforce planning and employee development to both parties.

Finally, it is useful here to refer to Hyman's distinction between the quantitative and qualitative bargaining demands. The former includes wages and other financial compensations and is the traditional bread and butter of collective bargaining. In contrast, qualitative demands involve 'actual conditions of work, the determination of effort levels and the control of production' (Hyman, 1994:126). Whereas quantitative demands are negotiated through the formal machinery of collective bargaining, qualitative demands are more closely related to the politics of the shop floor. Hyman argues that incorporating issues such as vocational training into bargaining strategies allows trade unions to 'focus on the "qualitative dimension of contemporary managerial discourse", allowing them to construct an agenda which appeals both to employers' desire to increase productivity whilst also offering something to members' individual interests' (1994:127). In the following section, we discuss the development of attempts to construct approaches to learning and development based on partnership between trade unions and employers.

Approaches based on social partnership

Some trade unions and many trade unionists believe that any form of partnership with management is a denial of the fundamental conflict of interest between workers and managers. Particularly at the level of the company or organisation, this may involve agreements covering issues such as flexible working or employment security and may involve new structures for consultation aimed at promoting more cooperative relationships between the parties. There are some well-publicised agreements, for example, between the Tesco supermarket chain and the Union of Shop, Distributive and Allied Trades Workers (USDAW: see Industrial Relations Services, 1997; Labour Research Department, 1998). The impact of these general purpose partnerships with employers is debated, but evidence suggests that they tend to weaken or attempt to bypass workplace trade union organisation (Kelly, 1996; Guest and Peccei, 1998) or involve trade unions in the legitimisation of the management of change. For some observers and some participants, the concept of partnership may be seen as an acceptance of management's objectives and incorporation. It is therefore seen as an emasculation of trade union purpose.

Partnerships on workplace learning can be distinguished here from these general purpose partnerships across a whole range of industrial relations issues as a means of establishing a cooperative arrangement with management on a single issue. The Ford Motor Company's EDAP and Unison's employer partnerships on the Return to Learn programme are examples of these (see Chapter 13 below). As outlined earlier, training and development is a policy arena in which there is some coincidence of interests between employers and trade unions, which explains the involvement of the social partners in the management of the broader institutional structures of vocational training in many European countries. This is not to argue that all training results in a 'win/win' situation for employers and employees, but rather that trade union involvement in decision-making processes at workplace level can contribute to the adoption of measures which are more rather than less favourable to employees.

To facilitate this, it helps if trade unions have an agenda in the workplace which is independent of management. This involves pursuing strategies which support workers' access to transferable skills and employee development programmes, which may conflict with employers' narrowly defined agenda for skills. Moreover, the development of union strategies towards workplace learning has the potential to contribute to trade unions' own organising agendas, serving as a recruitment tool and helping to develop new forms of representational activity (Munro and Rainbird, 2000). In order to achieve this, it is necessary to recognise that 'co-operation on training is not only compatible with conflict, but may require a conflictual capability of unions for its success' (Streeck, 1992). Well-organised, radical trade unionists will utilise a variety of approaches in the pursuit of their objectives. A methodology for working in an arena of joint interest in one area of their relationship with the employer does not compromise their 'capacity to fall out' over general terms and conditions of employment. Even where partnerships on learning and development have been agreed between the employer and the trade union, issues of funding, cover and release from work still have to be negotiated. This involves the recognition that different approaches may be appropriate towards different functions within management and in relation to different aspects of a workplace learning strategy.

In developing a strategy towards workplace learning, a number of elements need to be taken into consideration.

The recognition of different forms of workplace learning

In defining workplace learning as that which 'derives its purpose from the context of employment' (Sutherland, 1998:5), we are explicitly rejecting a transmission model of learning – in other words, that training is something that is done to a worker by someone else – in favour of a perspective which puts the emphasis on the worker as an active learner. Whilst we recognise the significance of course attendance, formal qualifications and other forms of 'articulated knowledge', there are many sources of learning which derive from the social relations of the work environment itself (see Chapter 12 below; Eraut *et al.*, 1998). In addition, forms of learning and development which are external to the work environment and not linked directly to the acquisition of work-related skills and competences may impact on workers' relationships at work, their possibilities and aspirations for job mobility. To phrase this in another way, to promote workers' interests, learning needs to open up opportunities for educational and job progression. It may do this through educational programmes such as Unison's Return to Learn which provides a second chance at education, along with routes into access courses and occupational qualifications. Equally, forms of job rotation, job shadowing and 'acting up' may create opportunities for learning about the work environment, enriching jobs and progressing.

This is not to deny the importance of accessing formal training programmes, particularly for groups of workers such as the low-paid, part-timers and those on temporary contracts, who have often had little access to it in the past. Apart from providing much needed competences and skills which may help them perform their jobs safely and efficiently, formal training signals the importance of different occupations and roles in relation to each other, suitability for promotion and, particularly where it involves release from work, may be perceived as a reward in itself. This involves questioning the types of training which the employer offers and, in particular, seeking access to forms of learning which provide skills recognised outside the immediate workplace, extending rather than restricting the workers' job mobility prospects in the external labour market. In particular, this requires a critical assessment of the value of forms of competence-based assessment and training in the form of National Vocational Qualifications/Scottish National Vocational Qualifications (NVQs/SNVQs). The accreditation of prior learning can be a positive experience for workers who otherwise have no formal qualifications, but the certification of competence does not necessarily involve new learning. There are also restrictions on progression routes where assessment is dependent on having access to performing more advanced tasks in the workplace. A workplace learning strategy based solely on the achievement of NVQs/SNVQs may therefore be limiting in terms of learning experiences and progression routes, even though it contributes to the achievement of National Education and Training Targets.

Trade unionists also need to be aware of the context in which training programmes are introduced: if it is at management's initiative and aimed at introducing changes to jobs which are unwelcome, they will be perceived as an imposition rather than a benefit by the workers concerned.

The identification of underlying principles of an approach

A fundamental principle underlying an approach to workplace learning is the significance not just of upholding equal opportunities but of attempting to redress past and present inequalities in access to learning. Whilst some groups of workers experience no problems of access to learning at work, others face considerable obstacles. They may have low expectations of themselves, which are reinforced by those of their managers and supervisors. Race, gender, age, family responsibilities, working patterns (shifts, night work) and employment status (part-time, short-term contract, agency staff, self-employed) have a significant bearing on access to learning opportunities at work (Arulampalam and Booth, 1998). They affect workers' confidence in taking up formal training and development programmes and their ability to overcome the barriers of time, money and encouragement that they may face (Leisten and Rainbird, 1999). Trade unions have a significant role to play in establishing a collective framework for learning and in creating a supportive and safe environment for learners. Whilst it is important to combat the marginalisation of groups of workers from learning opportunities, there are also dangers of targeting particular groups of workers for special treatment if it results in their stigmatisation (see Chapter 9 above). Therefore a fundamental issue is the question of establishing an entitlement to learning for all groups of workers.

Once an entitlement is established and expectations raised, it is important that these are not dampened. Therefore a second principle is that learning opportunities need to lead to progression routes within education, training or work. The question of reward for the acquisition of new skills and qualifications is problematic within a partnership framework, and this is more appropriately dealt with through the conventional collective bargaining arena. The recognition of achievement and the creation of progression routes into higher level qualifications are particularly significant to low-paid workers in dead-end jobs.

A third principle is that policies should promote solidarity amongst workers, both employed and unemployed. In other words, learning opportunities developed through partnerships with employers should not be restricted to favoured occupational groups or members of specific trade unions, as this can contribute to workforce division. Similarly, creative approaches, like the Danish experience of job rotation, can contribute to solidarity with the unemployed, in providing opportunities for work experience, in freeing up employees for educational leave and in creating opportunities for developing tutoring and mentoring skills.[6]

Finally, compulsion and coercion are not conducive to learning, so a final principle is that learning should be voluntary. The union role lies in providing structures of support and encouragement, particularly for non-traditional learners and for those who have particular difficulties in accessing opportunities.

The need to take the question of resources outside conflict

We argued earlier that locating access to learning in the context of collective bargaining could encourage the employer to view it as a cost rather than an investment. Trade unionists and managers are most likely to develop a joint problem-solving approach to workplace learning where resources are non-contentious or where both parties bring resources to the relationship. An example of the former is where a specific amount is allocated annually for this purpose: for example, through a statutory training levy, as in France, or in the annual allocation of funds to the Ford Motor Company's EDAP scheme. An example of the latter are the Unison/employer partnerships where the employer makes a per capita payment and allows paid leave for students whilst the union's contribution lies in its development work and educational provider role. A third model is where the state provides resources, as in the case of the DfEE's Union Learning Fund which has supported joint work around innovative learning projects between trade unions and employers.

Even where the question of the funding of workplace learning is removed from formal negotiations between employers and trade unions, fundamental questions about the distribution of resources for training and development between individuals and occupational groups begin to emerge. Trade unionists need to have a good understanding of the employer's business and work-force plans (assuming that they have them) and the financial state of the business, as well as the training and development needs of different groups of workers. This has consquences for the disclosure of information as well as relationships with the shopfloor.

Developing organisational capacity

If trade unions are to take their engagement in workplace learning partner-ships seriously, then this requires the development of new organisational capacity. Not only does it mean that shop stewards and officers will need to get to grips with a new range of issues on which to represent members' inter-ests, but with new approaches to working with management representatives, representatives of other trade unions and their own members. This has conse-quences for union education departments and potentially for the creation of new roles within branch structures.

Underpinning rights and entitlements

There is evidence that trade unions have been developing policies and practice towards workplace learning, both in terms of perspectives on the broader pol-icy issues (as evident in their involvement in the National Skills Task Force) and as an arena for workplace interventions. So far this has occurred within a voluntary framework. The weakness of a voluntary framework lies in the absence of statutory entitlements for individual workers to paid education and training leave and a requirement on the employer to allocate a proportion of payroll to training. Whilst the Labour government's ILAs attempt to establish the principle of joint contributions to a learning fund, the one-off nature of the allowance and its individual (as opposed to collective) nature undermine their effectiveness. Moreover, it does not take the form of an entitlement but resources for which individuals can bid. In the same way, although there is potential for trade unions to be involved in the UfI (Payne and Thompson, 1998) this is in delivery and legitimisation rather than workplace co-manage-ment of learning. As part of its legislation on trade union recognition, the Employment Relations Act (1999) has introduced for the first time a require-ment on the employer to consult with trade union representatives on training for workers within the bargaining unit on a six monthly basis. Nevertheless, this only applies to a minority of workplaces recognised under the new legis-lation.[7]

Conclusion

In a period in which workers are being told that they can no longer expect 'jobs for life', access to learning opportunities assumes a central role in guaranteeing their ability to adapt to changing circumstances at work. Trade unionists, therefore, have a responsibility to develop new approaches to learning at, for and through the workplace to ensure that their members have access to skills and competences which open up rather than close down opportunities in employment. Their involvement as stakeholders in decisions covering the provision of a wide range of learning opportunities for employee development, involving long-term planning for learning provision, needs to be based on an understanding of product markets, the changing nature of technology, developments in human resource management and processes of organisational restructuring. It can contribute to organisational and individual performance and to more preventative approaches to dealing with future restructuring and potential job loss. The involvement of trade unionists in workplace learning can help to stimulate the motivation to learn among members, and contribute to creating a safe and supportive environment in which learning can take place. Their involvement in a partnership with the employer lends legitimacy to the training and development programmes undertaken. They therefore have a responsibility to identify an agenda which is independent of the employer, based on a clear understanding of the context in which learning initiatives are being undertaken and where members' interests lie.

Under the Conservative government (1979–97), employee interests in relation to workplace learning were undermined by the withdrawal of statutory interventions in training, the marginalisation of trade unions from decision-making processes and the promotion of employers' interests as the interests of the economy as a whole (Keep and Huddleston, 1998). Employee interests continue to be poorly represented in the training system in general and in the workplace in particular. The voluntary approach to workplace learning led to some employers investing extensively in training whilst many others made very little, if any, provision. In particular, little activity takes place among small and medium-sized enterprises (SMEs) or the self-employed.

In the increasingly globalised economy, reluctant employers have to be encouraged to recognise the long-term benefits of workplace learning. Individuals who have been discouraged from learning have to be convinced that it can reinforce employment and career prospects as well as contribute to personal fulfilment and social well-being. Lifelong learning has to become a reality for small businesses and the self-employed.

The Labour government has stated its intention to 'encourage workplace partnership between employers, employees and their trade unions to promote learning' (DfEE, 1998:43). The limited requirement in the Employment Relations Act (1999) for employers to consult with trade union representatives on their training policy and plans provides a voluntary model for a partnership approach towards lifelong learning in the workplace, but would be strengthened if it were a statutory requirement. As part of this process, annual reports could be expected to reflect the nature and degree of investment in learning. Nevertheless, as yet, no effective legislative or institutional mechanisms have been introduced to require the allocation of resources to training, or to establish rights to education and training leave. As a minimum we would suggest that all employees should have an entitlement to learning for their own development, and that this should take a collective rather than individual form of application.

Trade unions will decide, within the context of their own experience and the nature of their relationships with employers, whether to pursue learning opportunities through traditional collective bargaining, learning partnerships, wider employment partnerships or a mixture of all three. As a contribution to that decision-making process we have examined in this chapter the rationale for trade union involvement in workplace learning. We have identified what can be achieved through adding training to the collective bargaining agenda and have argued that, whilst there are benefits to this approach, it also has limitations. Although on occasions unions are able to take a proactive stance, they are frequently restricted to responding to the employer's agenda for workplace change. More importantly, it means that initiatives are limited to organised workplaces and, as we argued earlier, this means that workers in many sectors of the economy, particularly in SMEs, are left outside these developments.

We have pointed to some of the issues raised by approaches based on partnership with employers, which are developing on a voluntary basis. They appear to provide opportunities for trade unionists to engage in innovative activities, which are proactive rather than defensive in nature and allow them to set the agenda with the employer. In providing learning opportunities from which members gain direct benefits in a context which is highly visible compared to much routine trade union activity, they have the potential to contribute to the establishment of a new relationship between unions and their membership base. This creates scope for redefining the benefits of trade union membership and, insofar as representatives set the agenda themselves, for raising significant questions about the entitlements to be established not just for members, but for the workforce as a whole, including those on non-standard contracts, potential employees and other members of the local community. Although the scope of partnership arrangements is potentially more inclusive than through traditional collective bargaining, coverage is still likely to be limited to the sectors of the economy covered by trade union organisation. Moreover, some managers continue to feel threatened by the prospect of a more confident and competent workforce and trade union representatives who understand and can articulate their members' learning needs. Managers and supervisors retain the capacity to block initiatives and provide release from work. The resources for training and development remain in the contested domain of employer/union relations and employers have yet to see union involvement as a partnership in a long-term planning process rather than as a last resort in crisis situations.

Although largely in an embryonic state, British trade unions are developing their capacity to respond to the workplace learning agenda in innovative ways. Initiatives such as the Union Learning Fund and the limited rights to consultation on workplace training can contribute to a more supportive environment for trade union involvement in workplace learning. Nevertheless, the absence of an underpinning framework of workers' rights to training and development and a system of institutional incentives to employers to invest in training prevents their wider dissemination.

Notes

1   See, for example, the British government's Green Paper *The Learning Age: a Renaissance for a New Britain* (DfEE, 1998) and the European Commission's Green Paper *Partnership for a New Organisation of Work* (1997).
2   We would argue that the distinction between price-oriented and skill-oriented strategies and their relationship to worker compliance with management objectives is more complex than Mahnkopf's formulation suggests. In the British context, some price-oriented strategies, dependent on the payment system, may involve a variety of challenges to management's right to manage, with gang piecework, for example, frequently determining levels of output, priorities in production and levels of earning. Equally, a skills-oriented strategy which is narrowly oriented to training can also lead to compliance with management objectives and productivity improvements.
3   Ufl has been heralded as a 'new type of institution' which will 'act as the hub of a brand new learning network, using modern technologies to link businesses and individuals to cost-effective, accessible and flexible education and training' (DfEE, 1998:18). Its role is partly as a source of information and advice, partly as a distributor of learning materials; it will be linked to locally accessible learning centres based in workplaces, libraries and shopping centres. The government is encouraging the creation of ILAs based on the principle of shared contributions between the state (£150), the individual (£25) and sometimes the employer as well. An initial tranche of funding was agreed by the incoming government in 1997 though it is not clear how ILAs will be sustained in the long term. The ULF was set up in 1998 and additional funds were allocated to it in 1999.
4   A survey conducted by Kennedy of 288 former Return to Learn students showed that 23 per cent had become involved or more involved in Unison after completing the course (Kennedy, 1995).

5   This has now been superseded by the 1997 Single Status agreement in local government which has introduced a single pay spine and includes clauses on codes of practice, equality of access, and the need for employers and recognised unions to cooperate on training and development (GMB/TGWU/Unison, 1997).

6   Job Rotation was piloted in Denmark in 1991. The WEA and the Glasgow Development Agency ran two EU ADAPT projects on the same lines in 1996 and 1997. This allowed unemployed people to be trained for six months before taking up six months' temporary employment. Employees were trained to act as mentors to them and their presence in the organisation allowed permanent employees to be released for training and development.

7   The view of the Department of Trade and Industry (DTI) is that this should encourage the wider adoption of good practice on a voluntary basis.

References

Arulampalam, W. and Booth, A. (1998) 'Training and labour market flexibility: is there a trade-off?', *British Journal of Industrial Relations*, 36, 4 (December), 521–36.

Blanpain, R., Engels, E. and Pellegrini, C. (eds) (1994) *Contractual Policies Concerning Continued Vocational Training in the European Community Member States*, Leuven: Peeters Press.

Cockburn, C. (1983) *Brothers: Male Dominance and Technological Change*, London: Pluto Press.

Cully, M., O'Reilly, A., Millward, N., Forth, J., Woodland, S., Dix, G. and Bryson, A. (1999) *The 1998 Workplace Employee Relations Survey. First Findings*, London: DTI.

DfEE (1998) *The Learning Age. A Renaissance for a New Britain*, London: DfEE.

Eraut, M., Alderton, J., Cole, G. and Senker, P. (1998) 'Learning from other people at work' in Coffield, F. (ed.), *Learning at Work*, Bristol: Policy Press.

European Commission (1997) *Partnership for a New Organisation of Work*, Brussels: European Commission.

Fryer, R. (1997) *Learning for the Twenty-First Century. First Report of the National Advisory Group for Continuing Education and Lifelong Learning*, Barnsley: Northern College.

Guest, D. and Peccei, R. (1998) 'The partnership company: bench marks for the future – report of the IPA survey', *Industrial Relations Services*, 655, May.

GMB/TGWU/Unison, (1997) *Single Status in Local Government A Member's Guide to the Proposed New National Agreement*. London GMB/TGWU/Unison.

Hall, M. (1998) 'Social partners make joint input to UK National Action Plan on employment', EIRO Feature, May, European Industrial Relations Observatory.

Heery, E. (1996) 'The new unionism' in Beardwell, I. (ed.), *Contemporary Industrial Relations: A Critical Analysis*, Oxford: Oxford University Press.

Heery, E., and Kelly, J. (1994) 'Professional, participative and managerial unionism: an interpretation of change in trade unions', *Work, Employment and Society*, 8, 1, 11–22.

Heidemann, W., Kruse, W., Paul-Kohlhoff, A. and Zeuner, C. (1994) *Social Dialogue and Further Education and Training in Europe. New Challenges for the Trade Unions*. Berlin: Sigma.

Hyman, R. (1994) 'Changing trade union identities and strategies', in Hyman, R. and Ferner, A. (eds), *New Frontiers in European Industrial Relations*, Oxford: Basil Blackwell.

Industrial Relations Review and Report (1991) 'New bargaining agenda for unions', *Industrial Relations Services; Employment Trends*, 492 (January) 9–14.

Industrial Relations Services (1997) 'Partnership at work: a survey', IRS Employment Trends, 645 (December).

Keep, E. and Huddleston, P. (1998) 'What do employers want from education? A question more easily asked than answered', paper presented to the 4th International Partnership conference, Trondheim, Norway, July.

Kelly, J. (1996) 'Union Militancy and Social Partnership', in Ackers, P., Smith, C. and Smith, P. (eds), *The New Workplace and Trade Unionism*, London: Routledge.

Kennedy, H. (1995) *Return to Learn. Unison's Fresh Approach to Trade Union Education*, London: Unison.

King, D. (1993) 'The Conservatives and training policy 1979–1992: from a tripartite to a neoliberal regime', *Political Studies*, XLI, 2, 214–235.

Labour Research Department (1998) 'Is partnership a bed of roses?', *Labour Research*, June, 11–12.

Leisten, R. and Rainbird, H. (1999) 'Unskilled, unqualified or just low paid? Preliminary findings of the employees' learning experiences survey', paper presented to 'Researching Work and Learning' conference, University of Leeds, 10–12 September.

McGivney, V. (1997) 'Adult participation in learning. Can we change the pattern?' in Coffield, F. (ed.), *A National Strategy for Lifelong Learning*, Newcastle: University of Newcastle.

Mahnkopf, B. (1991) 'The skill modernisation strategies of German trade unions; their impact on efficiency and equality', *British Journal of Industrial Relations*, 30, 1, 59–81.

Munro, A. and Rainbird, H. (2000) 'The new unionism and the new bargaining agenda: the example of the Unison/employer partnerships on workplace learning', *British Journal of Industrial Relations*, 38, 2, 223–240.

Payne, J. and Thompson, A. (1998) *Partnerships for Learning. Opportunities for Trade Unions and the University for Industry*, Leicester: NIACE.

Rainbird, H. and Vincent, C. (1996) 'Training: a new item on the bargaining agenda', in Leisink, P., Van Leemput, J. and Vilrokx, J. (eds), *The Challenges to Trade Unions in Europe. Innovation or Adaptation*, Cheltenham: Edward Elgar.

Ryan, P. (1999) 'The embedding of apprenticeship in industrial relations: British engineering, 1925–1965', in Ainley, P. and Rainbird, H., (eds), *Apprenticeship. Towards a New Paradigm of Learning*, London: Kogan Page.

Smith, P. (1995) 'Change in British Trade Unions Since 1945', *Work, Employment & Society*, Notes and Issues: Debate, 9, 1, 137–46.

Streeck, W. (1989) 'Skills and the limits of neo-liberalism: the enterprise of the future as a place of learning', *Work, Employment and Society*, 3, 1 (March) 80–104.

Streeck, W. (1994) 'Training and the new industrial relations; a strategic role for unions?', in Regini, M. (ed.), *The Future of Labour Movements*, London: Sage.

Sutherland, J. (1998) *Workplace Learning for the Twenty First Century. Report of the Workplace Learning Task Group*. London: Unison.

CHAPTER 11

Work placements for young people

Prue Huddleston

Introduction

A period of work placement, usually referred to as work experience, is now a feature of the school curriculum for virtually all young people in their last year of compulsory schooling. A recent DfEE survey revealed that: 'virtually all secondary schools with eligible pupils were involved in work experience placements. Nationally, in those schools, 98 per cent of the total number of pupils in their last year of compulsory schooling undertake such placements' (DfEE, 1999b:5). In addition, many young people beyond the age of compulsory schooling take part in work experience, or some other form of work-based or work-related activity as part of their full- or part-time education programmes.

Work experience is: 'a placement on an employer's premises in which a pupil carries out a particular task, or duty, more or less as would an employee, but with an emphasis on the learning aspects of the experience' (DfEE, 1996a). The Qualifications and Curriculum Authority (QCA), in providing guidance for successful practice in work experience, suggests that: 'The experience involves taking on the role of a young worker and engaging in work tasks, using and developing work skills, being involved in work processes and experiencing work environments' (QCA, 1998b:1).

The defining feature of work experience, as opposed to other forms of work-related learning, is that it should involve active participation by the young person. According to the most recent DfEE survey of education business links (DfEE, 1999b), the average length of placement per pupil is nine days.

The growth of work experience for young people has its roots in the early 1960s but it was not to assume its current scale until the early 1990s. Over these three decades a change in the focus of work experience can be discerned, namely a shift in its emphasis from what may be described as compensatory education for the few, often those described as 'less able', to a compulsory element of the curriculum for all pupils. Given that an average two-week pupil work experience takes up about as much time as half a GCSE course, the investment in terms of time and resource, both for schools and employers, is significant. Also the increasing numbers of pupils year on year requiring to be accommodated on employers' premises has placed a severe strain on employers and raised questions concerning the quality of such experiences.

The rationale for pupil work experience derives from concerns expressed intermittently throughout the past 30 years about the 'work-readiness' of young people, not just in terms of the occupational skills and knowledge required to undertake particular employment, but increasingly about dispositions and attitudes to work. In other words, emphasis was placed upon the workplace socialisation aspects of the experience: for example, the importance of punctuality, learning the rules and regimes of the workplace, fitting in.

In current policy terms, this is described as 'employability'. Although throughout the past 30 years there have been different names, the intention has been very similar. Pupil work experience has been seen as fulfilling a multiplicity of aims. The objectives set for it include: workplace socialisation; careers sampling; practical skills acquisition; contextualising learning; and the provision of a relatively 'risk free' environment in which pupils may experience the so-called realities of the workplace and so prepare themselves for real employment.

This chapter examines the rationale for work experience, set within the current debate concerning employability and key skills, and explores the proposition of work experience as a form of workplace socialisation in which young people are introduced to the practices of the workplace through observation and, to some extent, through active participation. Drawing on research from the field of cultural anthropology, it considers to what extent work experience provides a context for learning and, if so, what might be learned from such contexts. Results from fieldwork conducted in companies which regularly accept pupils on work experience provide insights into employers' perspectives on the nature and purpose of pupil work experience.

Finally, some conclusions are drawn about the extent to which work experience meets the objectives set for it and how apprenticeship as a model of learning can contribute to our understanding of what young people learn on work placement and in work.

The rationale for work experience: employability and key skills

Employability has been variously described as: 'the combination of knowledge, skills, attitudes and personal qualities which are valued by employers' (Industry in Education, 1996); 'the possession by an individual of the qualities and competences required to meet the changing needs of employers and customers and thereby help to realise his or her aspirations and potential in work' (CBI, 1998:6).

The term has assumed significance within the current policy debate on skills, although for those of us who remember the training initiatives of the early 1980s there is a sense of 'new wine in old bottles'. Once again it is the individual who is being exhorted to fit him or herself to the needs of employers. There is an extensive literature on the supposed skill requirements of employers, some of it contradictory and confusing. This is hardly surprising given the heterogeneous nature of employers. Also studies purporting to represent the views of employers are often conducted by organisations representing large employers and do not, therefore, canvass the views of SMEs. It is just such SMEs which provide the bulk of pupil work experience places (Huddleston and Keep, 1998).

It might be useful to reflect upon the current debate surrounding employability and ask why, at the present time, there is so much interest in the concept. Hillage and Pollard (1998) suggest that the public policy concern centres upon skill-based economic policies and work-based social policies. In other words, there is a recognition, on the one hand, of the need to improve the skill base in order to retain competitiveness within an increasingly global economy yet, on the other, there is the knowledge that a significant proportion of young people leave school without qualifications and with little intention of pursuing any further education and training. Amongst these are those who have been excluded, or excluded themselves, from the school system through persistent truancy. According to the Social Exclusion Unit 'each year at least one million children truant, and over 100,000 children are excluded temporarily. Some 13,000 are excluded permanently' (1998:1).

Employability not only refers to the ability to enter the labour market initially but also reflects the need for individuals to obtain new employment and to change direction within the labour market. In summary, it is concerned with gaining employment in the first place, keeping satisfactory employment and being able to access new employment opportunities.

In order to do this individuals require a range of occupationally-specific knowledge and skills, personal attributes and attitudes, the ability to transfer knowledge and skills to different situations, a certain mastery of key skills and an ability to present themselves in the job market. This includes, for example, the ability to complete a CV, or to present well at interview.

It should also be recognised that employability is not simply dependent upon the school leaver's or graduate's qualifications but upon a range of other external factors: for example, local labour market conditions and informal recruitment networks. It is simply not enough to suggest that it is the individual's responsibility to achieve employability because the issue of employability is far more complex. It is of little use to blame the victim without recognising the multi-causal nature of the problem.

What, then, is the function of a two-week work experience placement for school pupils in helping them achieve the 'holy grail' of employability? According to the CBI report, *In Search of Employability*, the concept embraces a range of skills and competences which include: values and attitudes compatible with work; basic skills (literacy and numeracy); key skills for the needs of work (unspecified); up-to-date and relevant knowledge and understanding; up-to-date job-specific skills; experience; mobility; career management skills (1998). A tall order indeed for any school, let alone a two-week work experience programme.

The 1998 *Skill Needs in Britain* survey (DfEE, 1999a) reported that employers identified general communication skills, numeracy skills and technical and practical skills as those most lacking in 16–17 year old employees. For 16–24 year olds the rates were: technical and practical skills (59 per cent), general communication skills (48 per cent), customer handling skills (46 per cent). Yet of those employers reported to have taken on new recruits within the 16–24 age band during the previous year, 41 per cent claimed to have provided no training for their young employees.

A recent British Chambers of Commerce (1998) report stated that SMEs were seeking particular employability and personal traits in their young recruits, including: reliability and trustworthiness; willingness to learn; motivation and enthusiasm; punctuality; and the ability to work in a team. The skills most lacking were reported as being the ability to write clearly and concisely (61 per cent of employers), and motivation and enthusiasm (56 per cent of employers). Similarly, the findings of a recent report by Andersen Consulting suggests that: 'Interpersonal skills, enthusiasm and initiative are as important to employers as formal qualifications' (1998:5).

If the purpose of pupil work experience is to achieve this multiplicity of aims, how well does it succeed? Or, perhaps more fundamentally, how can it succeed? How can its success be measured, or isolated from the other influences operating upon the young people during this formative stage of their education experience?

Workplace socialisation and contextualised learning

According to the QCA:

> Work experience can make a significant contribution to the learning of young peo-
> ple, provided that curriculum links are established, learning objectives identified
> and learning outcomes recorded and confirmed. In schools, well planned work expe-
> rience can help achieve the school aims and can contribute significantly to enhanc-
> ing the work-related curriculum at Key Stage 4. In colleges, work experience can pro-
> vide students with the opportunity to apply and develop the knowledge and skills
> necessary to succeed on vocational programmes and so prepare for employment in
> their chosen occupational field. (1998b:1)

Such rhetoric suggests that work experience may provide the elixir to re-
invigorate the curriculum which, when taken in liberal doses, will transform
allegedly work-shy youngsters into employable citizens. Some tensions immediately become apparent about the nature and purposes of work experience
for school pupils. For example, does it serve a broadly-based educative purpose or does it serve to aid the transition of young people from school to work
by enhancing their 'employability'? Shilling suggests that its purpose now
appears to be: 'to facilitate the acquisition of industrially relevant skills, attitudes and knowledge' (1989:157). Pupils, of course, may have entirely different views about the purposes of their work experience placements. These will
be explored more fully later in this chapter.

Watts identifies ten categories of work experience aims. These he lists as:
'enhancing, motivational, maturational, investigative, expansive, sampling,
preparatory, anticipatory, placing and custodial' (1983:17). He further suggests
that seven of the ten aims provide opportunities for curriculum enrichment:
for example, through 'enhancing' academic subjects, or through contributions
to personal and social education which emphasise the 'maturational' aim of
work experience. The motivational aim of work experience recognises that
some pupils may find practical, work-based activities more engaging than academic study. This aspect has recently been re-affirmed within the current provision for the disapplication of aspects of the National Curriculum at key stage
4 (14 to 16 years) for those pupils: 'who are in danger of becoming disaffected,
or for pupils who have not experienced much success at school or have ceased
to believe in themselves' (QCA, 1998a:3). Again, the concern is that this may
tie work experience too closely to the notion of compensatory education
alluded to earlier in this chapter.

Recent work in the field of cultural anthropology (Lave and Wenger, 1991;
Lave, 1993) provides some interesting insights into the relationship between
work and learning. Lave's work focuses upon the institution of apprenticeship

but there are a number of parallels which might usefully be drawn with the experience of the school pupil whilst on a work placement.

Lave's research emphasises the interconnectedness of the content and context of learning. She also stresses the importance of the relationship between apprentices and their adult mentors in the workplace. Lave describes the journey which apprentices make from their initial 'peripheral participation' in the workplace until they achieve 'full participation'. During the process they acquire not just the skills and knowledge necessary to undertake the work tasks, but also the adult identities which enable them to become full participating members of a 'community of practice'.

If we relate this to Watts' aims for work experience, some parallels might be drawn. For example, the 'enhancing' aim is designed to enable pupils to apply theoretical concepts learned in the classroom to a workplace context, whilst the 'anticipatory' aim seeks to introduce students to the routines and demands of the workplace in a more general sense. In other words, it introduces pupils to 'communities of practice'.

Engestrom (1994), drawing upon the work of the Russian psychologists, Vygotsky and Leontov, recognises the importance of structured teaching and learning to underpin the learning that occurs within social and workplace situations through individuals' interactions with others. For Engestrom, the components of effective learning are:

> ensuring that individuals have access to theoretical and experiential knowledge; the opportunity to engage in authentic tasks and interactions with others; the chance to develop their critical and intellectual capacities through the application of concepts and theories in practice; the opportunity to have their thinking and understanding enhanced through the guidance and teaching of others. (Engestrom, 1994:48)

Perhaps this better characterises an 'idealised' work experience model which aims to combine learning which takes place within the classroom with that occurring within workplace settings. Similarly, work experience supposedly allows young people to 'engage with authentic tasks', although the extent to which they are allowed to do this is a matter of conjecture. It also, allegedly, exposes them to the realities of the workplace and the demands and expectations of employers.

According to a recent Ofsted report on work-related aspects of the curriculum: 'While the school's key responsibility is to ensure that pupils gain the qualifications, skills and attitudes they need to improve their employability, it is also important that they should develop knowledge and understanding of the world of work and its demands' (1998b:4). It is important to notice the renewed interest in 'employability' and 'work-readiness' which has a distinct ring of *déjà vu* about it, one reminiscent of the compensatory education schemes for disadvantaged pupils during the 1960s and 1970s.

The debate surrounding pupil work experience continues to focus upon the twin issues of workplace socialisation and contextualised learning. Even this is to oversimplify the issue because the activity covers a broad spectrum of experiences for thousands of young people in countless workplaces across the country. What is lived and learned during those two weeks in Year 10 or 11 will be very much a personal experience. What pupil A experiences in the local garage will be very different from pupil B's experience at the corporate head-quarters of a multinational company. A placement with the corner shop hair-dresser will differ from a placement at the European parliament. All of these are based upon real examples collected during the research project discussed later in this chapter.

The development of work placement in England and Wales

The first reference to work experience for school pupils appears in the report of the Newsom Committee (Central Advisory Council for Education, 1963). Although highlighting the need for the school curriculum to be more 'outgo-ing' in its final year, particularly for those pupils of average or below average ability, it did not endorse work experience for all pupils; rather it suggested that: 'experiments enabling some pupils over the age of fifteen to participate to a limited extent, under the auspices of the school, in the world of work in industry, commerce, or other fields, should be carefully studied' (1963:79).

Throughout the remainder of the 1960s the debate concerning the use of work experience for those below school-leaving age focused not just on the educational desirability of such a process but on the legal implications of hav-ing young people below the statutory school-leaving age in workplaces. A sur-vey conducted by the Institute of Careers Officers in 1968/69 (Institute of Careers Officers, 1974) indicated that only about 2 per cent of pupils had undertaken work experience before leaving school. The raising of the school-leaving age to 16 in 1972 brought the debate concerning the need for a more 'outgoing' curriculum, possibly one including the use of work experience placements, to centre stage. It was clear that alternative approaches would have to be explored in an attempt to retain and engage those pupils who would previously have left school at 15.

To facilitate this process the Education (Work Experience) Act 1973 permit-ted pupils to undertake work experience on employers' premises, subject to some restrictions on particular locations or jobs, during their last year of com-pulsory schooling. Although some concerns about potential health and safety hazards continued to be raised, other more fundamental concerns relating to the educational merit of work experience placements began to be voiced. For many educational professionals, and possibly in the minds of parents and pupils alike, work experience was associated with schemes for the less able. In 1974, the Department of Education and Science (DES) attempted to dispel such concerns by issuing guidance pointing out that work experience: 'should have value for pupils of varying ability and aptitudes and should neither be designed as vocational training nor aimed at a limited range of ability' (DES, 1974, para. 8).

As the decade progressed there was a gradual increase in the number of pupils involved in work experience placements. However, these programmes were by no means open to all pupils, and in general they were still offered to those of lower ability, not to a whole year cohort (DES, 1979). Prime Minister James Callaghan's famous 1976 Ruskin College speech, in which he roundly criticised the education system for failing to produce the type of young people which industry required, once more focused attention on the relationship between education and the workplace. Work experience was seen by some as the potential centrepiece of such a relationship.

Rising youth unemployment in the early 1980s once again focused attention on the perceived need to develop a closer relationship between the worlds of education and work. There was an inclination to 'blame the victims' for their own unemployment by suggesting that they did not possess the right skills and attitudes to find employment. The reality, of course, was that there were simply insufficient jobs available within a rapidly contracting youth labour market (Finn, 1987).

Nevertheless, the government's response was to institute a range of schemes designed to train young people for suitable jobs, and a litany of acronyms bears testimony to them: for example, Work Experience on Employers' Premises (WEEP), the Youth Opportunities Programme (YOP), the Youth Training Scheme (YTS). All of these included substantial elements of work-based experience plus other elements variously referred to as: 'social skills', 'life skills', 'basic skills'. Again the implication was that the young people were inadequately prepared to enter the world of work because they could not: 'communicate', 'take messages', 'arrive punctually', or 'display good work habits'.

Although these work experience schemes were far more substantial than work experience for school pupils, trainees were paid an allowance and regarded as work-based trainees. Miller, Watts and Jamieson suggest that these youth unemployment schemes affected school-based work experience in three ways:

> Firstly, they caused some confusion in the minds of employers and trade unionists about the nature and purpose of work experience. Secondly, they did nothing to improve the image of work experience amongst teachers and students in schools. Thirdly, they reinforced the view that work experience was for the less able and for those who might have difficulty in obtaining employment. (1991:6)

By the mid-1980s, however, the picture had begun to change. The Technical and Vocational Education Initiative (TVEI), a programme specifically designed for the 14–18 age, range was introduced by the Manpower Services Commission (MSC) in 1983. By 1988 it covered all local education authorities (LEAs) and made work experience for all pupils a compulsory element of bids seeking funding from the initiative. In addition, there were further interventions by government through the Training Agency aimed at introducing a more work-related element to the school curriculum.

Throughout the 1980s the extent of work experience increased and employers were exhorted, mainly through the DTI, to provide the necessary additional placements required to meet the increased demand. The DTI's Education and Enterprise Initiative aimed to secure 700 000 work experience placements from employers each year (DTI, 1991).

The 1988 Education Act heralded the introduction of a National Curriculum with prescribed programmes of study and national testing at the ages of 7, 11, 14 and 16. From this point it became clear that if work experience was to survive it would have to tie its learning objectives more closely to National Curriculum outcomes. The DES issued revised guidance for both schools and employers in 1988 (DES, 1988a, 1988b) and these were further revised in 1996 (DfEE, 1996b, 1996c).

Work experience is now a well established landmark on the timetables of all Year 10/11 pupils in maintained schools, it has even become established within many independent schools as well. This being the case, why is it that government supports such a significant transfer of curriculum responsibility to hundreds of thousands of large, but overwhelmingly small and medium-sized, employers? What reasons could employers have for committing themselves to such an enterprise? The next section will examine some employers' responses to pupil work experience and will provide some pupils' perspectives.

The practice of work experience: the research evidence

In theory the opportunities for work experience placements are limitless, subject to certain legal restrictions: for example, those concerning health and safety, insurance, or equal opportunities. (For a fuller discussion, see Johns, 1997.) In practice, the choice is often smaller and will be dependent upon a number of factors: for instance, the number of local employers willing and able to provide placements; or the standing of one school *vis-à-vis* another within the community and, therefore, its ability to engage employers. It is well known that some employers have 'preferred' schools. The shortage of placements in some sectors and their abundance in others can further exacerbate the problem, resulting in pupils being inappropriately placed. These are just some examples of quantitative issues, whereas the issue of quality is a much more contentious one.

A three-year study of pupil work experience undertaken by the Centre for Education and Industry (CEI) at the University of Warwick has indicated that the most frequently occurring pupil work experience placements tend to be in the retailing, business administration, health, local government and education sectors. Whether pupils make their own selection from a range of possible company opportunities, or are selected by other means (for example, by teachers 'guiding' particular pupils into particular jobs) the matching process is crucially important. A representative from a well known chocolate manufacturer once told a college work placement organiser: 'Don't send me any overweight students, they are not good for the company's image.'

Some pupils may organise their own placements and may be advantaged by the fact that their parents and relatives have 'connections in high places' and may be able to arrange placements in 'blue chip' companies or with distinguished professionals. Clearly, this results in different experiences for different young people structured along class, and often gender, lines.

Miller, Watts and Jamieson draw our attention to the fact that there are three parties involved in the matching process: employers, pupils and teachers. They point out that there may be tensions between the concerns of each party since the focus of each may differ. They illustrate this by suggesting that the employer will be concerned with 'task and social competence', the pupil with possible 'career orientated interests' and the teacher with 'curricular aims' (1991:208). They conclude that a thorough understanding of the aims of work experience is central to resolving such difficulties. However, since the aims appear to be multiple, and in some cases contested, or at least different for different types of pupil, the tension may not be easy to resolve.

In 1997, the CEI was commissioned by the Education Business Links Division of the DfEE to undertake research into pupil work experience with a particular focus upon the potential learning outcomes of such activities. Previous research in the field (Hillage *et al.* 1996) had indicated that many pupils do not discuss possible learning outcomes with employers when negotiating work experience placements. 'Specific learning outcomes, as opposed to general outcomes such as "learning about the world of work" were rarely seen as the main objects of work experience placements' (Hillage *et al.*, 1996:8).

The Warwick study aimed to identify the potential learning opportunities across a wide range of business sectors for work experience pupils to undertake both work-specific tasks and to develop key skills whilst on placement with a company. The results of the study were presented in a series of frameworks. One of these – Work Experience: The Learning Framework – aimed to: 'develop and disseminate a framework for learning from pre-16 experience, thereby helping students, employers and teachers to identify learning outcomes and enhancing links with the school curriculum' (CEI, 1997:3).

The initial survey focused upon three of the most popular categories of work experience placement: retail, office or clerical, and manufacturing/workshop. These were supplemented in subsequent years with further surveys in different sectors. The current number of frameworks now totals seventeen. For each sector fieldwork visits were made to approximately 24 employers, all of whom had experience of providing work placements for school pupils. The company sample included SMEs as well as large companies.

In each company interviews were conducted with the member of staff responsible for work experience. Questions focused upon: the company background and its work experience policy; tasks undertaken by students whilst on work experience; differences, if any, between tasks for pre-16 and post-16 students; opportunities for key skill development within work experience placements.

In addition, managers were asked to prioritise the main aims of pre-16 work experience from a business perspective. They were presented with five aims and asked to rank them in order of importance. In framing the research question the project team drew upon the earlier research conducted by Miller, Watts and Jamieson (1991) concerning the aims of pupils' work experience. Aims were classified as: 'Understanding the world of work; developing personal and social skills; employability; testing a vocational preference; relevance of school subjects to work' (CEI, 1997).

Overwhelmingly, for pre-16 pupils, employers saw 'understanding the world of work' as the priority aim of work experience, with 'developing personal and social skills' and 'employability' as the second and third most desirable aims. Given the current debate on employability it might be argued that the two are not mutually exclusive. In every case, 'relevance of school subjects to work' was ranked as fifth in the list of priority aims.

At the post-16 stage, however, priorities tended to shift towards 'testing a vocational preference' and 'practising vocational skills' although, in every case, the 'relevance of school subjects to work' was again ranked last in the list of priorities. Managers suggested, amongst other things, that:

Students need to understand work discipline and taking responsibility. Work in retail is hard. (Manager, High Street chain store)

Students lack basic social skills and do not have the basic communication and numeric skills. (Personnel manager, building society)

Students need to be more positive about manufacturing industry. Many of them have an outdated view of it being a dirty environment. (Engineer, textile manufacturer)

Schools should understand the social skills and interview skills required. Some students cannot present themselves well at all. (Managing Director, small construction firm)

In terms of actual job tasks undertaken, the research team identified that there were a wide range of opportunities available for pupils to 'help someone do a job' (most frequently cited); 'do an actual job' (second most frequent); and 'observe someone do a job' (third frequency). There was least opportunity for students to undertake 'specially constructed tasks'. This is hardly surprising since employers could scarcely be expected to design a wide range of special tasks for pupils to undertake whilst on work experience. There were, however, some notable examples where pupils could work their way through portfolios of activities which would in turn provide evidence for GCSE coursework, or elements of NVQs. The research team identified that there were plenty of naturally occurring opportunities for young people to learn from their experiences, but that these needed to be structured in a way which made them understandable to the young people themselves. As one 15 year old said of his placement in a hotel: ' I learned that there are a lot of people working here with no qualifications at all, the pay's lousy and the job's rubbish, it's been a waste of time.' It is tempting to suggest that he had learned a great deal more than he realised.

For other pupils the learning outcomes, or indeed opportunities, were quite different but served very different ends: for example, 'It's been great I've been offered a summer job here as a result' (pupil reflecting on his experience with a veterinary practice); and another said: 'I went into court and watched the barristers at work, I had to buy a special black outfit suitable for court, it was very exciting' (pupil talking about her placement at a distinguished QC's chambers; placement arranged through family connections).

A recent conference paper presented by Ofsted suggested that there are three main challenges to be confronted if the government's aim to improve school-business links by the year 2002 is to be achieved: 'to link work-related activities more strongly to pupils' study in school on an everyday basis; to provide coherent experiences over time; to provide good quality work experience placements with clear aims and objectives and to give support to vocational areas in GNVQ courses' (1998a:4). It is interesting to note that the first item is exactly the area which employers interviewed during the CEI study reported as being least important. They regarded what might be described as the 'workplace socialisation' aspect as being far more important.

The CEI research identified a wide range of learning opportunities available for pupils whilst on work experience, both work-specific tasks (such as filing, booking appointments or stacking shelves) and those which might be described as developing key skills (such as reading and responding to written material, or working in a team). However, it is clear that pupils were also learning a great deal more. This is hardly surprising 'given the complex interactions of human, social, technical and practical processes at the workplace' (Benett, 1999:286). The question of assessment is an even more complex issue since the variability of experiences, quality of supervision and learning opportunities available will significantly influence what can be learned or assessed, and whether such assessment would be valid.

Real work and work experience

Ahier and Moore suggest that it has been customary to think of work experience as designed, amongst other things, to introduce: 'young people to the workplace, the routines and disciplines of employment and the nature of life in a public institution very different from home and a school' (1999:236). In other words, it serves an important function in aiding the transition from school to work. Such notions of work experience were fully explored within earlier studies on pupil work experience (Watts, 1983; Miller, Watts and Jamieson, 1991). More recently, studies of work experience have attempted to focus upon the potential for curricular outcomes and to explore the concept of employability, although this may be the sheep's clothing of the old wolf formerly known as 'social skills' or 'life skills', which was much beloved of the compensatory education schemes.

Nevertheless, the contemporary labour market is very different from that existing in the early 1980s: the staying-on rate of 16 year olds in full-time education has significantly increased, and substantial numbers of (supposedly) full-time pupils have part-time jobs. (For a fuller discussion see Huddleston and Unwin, 1998.) To this extent they have significant experience of a wide variety of workplaces, many of them holding down two or three part-time jobs at any one time. Other young people are engaged in the informal economy and show particular flair in the areas of enterprise and market knowledge. They clearly possess a range of skills which make them successful and employable within that context.

It would be interesting to investigate to what extent employers find these young people unemployable and lacking in the necessary 'social and interpersonal skills' cited both in current policy rhetoric and in the research outlined above. Given that most leading supermarket chains and fast food retail outlets are heavily dependent on part-time student labour, and given that such retailers also pride themselves on high levels of customer service, there appears to be an inherent contradiction in alleged 'employers' perceptions'. It is inconceivable to imagine that such major employers actually engage labour which is 'unfit for the job' or which is 'lacking in basic skills'. Is 'employability', therefore, merely another device for scapegoating those who 'do not quite fit the bill'?

It might be argued that the experiences which young people gain from their part-time and vacation jobs are as valuable, if not more so, in introducing young people to the demands of employment as are two weeks' work experience. Learning, which may occur quite naturally in such situations, is infrequently drawn upon within the context of the National Curriculum and within formal learning, and yet compulsory pupil work experience, it is suggested, is an important element in the preparation of young people for adult and working life. What many young people enjoy about their weekend and holiday jobs is that they are real jobs which carry with them real adult responsibilities. No amount of workplace simulation can compare with a busy Friday night on a supermarket checkout.

Most of the aims elaborated by Watts (1983) for pupil work experience would apply equally to young people's part-time employment. In addition to the obvious 'maturational' aspects of such work, the 'preparatory' and 'anticipatory' aspects are equally important. It might also be argued that Lave's work on learning in apprenticeship (1993) can be used as a model for investigating the ways in which young people learn through their experiences of part-time employment.

What then, is the purpose of a compulsory, structured period of work experience, which can take up to two weeks of curriculum time, during the final year of compulsory schooling, often supplemented by further periods post-16? Why is this period being extended for those young people who are finding the National Curriculum either too challenging or de-motivating?

Extended work experience placements and vocational link courses between schools and further education colleges are being offered to 14–16 year olds who are experiencing difficulty with the full National Curriculum or who are in danger of exclusion from school. What is yet unknown is the extent to which this type of curriculum is more attractive to some young people and also the extent to which it will result in the much lauded 'employability'. However, some early results from the New Start initiative (DfEE, 1998) indicate that as well as appreciating the work-relatedness of the curriculum offering, it is often the more adult environment of the college or the workplace which is enjoyed by the young people. In other words, it is the opportunity to participate in 'communities of practice', to use Lave's model, which is appreciated.

Conclusion

It is not easy to find the answers to some of the questions raised in this chapter because the process of work experience has been used to meet a variety of aims; some concerned with the socialisation of young people into the workplace, others concerned with youth/adult transitions, others focusing upon potential careers sampling (the list is by no means exhaustive, or mutually exclusive).

For employers the process has sometimes been used to engage in some informal recruitment, particularly in areas where there is a shortage of good young recruits. The CEI research found examples of work experience pupils being offered employment: in one large motor manufacturer, preference was given to applicants who had completed a work experience with the company. Many companies see work experience as an opportunity to influence potential future customers. There are some public relations issues, too, for firms and their local communities, particularly where the company's product may have an environmental impact. Some companies interviewed during the course of the CEI research believed that there were staff development benefits accruing from company staff working with young people and acting as mentors.

In summary, from the perspective of employers, accepting school pupils on work experience can serve a multiplicity of aims. These include:

Raising educational standards, both among potential recruits and more widely;
Developing existing staff;
Fulfilling social and community responsibilities;
Improving society's – and in particular young people's knowledge and understanding of, and influencing attitudes to, industry and commerce;
Enhancing the reputation of the firm and its products. (Miller *et al.*, 1995)

What has not been fully explored, although the Learning Frameworks research has attempted to chart some of the learning outcomes, is the extent to which the work of Lave and Wenger might be used as a framework to consider what is happening during a pupil's work experience. Guile and Young rightly remind us of the need to reconsider 'the relationship between learning and work and the scope of workplaces as sites of learning' (1998:186). This would seem a productive way forward in thinking about what is learned during a period of pupil work experience and about how it is learned.

Watts has elaborated an extensive range of objectives for pupil work experience which is so comprehensive that it is hard to imagine how they might all be accomplished in two weeks (1983). For such objectives to be achieved opportunities for learning have to be identified in advance, and ideally every situation would have to be mapped. Clearly, this could not be undertaken by all secondary schools which currently engage in placing their pupils on work experience, and neither could employers be expected to undertake such an exercise. However, young people and their teachers might be encouraged to reflect much more about the ways in which learning occurs and to recognise that what is learned outside a formal, institutional setting can be as powerful, if not more so, as that which is learned in the classroom.

The renewed interest in the 'work-based' route for post-16 education and training, through Modern Apprenticeships and National Traineeships, suggests that, at the very least, pupil work experience provides an opportunity for pupils to encounter the workplace as a site for learning and to consider ways in which such learning takes place. This might equally apply to their part-time and holiday jobs. Lave's work on apprenticeship provides a model of learning which can contribute to our understanding of pupils' learning both during work experience and 'real work'. This supports Engestrom's view that theoretical knowledge is needed to underpin what is learned in social and workplace situations and that this requires a pedagogy which will enable young people to interpret their experiences of work and workplaces and to draw upon such learning.

References

Ahier, J. and Moore, R. (1999) 'Big pictures and fine detail: school work experience policy and the local labour market in the 1990s', in Ahier, J. and Esland, G. (eds), *Education, Training and the Future of Work 1*, London: Routledge.

Andersen Consulting (1998) *The Attributes of Youth: Young People, Education and Employability*, London: Andersen Consulting.

Benett, Y. (1999) 'The validity and reliability of assessments and self-assessments of work-based learning', in Murphy, P. (ed.), *Learners, Learning and Assessment*, London: Paul Chapman Publishing.

British Chambers of Commerce (1998) *Skills for Competitiveness*, London: British Chambers of Commerce.

CBI (1998) *In Search of Employability*, London: CBI.

CEI (1997) 'Work experience in the retail environment', unpublished report for the Department for Education and Employment, CEI, University of Warwick.

Central Advisory Council for Education (1963) *Half Our Future* (Newsom Report), London: HMSO.

DES (1974) *Work Experience*, Circular 7/74, London: DES.

DES (1979) *Aspects of Secondary Education in England*, London: HMSO.

DES (1988a) *Education at Work: A Guide for Employers*, London: HMSO.

DES (1988b) *Education at Work: A Guide for Schools*, London: HMSO.

DfEE (1996a) *Equipping Young People for Working Life*, London: DfEE.

DfEE (1996b) *Work Experience: A Guide for Employers*, London: DfEE.

DfEE (1996c) *Work Experience: A Guide for Schools*, London: DfEE.

DfEE (1998) *New Start*, 3 (July) London: DfEE.

DfEE (1999a) *Skill Needs in Britain, 1998*. Sheffield: DfEE, British Chambers of Commerce.

DfEE (1999b) *Survey of School Business Links in England: 1997/98*, Statistical Bulletin, 2, 99, London: The Stationery Office.

Engestrom, Y. (1994) *Training for Change: New Approach to Instruction and Learning in Working Life*, Geneva: ILO.

Finn, D. (1987) *Training without Jobs*, London: Macmillan.

Guile, D. and Young, M. (1998) ' Apprenticeship as a conceptual basis for a social theory of learning', *Journal of Vocational Education and Training*, 50, 2, 173–93.

Hillage, J. and Pollard, E. (1998) *Employability: Developing a Framework for Policy Analysis*, DfEE Research Report, 85, Sheffield: DfEE.

Hillage, J. *et al.* (1996) *Pre-16 Work Experience in England and Wales*, Brighton: Institute for Employment Studies.

Huddleston, P. and Keep, E. (1998) 'What do employers want from education? Questions more easily asked than answered: re-assessed', paper presented at the International Partnership Network conference, Trondheim, Norway, July.

Huddleston, P. and Unwin, L. (1998) 'Stakeholders, skills and star-gazing: the problematic relationships between education, training and the labour market', in Stanton, G. and Richardson, W. (Eds), *Qualifications for the Future*, London: Further Education Development Agency.

Industry in Education (1996) *Towards Employability*, London: Industry in Education Trust.

Institute of Careers Officers (1974) *Work Experience in British Secondary Schools*, 2nd edn, Stourbridge: Institute of Careers Officers.

Johns, A. (1997) *Work Experience and the Law*, Coventry: CEI, University of Warwick.

Lave, J. (1993) 'The practice of learning', in Chaiklen, S. and Lave, J. (eds), *Understanding Practice*, Cambridge: Cambridge University Press.

Lave, J. and Wenger, E. (1991) *Situated Learning*, Cambridge: Cambridge University Press.

Miller, A. D., Watts, A. G. and Jamieson, I. M. (1991) *Rethinking Work Experience*, London: Falmer Press.

Miller, A. D., Cramphorn, J., Huddleston, P. and Woolhouse, J. (1995) *Making Education our Business*, London: DFE/ED/ESSO.

Ofsted (1998a) 'Schools in partnership with employers: Ofsted findings', paper presented at the CEI Annual Conference, Leicester, 1998.

Ofsted (1998b) *Work-Related Aspects of the Curriculum in Secondary Schools*, London: Ofsted.

QCA (1998a) *Disapplication of the National Curriculum at Key Stage 4 using Section 363 of the 1996 Education Act for a Wider Focus on Work-related Learning. Guidance for Schools*, London: QCA.

QCA (1998b) *Learning from Work Experience*, London: QCA.

Shilling, C. (1989) *Schooling for Work in Capitalist Britain*, London: Falmer Press.

Social Exclusion Unit (1998) *Truancy and School Exclusion*, Report by the Social Exclusion Unit, Cm 3957, London: HMSO.

Watts, A. G. (1983) *Work Experience and Schools*, London: Heinemann.

CHAPTER 12

What engineers learn in the workplace and how they learn it*

Peter Senker

Introduction

Two linked and fundamental misapprehensions permeate policy discourse on learning relevant to performance in the workplace: that learning takes place almost exclusively during formal education and training courses, and that learning inputs and outputs can be measured in terms of parameters such as the costs of education and training, the time spent on them, and qualifications achieved.

Policy discourse relating to learning and to the 'Learning Society' focuses mainly on formal education and training. Provision is defined in terms of how training is delivered or facilitated. Goals are defined in terms of the achievement of qualifications with much less attention to gains in knowledge, skills or capability which are not assessed formally (Eraut *et al.*, 1998a). The dominance of such discourse is illustrated by a British government official who uses survey data as a basis for the extreme statement that 'just under half [of the

* This chapter draws heavily on a study of knowledge and skills in employment inspired and led by Michael Eraut, and funded by 'The Learning Society' Programme of the ESRC. I am also most grateful to Geoff Mason, Kevin McCormick, Jane Millar and Helen Rainbird for their perceptive comments on earlier drafts.

working age population] has done no learning in the last three years' (Stuart, 1997). This discourse owes its supremacy to the perception that widening access to formal education and training is the only way to provide and stimulate learning, and to the success in promoting their wares to the public and the Government of those who provide, promote and study formal work-related education and training. These are issues with world-wide implications. A recent report from the ILO recognises the problems of measuring changes in the skill composition of the labour force. However, its discussion of skills issues concentrates unduly on formal education and training, and its recommendations are unduly biased towards the need to make improvements in the efficiency and governance of training systems, placing insufficient emphasis on the need to improve the workplace as a learning environment (ILO, 1998). So far, however, the political emphasis on formal education and training may be greater in Britain than in most other countries, and Britain therefore provides a good environment in which to study these phenomena.

The British Government's recent Green Paper (DfEE, 1998) assumes that learning happens almost exclusively in formal education and training settings and that such learning is directly related to effectiveness at work. It neglects to consider enriching work as a means of enhancing its potential for stimulating learning. Indeed, it has been suggested that the three main political parties in Britain recognise the need for a strategic and policy framework for lifelong learning on the basis of the assumption that lifelong learning is only about 'widening participation ... in the further and higher education sectors' (McGivney, 1997). Researchers generally make similar assumptions: a paper by distinguished academics which examines the concept of the learning organisation is concerned almost exclusively with training (Raper *et al.*, 1997).

The prevailing ideology amongst politicians is that everything significant to policy can be measured: in the case of the issues discussed here, that learning can be measured in terms of qualifications achieved. In some policy areas, quantification can indeed provide a sound basis on which policy can be developed. Provided that key parameters and the chains of causality which link them can be identified, progress in achieving policy objectives over time can be monitored by measuring the relevant parameters periodically. If the parameters do not reach the targets set for them, policies can be modified in an attempt to align future progress more closely with targets. In contrast, it is contended here that learning cannot be quantified in ways which comply with these conditions, and therefore that quantification cannot provide a sound basis for policy development.

The British National Adult Learning Survey (NALS) made determined efforts to quantify work-based learning. This was a carefully thought-out study designed to 'estimate the number and characteristics of people taking part in learning of a range of different types' (Beinart and Smith, 1998:33). The survey definition of learning 'was not restricted to education and training as conventionally understood – viz. periods of instruction received from a teacher or trainer'. The survey designers faced problems such as how to capture information about self-directed learning, and how to communicate their definition of learning to respondents during a survey interview. They tackled these problems ingeniously, asking respondents about their experience of five types of 'Taught learning' and four types of 'Non-taught learning'. Non-taught learning included studying for qualifications without taking part in a taught course; supervised learning while doing a job (for example, when a manager spent time helping respondents to learn); time spent keeping up to date, (for example, by reading books or manuals or attending seminars); and deliberately trying to teach themselves without taking part in a taught course. But it will be shown that even this broad definition excludes major elements of people's learning at work.

The chapter continues with a brief discussion of the nature of learning in specialist education and training institutions and in the workplace. This is followed by a discussion of what engineers and technicians need to know in order to carry out their work, a brief review of their initial education and training, and some findings from empirical research on the development of engineering knowledge and skills in employment. Discussion of these issues concludes with the suggestion that, since learning as an integral part of work activities is very important, more research is needed to understand it better, so as to place policy formation on a firmer basis.

Learning relevant to employment

There are two principal types of site at which learning relevant to employment takes place: in education and training institutions, and in the workplace.

Learning in education and training institutions

Education and training institutions are primarily concerned to train and educate people. In practice, ensuring that the skills and knowledge imparted will contribute to performance in work is often secondary to the objective of passing on the accumulated knowledge and wisdom of the teacher or trainer. The relative autonomy of education and training institutions from the world of work has often led to major divergences between educational goals and the goals of the wider society and economy. In the past such divergences have sometimes persisted for centuries. The introduction of new types of knowledge into the curriculum of universities and other academic institutions has often been a slow and painful process. The resistance of those within the academic system wishing to preserve the place in the curriculum held by disciplines which have long lost their relevance to society and work has often been formidable and long-lasting. By the early twentieth century the bias against university studies related to industrial needs had been eroded by fears about falling growth in industrial production, increased foreign competition and changes in industrial structure (Senker and Senker, 1997). More recently, there have been extensive efforts to try to bring the activities of educational institutions into closer accord with the needs of employment (Senker and Senker, 1994). The interview material presented later in this chapter indicates that such efforts have achieved only limited success.

Learning in the workplace

The workplace can be a creative and motivating site for learning. The learning that takes place at the workplace can be divided into 'organised learning', in which the employer makes deliberate attempts to enhance the learning of employees, typified by on-the-job training and apprenticeship, and also employees learning in the normal course of their work.

Apprenticeship is organised by employers in workplaces and its aims include facilitating the learning of newcomers to an organisation. Lave (1991:65) considers learning as a process of becoming a member of a sustained community of practice. Newcomers become old-timers when their initial 'legitimate peripheral participation' is transformed into full participation in communities of practice. She suggests that apprenticeship essentially involves exposure to on-going practice but does not necessarily involve intentional guidance and instruction. 'Knowledge and skill develop ... as an integral part of the process ... of becoming like master practitioners within a community of practice' (1991:71).

Until the sixteenth century at least, the knowledge and skills acquired by apprentices were almost exclusively tacit: heuristic, subjective and internalised and learned through practical examples, experience and practice. Neither the craftsman nor the apprentice had any knowledge of science or scientific principles (Senker, 1996).

In advanced countries today, engineers need articulated knowledge, skills and tacit knowledge, and to 'assemble' them so as to achieve competent performance (Anderson, 1983:4–5). Articulated knowledge 'is transmissible in formal systematic language and includes general scientific principles and laws. Such principles may be written down in detail in manuals and textbooks and taught to students in formal education and training environment' (Senker, 1993) Similarly, knowledge of information – such as catalogue knowledge (know-what) and explanatory knowledge (know why) – is symbolic in nature and more readily transmittable than contextually sensitive encultured knowledge such as process, social and experiential knowledge. (Millar, Demaid and Quintas, 1997).

Fundamental concepts can provide a framework on which subsequent knowledge and skills can be built. This is illustrated by an experiment in which the performance of non-literate subjects was compared with those of subjects who had recently acquired literacy skills. In one experiment, subjects were given pictures of a hammer, a saw, a log and a hatchet, and asked to say which three went together. Literate subjects were generally able to say that hammer, hatchet and saw were grouped together, as all were tools. Non-literate subjects found it difficult to perceive this (Wertsch, 1985).

Tacit knowledge has been characterised as the knowledge of techniques, methods and designs that work in certain ways and with certain consequences, even when one cannot explain exactly why (Rosenberg, 1982). The essence of tacit knowledge is knowledge of how to do things without knowing how we do them: examples include ability to ride a bicycle or to swim (Polanyi, 1986). Research by Eraut confirmed Polanyi's view that knowledge use is a largely tacit process (Eraut *et al.*, 1995). Some tacit knowledge is specific to an individual firms' own products and production processes (Senker, 1993). Skilled members of a community of practitioners – such as teams of engineers working in a company – are often 'unaware of the details of their problem-solving behaviour, the rules they follow and the information they draw on' (Millar, Demaid and Quintas 1997).

Learning and performance are highly dependent on contextual factors and cognitive processes are tied to the context at the time of knowledge acquisition. Learning does not occur naturally; it involves active 'mastery', which is a process of internalisation. An operation which initially represented an external activity begins to occur internally. Interpersonal processes are then transformed into intra-personal ones, and this process involves a series of developmental events (Millar, 1995). The acquisition of some types of knowledge and skills tends to be more context-dependent than the acquisition of other types of knowledge. In particular, the acquisition of articulated knowledge may be less context-dependent than the acquisition of tacit knowledge.

The pattern through which knowledge and skills are acquired, and the efficiency of the learning process, depend both on how people learn and on the relative cost-effectiveness of various learning strategies, and in particular on the relative efficiency of 'on-the-job' learning and formal 'off-the-job' education and training. In general, the more specialist the work involved; the more rapid the changes in the job – for example, resulting from changes in work organisation and technology – and the more efficient it is to acquire the knowledge and skills they need 'on-the-job'.

Vygotsky's analysis of the relationships between teaching and learning is extremely complex, and there is only space to touch on it here. Essentially, while people can accomplish more with help and support than they can alone, they can only learn what is within their range: within their 'zone of proximal development' (Newman and Holzman, 1993). Teaching methods such as lectures, tutorials, written information and educational telecommunications represent indirect experience for the learner (Griffey and Hughes, 1997). If there is a training intervention, and the aims and content are remote from existing experience in content or time, then it may be rejected. Experiential learning derived from interaction with the working environment is often more effective (Kolb, 1984). Examples of experiential learning are given later in the chapter.

What professional engineers and engineering technicians need to learn

A high proportion of engineering activity still takes place in the absence of 'deep scientific knowledge of why things perform the way they do' (Rosenberg, 1982). Most technology is 'specific, complex, often tacit and cumulative in its development' (Pavitt, 1987). It embodies encultured knowledge which is intrinsically tied to its context, being generated and situated in use. Engineers' needs for knowledge and understanding are significantly different from those of scientists. The basic goal of the physicist is knowledge about the physical world. In contrast, engineers need to predict the performance of the objects they design, and require analytical tools to carry out design calculations. Scientific knowledge must be reformulated to make it useful for engineers. In the case of fluid mechanics, physicists concentrate on the solution of differential equations of motion. In contrast, engineers need analytical tools to help them to understand problems involving the flow of fluids in devices such as engines, rockets and boilers. But science is not always heavily involved in important developments in engineering. For example, in the early 1930s, most metal aeroplanes designed in the USA were held together by rivets with heads protruding beyond the external surface of the aircraft. This caused air resistance. Ten years later, almost all aircraft had rivets flush with the surface. This development was important because, for civil aircraft, as speeds went up, the costs of dragging exposed rivet heads through the air increased; for military aircraft, as other methods of increasing top speed reached their limits, the gains from getting the rivet heads out of the airstream looked increasingly attractive. The development of flush rivets required extensive and highly complicated learning activity throughout the industry, involving much trial and error and learning from experience, but hardly involving science at all (Vincenti, 1990:112–36, 170–90) Engineers usually work in teams, as in this example; accordingly, personal and communications skills are crucial. Over many years, numerous reports have complained about the poor communications skills of many engineers in Britain (for example, see Finniston, 1980; Beuret and Webb, 1983).

How engineers and technicians learn

Initial education and training

Initial engineering education and training of engineers and technicians in Britain has changed extensively in the last several years. However, some broad patterns have persisted for many years. Until the age of 16, all receive education at school which includes subjects of particular relevance to engineering such as mathematics, science and English language. Between the ages of 16 and 19, some of those aspiring to do craft and technician work enter employment as apprentices or trainees and participate to varying extents in part-time work-related training and theoretical study. Others take full-time vocational courses at colleges of further education.

The majority of those who aspire to be professional engineers continue at school until 18 or 19, specialising in subjects such as mathematics and science, and go on to study engineering or related courses at university. A minority take alternative routes (for example, taking full-time vocational courses at colleges of further education or entering employment as apprentices) as first steps towards eventually achieving professional engineering status, often, but not invariably, taking a university degree at a later stage in their career.

Development of knowledge and skills in employment

A recent study included interviews with people in large and medium-sized organisations in three sectors: business, engineering and healthcare (Eraut *et al.*, 1998a). The business organisations were all large: insurance companies, a bank and an electricity supply company, in which the people interviewed were non-technical and involved in managing and marketing services. Engineers and technicians were interviewed in three companies mainly engaged in developing engineering products, and in two large public service organisations whose main function lay outside engineering; these organisations were working in an environment of rapid technological change. Nurses, nursing assistants, radiographers and cardiac technicians were interviewed in the healthcare sector.

The strategy was to ask about the respondent's job, recent tasks, duties and problems; to discuss the nature of the competence/expertise required to do it; and to ask how the necessary expertise was acquired and the extent to which it was changing. Questions were also asked about different sources of learning and respondents were encouraged to elaborate on salient learning episodes.

One of the key findings was that, in these occupations formal education and training provide only a small part of what is learned at work. Indeed, most of the learning described in our interviews was non-formal, neither clearly specified nor planned. It arose naturally out of the demands and challenges of work-solving problems, improving quality and/or productivity, or coping with change – and out of social interactions in the workplace with colleagues, customers or clients. Responding to such challenges entails both working and learning – one cannot be separated from the other. In retrospect it may be described as learning from experience.

Most of engineers' learning occurs at the same time as work, and as an integral part of work activities, and would therefore be excluded from the scope of the NALS survey discussed above. Initial education and training (engineering degrees, apprenticeships and so on) can be important as foundations on which learning at work can be built; and short training courses can sometimes be useful. But learning arises largely out of the challenges posed by work – for example, solving problems, improving quality, getting things done, coping with change – and out of interactions with colleagues and customers.

Research evidence indicates that experience plays a major role in building up a knowledge base which produces expertise (Griffey and Hughes, 1997; Eraut *et al.*, 1998a). Interviews demonstrated the relatively small role of formal education and 'off-the-job' training in engineers' learning (Eraut *et al.*, 1998a); it was also confirmed that engineers need 'enormously diverse and complex kinds of knowledge' (Vincenti, 1990:8–9). For example, in discussing the usefulness of his undergraduate degree in nuclear engineering, a senior staff engineer in his late thirties said:

> There are two or three aspects which I use very very rarely but when I use them they're useful, principles like part of the degree was thermal modelling, thermal calculations, I occasionally have to apply that, but to a very very low degree ... I don't sit down and work through partial differential equations. I just have one or two very simple equations which I will then put into a spreadsheet ... I know what stress analysis is but I'll look it up in a book... probably a little bit more useful is the general knowledge that it gives you in terms of subatomic particles and X-rays .

A development engineer in her late twenties also questioned the relevance of her undergraduate degree: 'I think a lot of what I did in my degree course was done because we had to pass the exams and you could forget it as soon as the exams were over.'

A senior software designer in his late twenties had taken a degree in Information Systems Design and had found this rather useful. But he emphasised the usefulness of the year's company placement included in the degree programme. (He had taken a four year course with one year out.)

> I thought that was a good idea as well to have a year out, because clients look up on programming and software design. If you've got some experience, you've got a bit

of an edge over perhaps someone who's done a three-year course... There's various methodologies within programming that you can adopt and we were taught ... representation of diagrams, disciplines, for instance, data flow diagrams.

He also emphasised the significance of a university degree as an entry requirement for getting a job in software design: employers need to be reassured that their prospective employees are suitable, and their possession of a degree provided such reassurance. A notable benefit of the degree course was being taught to carry out projects to time:

> We were pushed all the time, weekly deadlines, and ... if you were one minute late, your deadline, you get no mark ... that helped me to get my stuff done, and I spent a few sleepless nights not going to bed ... and delivered the stuff on time, and then collapsed ... it woke me up quite substantially to the real world ... cope with pressure situation, you've got to deliver your products, you've got to be there on the dot ... that was very good... sort of indirect training, but that was what the lecturers intended.

The sheer complexity and variability of engineers' learning processes and the extent to which most are embedded in day-to-day work is remarkable. A senior engineer learned much of what he knows through experience: 'there was an enormous great machine that we were building ... and there was no one to run it, so basically I sort of thrust myself in it and said ... "I'll do it, I'm quite happy to, to have a go at it".'

Learning from experience often involves learning from mistakes: his subsequent work involved supervising:

> I made some mistakes and I learned through those mistakes ... one of my ... maxims is always to have a certain amount of work lined up for the guys working below. At that time it never really struck me so these guys would be coming up to me saying 'What do I do now?' ... I'll be thinking 'Crikey, I don't know, what do you do now?' So ... you gradually learn immediately that you gotta start planning these guys' workload ... as opposed to just go to one of them and say 'Oy! ... could you do this please' ... You learn that you should really go through the proper route, you talk to the supervisor first.

Another vital part of learning from experience is learning from colleagues:

> I was identified as somebody who could fix problems ... I then had a team of designers assigned to me ... I worked with, in fact I still work with ... a supervisor in the drawing office ...who is about forty-five and he's got a wealth of experience in design so ... through talking to him, bouncing ideas off him ... we ... had a good synergy where he's got a lot of experience in manufacturability ... I would be good at identifying ... the root cause of the problem ... the root cause is we don't have ...

enough force at this point … or this bit cracks because it's not expanding, so I would identify the problem and then John and I would sit down and we'd bounce ideas and I'd say 'You could do this by doing this' and he'd say 'It's a little bit complicated, can't we do it this way? …

Then a major project came along … designing a machine from scratch … we had to make sure that we got all the bits … we had come to manage all the people underneath us so they were always working as efficiently as possible on the right thing … a lot of my learning at that point … came from … my immediate manager who was a very dynamic person… I learned a lot of design for cost from him … and also the management of the qualification of the machine. It's one thing to build the machine, but when you're doing a new machine you have to qualify at the end of it to prove that it does what it's supposed to do, and he was very good at quantifying how to do that and I learned a lot.

Similarly, a development engineer in her late twenties doing very different work recounts how she learned from past mistakes:

a big problem of test failures … also the rework cost us money and time. So quality did a study … what came out of that said we don't understand the fail rate, we don't understand what's happening. Now the company are very hot on … quality improvement teams … I said I'm quite interested in that … so we set up a chain, it was myself from development, we had a production engineer, two guys from the shopfloor, somebody from inspection, and also a quality manager, was what we called a facilitator … we set up regular meetings… We set up a database, so every [product] that failed we looked right, why did it fail, I've now got six months' work data that says right, if the [product] fails let's try this, this and this, don't try anything else because it doesn't work. We do all sorts of analysis using various quality tools that we're taught throughout the company… And we said … the [product] seizes, it must be because two bits don't fit … So we've got to do something about that. So we went back and we found we were getting a certain number of things oversized, it was particularly sensitive to dirt, so we went 'What the hell is this dirt', we got the bits picked out of the [product] and it was blue fibres … blue rags that they use around the shop for wiping down … we got them banned from the machine and we've got lint-free paper now instead of the wipes … that was something that we didn't think of. And we learned an awful lot about the product itself and what to account for with regards to component errors … it's not necessarily the obvious thing that you would think of … and we've learned a lot more about the product which we now feed into the rework side of things … so our rework has come down from sort of thirty per cent to zero.

It is interesting to note the attempt to capture past experience in a database, and the significant but relatively small role played by formal training courses run by the company on 'quality tools'. The central feature of this example is that a team was established to diagnose and remedy problems which occurred through past failures, and the team all learned from each other.

Moreover, this development engineer believed that her learning from colleagues was not confined to technical matters:

I learned ... from watching how other people are, how the good chairman chairs a meeting, and how a poor chairman chairs a meeting ... trying to stop it deteriorating into general chat and bring it back into focus. 'Will you do this?' making sure that people are prepared to take on actions and they understand what they're doing, they don't just take it on and 'I haven't got a clue but she said I've got to do it.' ... making sure people know what they've got to do and when they've got to do it by, so you do that ... by observation... If I got problem I say 'I haven't got a clue how to do this', I've got maybe a little bit of idea then I go and say right, 'let's do it like this, is this approach right', and then I gotta talk it through with somebody ... who's been helpful in the past, who perhaps has been here a long time, has a lot of experience, done a similar thing in the past ... Just by working with people, you find out who is good with the knowledge and who says things just for the sake of saying to get you off their back. And ... again, it's by observation.

These themes of learning from experience, learning from each other and learning from mistakes cropped up frequently in the interviews, in a vast variety of contexts. A senior software designer who also works in customer support stated:

The first time I was on call, it was a very nervous situation ... you've got to have a technical eye to start with. The second part is dealing with customers, something like telephone manner, that's got to be good ... cos sometimes when you want to scream and say ... 'you stupid idiot' ... you've just got to bite your tongue and say ... 'I think we should do it this way' and ... that's something I wasn't taught during my graduate course ... take customers through ... 'Click that down, move it to that button, bring that menu down, and release that button, and then this'll pop up'... You can't get someone off the street ... and put them on call ... they've got to have knowledge of the system that's been developed at [the organisation] ... the support manager came up to me and said, would you like to go and support ... nobody was trained in the support role ... we learn from our associates, they take you through it.

If you make a mistake, as long as you learn from it and don't make the same mistake, that's how we work. I'm always in the situation where, it's like life, if you make a mistake and you learn from it, that's good, you're progressing. If you ... make the same mistake again, then you're wasting your time, you've not learned anything. Try and learn from your mistakes ... that's one of my personal approaches. But ... most of my job ... I've learned through qualified people in the job already, senior principal people ... If you've got a problem ... 'can you give me a hand on this?' ... If we get a situation where somebody's working alone and they can't come back to me and say can you give me help, I can't do this ... I think we've failed him ... if he's got a problem, say ... downloading a piece of software ... I show them what to do ... One day ... this guy came up to me, and ... this guy he's probably one of the best people ... in knowledge of [the product] ... I asked him a question, and we sat down at a table ... and he showed me what to do, and I said, 'Oh, didn't you know how to do this?', and it was just ... a simple command, but he never knew that UNIX command, and he said, 'Oh right, I've learnt something today', and I actually taught him something, and he's taught me something.

Off-the-job-training

Training courses generally provide a rather small proportion of engineers' work-related learning. For example, a control software manager 'did do quite a bit of CAD [computer-aided design] training at one point because I was sort of doing system administration for a UNIX based CAD system ... I did do quite a bit of that which I haven't really used since although the UNIX may prove useful if we ever move that way.'

The only training this company gave a development engineer was seeing videos primarily intended for 'American sales engineers ... we were expected to sit for hours on end in front of a video of someone giving a seminar to sales-men, who obviously asked marketing, sales type questions, which were not at all applicable to how the machine worked ... it was useless.'

However, there seem to be three principal exceptions to the general rule that training courses are relatively unimportant: safety training; initial engineering courses offered by companies to introduce their engineers and technicians to the highly specialised technologies which some companies use; and manage-ment courses, typically offered to engineers progressing into management positions in their thirties.

For example, a reliability engineer had received 'lots of training on things to do with safety ... new regulations that come out, but ... my electronic knowl-edge, I've never seen anything from [the company] to help improve that'. But companies were sometimes reluctant to provide much-needed safety training. A development technician:

> was told when I came here that we will be sent on training courses, and updated on things on a regular basis, at least once or twice a year: it hasn't materialised – I had a moan, a lot of serious moans about the lack of electrical expertise within the depart-ment, and it was only when there were a couple of near-miss accidents that they finally conceded.

A company providing a specialised service which requires sophisticated engineering support operates a training centre which is highly regarded by its engineers. According to one of the engineers:

> the [company] has excellent engineering training ... the fundamentals course ... deals with the basic principles ... four weeks ... I wouldn't fault any of the engi-neering training ... that's as good as you could hope for, but what is very difficult to learn other than by doing it is the sort of interpersonal and diplomatic side of the job which has become so much more important in the last two or three years.

A systems engineer went to the same training centre and learned 'funda-mentals, which are still fundamental ... even today ... digital distribution, it's still the same as it always was, the principles are still the same, and I've always found that it helps you understand all the systems'. But a senior Head of Project Operations found these courses less useful: 'I don't regard them as being the key part of getting to know things. I think what's been my driver is to be able to drill down into an organisation and find out how it all works.' In another company designing specialised products, a systems engineer had been on a six-week course: 'they structured it well ... you had practical exercises, quite frequently ... they would actually put faults on the hardware, and then you would have to find out the faults.'

Management courses were highly rated by several engineers – but it was very important to ensure that the timing coincided with their assumption of management responsibilities. A marketing quality coordinator had stated:

> I've gained a lot of further skills and am becoming more financially aware, that's for certain through the CIM [Certificate in Management] course ... The timing has been very important ... I've got the necessary tools ... I've never read so much in all my life ... I do a tremendous amount of research and that has helped me. A really good example I think ... if when we did the finance module. I wasn't very financially aware at all ... I took a project ... to make a compensation claim from one of our suppliers and I put a paper together ... they used the document to present to the supplier ... I'm pleased to say that just this week, again the timing is unbelievable, that has actually been paid out by the supplier... A year ago I just would not have had the skills ... to do something like that.

At another company, a duty engineer went on a CMS Certificate in Management course:

> that was my Ladybird guide to management – it was very broad brush, I learnt ... how to deal with disciplinary matters, I learnt how to re-scratch the surface on individual's behaviours, how they interact within groups, then we go down the finance side, and the marketing side, marketing and finance ... My ... style in interaction with my colleagues, and my communication with these colleagues and customers, I have completely moved ground from an aggressive stance ... and have far more empathy with what these individuals are going through and the roadblocks that they have to move around, whereas before ... I never really considered their thoughts.

Discussion and conclusions

Most of engineers' work-related learning takes place at the workplace and is inextricably embodied in other work activities. The same applies to the other occupations considered in our study such as people involved in managing and marketing services in large business organisations together with nurses, nursing assistants, radiographers and cardiac technicians. Clearly, this is not a purely British phenomenon. The results of research in Holland also suggest that the amount of learning and informal training (for example, employees teaching their peers) that takes place in the workplace is very significant. 'The problem is that it is not measurable, only the formal on-the-job training programmes can be measured' (Mulder and Tjepkema, 1999).

A very small proportion of learning at the workplace is recognised by qualifications such as NVQs, the vast majority of which are acquired near the beginning of working life. However, the continuous workplace learning which takes place in relatively high-level professional and managerial occupations may not be reflected fully in the experience of less highly-skilled workers. Indeed, the workplace learning of workers in less highly-skilled occupations may be more heavily concentrated at the beginning of working life, and a significant proportion of it may possibly be reflected in the achievement of NVQs. Nevertheless, the general conclusion that it is impossible to quantify work-related learning realistically is inescapable, however unpalatable such a conclusion may be to some politicians and researchers.

Business organisation, practices and technology are changing rapidly, and people move from job to job frequently. As soon as – or even before – one job is 'mastered', the engineer moves to new work, generally but not invariably within the same organisation. Sometimes a change involves a new job title within the same or different department; sometimes it is a change of role which is not necessarily recognised formally. The rate of change is such that everyone, whether senior or junior, needs to learn continually, often from each other. Many engineers' working lives could be described as 'continual apprenticeship', if, following Lave (1991), we broaden the concept to include examples of legitimate peripheral participation which are not normally recognised as apprenticeship, and which do not necessarily take place in the initial stages of working life.

Other forms of initial education and training – such as university degree courses, technician vocational education and training and specialised engineering training by companies – play roles in providing theoretical foundations, in helping people 'learn to learn' and, not least, by providing experience (project-based learning) in problem-solving. Inevitably, most engineers' formal education is very inefficient in terms of meeting the eventual learning needs of any one individual, as it aims to be broad enough to provide the foundations for the vast variety of jobs which engineers eventually do, and it mainly takes place outside the workplace context which is most conducive to effective learning. But some of it can be justified in terms of providing essential principles on which subsequent learning can be based, and some by economies of scale in preparing teaching materials and presenting them to large numbers of students. Safety training can be vital, and may sometimes be neglected, and management courses for engineers moving into supervision or management can be invaluable. But, with some important exceptions, off-the-job training courses play roles in engineers' learning which are generally minor in relation to learning from work experience, from mistakes, and through communication between colleagues.

British government attempts to promote 'The Learning Age' are based on a false premise: that most work-related learning takes place in formal education and training settings. The success of government attempts to promote lifelong learning will be measured quantitatively (for example, in terms of the numbers of people achieving qualifications such as NVQs). It is suggested here that such measures are totally inappropriate. Success or failure in meeting the British government's objective of investing 'in human capital … as the foundation of success in the knowledge-based global economy' (DfEE, 1998) cannot be measured in this way, as they only assess a relatively small proportion of employees' learning. As illustrated in the interview material, learning flows in many directions: within departments, between departments and functions, and between different levels in the same function. For example, a senior (graduate) may contribute theoretical insights, but a technician may make a complementary contribution based on long experience.

At present, engineers' learning in the workplace in Britain is mainly opportunistic. This implies that there may be scope for individuals and organisations to exploit the potential of the workplace as a learning environment more systematically. The culture and employment policies and practices of Japanese companies seem to be more conducive to the effective use of the workplace as a learning environment than those of British companies, and it may be that the strength of Japanese engineering derives from this to a significant extent. There is evidence that the strength of Japanese engineering relative to British arises more from companies' efforts to ensure that their engineers get balanced experience in work, rather than to the quality of Japanese initial education or subsequent formal training. The dominance of education and training-oriented discourse in this country is such that few would dare to express such a view, even when they themselves present evidence which supports it. For example, Kynch reviews evidence of the relative weakness of higher education in engineering in Japan, and is driven to the tentative view that 'in certain circumstances, work experience may dwarf degree study as a source of useful skills', and even to express doubt about 'the assumed link between learning acquired in higher education and required in work' (1995:23–4).

The research data presented in this chapter indicates that the quality and quantity of the learning opportunities afforded by experience at work are the primary factor affecting the quantity and quality of engineers' learning (Eraut *et al.*, 1998a, 1998b, 1999). This conclusion applies also to the other occupational areas considered in this study, and probably also applies to many other occupations.

Further research would be needed to verify this, as the study reported here suffers from the limitations which apply to most studies which could be classified broadly under the heading of educational research: it was on far too small a scale to provide a sound basis for development of policy (Hargreaves, 1998). If, as suggested in this chapter, learning as an integral part of work activities represents a major factor in learning, more research on learning at work is needed as a basis for development of policies designed to lead to the creation of a 'learning society'.

References

Anderson, J. R. (1983) *The Architecture of Cognition*, Cambridge, Mass.: Harvard University Press.

Beinart, S. and Smith, P. (1998) *National Adult Learning Survey, 1997* (NALS), London: DfEE.

Beuret, G. and Webb, A. (1983) *Goals of Engineering Education: Engineers – Servants or Saviours?*, London: Council for National Academic Awards.

DfEE (1998) *The Learning Age: A Renaissance for a New Britain*, London: DfEE, Cm 3790.

Eraut, M., Alderton, J., Cole, G. and Senker, P. (1998a) 'Development of knowledge and skills in employment', University of Sussex Institute of Education, *Research Report 5*.

Eraut, M., Alderton, J., Cole, G. and Senker, P. (1998b) 'Learning from other people at work', in Coffield, F. (ed.), *Learning at Work*, Bristol: Policy Press.

Eraut, M., Alderton J., Cole, G. and Senker, P. (1999) 'The impact of the manager on learning in the workplace', in Coffield, F. (ed.), *Speaking Truth to Power: Research and Policy on Lifelong Learning*, Bristol: Policy Press.

Finniston, Sir M. (Chairman) (1980) *Engineering Our Future: Report of the Committee of Inquiry into the Engineering Profession* (The Finniston Report), London: HMSO.

Griffey. S. and Hughes, J. (1997) 'VET and HRD and the ideal learning environment', paper presented to the Journal of Vocational Education and Training Second International Conference, 'Policy and Practice in VET', University of Huddersfield.

Hargreaves, D. H. (1998) 'Teaching as a research-based profession; possibilities and prospects', The Teacher Training Agency, Annual lecture, 1996 mimeo, cited in Tooley, J., *Educational Research: A Critique*, London: Office for Standards in Education.

ILO (1998) *World Employment Report 1998–99: Employability in the Global Economy: How Training Matters*, Geneva: ILO.

Kolb, D. A. (1984) *Experiential Learning: Experience as the Source of Learning and Development*, Englewood Cliffs, NJ: Prentice-Hall.

Kynch, C. (1995) 'Engineering expertise – not enough of the right type in the right place?', paper for ESRC study group on the Economics of Education.

Lave J. (1991) 'Situated learning in communities of practice', in Resnick, L. and Levine, J. (eds), *Perspectives on Socially Shared Cognition*, Washington: American Psychological Association.

McGivney, V. (1997) 'Adult participation in learning: can we change the pattern? in Coffield, F. (ed.), *A National Startegy for Lifelong Learning*, Newcastle, University of Newcastle.

Millar, J. (1995) 'Interactive learning in situated software practice: factors mediating the new production of knowledge', unpublished D. Phil Thesis, University of Sussex.

Millar, J., Demaid, A. and Quintas, P. (1997) 'Trans-organizational innovation: a framework for research', *Technology Analysis and Strategic Management*, 9, 4, 399–418.

Mulder, M. and Tjepkema, S. (1999) 'Training and development in the Netherlands', *International Journal of Training and Development*, 3, 1, 63–73.

Newman, F. and Holzman, L. (1993) *Leve Vygotsky, Revolutionary Scientist*, London: Routledge.

Pavitt, K. (1987) 'The objectives of technology policy', *Science and Public Policy*, 14, 4, 182–8.

Polanyi, M. (1966) *The Tacit Dimension*, London: Routledge & Kegan Paul.

Raper, P., Ashton, D., Felstead, A. and Storey, J. (1997) 'Towards the learning organisation? Explaining current trends in training practice in the UK', *International Journal of Training and Development*, 1, 1, 9–21.

Rosenberg, N. (1982) 'How exogenous is science?', in Resnick, L., Levine, J. and Teasley, S. D. (eds), *Inside the Black Box, Technology and Economics*, Cambridge, Mass.: Cambridge University Press.

Senker, J. (1993) 'The contribution of tacit knowledge to innovation', *AI and Society*, 7, 209–24.

Senker, J. and Senker, P. (1997) 'Implications of industrial relationships for universities: a case study of the UK Teaching Company Scheme', *Science and Public Policy*, 24, 3, 173–82.

Senker, P. (1996), 'The production of occupational competence: towards a framework of analysis', in Banerjee, P. and Sato, Y. (eds), *Skill and Technological Change: Societies and Institutions in International Perspective*, New Delhi: Har-Anand.

Senker, P. and Senker, J. (1994) 'Transferring technology and expertise from universities to industry: Britain's Teaching Company Scheme', *New Technology, Work and Employment*, 9, 2, 81–92.

Stuart, N. (1997) 'The Policy of UK Government on Lifelong Learning', in Coffield, F. (ed.), *A National Strategy for Lifelong Learning*, University of Newcastle.

Vincenti, W. G. (1990) *What Engineers Know and How They Know It: Analytical Studies from Aeronautical History*, Baltimore, MD: John Hopkins University Press.

Wertsch, J. V. (1985) *Culture, Communication and Cognition: Vygotskian Perspectives*, Cambridge: Cambridge University Press.

CHAPTER 13

Adult learning and the workplace*

Peter Caldwell

Introduction

Changes in employment, occupational structure and society more widely are encouraging a re-think of the ways we look at VET in the workplace, especially as this relates to low-paid workers. These changes are dramatic, and seriously upset and challenge existing notions of skills, education and training. This chapter focuses on the development of wider adult learning opportunities in the workplace. These opportunities partly concern changes within VET, but also have a much wider scope and significance.

It is in the context of these changes in employment and occupational structure, which are discussed below in more detail, that debates about lifelong learning have arisen. The argument for lifelong learning derives in part from a shift away from a dominant and predictable pattern of a life *cycle* (within which education could play a clearly defined part, mainly in the early years of life) into diverse and unpredictable life *courses*. The variety in employment, family, social and leisure lives means that people have different educational needs for different purposes at different times of their lives. The notion of lifelong learning should not be seen as replacing one system with another

* I would like to thank Helen Rainbird for her help in preparing this chapter whilst acknowledging that any limitations and errors remain my own responsibility.

but developing a much more flexible, diverse and responsive approach to learning.

Linked to this, there is an argument that education and training should be de-institutionalised. Education should not be a matter of attending courses, mainly in educational buildings. It should be something that is available when and where the interest and motivation exists (for instance, in the workplace, neighbourhood, leisure centre, shopping mall or home) and it should be something that the users can help to shape around their own needs, capacities and inclinations.

The development of workplace learning is very significant within this perspective. The workplace can provide a *site* for learning that is convenient and accessible and an opportunity to learn with peers; and it links in with, and builds upon, the motivation for self-improvement provided by employment. In addition the workplace *may* provide an infrastructure of support for learning: not just space, materials and equipment, ways of organising access to teachers and advisers, but also support from fellow workers, managers and union representatives.

Here 'workplace learning' includes learning opportunities physically located in the workplace (such as through workplace learning centres) and those organised in a workplace context (such as employee development schemes) that may encourage and support participation in courses provided outside the workplace. The potential scope of workplace learning *centres* is illustrated by the aim, stated in the Kennedy Report into *Widening Participation in Further Education*, for 50 000 workplace learning centres covering a third of the workforce to be established over next 20 years (Kennedy, 1997:8).

At one level there seems to be a widespread consensus about the importance of workplace learning and the form it should take. However, this agreement around the desire for a more flexible and de-institutionalised approach to education masks a range of tensions and inconsistencies. These revolve around questions about both the *purpose of* and the *constituency for* lifelong workplace learning. There is a crucial tension between a vocationally-driven 'competitiveness agenda' and one centred around personal development. Korsgaard, for instance, charts a shift from humanistic (UNESCO) to economic (OECD) interpretations of lifelong learning as national governments are increasingly oriented away from welfare state measures and towards policies designed primarily to equip their national economy (and labour force as part of this) to compete in global markets (Korsgaard, 1997:18).

Should lifelong learning be driven above all by the need for the UK economy to compete in global markets? Or is its starting point the requirement of individuals to be able to survive and negotiate their way though the unpredictability and uncertainty of modern life?

Overlapping with this is the question: education for whom? Has lifelong learning a mission to reach the non-participants and particularly those who missed out on their initial education? Or should it be there for those willing and able to seize the opportunities and make the most of the resources available? Is it primarily about employees, especially the younger, ambitious and mobile ones who are well placed to take advantage of this more individualised approach? Or is there a concern with inclusivity and addressing inequalities in the labour market?

These tensions between 'competitiveness' and personal development, and between a focus on 'new learners' and on existing successful ones, run through all the debates and practices on workplace learning.

Taking a perspective from adult education, this chapter addresses a number of questions concerning the changing relationship between adult learning and the workplace. First, to what extent is the workplace and employment providing a context for the development of broadly non-vocational education amongst working-class adults? Second, how are the different players – government, employers, trade unions, employees and educators – responding to this changing context? Third, it will assess the impact of these developments in the workplace and conclude by identifying some of the main issues around learning that are emerging and need to be addressed by practitioners.

The changing context of employment

How do changes in employment affect learning in the workplace? First, there is the shift towards a post-industrial society with a shrinking minority of employees engaged in manufacturing and extractive industries. There has been a fall in manufacturing employment 'from about 7.5 million employees in the UK in the early 1970's to just over 5 million in 1990. In contrast, non-manufacturing employment has risen from 14.5 million to 17.5 million over the same period, with services employing over 15.4 million people' (Grint, 1998:153). This expansion of service sector employment generates a requirement for a range of information handling and 'people related' skills. Noon and Blyton refer to the importance of 'emotion work' for many service workers, such as flight attendants, nurses and supermarket checkout assistants. For example, for most supermarket checkout operators, it is no longer sufficient to charge up the goods speedily and handle cash, cheques and credit cards accurately; this has also has to be a service performed 'with a smile', a friendly greeting, gaining eye contact and a farewell (1997:121). Bank workers have to 'look happy in their work' and flight attendants appear calm and reassuring, whatever their alarm or fright. Many employers who have invested in workplace learning have done so in response to this more competitive environment. Scottish Power, with an avant garde approach to learning centres 'has had to adapt fast to the pressures of competition, constant change, and increasing emphasis on the customer' (IRS, 1997).

In addition, the notion of a move towards a post-Fordist society (Piore and Sabel, 1984), with flexible teams of workers responding to rapidly changing market demands, puts a premium on developing flexible, multi-skilled and autonomous employees with teamworking and problem-solving skills. The trend towards generic working amongst ancillary workers in the NHS illustrates this. In one study of workplace learning, a manager in a healthcare trust commented that 'the work of healthcare assistants is not professionalised but is highly skilled'. He described the role as requiring compassion, tolerance, an ability to normalise conditions for clients, ability to treat clients as individuals, ability to deal with their own and other people's stress (Munro, Rainbird and Holly, 1997:12). Equally, trends towards decentralisation and de-layering, along with quality assurance systems that pinpoint individual accountability, place considerable demands on what have been considered unskilled and routine workers. Payne links the introduction of the path-finding Basic Skills programme at Baxi in 1990 to the introduction of a flatter management structure, team working and Total Quality Management (Payne, 1996:224).

These occupational shifts have begun to impact upon education and training in the workplace in some sectors. The impact has of course been uneven, but certain trends are evident. First, there is a focus on the need to provide training for groups who have traditionally been ignored for, as a recent study shows 'all the evidence ... points to a persisting lack of training for the low skilled and qualified workers' (McGivney, 1994:30). A more competitive 'market' environment in public and private service sectors, as well as changes discussed above, places increased pressures on front-line staff such as care assistants, checkout staff and receptionists.

Second, they problematise the distinction between vocational training and education for personal development as today's front-line service workers (in public and private sectors) require not just greater information-handling skills but also the capacity to relate to people in a range of unpredictable and difficult circumstances. This requires self-confidence, communication and negotiating skills, capacity for initiative and ability to weigh situations up and make judgements. These skills and attributes are often seen as an outcome of wider liberal education, with its emphasis on personal development.

Moreover, and third, many workers need contextual understanding in order to be able to deliver an appropriate and sensitive support to clients. Thus an inner-city care worker needs an understanding of the background and circumstances of her clients' lives in order to be able to deliver an appropriate and sensitive support.

If these pressures exist on employers' demand for skills in work, what about employees? It is a commonplace nowadays to refer to the end of the lifetime career and the expectation instead that employers should provide training for employability rather than employment. For many the experience has been one of increasing insecurity and unpredictability in working life. It was reported in 1996 that 40 per cent of British employees feared for their jobs while 60 per cent argued that insecurity has been rising (Grint, 1998:313), and insecurity is greater for less well-paid and qualified workers. Nevertheless, employers are increasingly asking of their workers that they plan their own careers, and workers too are aware of the dangers of becoming boxed into particular career paths. A common theme amongst some employers is to expect employees to take responsibility for their own training, as this comment from a manager at Standard Life illustrates:

> in the past, people tended to wait for their managers to suggest training. Now, we expect people to identify the training they need to do their present job and to develop their role in the future. We believe everyone in the organisation should be learning, because if you don't develop, you won't remain employable in an environment that is changing so rapidly. (Adams, 1997)

If insecurity is one driving force, for some groups of workers, too, there are more opportunities both in employment and in education. Employment in some areas, such as professional and middle management grades in the public and voluntary sectors, are becoming more accessible to women workers (Crompton, 1997:46–7). In other areas, such as nursing and social work, skill shortages are leading to greater opportunities for adults to re-train and enter professions, and the restructuring of work – for instance, the development of generic working in the health and care sectors again creates scope for limited enhancement and progression amongst traditional groups of manual staff, such as cleaners and catering assistants.

Government policies

It was widely accepted in the 1980s that the UK system of VET was weak and in need for reform. The thrust and nature of reforms introduced by the 1979–97 Conservative Government have been discussed extensively elsewhere (for example, Keep, 1993; Field, 1996). From the point of view of this chapter it is important to briefly summarise developments in adult education. The key is a continuing process of restructuring that favours, and mainstreams, under the growing influence of central government, areas such as adult basic education and access provision, and marginalises more liberal and leisure-based provision. This had the effect of strengthening vocational and qualification-bearing courses and deprived adult education of some of its traditional flexibility and student-centredness. But there were benefits too. Both further education colleges and – to an extent – universities became more open to working-class adults, and a range of new programmes, such as access and Return to Learn, flourished (Caldwell, 1991).

With the election of 'New Labour' in 1997, lifelong learning received a high profile with a number of reports and initiatives. NAGCELL, which broadly represented the contemporary adult education establishment, was established in June 1997 and reported in late 1997 and May 1999. A Green Paper, *The Learning Age*, was published in Spring 1998 and consultations were completed in Spring 1999. There are a number of key items in the emerging policy agenda that are clearly relevant to workplace learning. These include: ILAs, the UFI, the ULF and measures to encourage widening participation in further and higher education. Some of these are discussed below.

In important ways, this political context is now proving more favourable to the development of adult learning in the workplace. Whilst employers continue to occupy a key role, this is balanced to an extent by granting greater legitimacy to trade unions and the involvement in policy-making of key members of the adult education establishment. Union initiatives, such as Unison's Return to Learn scheme, have been positively received by Government spokespersons, and union experience and perspectives have been considered. For example, the first NAGCELL Report contained a section on workplace learning (which was drafted by the then Director of Education and Training for Unison, Jim Sutherland) which called for a structure of employee representation and learning agreements modelled on the successful safety representatives regulations (Fryer, 1997). This would provide a way through which the learning needs of employees could be effectively articulated. Whilst this approach has not been fully endorsed, the Government has placed a strong emphasis on partnership in the workplace and created a mood favourable to greater trade union involvement.

Additionally, senior members of university continuing education departments, residential colleges, National Association for Adult and Continuing Education and further education colleges have been drawn more fully into the policy-making community. This has enabled discussions on workplace learning to be informed by an awareness of insights from adult education, particularly the importance of a broader, more liberal strand of provision.

The tensions between the contrasting agendas remain but the balance may have shifted in important ways. Commitment to a vocationally-driven 'competitiveness agenda' remains powerful but there is also an acknowledgement of other educational impulses such as citizenship and personal development. Second, whilst much of the methodology of lifelong learning may, as argued below, prove more congenial to successful and established learners than to new ones, there is a robust government commitment to widening participation as illustrated, for example, by financial incentives for colleges and universities to recruit more students from educationally disadvantaged backgrounds.

Consideration of the early impact of New Labour on workplace learning is complicated by the particular ways through which state policy is designed to shape lifelong workplace learning. The role of government is expressed well in the recent White Paper, *Learning to Succeed*, 'The Government's role in the new arrangements will be to steer the system, to set the necessary economic, social and economic framework' (DfEE, 1999:15). Thus, rather than founding a new institution, such as the Open University, the aim is to use the powers of government to both stimulate demand and re-shape supply, particularly by encouraging new partnerships between employers and educational organisations as well as trade unions and voluntary and community organisations. A vision of what the Government would like to see can be discerned (and is outlined below), but its development remains inchoate, dependent upon the actions of non-governmental organisations.

This notion of an enabling state is illustrated in the various lifelong learning initiatives. Both of the 'big ideas' in *The Learning Age* encapsulate this tension between competing agendas.

Individual Learning Accounts (ILAs) are a mechanism through which individuals are encouraged, by a variety of measures such as fee reductions and tax incentives, to save and borrow for learning through opening up a specific account. The idea was piloted in 1998/9 and TECs are aiming to launch the first million accounts in 1999–2000. ILAs have to be used for vocationally relevant courses that would not normally be provided by the employer. They will have a stronger appeal to those with the resources and motivation to save for their own, or other people's, future learning; as research prior to their launch concluded, 'ILAs are a product for employees who are motivated and who have disposable income' (Corney, Jones and Maxted, 1998). The problem this poses for widening participation and involving 'new learners' is recognised by government, who have used TECs to help set up a million subsidised accounts. Here TECs have been asked for some of the subsidised accounts to target traditional non-participants such as low-paid and part-time workers and employees in SMEs. Research, however, questioned how far ILAs would be *sustained* amongst committed employees on low pay (Corney, Jones and Maxted, 1998:20).

The University for Industry (UfI) is due to be launched in 2000 and start-up arrangements are well under way. Despite its name, the UfI is not mainly concerned with Higher Education level provision. The aim of the UfI is to prompt and shape the development of thousands of learning centres in workplaces and in the community. UfI will prompt these though huge marketing activities, the provision of advice and guidance and the commissioning of new programmes. The UfI vision of a learning centre is an accessible setting where the individual can go along, be welcomed, receive guidance and enrol on (and in many cases study) individual computer-based learning packages. Thus there is a drive to decentralise the provision of learning opportunities, making them much more available, but the learning itself is to be much more individual, flexible and led by Information and Communication Technology (ICT). The latter is seen as cost-effective and – in many cases – more attractive to many potential learners. This promotion of flexible and independent ICT-based workplace learning will have a strong appeal for more mobile and confident educational achievers. However, the vision will require strenuous efforts in order to make it accessible to the millions on the periphery; such as older workers and those lacking recent educational success.

The importance of the widening participation agenda is demonstrated by the way the UfI has identified basic skills training as a key priority. In addition it is likely that public funds for priority areas such as basic skills training will be channelled through organisations, such as workplace learning centres, that are recognised by the UfI. It is acknowledged by government that a key problem is the long tail of low skill and educational attainment within the UK workforce. Thus the Kennedy Report refers to 60 per cent of adults having qualification levels below Level Three (equivalent to A level) (Kennedy, 1997), and the Moser Report on basic skills (Moser, 1998) suggests that little progress has been made in denting the substantial numbers of adults with poor and low literacy and numeracy levels. Whilst the emphasis on basic skills indicates a commitment to educationally disadvantaged adults, it is not entirely unproblematic. There are elements of moral panic involved with a tendency to blame employees and the education system for the 'skills crisis', whilst it is by no means clear that employers desire, or would make effective use of, better educated employees (see Chapter 9 above).

Also launched in 1998 was the Union Learning Fund (ULF) which is discussed below and is designed to encourage unions to become involved in workplace learning initiatives.

It is possible, then, to discern the broad outlines of a government policy towards workplace learning that is vocationally centred but not constrained by this, flexible, delivered in a localised and frequently individualised fashion and intending to make extensive use of the information superhighway

Employers and the growth of employee development

How have employers responded to the changes in employment which are summarised above? There has been no clear pattern of employer response, but rather a range of responses relating to the circumstances of the enterprise: for example, different product and labour markets and the interests and enthusiasms of individuals and groups.

Within the private sector it is possible to identify a number of large employers, competing in international product markets and with an established commitment to HRD strategies who have invested significantly in workplace learning and employee development (ED). Such employers include British Aerospace, Rover, Unipart and Jaguar. Investment includes computer-based open learning centres and links with higher and further education providers.

These schemes could be seen as *business-led*, following a *competitiveness agenda* and with a relatively weak awareness of widening participation.

However, other employers, particularly those operating in low-skill labour markets and organising production around repetitive flow line methods, have not followed suit. It is also widely acknowledged that SMEs have had diffi- culty embracing workplace learning and employee development (Fryer, 1997).

The private sector scheme with the highest profile within adult education, the Ford Motor Company's EDAP scheme, has its roots in a particular context and could be described as following a *micro-corporatist* approach. Although the scheme arose, strictly speaking, as an employer response to an element in the Ford unions' pay claim, EDAP was seen by management as a key 'non-adver- sarial initiative' forming part of a prolonged attempt to re-structure industrial relations following failed initiatives around quality circles and employee involvement. Key to this approach was the allocation to Ford unions, at plant level, of a central role in administering the scheme, along with a strong empha- sis on involvement by shopfloor workers (McCarthy, 1990; Caldwell, 1991). Thus, although Ford EDAP makes an important contribution to workplace learning, it was driven by industrial relations concerns.

Whilst EDAP, and similar schemes such as Peugeot's, promote wider access to existing educational programmes, some other schemes, especially in the public services, focus on *curriculum innovation*. Sheffield City Council's 'Take Ten' scheme, possibly the first employee development scheme, provides a sec- ond chance/civic education programme for council workers, and other local authorities (Humberside, Glasgow and Derbyshire) have also developed schemes, although not based on the Sheffield model. Workbase's pioneering basic educational work was based on carefully constructed courses designed specifically for low-paid employees and the context within which they worked. More recently, Unison's *partnership approach to workplace learning* (dis- tinctive as a trade union-led initiative operated in partnership with the WEA) has been built around developing tailor-made courses that address the experi- ence and aspirations of public service employees.

Two key strands within employer workplace learning are evident. They are not mutually exclusive. First there is the growth of what could be called *resource-based learning* (RBL). This is based on seeing individual employees as responsible for planning their own training/education. The employer pro- vides workplace learning centres with a range of mainly computer-based open learning packages, along with some guidance and administration. In these cases there are different lines into management and career structures; in some instances managers act as mentors and training is seen as a key element in career progression.

Standard Life recently established a large open learning centre at its head- quarters in Edinburgh. One of the reasons was that a recent customer survey has shown that 'Although they felt we were highly trustworthy and gave a superb investment performance, they told us we were difficult to do business with, arrogant and slow ... *people* are now our main source of competitive advantage' (emphasis in original). They replaced popular courses with computer-based training or CD-ROM materials and estimate that they will have paid for the investment in the learning centre in two years just by dropping two courses (Adams, 1997). The learning centre was linked to the company's policy of self-managed learning referred to above.

A second strand is based on the notion of an *employee entitlement*. This is encourages individual participation in education/training and usually involves a wide choice, including non-vocational courses. In some instances, such as Ford, employees are discouraged from following job-related programmes. In these cases paid 'time off' is rarely provided. What is usually provided is the entitlement to payment of course fees, up to a ceiling, usually in the range £50 to £250. In most cases some guidance is provided. Here there are less clear lines into management and career structures, and sometimes they are specifically separated. These schemes usually have an awareness of inclusivity and widening participation

Trade unions and workplace learning

Trade unions can contribute to workplace learning in a number of ways: as providers of courses for union members (especially activists), and as bargainers articulating membership needs. In addition the TUC has represented union views to government on a wide range of training and educational questions.

Trade union education historically has been a key element within non-vocational workplace education. In the inter-war years, union educational programmes contained a mixture of training for voluntary officers and representative roles alongside broader educational issues. In the post-war period some unions, especially the miners, developed substantial liberal educational programmes based on paid release from work and run in conjunction with university extra-mural departments (Croucher and Halstead, 1990). Unions could be seen as forerunners of the 'Access to Higher Education Movement' in their work with the WEA, universities and Ruskin College, and many trade unionists progressed to full-time university study (Holford, 1993).

At the same time there was a growth in shop-steward training, again based on paid release from work. In recent years the 'training model' has predominated over the more liberal 'industrial studies' model, although shop-steward training contains important educational and confidence building strands. In the 1970s and 1980s, the TUC was prominent both in organising substantial shop-stewards' training programmes and – until the ending of the Manpower Services Commission – in tripartite training schemes for young people and the adult unemployed. The maintenance of substantial shop-steward training programmes, mainly provided in collaboration with the further education sector, was an important achievement in the years of trade union retreat following 1979.

Whilst craft unions have historically been closely involved in regulating apprenticeship training schemes, training has not been a major bargaining priority for post-war unionism (Rainbird, 1990). This was acknowledged recently by the TUC: 'TUC research projects ... concluded that trade union involvement in, and knowledge about workplace training was extremely limited' (TUC, 1998). More recently, the TUC *Bargaining for Skills* projects have had important successes in some TUC regions in prompting workplace trade union interest and activity in collective bargaining around training issues.

Unions played a key role in Ford's EDAP, and this is discussed in more detail below. Significantly, though, unions did not play a strong role in generalising the Ford experience and subsequent employee entitlement schemes have contained a less marked trade union contribution.

The election of New Labour opened up significant prospects for trade union involvement in lifelong learning with a much more supportive policy climate and positive comments about unions in the NAGCELL Report, *The Learning Age* and the Moser Report. The government has not restored public funding for shop-steward training (which was ended in the later years of the previous Conservative administration) but has established the ULF. This financially supports union pilot initiatives that address the lifelong learning agenda in workplaces: for instance, by providing employee education, extending the use of ICT and identifying and training union learning representatives or lifelong learning advisers. Again the fund encourages unions to work in partnership with employers and educational organisations.

The TUC has seized the opportunities to identify a role for unions seeking to promote, and help influence, initiatives such as the UfI and developing the role of union learning representatives as advocates of lifelong learning and providers of front-line advice and guidance to employees. The education work of individual unions, particularly Unison, has expanded greatly in this more favourable environment. In the area of basic skills, the TUC is involved in brokering relations between unions and state organisations (such as the Basic Skills Agency), and providing a union perspective within course development and staff training.

Lifelong learning offers great opportunities for trade union renewal and growth. Unions can provide, or help to provide, learning opportunities for members, learning can provide a fruitful area to develop workplace bargaining and the experience of learning can encourage union members to become more active in their union. Many of those involved in providing education within trade unions remained wedded to the representative training model and are reluctant to see, let alone build upon, the impulses unlocked by programmes involving their wider membership. Unison programmes, for example, have been criticised as they do not have any demonstrable effect in terms of encouraging members who participated to become union activists. Follow-up studies of Unison programmes have suggested that some members have gone on to become representatives or branch officers, but the key research finding was identifying the development of 'active members'. These were members who took on various informal roles in support of the union – for example, circulating information, encouraging discussion and persuading members to take part in union ballots – rather than taking up formal positions (Kennedy, 1995: Caldwell, 1998).

There are important issues about how lifelong learning links into trade union renewal and growth. For unions, changes in employment may tend to limit the relevance of the model of the activist and representative as a person making a long-term, formal, voluntary commitment to their union. Union leaderships may well have to encourage and recognise flexible and diverse forms of involvement that arise from the more transient and insecure nature of employment as well as the complex and competing pressures on members' time and energy. Lifelong learning programmes may well offer a point of entry for these new activists, as well as providing insights into how trade union educational programmes themselves can be re-fashioned.

What have we learned so far?

Whilst workplace learning has developed unevenly and only in a small minority of workplaces, it is still possible to draw some lessons. The first striking conclusion that can be drawn is that, whilst evidence varies greatly between different schemes and contexts, there can be little doubt that workplace learning can succeed in drawing in many thousands of new learners. Why is this?

The workplace can be an important context and site for learning. It addresses the needs of groups such as shift workers, especially those on rotating shift patterns for whom attendance at a weekly course, meeting at the same time each week, would be an impossibility. Payne states that the major group to benefit at Ford were shift workers, referring to 'the substantial proportion of courses taking place on Ford premises to fit in with shift work'. He also refers to workers at Baxi with a shift system on a three-week rota who were allowed to change their shift once a week to fit in with courses (Payne, 1996:231). The context of employment, especially where there is a union and sympathetic training managers, enables practical and logistical problems such as these to be dealt with in satisfactory way.

A key feature of workplace support is the provision of paid educational leave (PEL) for some, or all, study time. Within the EDAP scheme, employees have to study in their own time. However some workplace learning schemes do provide PEL; this has been an entitlement for trade union representatives attending approved courses since 1975 and is a feature of some of the recent employee development schemes. Employees on Unison's Workplace Partnership programmes are granted the equivalent of ten days' PEL which covers the study group and day school element of the Return to Learn course. At Baxi half of the study takes place in the employee's own time and the other half during paid release from work (Payne, 1996:224). Recognition of the importance of PEL is provided in the Moser Report which proposes government funding to permit basic skills students to have 13 days' PEL to support their study activities (Moser, 1998).

An interesting series of insights into the role of workplace education in widening participation is provided by Beattie, a local educational adviser working in Ford's Dagenham plant (Beattie, 1997). The workforce are predominately manual workers and he estimated 42 per cent participated in EDAP against a 'benchmark' figure of 16 per cent, derived from national surveys of the participation rates of manual workers in education. He concludes that hostility towards education amongst these groups might be less than expected, and that the EDAP scheme did not so much provide reasons for participation as 'give a push'. Why did they participate? Financial incentives were certainly important: as one Ford worker put it, 'Anything you get for free, you never turn down, never.' In addition, the presence of a supportive educational organisation within the workplace helped simplify procedures and provide support: for example, the local education adviser helped to by-pass complicated and inconvenient enrolment systems. Finally, 'in plant' courses proved extremely popular: some employees would say, 'I'd like to do a course. What's available in-house?' Partly, as one person said, 'It's very, very convenient' but there is also the positive attraction of studying alongside peers, removing the embarrassment of studying, and revealing weaknesses, in front of strangers, especially if the expectation is that the majority of the others will be much younger.

The scope for the practice of workplace learning to begin to lead to a learning culture was captured in a study of manual employees at Leeds University who were undertaking the Unison Return to Learn course. Their manager reported:

> there's a little sub-team that are quite supportive of each other. I've seen them doing their homework in the canteen helping each other out. I've also seen some of those who aren't on the course, not being patronising but trying to help those who are on the course. So the whole thing's started to gel and there is almost a subculture of learning going on around the place. (Munro, Rainbird and Holly, 1997:18).

This does not mean that the workplace is an unproblematic site for learning. Productive partnerships between employers, unions, educators and TECs in the interest of expanding employee education are *possible* but not *inevitable*.

Accounts like this tend to focus on areas of good practice and of potential, whereas the overall picture is much more depressing. Surveying basic skills provision, for example, the Moser Report stated:

> We start from a position where workplace provision [of basic skills] is regrettably limited. Many employers do not see it as their responsibility to take on the improvement of basic skills. We were struck – and shocked – by this limited commitment within industry and business generally. It represents one of the most important areas for change ... Employers in general ... do not have the expertise to tackle basic skills. (1998:48)

Trying to build workplace education is difficult for a number of reasons. First, within the workplace individuals are much more visible and exposed than they are at home. Becoming involved in education can lead to criticism and/or banter from fellow workers, as was observed in the Leeds Programme: 'when you get a fairly aggressive group of building trade workers, showing a weakness isn't something you try to do too often ... Admitting you need a bit of help is a brave act.' And, as one of the students said, 'Verbally, I've had quite a lot of tripe from my fellow working man, whether it's joking or a bit snide' (Munro, Rainbird and Holly, 1997:17). There can also be a reluctance to expose weaknesses to managers as this could lead to criticism or potentially dismissal or re-deployment.

This latter point is compounded by the differences and tensions within management around training issues. Educational and training initiatives usually derive from central specialist managers (training, human resource development) and there are frequently difficulties involved in gaining the support and cooperation of line management. Studies have identified line management suspicion and reluctance to release staff (Quintana, 1998:40), and have also identified the need for cultural changes to be seen, 'not just in terms of modifying the attitudes and behaviour of shop-floor workers, but also those of supervisory management' (Payne, 1996:224). Successful schemes need an 'enthusiastic local actor': as Munro, Rainbird and Holly argue, in the case of Leeds University, 'the particular support of the UNISERV manager has been key to the success of the course' (1997:19).

In this setting trade unions can play an important and positive role. They have a vision of how education can contribute to social change and have experience of workplace education gained from shop-steward training. Trade unions too have a commitment to equity and are well placed to ensure that opportunities are widely shared amongst employees. Certainly it was the case that workplace trade unionists were key to developing and shaping EDAP. In addition, unions can be crucial in encouraging participation: 'Union-led programmes are often seen by employees as safe, credible and relevant' (Moser, 1998:50). Moser also refers to union experience in the field, their possible bargaining role and the notion of union 'learning reps'. Trade union representatives will usually have an awareness of many of the practical constraints and issues facing employees, and the experience in local negotiations and problem-solving that can help in overcoming them.

Unions too can be *instigators* of education. Unison see their workplace partnerships as 'an answer to a problem' rather than a 'demand', and most programmes derive from union approaches. At a local level, it was found that, 'At the Coventry Health Care Trust the key actor was the part-time (Unison) equal opportunities and education officer whose persistence ... resulted in the eventual agreement' (Quintana, 1998:40).

A further important lesson is that non-vocational education can play an important part in workplace education and can have life-changing effects on some individuals and a positive impact on many. Non-vocational and more liberal programmes often have a wide appeal and can act as a bridge into education for new learners. This was recognised, for instance, in the Kennedy Report: 'For many 'new' learners, non-Schedule 2 [i.e. courses generally *not* funded through the Further Education Funding Council] courses provide essential first steps to more formal learning and accreditation' (1997:33). Shorter general courses can break the ice, remove some of the fears of returning to education and begin to develop some of the habits and skills involved in successful study. Whilst this argument is widely accepted amongst adult educators, there remain important issues in finding suitable pathways and opportunities to enable this progression to take place.

The argument about a wider and more liberal education within workplace learning goes further than stating its role as a bridge into more formal study, however. This wider education actually addresses directly many of the needs of the employee in the modern labour market, helping to encourage a more critical, confident and questioning person, more capable of solving problems and taking initiatives. This transforming role of education is stated well by this student:

> I think now I feel that I've got a right to question, which I never thought before because you're working class, you pay your taxes, you go to work and that's it, and they know better. I think I've changed in my views, because I feel now I've got a mind of my own, and I can question, whether or not my questions are relevant or sensible, but I like to think now that I can listen to something and think 'No, I don't believe that' or 'That's not my view'. Before I wouldn't, I'd think they're more educated ... I've gained confidence in my own ability to think or to question. (Kennedy, 1995:10–11)

Very often too, this broadens the horizons, encouraging people to consider options way beyond the obvious next step. Whilst the achievements and potential contribution of this modern liberal education can be demonstrated from a range of case studies, its future development is linked to issues of curriculum, teaching methods and staffing.

To what extent is the development of workplace learning a case of extending access to the existing curriculum offered, ensuring wider take-up of vocational training and the provision of adult, further and higher education provided by colleges and universities? Certainly this is a part of it, and key initiatives such as EDAP and the TUC's Bargaining for Skills projects mainly centre on this. At the same time, the adult education tradition is also about curriculum development and reform, building programmes around the interests of new student groups and arguing that a wide and stretching curriculum should be available for all. It contests the view that different 'levels of education' are appropriate for different 'levels' of employee. The earlier discussion of employment changes points the way to an emerging curriculum that bridges the vocational/non-vocational divide, addresses the different aspects of employees' lives and provides a critical and experientially based education.

In addition, there are other contemporary critiques articulated (for instance, in Moser, 1998 and *Learning to Succeed* DfEE, 1999) of the fragmented nature of the adult and further education curriculum. These discussions have formed the background to the move towards a credit framework system and towards some form of national curriculum in adult education. However, if these reforms are to be successful for adult students they will need to recognise two key aspects of their experience. First they want to learn at their own pace (with occasional spurts and interruptions) and they benefit from education that builds upon the diverse motives and impulses that lead people into adult education. This diversity needs to have a strong multicultural emphasis and acknowledge the central role of women students.

Linked to arguments about the workplace curriculum are debates about teaching and learning methods. Much of the success with educationally disadvantaged adult students generally has been based on developing adult education good practice. Teaching has mainly taken place in groups with a professional tutor, different activities and plenty of discussion and experiential learning. There are usually good staff/student ratios (in the 1:10/1:15 range) and the tutor is able to get to know the group and help them to work together, providing guidance and individual pastoral support. Tutors – as employees of educational organisations – provide independence and a professional ethos that can respect confidentiality and is independent of the management structure. More recently, too, there have been experiments with developing different models of champions, mentors and role models in order to provide further support for students. Voluntary Educational Advisers have developed within the WEA; they are former students who wish to 'put something back'. They work with new students providing support, encouragement and advice as well as helping to promote learning in their workplaces and communities. These are all important ideas, but largely untested at this stage. Unions are beginning to develop specialist voluntary roles to support and encourage learning; examples are Unison's Lifelong Learning Advisors and the (slightly different) TUC union learning reps (TUC, 1999).

The approach has been kept flexible to cater for varying student needs and a range of outcomes. At the same time, group learning has provided an essential structure and framework through which people have learned and progressed. Central to the learning process has been the importance of confidence-building as an underpinning theme and gateway to further learning. Students' evaluations invariably refer to the benefits of group and mutual support. The course is often experienced as a difficult journey, the students realising that they 'are all in the same boat' and supporting each other as they go.

The UfI, which is driving the development of workplace learning centres, is firmly wedded to learning through information technology. Their vision is providing adults with individual access to learning opportunities through computer packages and CD-ROMs. Learning centres would provide guidance and some learning support. Where tuition were available, this would be mainly provided 'at-a-distance' through e-mail. This approach is seen as more cost-effective and as more attractive to many potential learners, being much more flexible and avoiding the stigma attached to acknowledging basic skills needs. There is little doubt that ICT contains great attractions for new learners but there must be important questions about how far these groups can be retained and developed without substantial personal and social support. Thus a recent commentary on Adult Basic Education (ABE), with its tradition of one-to-one tuition, recognised the role for individual learning but added, 'the flexibility in timing offered by open learning was welcomed by many adults, but not all ABE students were able to benefit from such self-organised study methods, which offered less opportunity for the discussion and mutual support that proved to be an important part of developing confidence to tackle basic skills' (Hamilton, 1996:156). The argument here is not simply about the role of tutors and group learning, but also about the importance of organising and 'face-to-face outreach' activities as part of preparation for workplace programmes (Wolfe, 1987:95).

Conclusion

This chapter has traced the history of recent developments in workplace learning and outlined the contemporary context. The changing experience of employment has led to a greater demand for a range of educational and training opportunities, including a wider, more liberal, education that addresses personal development as well as vocational needs. This opens up the possibility that the workplace can be made into a site where a wide range of learning takes place, involving large numbers of people.

A minority of employers are beginning to think about this in various ways, in some instances following pressure or proposals from trade unions. Different strands of employee development and learning centres and programmes are emerging. Their significance so far is to demonstrate the potential of workplace learning and suggest ways in which it could be approached. The election of New Labour and its lifelong learning agenda are giving an added impetus to these developments. Policy initiatives are slowly beginning to shape the landscape, but its future contours are unclear.

These are all positive changes and cause for great optimism and enthusiasm amongst adult educators. However, the picture is complex and uneven and there are many competing priorities and narratives. In particular there remains a very powerful vocationally centred 'competitiveness agenda' which may significantly limit who becomes involved in workplace learning and what they get out of it. If workplace learning is to live up to its potential to change the lives of hundreds of thousands of employees, other agendas and priorities will have to be heard and recognised. In particular this will mean an unending search for ways to involve and enthuse all employees, especially the sceptics and the non-participants, and a willingness to develop a curriculum and methodology that addresses the diversity of their interests and motivation. This openness in attracting people into learning will need to be matched and sustained in the learning process itself. The challenge will be to combine flexibility and accessibility with those elements of personal support and the experience of a 'community of learning' that have played such an important part for past and present generations of adult students. If this is possible, the scope exists to make workplaces the site of relevant, exciting and stretching adult education and thus make a substantial contribution to developing lifelong learning in the UK.

References

Adams, K. (1997) 'Standard Life launches new open learning centres', IRS *Employee Development Bulletin*, 89, 12–13.

Beattie, A. (1997) *Working People and Lifelong Learning*, Leicester: NIACE.

Caldwell, P. (1991) 'A novel route to employee development? Ford EDAP: problems and opportunities for unionised workers', unpublished paper presented to the ninth International Conference on the Organisation and Control of the Labour Process, Manchester.

Caldwell, P. (1998) 'Labour education and 'New Unionism' in the UK: the case of UNISON', unpublished paper presented to the 1998 UCLEA/AFL-CIO Education Conference, San José.

Corney, M., Jones, H. L. and Maxted, P. (March 1998) *Individual Learning Accounts: Research Consortium 1V*, Hythe: MC Consultancy.

Crompton, R. (1997) *Women and Work in Modern Britain*, Oxford: Oxford University Press.

Croucher, R. and Halstead, J. (1990) 'The origin of liberal adult education for miners at Sheffield in the post-war period: a study in adult education and the working class', *Trade Union Studies Journal*, 21, 3–14.

DfEE (1998) *The Learning Age: A Renaissance for New Britain*, London: DfEE.

DfEE (1999) *Learning to Succeed. A New Framework for Post-16 Learning*, London: DfEE.

Field, J. (1996) 'Learning for work: vocational education and training', in Fieldhouse, R. and associates, *A History of Modern British Adult Education*, Leicester: NIACE.

Fryer, R. (1997) *Learning for the Twenty First Century*. First report of the National Advisory Group for Continuing Education and Lifelong Learning, Barnsley: Northern College.

Grint, S. (1998) *The Sociology of Work*, Cambridge: Polity.

Hamilton, M. (1996) 'Literacy and adult basic education', in Fieldhouse, R. and associates, *A History of Modern British Adult Education*, Leicester: NIACE.

Holford, J. (1993) *Union Education in Britain: A TUC Activity*, Nottingham: Department of Adult Education, University of Nottingham.

IRS (1997) 'Scottish Power opens the doors to learning', *Employee Development Bulletin*, October, 12–15.

Keep, E. (1993) 'Missing, presumed skilled: training policy in the UK', in Edwards, R., Sieminski, S. and Zeldin, D., *Adult Learners, Education and Training*, London: Routledge.

Kennedy, H. (1995) *Return to Learn: UNISON's Fresh Approach to Trade Union Education*, London: Unison.

Kennedy, H. (1997) *Learning Works: Widening Participation in Further Education*, Coventry: Further Education Funding Council.

Korsgaard, O. (1997) 'The impact of globalisation on adult education', in Walters, S. (ed.), *Globalisation, Adult Education and Training: Impacts and Issues*, Leicester: NIACE.

McCarthy, J. (1990) 'In Pursuit of Jointness: A Study of the Employee Development programme within Ford UK', unpublished MA Dissertation, University of Warwick.

McGivney, V. (1994) *Wasted Potential: Training and Career Progression for Part-time and Temporary Workers*, Leicester: NIACE.

Moser, K. (1998) *A Fresh Start. Improving Literacy and Numeracy*, Sudbury: DfEE.

Munro, A., Rainbird, H. and Holly, L. (1997) *Partners in Workplace Learning: A Report on the UNISON/Employer Learning and Development Programme*, London: Unison.

NAGCELL (1999) *Creating Learning Cultures: New Steps in Achieving the Learning Age: Second Report of the National Advisory Group for Continuing Education and Lifelong Learning*, NAGCELL.

Noon, N. and Blyton, P. (1997) *The Realities of Work*, London: Macmillan.

Payne, J. (1996) 'Who really benefits from employee development schemes?', in Raggatt, P., Edwards, R. and Small, N. (eds), *The Learning Society*, London: Routledge/Open University.

Piore, M. J. and Sabel, M. (1984) *The Second Industrial Divide: Possibilities for Prosperity*, New York: Basic Books.

Quintana, M. (1998) 'Training: A New Item on the Bargaining Agenda?' unpublished MA Dissertation, Warwick Business School.

Rainbird, H. (1990) Training Matters. Union Perspectives on Industrial restructuring and Training, Oxford: Basil Blackwell.

TUC (1998) *Learning Services Report*, London: TUC.

TUC (1999) *Learning with the Unions. A Showcase of Successful Projects Sponsored by the Union Learning Fund*, London: TUC.

University of Leeds (1993) *Adult Learners at Work*, Leeds: Department of Adult Continuing Education, University of Leeds.

Wolfe, M. (1987) 'Workbase (London)', in Mace, J. and Yarnitt, M. (eds), *Time Off to Learn*, London: Methuen.

CHAPTER 14

Workplace learning and the limits to evaluation

Lesley Holly and Helen Rainbird

Introduction

Taken at face value, it would appear uncontentious that workplace learning and, indeed, any kind of training and development should certainly have a strong relationship to ideas about continuous improvement. Whether investments in employees' learning are regarded as an investment or as a cost, at some stage account has to be made for this expenditure and its impact assessed. To reveal that relationship, some kinds of evaluation practice could be employed. Of course, in the real world the terms 'evaluation', 'continuous improvement' and even 'learning', 'training' and 'development' are areas of competing definitions; they have links with different academic disciplines and have different historical and cultural roots. For all these reasons putting these terms together does not lead to an unproblematic understanding of what each means in relation to the other. This is especially the case in the context of the workplace where, as many contributions in this book have indicated, the complexities of organisational reality and the conflicting objectives of different aspects of human resource strategies intervene.

Even so, the ways in which improvement can be assessed are problematic. The indicators for measuring learning as well as for measuring their impact in the workplace are far from straightforward. Some outcomes of learning events are relatively easy to measure: for example, by attendance figures, by the proportion of participants rating the course as satisfactory, by the achievement of formal qualifications and through the assessment of competence. But what do these measurements tell us about learning? They tell us about formal events and procedures in which a transmission model of learning operates. In the case of competence-based assessment (for example, NVQs) it tells us that tasks can be performed, but not about the underpinning knowledge. These indicators tell us very little about the actual process of learning and the relationship of this knowledge to workplace practice (see Chapter 12 above, and Eraut *et al.*, 1998). Where inputs are relatively easy to identify (for example, with an off-the-job training course), it may be feasible to measure the direct and indirect costs of employees' attendance and release from productive work. It is much harder to measure the impact of that expenditure on particular work processes. Many aspects of training are even harder to assess, such as their impact on motivation and commitment. These are notoriously difficult to quantify except through indirect measures such as improved retention rates and reduced industrial disputes. Other developments in the employment relationship, such as work intensification, deskilling and redundancy programmes, which are outside the control of training professionals, may impact negatively on the motivation to learn and to work more generally.

The process of evaluation also has to address a fundamental problem, which is that although individuals have many ways of learning work-related skills, these are operationalised in social environments. Organisational and contextual constraints may prevent the realisation of the potential of new knowledge and skills. It is here that the individual's location in a 'community of practice' (to use Lave and Wenger's term, 1991) may create both positive and negative incentives for individuals to learn, to practise and to share skills. The point here is not so much that evaluation lacks sound tools for measuring inputs and outputs and the relationship between them, but that if the parameters of measurement are narrowly defined, then complex interrelationships between particular strategies, their learning outcomes and other contextual factors which may cross-cut them may be overlooked.

In this chapter we examine the rationale for evaluation. First, for reasons of clarity we locate the history of the terms 'evaluation' and 'continuous improvement' and 'training' before discussing some examples of how these three concepts have been brought together to influence evaluation practices. In the second section we examine the relationship between the planning of training and its evaluation. This involves considering its relationship to the business strategy of organisations; its use by training providers; and in relation to particular training interventions. Third, we examine the significance of context to the evaluation process. This includes an examination of factors relating to the organisation itself, to specific production processes, the interplay of training and work organisation, management objectives and political context. This is followed by a conclusion.

Evaluating training and continuous improvement

Evaluation has been defined as 'any activity that throughout the planning and delivery of innovative programmes enables those involved to learn and make judgements about the starting assumptions, implementation processes and outcomes of the innovation concerned' (Stern, 1990, quoted in Employment Department, 1992:1). It therefore involves a consideration of evaluation needs at the stage of project design; it allows judgements to be made about the progress of the innovations; it emphasises learning and improvement; it should recognise the different parties with a stake in the evaluation process; it emphases the utilisation and dissemination of the evaluation information; and it leads to the reappraisal of actions and policies (Employment Department, 1992).

The European Commissioner, Erkki Liikamen, has argued that as far as public programmes are concerned, evaluation is central to the resource allocation process (Stern, 1997). Evaluation has, at least in theory, become an integral part of programme design and management procedures in the EU. The version of evaluation identified by the commissioner is resonant with the methods of evaluation research developed in the USA in the 1960s. Stame argues that this period was characterised by a pragmatic political culture and decentralised system where evaluation was associated with programmes which aimed to achieve a result over a specified period and with specific resources (1998). As a result, evaluation focused on whether the particular policies under review had been successful in achieving the outcomes desired. This assumes, of course that the outcomes were clearly specified at the start.

An alternative model of evaluation emphasises providing feedback on the policy or programme in question. A definition by Norris encompasses both aspects: 'most definitions of evaluation suggest that its purpose is to conceive, obtain and provide information which decision makers in their various forms … can use to make decisions about the future of specified programmes or policies' (Norris, 1990:19). Implicit in these definitions is the assumption of accountability. Increasingly during the 1990s public bodies have become subject to the demand that internal processes are made more accessible to the public gaze. This political dimension to evaluation developed in the 1980s when market forces and consumer rights dominated political agendas. With the shift of the role of the public sector from direct provider to an enabler of services, evaluation and quality assurance systems had a role to play in the management of contracts where more direct forms of management are not available

(Corfield, 1997). Increasingly professionals in the public services are held to account through a variety of evaluative practices. Evaluation has become more than mere accountability. Pawson and Tilley argue, 'The nature of surveillance in post-industrial society has changed. The army of evaluators continues to grow. Instead of hands-on-the-shoulder control from the centre, the modern bureaucracy is managed by opening every activity to "review", "appraisal", "audit", "quality assurance", "performance-rating" and indeed "evaluation" ' (Pawson and Tilley, 1997:1).

Whereas the origins of evaluation derive from the USA and free market ideologies, those of continuous improvement derive from Japanese management techniques such as TQM which aim to rationalise work organisation to minimise waste and maximise efficiency (Geary, 1995). Gallaher and Smith note its influence on education and training and its acceptance as 'an integral part of the lexicon of organisational literature' (Gallaher and Smith, 1998). Quality and quality assurance underpin TQM, with its emphasis on 'getting it right first time' and on management systems that are 'fit for purpose'. Quality assurance has been defined as 'putting in place a framework which is designed to maximise the chances of achieving particular goals as a matter of course' (Tovey, 1994:11). Nevertheless, the appropriateness of these management systems which have their roots in commerce and industry to educational contexts is questionable. Their customer-centred definition of quality assumes that the market is the major organising principle for all institutions, both public and private. It is undeniable that the 'customer' has become an increasingly important organising principle in the public sector but, as Tovey argues, to focus all attention on the relationship with the customer is to limit the range of meanings which the term 'quality' could encompass (1994).

Quality assurance procedures are usually outlined in a manual. The subject matter is not simply procedural but may move into areas of policy. The incorporation of quality assurance into evaluation practices has become popular practice in public bodies because it meets the demand for accountability and combines it with the self-reflexivity which the best evaluation practice promotes. In 1980s and 1990s the evaluation of programmes receiving public finance sometimes involved evaluation by external researchers, but self-evaluation was often a condition for the receipt of funding. For example, the Open Learning Programme was funded in 1983 through the Open Tec Programme of the Manpower Services Commission. It aimed to develop educational and training materials and to set up distance-learning methods of delivering training to students. Self-evaluation was an integral part of this programme. The evaluation handbook for managers suggested that information was needed for three purposes in relation to the project: for good project management; for project evaluation (to see what has been achieved and whether it should be continued or modified); and to help the Open Tec Unit of the Manpower Services Commission evaluate the achievements of the whole programme (Hilgendorf and Tavistock Institute, 1994). This self-evaluation activity was also seen as a mechanism for managers to gather material and feedback for future decision-making. Quality assurance and self-evaluation were linked in evaluative activities which were designed to deliver both assurances of quality and accountability.

Evaluation has a wider remit than quality assurance, with its focus on customers. For any programme there is a range of interested parties, or stakeholders, who have an interest in knowing how a programme is working. Sommerlad describes stakeholders as people who 'care about the programme and its effectiveness; influence programme decisions and the context in which it operates; are the intended beneficiaries (eg students, employers); are users of the evaluation findings (eg the wider academic audience)' (Sommerlad, 1991:11). Some forms of managerial evaluation which are developing as part of new systems of public sector management are potentially rather limited, neglecting other stakeholder interests such as those indicated above.

Sommerlad suggests that if a culture of evaluation could become embedded within institutional culture and processes then it could provide the underpinnings for establishing the 'learning organisation' (Sommerlad, 1992:11). The objective of achieving organisational learning may therefore promote the growth of self-evaluation practices. Self-evaluation has many advantages for organisations. If it is built into the everyday practice of organisations, it becomes integral to all activities and therefore findings are more likely to be acted upon. The capacity for self-reflection and change are potentially increased and the process of evaluation itself is a developmental activity (Stern, 1991). Nevertheless, self-evaluation may also have shortcomings. It is a time-consuming activity and not all staff have the necessary competence to carry it out. Evaluation questions may be narrowed to course level activity and it is difficult to consider wider evaluation questions, especially of a cross-organisational nature. In this inspection of detail, larger concerns can disappear.

The relationship between planning and evaluation procedures

In the previous section we outlined how evaluation has been developed as a tool with multiple objectives. In this section and the following section, we draw on the findings of a research project on 'The evaluation of quality in continuing vocational training'[1] to explore the contextual factors which determine the effectiveness of tools for the planning and evaluation of training. The objective of the project was to examine how evaluation was used, including its use in organisations and educational institutions, as well as in its application to specific programmes. The case study organisations were: a motor manufacturer (Small and Medium Cars, Rover Group); a process plant (British Sugar); a higher education institution using distance learning techniques (The Open University); a local authority (Northamptonshire County Council); and a trade union education department (the public sector union Unison). In each case general evaluation procedures were examined as well as those relating to a specific programme or initiative. These were, respectively: the Leading to Excellence programme for team leaders and managers; engineering training for the Additional Skills initiative; The Effective Manager, run by the Open University Business School; the introduction of the IIP quality assurance procedures; and the Return to Learn programme run as a membership development service.

In examining the broader system of continuing vocational training (CVT) in Britain, initially it seemed that there was little external regulation affecting the way companies organised their training activities. There is no legal requirement on them to spend a percentage of the payroll on training or to publish details of their investment in training in their annual reports. Equally, there are no formal requirements for them to consult and inform employee representatives about their training plans. Many of these features can be found in other European training systems (see Blanpain, Engels and Pellegrini, 1994). The 1998 Workplace Employee Relations Survey shows that management is more likely to consult or inform union or non-union representatives on training rather than to negotiate it with them (Cully *et al.*, 1999:104). Quality assurance systems for training, such as the IIP award, are voluntary. There is therefore no national model, as such, for evaluating CVT, though similar tools may be adopted as 'good practice' is disseminated. Organisations, whether private sector companies or public sector bodies, will have internal systems for evaluating their training systems and programmes in order to ensure that they can deliver their business strategies. They may draw on external quality assurance systems such as BS5750 and the IIP award as a means of providing guarantees to customers and other external agencies. Direct regulation is greater with providers. The public sector is a major provider of CVT (higher education and further education) and here a range of mechanisms provide public accountability for teaching and research output, but also allow for the comparability of students' attainment between institutions: for example, through the national Credit Accumulation and Transfer Scheme (CATS). Amongst private sector providers, the rationale for evaluation lies in providing accountability for receipt of public funds and a guarantee of value for money to customers.

In examining individual case study organisations, it is clear that different forms of evaluation can serve different purposes. Whilst an organisation may need to evaluate the effectiveness of its own systems for delivering its business strategy, it may also evaluate particular training interventions where it is in an internal provider role or is a customer of another provider. The extent to which evaluation establishes value for money, serves as a badge of quality, allows for leverage in the allocation of resources or contributes to processes of continuous improvement will vary according to context and to the purpose of the mechanisms established. In the following sections, a range of tools for identifying training needs are examined and, as a consequence, their relationship to the task of evaluation.

Mechanisms for business planning

Training needs are identified through a range of processes and activities. Central to this is the business planning process. This will involve the identification of factors which are critical to the organisation's success in achieving its objectives which might concern levels of customer satisfaction, market share, increasing profit margins and reputation. This may involve company-wide programmes aimed at increasing corporate learning and innovation, and initiatives aimed at senior management, which will be translated into the business planning process at the level of individual business units. Training policy will therefore involve the identification of training needs at varying levels, as well as processes for managing learning. Planning will be based on a range of factors such as a conception of the organisation's mission and purpose as well as the evidence provided through personnel records, skills audits and records of course attendance. There will be a number of processes which can serve as tools for evaluation: some will be integrated into the business planning process; others will be linked to auditing procedures and self-assessment, and also to reporting procedures relating to training and development.

Mechanisms for identifying employees' needs

The most common mechanism for identifying individual training need is through the appraisal process, although this goes by various names. However, as emphasised in Chapters 3 and 4 in this volume, there are variations in the extent to which development needs are separated from the assessment of performance and how these conflicting objectives are resolved. There are also tensions between individual workers' need for development and the organisation's need for job effectiveness. Other mechanisms for establishing employees' training needs are skill matrices, employee attitude surveys and surveys geared specifically towards learning and development. Where employees have an entitlement to training and development – for example, through an entitlement to the payment of fees or to educational leave – individual employees may have more scope for identifying their broader development needs independently of their employer. At its best, appraisal can be a mechanism for reflecting on and evaluating learning experiences and identifying new areas for development.

Mechanisms for influencing course provision

There are various stages at which evaluation can be used to influence training provision. Where organisations are in the provider role, there are ways in which evaluation procedures – or an ex ante evaluation – can be incorporated at design stage: for example, senior managers or specialists may be involved in the design of corporate change programmes. External checks and reviews conducted by experts or appropriate professional bodies may also be used. Formative evaluation, using course questionnaires, may be issued to participants during or on completion of a particular course. They will be asked to rate programmes in terms of whether their expectations and objectives have been met, their relevance, and the quality of the presentations and course materials. Skills and knowledge tests may also be employed. However, the nature of provision and the degree to which it can be improved in line with this feedback will vary. This will affect the focus and nature of evaluation procedures, and this issue will be discussed in greater depth in the examination of the case studies below.

Where an organisation purchases training from an external provider, the scope for influencing provision in response to the findings of evaluation will depend on the market power of the purchaser, as well as the responsiveness of the provider. For example, large companies may be able to negotiate customised provision from local further education colleges or universities because of the numbers of employees using their facilities and the scale of resources invested in them. In contrast, small organisations may have less scope for suggesting changes in courses and may opt for alternative sources of provision.

Mechanisms for debriefing, feeding back or applying knowledge in the work context

Some organisations may encourage the debriefing of training programme participants by their line managers or the cascading of new skills and knowledge to the wider work group. This may be achieved on a one-off basis or through a regular forum such as team briefings, where these are part of the organisational culture. Equally, the design of training programmes can encourage participants to develop projects for transferring knowledge into the workplace.

The organisational context of evaluation

In the following sections CVT evaluation procedures are examined in the light of contextual factors affecting the five case study organisations. This involves a consideration of factors such as the nature of the production process and the susceptibility of the training intervention to improvement at different stages in its development, as well as the ways in which the internal politics of the organisation affect the prioritisation and targeting of resources for training and development.

Opportunities for evaluation afforded by the nature of the production process

In Small and Medium Cars, part of the Rover Group, a wide range of planning and evaluation practices were in evidence in relation to the corporate level, the assessment of individual needs and the evaluation of particular training interventions. It useful to examine how, even within a single organisation, differences in the nature of the production process will affect the mechanisms used for identifying training needs, the forms of evaluation used and the extent to which they can be linked directly to processes of continuous improvement.

In the paint engineering section, for example, a small group of engineers was working on a new process and projects linked to the installation of a new paint shop. Staff participated in a range of training activities: technical courses; courses to keep abreast of developments in paint technology, including courses run by paint manufacturers; seminars on environmental issues; and regular team-building weekends. Skills matrices were used to identify gaps in individuals' knowledge, alongside development reviewing. Close links were maintained with the Research and Design function, which was on a separate site, and training was seen as being integrated into the well-being of the department. Since the work of the team was not tied to the track, it was relatively easy for release for training to be arranged, compared to some of the other departments. The results of these training activities were not assessed through a formal mechanism, but participants would provide feedback to the entire team at weekly team meetings.

In contrast, the body-in-white section is where body shells are assembled in a non-painted condition. It is an automated line with robots, transfer systems and automated kit. There were more than 250 employees working in this section on a three-shift system. Training needs were identified through the use of a matrix system, and development reviewing and job rotation were used as a means of extending knowledge of the different elements of the production process. Individuals had access to £100 per annum for personal development under the Rover Employee Assisted Learning (REAL) scheme. In this section, it was anticipated that new working patterns (job rotation), and the training to facilitate them, would made the work less monotonous and reduce the incidence of repetitive strain injury. A system of 'total productive maintenance' had been introduced to encourage employees to take responsibility for the routine maintenance of their equipment. In this section it was anticipated that the impact of the training would be measurable in terms of a reduction in employee absenteeism and sickness on the one hand, and the reduction in downtime of equipment on the other. However, it is difficult to dissociate the effect of training from the impact of job rotation, because they facilitate each other. Moreover, the majority of training is in-house. New operatives undertake an induction programme and 'work shadowing' of experienced employees. Because the company is 'lean' and the production process is continuous, it is extremely difficult to provide cover for course attendance. Training which is off-the-line also requires overtime payments to be made.

Rectification is a repair facility employing more than 30 people, organised on a two-shift system. When car bodies come off the track they are checked for quality. If they fail to meet the quality standard, operators assess and conduct the repairs. One feature of the workload in this section is its unpredictability: the quality of paint finish varies with atmospheric conditions, temperature, process issues and worker error. Training strategy is linked to the evaluation of performance, and this is measured in terms of volume and quality through system process charting. Two car bodies are audited for quality on each shift and this can be used for assessing the quality of training. At the time of interviewing, personal development reviewing was being introduced in this section. Skill matrices were used to identify training needs and there was some job rotation. The main tool for evaluating training was the charting and auditing of production, as this allowed the identification of problems and for remedial action to be taken.

The conformance department is made up of industrial, technical and quality engineers and provides technical support to a car build line. The department is the link between the design and process offices and those that build the car on the shopfloor. There were just over 20 employees in this department, including engineers, staff and hourly paid workers. In this department there were no training strategies as such, but general strategies for manufacturing and consultation with colleagues. Personal development reviewing was used to identify individual training needs. When a new model is introduced, this mechanism is used to identify training needs. Styling and design engineers work on the new model and then it is tested. Proving vehicles are built, using track workers who understand the process. This kind of training is process- and product-related rather than job-related. There is no formalised system for evaluating training because the members of the department have individual specialist skills and there is no intention for them to be equally skilled in all disciplines.

Although this is not an exhaustive review, it does point to the extent to which the nature of the production process itself generates measures which can be used to assess training needs and to evaluate the effectiveness of training interventions. Where training is for specific, task-related purposes it is more easily measurable in terms of production outputs. Measurement is easiest where there are restricted opportunities for learning generated by the labour process itself: it is most in evidence in areas where job rotation is used to reduce monotony. Where work is project-based, linked to the design process and involves continuous change, the nature of the work generates more complex forms of learning, which are not easily captured by simple measures. In these areas, general forms of communication within the work group are used to disseminate new knowledge and formal evaluation tools are least in evidence. It is in these contexts that appraisal is more likely to be linked to personal development rather than task- or job-related training.

Evaluating programmes of cultural change

Many organisations use programmes of cultural change to bring about improvements in quality. Leading to Excellence at the Rover Company's Small and Medium Cars business unit is an example of a programme which aimed to develop team leaders to deliver the company's quality objectives. The need for the programme was identified by members of the senior management team and an action team was set up to develop it, involving line managers, functional specialists and training specialists. It was a week-long programme, delivered off-the-job, and it was anticipated that participants' managers would brief them before attendance and debrief them on their return to normal working. It was intended that all team leaders in the business unit would attend the course and that each participant would produce a 'delivery action plan' to apply to their own workplace. The programme evaluation required participants to complete a questionnaire each day and included a learning review on the last day. The results of this evaluation were fed back to the members of the senior management team. External accreditation was also provided for the workplace assignments.

The measures for evaluating the programme outlined above are relatively straightforward and relate to the training department's provider role. In the context of an organisation in which there have been a series of initiatives on quality improvement, it is much harder to isolate the effect on cultural change and performance. Managers referred to the possibility of using qualitative measures, such as the extent to which the language of the programme was in evidence, or a subjective perception that individuals had benefited from it (as evident in initiatives they had taken). Moreover, because of the 'sheep dip' approach adopted, participants included staff who had already attended courses on quality management, and others who had recently been promoted to team leader roles. The former felt that the programme served as a refresher, whereas the latter were more enthusiastic about it. A number of participants emphasised the relational aspects of the programme and how the mix of staff from different parts of the company had contributed to their awareness of different aspects of the business, facilitating communication and networking.

In this instance, it is difficult to separate out the effect of a single initiative from on-going developments aimed at quality improvement. Individual participants clearly valued the way in which the programme helped them understand how their section fitted into the wider picture of the company and its quality strategy. A measure of success will lie in the extent to which these various initiatives are translated into team leaders' taking responsibility for introducing process improvements. By definition, changes of this nature and amplitude are long term rather than short term, and their impact can not be measured in a mechanistic way.

Evaluating the impact of training and changes in work organisation

The Additional Skills Training programme was introduced at British Sugar in 1990 (see Incomes Data Services, 1992). There were a number of reasons for its introduction. Management wanted to reduce headcount and to increase flexibility in order to maintain the company's competitive position. This was partly driven by technological change but was also linked to the flattening of hierarchical structures. Process workers were to take responsibility for routine maintenance by acquiring additional skills, and mechanical and electrical maintenance workers were to learn each other's skills. When training modules are successfully completed, workers are promoted to new technician pay grades. Two significant factors affect the company's the business strategy. First, the EU sets quotas for sugar production so that increased profits can only be secured through greater efficiency and not by an expansion of market share. Second, the work is seasonal in nature: sugar beet harvesting takes place between September and December and processing at the plants between September and March. During the beet processing campaign, the permanent workforce is joined by a seasonal workforce of temporary staff.

British Sugar invests a considerable amount in training, both for the permanent staff in different grades and functions and for the seasonal staff. The cost of the Additional Skills Training initiative was substantial: £5 million over a five-year period. It involved six or twelve weeks training off-the-job at an Engineering Training Authority (EnTrA) centre, followed by twelve weeks' consolidation in the workplace. In order to achieve the full benefits of the new training, a number of changes in work organisation were necessary. This included the introduction of teamworking, the use of job rotation to ensure that new skills were utilised and a new emphasis on preventative maintenance. Training and work organisation interact with each other: training was the mechanism for acquiring new skills which facilitated job rotation, teamworking and the changing division of labour, whilst these changes in work organisation created the opportunities for workers to use and maintain the new skills.

In this example, an enormous investment in training took place and, significantly it took place in an organisation which has a five-year business plan. This compares to the lack of business planning, and difficulties of formulating and implementing training strategies reported in many companies in Chapters 2, 3 and 4 in this volume. The nature of the evaluation of the initiative took a number of forms. Employees' progress on the courses was monitored, as well as their attainment of certificates and the application of their skills to the workplace. Factory managers were required to report on the contribution of multi-skilling and the reassessment of tasks to the achievement of their factory's business plan. The cost of the programme has been kept in the background, because the business case for multi-skilling lies in its long-term rather than short-term benefits. Initially, there may be a dip in profits as newly trained workers begin to use their newly acquired skills, and it takes time for a multi-skilled team to operate effectively together. For the company, the ultimate evaluation takes place in the boardroom and concerns how the programme has contributed in the long-term to business performance.

Course development as a labour process: targeting evaluation at the stages where it can have a positive impact

The Open University was set up in 1969 to provide undergraduate education in a range of academic subjects through multimedia delivery and supported open learning. Its provision now extends to continuing education, including professional and scientific up-dating as well as postgraduate programmes and the supervision of degrees by research. Courses are delivered to students in their own homes, involving 12–14 hours' study per week over the academic year, combining customised text books (developed by the university's course teams), television and radio programmes. Students are supported though correspondence with tutors and counsellors through a network of local and regional study centres. Residential and day schools are also held in the regions. Unlike other British universities, the Open University is organised on the principle of open access: there is no required educational level for students as a precondition of entry.

The nature of the design, development and delivery of distance learning materials has consequences for evaluation procedures. The starting costs of developing new teaching materials and television programmes are enormous but, once in place, delivery costs are relatively low compared to conventional face-to-face teaching methods. Therefore quality assessment procedures have focused on the design and development phases of the production of new courses and their 'first presentation' to students. The emphasis here is on getting it 'right first time' through evaluation ex ante. The process of course development involves a series of external checks and reviews; in other words, quality assurance procedures are front-end loaded because the capacity of the system for continuous improvement is much lower once the course materials have been developed. Therefore the process of course approval is central to the evaluation of quality. It involves planning and approval processes for resources and academic planning; the use of tools to ensure internal coherence in the structure of the programme; market research; the involvement of staff in the broader academic community to identify course content; and the use of peer review.

Other mechanisms of evaluation focus on delivery. The focus here is on the assessment of assignments. Tutors' feedback to students is seen both as a learning mechanism and as a means of measuring achievement. Therefore the sampling and monitoring of assessment is important in evaluating the quality of the learning experience and in ensuring the comparability of grading. Questionnaires are also issued to students on residential and day schools by the regions and there is more flexibility at this level to respond to student feedback.

The Open University has its own internal evaluation procedures. The Institute of Educational Technology provides educational evaluation services which contribute to the development of teaching approaches and to quality improvement. It is a national centre of excellence for research on educational evaluation. Since 1993, the University has also been subject to scrutiny by the Higher Education Funding Council for England, from which it receives a major part of its funding. This is the national system for assessing teaching quality in universities. It is conducted by subject discipline and involves both self-assessment and assessment by an external panel of experts. The Open University uses a range of evaluation tools linked to its provider role which are shaped by the nature of course provision; it is also subject to external scrutiny and accountability to the state.

Evaluation and the introduction of a quality standard

In this example, the IIP standard was introduced at Northamptonshire County Council in order to align training and development strategy to service delivery strategy. The standard has been developed to ensure that resources committed to training and development are put to effective use and it provides a bench mark for measuring progress towards improved business performance. The adoption of the IIP framework is aimed at supporting the organisation in achieving its own goals. Initially an organisation registers its commitment to achieving the award. An assessment is then made of evidence that particular departments have reached the standard. This would include documentary evidence and an interview with 15 per cent of the relevant workforce. The award is reassessed every three years.

Evaluation is central to the achievement of the award through four principles which underlie the standard: commitment, planning, action and evaluation. The coordinator for training and development in the Education Department stated that the award concerned corporate strategy, investment in the workforce and its evaluation, and the ways they could be improved. In this department a number of developments are directly attributable to IIP: for example, all staff were given an up-to-date job description, appraisal was introduced as a means of identifying training and development needs, and an induction pack for new employees was produced. Managers are required to formulate training plans for their service areas and to use feedback from the public and employees to identify training and development activities. Management training and development, including self-development, are central to these processes.

There has been no systematic evaluation of the IIP process itself at the County Council, although its impact has been assessed at policy meetings and through feedback from individual departments. It has been seen as assisting the development of training and development strategy overall, and in contributing to meeting the County Council's service delivery objectives, on the one hand, and its commitment to equal opportunities for its employees, on the other.

Evaluating an entitlement for non-traditional learners

Unison is unusual in the British trade union movement in having a large Department of Education and Training which provides courses for membership development as well as the more traditional trade union education for activists and representatives (see Rainbird and Munro, 2000). Because of the range of courses and provision offered, different approaches to evaluation have developed for different programmes. Every project must have a business plan and have quality assurance procedures built in before it is validated. This includes meeting the requirements of professional bodies where courses lead to professional qualifications. The union has a computerised system for tracking student enrolment and progression, including the quality of tutor feedback.

The Return to Learn (R2L) programme was originally set up by the National Union of Public Employees (NUPE) in the West Midlands, and aimed at its predominantly manual membership. When Unison was formed in 1993 through the merger between NUPE, COHSE and NALGO, the programme was extended nationally. It offers educational opportunities to members who wish to return to education. It is targeted at groups of workers such as women, part-timers, the low paid, black workers and manual workers. The course is delivered by the WEA to small groups of students with support from a personal tutor. It takes approximately 9–10 months to complete and includes two residential weekend schools. The programme is unusual insofar as it is aimed at ordinary members rather than activists.

The evaluation of the quality of the programme is seen as very complex, because students joining the course have a variety of objectives and need different kinds of support. These may relate to career ambitions, a desire to become more active in the union or general personal development. There is therefore no simple output notion of quality, though accreditation of achievement provides a formal structure for evaluation. Quality is seen as dependent on the ability of the programme to provide support necessary for the students to achieve their own aims and ambitions. Therefore some of the criteria concern factors such as whether the target group of students is being reached, whether the students receive what they are entitled to in relation to tutor feedback, for example, as well as more conventional measures of retention and completion.

There are a number of mechanisms built into the programme for reviewing and improving provision which form part of the guidance for WEA tutors and organisers. One student assignment requires students to review the course. In addition, students who have completed the course can become voluntary education advisers (VEAs) who act as advocates and sources of support for students at different stages of the course, from initial publicity and recruitment to completion. A Curriculum and Review group meets periodically and materials are continually revised on a just-in-time basis. In addition to more traditional evaluation processes, Unison commissioned a research report which involved a postal survey of 288 former students (Kennedy, 1995). This served a dual purpose: first, it provided detailed information of students' views of the programme; second, it has been used to demonstrate the value of the R2L programme within Unison and to justify continued expenditure on it.

Like much educational provision, the course quality of R2L is monitored through validation and moderation procedures as well as innovative procedures involving student review and peer support. NUPE's decision to create an educational entitlement for members in the most disadvantaged sections of the public sector workforce took place at a time when their jobs were under attack through compulsory competitive tendering and the privatisation of public services. When Unison was created in 1993, objectives were set to achieve proportionality and fair representation in union structures. R2L was perceived as having the potential to encourage underrepresented groups to be active in the union in whatever ways they felt were appropriate. Unison makes a substantial resource commitment to R2L and this has had to be justified within the union. This has been achieved by demonstrating the benefits to individual members, as well as the benefits in achieving organisational objectives.

Conclusion

In this chapter we have reviewed the relationship between training, evaluation and continuous improvement with reference to practices in organisations, in providers and in relation to particular training programmes or events. Some of these mechanisms have a *provider/customer focus* (for example, participants' feedback on courses). Others have a *provider/funder focus*, which allows the funding body or department to monitor the quality of provision and may also allow for the recognition of attainment. Equally an organisation may use evaluation to assess the relationship between its training and development strategy and its business strategy, and this will have a *procedural focus*. Depending on their objectives and functions, organisations will draw on various combinations to assess their activities.

Evaluation can be a useful tool in many contexts, but it also has its limitations. It is most effective when designed for a specific purpose and aimed at assessing the impact of an intervention with easily identifiable or measurable outcomes. This is 'realistic evaluation' (Pawson and Tilley, 1997). Where a training programme has a range of objectives, or where the stakeholders have a range of different – and even conflicting – objectives for their involvement in a programme, as Huddleston reports in her examination of work experience in Chapter 11, this lack of clarity makes the task of evaluation difficult. In the same way, evaluation tools are less able to measure of the contribution of specific training interventions to more complex change processes, where training is only one of a number of factors contributing to the intended outcome. This is especially the case where the desired changes are long term rather than immediate in their impact.

The transfer of new knowledge to the work environment is a key objective of training interventions. The analysis of the case studies shows that this is most easily assessed where the training is task-specific and has an impact on the production process in terms of measurable outputs. The more the intervention is related to individual development and the process of learning itself, rather than the needs of the job or the task, the harder evaluation becomes. As Senker argues in Chapter 12, an enormous amount of learning takes place at work but much of it is not measurable. Moreover, if the focus is on the learners' needs and learners are seen as stakeholders in the process, the nature of intervention shifts, as do the criteria by which success may be judged. Evaluation has developed as a managerial tool for ensuring value for money for the state, for the employer, for the provider, and for the customer. It is one measure, but by no means the only measure for assessing the quality of a learning experience.

Notes

1   This project was funded by the European Commission's Leonardo programme and was coordinated by the Centro di Studi Economici e Sociale (CESOS), Rome. The British case studies were conducted by Lesley Holly, Anne Munro and Helen Rainbird and were based on a series of open-ended interviews conducted in the case study organisations in the summer of 1996. See CESOS, *Quality Appraisal and Cost-benefit Analysis in Vocational Training Initiatives and Structures: Case Studies,* Volume 1 (CESOS, Rome 1996) for a full report of the findings.

References

Blanpain, R., Engels, C. and Pellegrini, C. (eds) (1994) *Contractual Policies Concerning Continued Vocational Training in the European Community Member States,* Leuven: Peeters Press.

Corfield, J. (1997) 'The contract state and managing at a distance', unpublished Masters dissertation, Northampton: University College Northampton.

Cully, M., Woodland, S., O'Reilly, A. and Dix, G. (1999) *Britain at Work. As Depicted by the 1998 Workplace Employee Relations Survey,* London: Routledge.

Employment Department (1992) *A Guide to Local Evaluation,* London: Employment Department and EDRU, Tavistock Institute of Human Relations.

Eraut, M., Alderton, J., Cole, G. and Senker, P. (1998) 'Learning from other people at work', in Coffield, F. (ed.), *Learning at Work,* University of Bristol: Policy Press.

Francis, M. H. (1997) 'En route to TQM', *Training for Quality,* 5, 2.

Gallaher, J. D. and Smith, D. H. (1998) 'Applying total quality management to education and training', *Training Strategies for Tomorrow,* 1, 4.

Geary, J. (1995) 'Work practices: the structure of work', in Edwards, P. (ed.), *Industrial Relations. Theory and Practice in Britain,* Oxford: Basil Blackwell.

Hilgendorf, L. and The Tavistock Institute of Human Relations (1984) *Self Evaluation by Open Learning Projects,* London: HMSO.

Incomes Data Services (1992) 'British Sugar', *IDS Study* No. 500, February, 9–11.

Kennedy, H. (1995) *Return to Learn. UNISON's Fresh Approach to Trade Union Education,* London: UNISON.

Lave, J. and Wenger, E. (1991) *Situated Learning. Legitimate Peripheral Participation*, Cambridge: Cambridge University Press.

Norris, N. (1990) *Understanding Educational Evaluation*, London: Kogan Page.

Pawson, R. and Tilley, N. (1997) *Realistic Evaluation*, London: Sage.

Pollit, C. (1997) 'Two kinds of evaluation', *Evaluation*, 3, 4.

Rainbird, H. and Munro, A. (2000) 'Unison's approach to lifelong learning', in Terry, M. (ed.), *Redefining Public Service Unionism: Unison and the Future of Trade Unions*, London: Routledge.

Sommerlad, E. (1992) *A Guide to Local Evaluation*, Employment Department and EDRU, Tavistock Institute of Human Relations.

Stame, N. (1998) 'Discussion', *Evaluation*, 4, 1, January, 92–103.

Stern, E. (1991) 'The characteristics of programmes and their evaluation', Tavistock Institute of Human Relations.

Stern, E. (1997) 'Interview with Erkki Liikanen', *Evaluation*, 3, 2, 237–43 (April).

Tovey, P. (1994) *Quality Assurance in Continuing Professional Education. An Analysis*, London: Routledge.

Index